Child
of
Mine

Child of Mine

Feeding with Love and Good Sense

Ellyn Satter, R.D., M.S., M.S.S.W.

Bull Publishing Co.

Copyright © 1983, 1986, 1991 (updated RDAs, new cover)
Ellyn Satter

Bull Publishing Company
P.O. Box 208
Palo Alto, CA 94302-0208
(415) 322-2855

ISBN 0-923521-14-3

Library of Congress Cataloging-in-Publication Data
Satter, Ellyn.
    Child of mine : feeding with love and good sense / Ellyn Satter.
        p.   cm.
    Includes bibliographical references and index.
    ISBN 0-923521-14-3 : $14.95
    1. Infants—Nutrition.   I. Title.
    RJ216.S376   1991   91-3632
    649'.3—dc20   CIP

Distributed in the United States by:
Publishers Group West
4065 Hollis Street
Emeryville, CA 94608

Cover Design: Robb Pawlak
Cover Photograph: Barry Shapiro
Cover Model: Nicholas Armour
Interior Design: Michelle Taverniti
Design Assistant: Margaret Panofsky

Contents

Feeding—from Pregnancy
Through the Toddler Period

Special Issues in Feeding

Of Current Interest

Acknowledgements

This book did not come from me alone. Many friends, associates and colleagues gave generously of their time, expertise and encouragement, and I thank them.

For professional technical evaluation of parts or all of the book:

Barbara Abrams, R.D., M.S.
Alfred Harper, PhD
Virginia Dykstal, R.N., C.P.N.P.
Patricia Joo, M.D.
Barbara Brew, M.D.
Ellyn Kroupa, M.A.
Terri Cohn, P.A.
Deborah Roussos, R.D., M.S.

Donna Oberg, R.D., M.S.
Gloria Green, R.D.
Laurie Fjeldstad, R.N., B.S.
Robert Jackson, M.D.
B. U. Li, M.D.
Marshall Cusic, Jr., M.D.
Albert Stunkard, M.D.
Donald Williams, A.C.S.W.

For help in reading the manuscript, editing, criticizing, reacting and supporting:

Laura Dennison
June Roffler
Elana Stern

Virginia Huber
Polly Colby

For expert and cheerful typing, always at the last minute:

Ruby Olson
Findley Cook
Clara Páez de Peña
Barbara Boyle

Pam Morgan
Kjerstin Satter
Lesley Rode
Joanne Prange

To the Reader

This is a book about feeding and the feeding relationship. It is a book that attempts to help you find the moderate middle ground between extremism and unconcern, between being domineering with your child's nutritional care and being neglectful. You need to know how to provide a nutritionally wholesome diet, but you also need to know how to feed in such a way that you nurture your child's sense of security, autonomy, and respect for himself and his body.

I intend this book to be a handbook and companion to you as you negotiate the four-year period from pregnancy through the toddler period (roughly age three). Because it should serve you as a reference book, I want you to be able to open it at any point and get the information you need. That means that some of the points must be made more than once. For instance, we will talk about calcium in the chapter on pregnancy and again, in greater detail, in the toddler chapter. Some subjects are covered in one place in considerable detail (not necessarily the first time the topic is raised), and at other times more briefly. Extensive cross referencing with page numbers or chapter names will help you to check back and forth as you go along.

I'm not going to tell you to change your child's diet to try to avoid cancer and heart disease. I don't think the evidence is good enough to give any clear direction. What I have done is give you advice about presenting a moderate and wholesome diet and guidelines to solving some of the nutritional problems of childhood: problems like selecting food that is appropriate for your child both developmentally and nutritionally; problems like feeding yourself well so you can produce a healthy baby and provide enough breast-milk; problems like doing all you can to prevent obesity; and problems like avoiding making the inevitable battles of the toddler period battles over food.

The three chapters of the book, Special Issues in Feeding, present information that will be helpful to you during the whole four years we discuss in the book. Chapter 9, Diarrhea, talks about managing diarrhea in children from infancy through toddlerhood. Chapter 10, Regulation of Food Intake, and Chapter 11, Obesity, discuss issues that are of major concern to most parents, are often misunderstood and mishandled, and can exert a major disrupting influence throughout your child's growing-up years. Read them early and often. You hear and read so much misinformation in this area that you will need to be reminded frequently about what is reasonable and real.

I have indicated scientific references so you can check out, if you want to, the evidence backing up what I say. While I have made some recommendations, the intent is to give you enough information so you can make your own decisions about your own child. As one young mother observed, "my baby sounds like all of those you talked about." Like the mothers I talk about, she had to make her observations and come up with solutions that were right for both of them.

Through it all, the important things to remember are 1) to enjoy your baby and 2) to trust yourself. If you do that, you can do a lot of things "wrong" and it won't make any difference.

Note on First Expanded Edition. In this First Expanded Edition of *Child of Mine*, the "Of Current Interest" section is new. This section includes two chapters, "The Feeding Relationship" and "Eating Disorders." The rest of the book remains the same.

In the three years since *Child of Mine* was published, I have learned more about feeding. Rather than waiting for a second edition, I want to share it now with you. There is a real need. Increasingly, parents and professionals tell stories about distorted feeding. Some of these situations are dreadful, and go on, with an enormous amount of pain and sacrifice, for years.

Parents are having trouble feeding themselves and feeding their children. They worry that their child eats too much or too little, grows too well or too poorly. Or they get caught up with their child in battles about eating that get bad enough to positively wreck meal time and other times. The struggle over feeding and growth can, at times, spoil an entire relationship.

Eating disorders in adults are on the increase, and they are having an impact on children's eating. Parents with severe difficulties with their own eating have a hard time parenting appropriately with food. Someone who doesn't know how to eat normally has great difficulty trusting a child to do so.

People not only need to know how to choose good food for their child, they need to know how to behave helpfully when they offer it. And they need to know when they are having serious difficulty in the area of feeding. I hope these two new chapters will help.

1
Introduction: History of Child Feeding

It is convenient, and sensible, to feed babies with food that is nutritionally appropriate and that they can ingest and digest most easily. The practical approach then, would be to nipple-feed breastmilk or another appropriate milk feeding as long as babies need to be held in a cuddling and supported position; and then, when they can sit up and can learn to swallow other foods, our practicality would lead us to progress them rapidly to table foods.

Unfortunately, this sensible approach has, as long as anyone can record or remember, been distorted by folk "wisdom," nutritional "knowledge" and social pressure. The attitudes of parents (which represent the attitudes of the times they live in) are evident from the way they feed their child. And, even in these enlightened times, our feeding attitudes and practices are often inconsistent with what we have (or should have) learned.

1

For me, one of the startling things about having a baby was coming slap up against what seemed to be the realization that I didn't know the simplest, most basic fact about taking care of one.

I knew I was *generally* ignorant. What I wasn't prepared for was the fine and exquisite detail of my ignorance. For example, I was very puzzled when the pediatrician told me that Kjerstin, my new-born daughter, would eat less frequently at night than during the day. How in the world did an infant know the difference between night and day? The pediatrician seemed to take it for granted that she would, so I didn't ask. I decided to wait and see. She slept longer at night (as do most, but not all babies). Fortunately Kjerstin seemed to know more about it than I did—a trend, I might add, that continued.

I thought I had her feeding regimen all figured out: I would breastfeed her and some day I would start feeding her solid foods. Just when, I didn't know, but I figured I would think about that when the time came. It had never occurred to me that I couldn't breastfeed, so I did. The obstetrical ward nurses helped us with some of the mechanics of it, and it went fine. Kjerstin seemed to know all about it. She cried when she was hungry, stopped eating when she was full, and even established herself on a nice feeding schedule. She knew the details, it seemed; all I had to do was provide backup and support.

It seemed to me that things were going well, particularly when we went to the pediatrician after the first month and found out that she had gained over two pounds. She was eating well and sleeping well and seemed to be satisfied and happy with her feeding regimen. She was waking up only once a night and eating at comfortably-spaced intervals throughout the day. Even though I knew little about feeding babies, that seemed right to me.

I must have led a very sheltered life. I was surprised when the pediatrician told me that it was time to start solid food. It hadn't occurred to me to even wonder about that yet. Breastfeeding seemed right for the way she was at that age. More ignorance, more details, I assumed, and went along with what the pediatrician said.

Solid foods, she said, would solve a lot of the problems that we were having. (We were having problems? I didn't know enough about the details to know we were having problems!) It was time, she said, that my daughter was sleeping through the night and she was just "putting something over on me" in insisting on getting up for that night feeding. (Actually, I was rather enjoying that night feeding, especially since my breasts got so full and uncomfortable I couldn't sleep.) Cereal would help that. Furthermore, Kjerstin was starting to get a little plump from "all that breastmilk," and was looking like a "fat little milk baby."

Cereal would take care of that, too, and I was to start her on it right away. It was to be given before the breastfeeding so she would be hungry enough to take it. Further, I was to get a demitasse spoon and put the solid feeding far enough back on her tongue so it would just slip right down and not be spit out on her chin. I was told to hold her on my lap with her head in the crook of my elbow, so she would be secure and at the right angle to let the mush slide right down her throat.

We worked very well at that, because by the second month Kjerstin was eating, two, two-ounce bowls of cereal a day and hardly spitting out a drop. She couldn't. I was practically putting it directly into her esophagus. The pediatrician praised us and rewarded us with another little tear-off sheet from the baby-food company, instructing me to now feed not only baby cereal, but also fruit and vegetable.

On the way home we made a quick stop at the grocery store, and the next day our family left for a three-week camping trip with Kjerstin, armed with an ice chest filled with milk, boxes of baby cereal, and dozens of little bottles with fruit and vegetables in them. What a trial it was to haul all that stuff along and keep it cool that whole time!

3

I can feel my blood pressure rising as I write this. Or maybe that flush spreading across my face is embarrassment, as I remember how guillible I was and how colossally ignorant, to accept that crazy, inaccurate advice in a field that was supposed to be my own. But at the same time I am struck by how much more sensibly I had been feeding her when I had been ignorant. I had been paying attention to her signals and feeding her in a way that seemed right for her developmentally. It was only after we got all those *details* that we really got off on the wrong track.

How my husband and I knocked ourselves out to push all that unnecessary food into that cooperative, vulnerable little baby. Well, my only reassurance is that I don't think it hurt her. She seemed to grow well and do well and had no major crises with diarrhea or dehydration, so I hope we did no harm. But we sure went to a great deal of unnecessary work, and we certainly gave her no positive benefit from the crazy, complicated feeding regimen we had her on.

By the time the boys, Lucas and Curtis, were born, I was able to defend myself against the details. I trusted my breastfeeding and delayed the addition of solids, even though they were both chubby, robust kids with great appetites.

I can remember going on a bike trip when Lucas was three months old. He rode on my back in a pack. When we stopped for lunch, he got off my back to breastfeed and that was that: not a spoon or a bottle in sight. How nice that was! All we needed was a few disposable diapers and we were ready for action. With Curtis, I was even more casual. Even though he ate often and irregularly and grew very fast, I knew breastmilk was all he needed at first. I had finally made my peace with the details.

The pediatrician has simplified things, too. In the time since my first-born in 1966, she has moderated her baby-feeding advice. The trend in baby-feeding has changed, and to a certain extent she has gone along with the trend.

4

Feeding babies is not complicated. Like me with my first baby, where most people get into trouble with feeding their children is in trying to make it more complicated than it really is. It seems that the most difficult task for a modern parent is to sort through the chaff of conflicting advice and information, to find the grain of common sense.

Most of us haven't experienced an infant until we have our own, so we must learn from relatives, from other parents, from professionals, from books. In raising kids, one of the easiest things to do is get advice. That's especially true about advice on feeding. Since everyone eats, everyone knows about feeding. A crowd gathers. What one person suggests, the other contradicts.

Feeding patterns for infants have changed so drastically in the last few years that you will probably get as many versions of appropriate feeding practices as people you consult. You can even find considerable variation in the recommendations of doctors, nurses, and dietitians.

You might say some people are more up-to-date than others. On the other hand, you might not want to say that, because sometimes being "modern" only means being fashionable. Some fashionable theories prove that babies have a remarkable capacity to adapt to the whims of their caretakers, and seem to do pretty well on a wide variety of feeding approaches.

Too often common infant feeding practice is based on only that—common practice. It need not be so. As with all other behaviors, as the infant grows and develops, abilities change and patterns of feeding change.

Nutritional needs vary as the child grows. The mouth muscle patterns vary at different ages—sucking patterns of early infancy give away to swallowing patterns, and finally chewing patterns appear. The digestive tract matures, from one adapted to milk digestion to one able to handle a wide range of food. The child continually develops her awareness and mastery of her environment. Along with this comes imitation of eating patterns of older people, and she will feel compelled at appropriate ages to adopt more-nearly-mature eating behaviors, just as she is driven to crawl, to stand and finally to walk.

To be able to know what you're doing and why you're doing it, as you feed your baby appropriately at different ages, you need to understand:

1. Your infant's nutritional needs at different ages.
2. How growth and development are related to eating.
3. Signals that indicate readiness for maturing eating styles.
4. Appropriate eating styles for a given level of growth, development and nutritional need.

Given this understanding, you will be able to feed your infant with flexibility, based on a clear understanding of what he needs and is able to do at different stages of maturation. This is important, as different infants mature at different rates. You need to be able to adapt your feeding style to fit your infant.

When you match feeding practices to the child's developmental needs, the feeding regimen goes something like this:

- Give the baby breastmilk (supplemented with Vitamin D and flouride) or formula, only, for the first four to six months of life.
- When he can sit, supported, begin offering iron-fortified baby cereals mixed with formula or milk. Do this after the breast or bottle feeding.
- When your baby turns his head or otherwise indicates he's full, take his word for it.
- After he is taking about ⅓ to ½ cup of mixed-up cereal a day, gradually begin offering a variety of fork-mashed, unseasoned table foods, always after the milk feeding.
- At around 8–10 months when the baby is able to sit alone, shows an interest in the family table, and is adept at conveying things to his mouth, start putting him up to the table at mealtime, where he can

6

feed himself a variety of soft food that won't choke him. Offer an assortment that is likely to add up to a nutritious diet.

- At the same time (if he hasn't already) he is ready to start drinking with assistance from the cup.
- Now postpone the breast or bottle feeding until after the meal, and give formula or whole milk in a cup along with the meal.
- As he eats more at mealtime and drinks from the cup, he will gradually lose interest in the breast or bottle and can generally be weaned, one feeding at a time, with no hassle. At this point, he is getting more of his nutritional needs from a variety of foods, and formula or breastmilk becomes less important nutritionally.
- Once he is well-established on table food, it is all right to switch to whole milk, or to whole evaporated milk diluted one-to-one with water.

All of this development in eating takes place by age one year. About the only real change in eating you see after that is when the child gets his two-year molars, sometime in the second year, and can chew more efficiently. Then he can handle tougher, chewier foods.

And that's all there is to it: breast or formula alone for the first 4–6 months, beginning solids after that, and self feeding of table foods beginning around 8–10 months.

Working with Health Professionals

As my kids were growing up, I often got the feeling that pediatricians were putting themselves in charge of *my* children. It seemed that they weren't advising—they were dictating. I was expected to go along with their pronouncements without question. Those are the traditional roles of the patient and the physician: the physician is in charge of the patient's health care. The "good" patient has been the *compliant* one; that certainly has been an apt word, because being compliant means, "to accept or comply tacitly; to accept as inevitable or indisputable; to yield."

It's a good thing those times are passing. That kind of behavior by a parent may save time in the doctor's office, but it surely doesn't make a very good mental set for all the responsibility of raising kids.

It is kind of a chicken-and-egg question to try to decide which started to change first, patient or physician attitudes—but the relationship definitely is changing. People are expecting to retain responsibility for the health care of themselves and their children. They are looking to health care providers as consultants, as people to whom they can turn for information and recommendations. Along with that comes the patient's expectation that she will be able to understand the reasons for what she is doing, so she can take reasonably informed courses of action.

In their turn, health care providers are expecting to act more as consultants and resource people to parents. They are realizing that what the parent needs most of all is confidence in his or her own ability to make decisions. Therefore they are doing more informing, and educating, and giving advice, leaving the bulk of the decision making up to the parents. Nurses in pediatrics are doing what they call "anticipatory guidance"—telling parents ahead of time what to expect from their children, so parents will be prepared to interpret and handle changes.

Some parents don't like this approach any more than some health practitioners. They would much rather do it the old way. Here is hoping that those parents and practitioners find each other. Meanwhile, I am assuming that you want to be informed enough to make your own decisions.

In this book I will be your consultant as you struggle with this important business of caring for your child nutritionally. I will try to give you the nutrition information and tools you will need to make your own decisions. I want you to know the important nutritional issues and pros and cons about some of these issues. I will try to anticipate some of the problems you will be encountering and give suggestions about ways of handling those problems. I want to support you in developing your own confidence about caring for your child nutritionally.

All of this comes from my absolutely firm conviction that you are the person in charge, and that the rest of us are, at best, playing supportive roles.

Historical Perspective on Infant Feeding

It seems to me that a logical way to get started with the process is to take a look at what has gone before. Getting a perspective on infant feeding can help, I think, in a couple of ways. First, it can help you in fielding advice. Say, somebody is telling you that you should be doing something. If you can think, "Ah, yes, that is the way they did things back in the forties and the reason that they did that was this-and-this," you are going to be much more secure in accepting or rejecting that piece of advice. Second, a brief review of the recent history of infant feeding can provide us with an introduction to some of the important issues in infant feeding. It's kind of like telling a story to make a point: we can have some fun with this and conduct our business at the same time.

The recent history of infant feeding tells about the attitudes of parents toward babies, changing influences on families over the years, and the development of the science of nutrition and modern food technology. You will find remnants of some of the older ideas in a lot of the advice you get about infant feeding.

Until the early part of the 20th century, the infant who could not be breastfed usually could not survive. The technology was not available to provide the infant with a sanitary feeding that was digestible and nutritionally complete. It was not until the 1920's that a consistently safe and reliable substitute for breastmilk was available. By that time sanitation in milk production and handling had improved to the point where people had a better chance of getting fresh, wholesome milk.

9

Techniques of sterilization had been developed that prevented the bacterial contamination and dysentery that had been common in an artificially fed infant. Safer water supplies were developed. Easily cleaned and sterilized bottles and nipples were available. It was discovered that boiling cows' milk softened the milk curd formed in the infant's stomach, making it more digestible.

It was noted that since cows' milk is more concentrated than human milk, levels of calcium, phosphorus and protein were unnecessarily high, and that getting rid of the excess as waste products put an unnecessary load on the baby's kidneys. It was therefore helpful to dilute the formula with water. Then to make up for the calories lost through dilution, extra carbohydrate, generally sugar or syrup, was added. The diluted, carbohydrate-enriched mixture then more closely approximated human milk in composition.

In the 1920's and 1930's vitamin C was isolated and identified as the preventative of the scurvy possible in bottle-fed infants. Cod-liver oil came into use as a source of vitamin D to prevent rickets. The acceptance of canned, sterilized evaporated milk as the basis for infant formula (which, ironically, had been around ever since Gail Borden patented it in 1856) represented a great breakthrough in safety and convenience. Formula, based on canned milk, along with supplements of codliver oil and vitamin C, represented an artificial feed that was nutritious, convenient, safe and economical. (Later evaporated milk was fortified with vitamin D.)

It was the SCIENTIFIC AGE of feeding babies: formulas were adjusted to fit the age of the child, quantities to be fed were pre-selected in the doctor's office, and frequencies of feeding were rigidly controlled. Breastfeeding was considered old-fashioned and non-scientific, and the trend away from breastfeeding began. The percentage of newborns who were breastfed dropped to 65% in the 1940's and 25% in the late 50's.

The scientific age has continued, until now there are many commercial formulas on the market. They are based on pretty much the same principle: cows' milk modified by boiling, dilution, increase of calories with added carbohydrate, and supplementation with essential nutrients.

Trends in the introduction of solid foods have changed as rapidly as those related to the milk feeding. Early in the 1900's infants were kept on breastmilk alone until about age one year. However, as artificial feeding became more popular, some of the more adventurous parents and physicians began offering solids at an earlier age. The infants seemed to accommodate this, and continued to grow well, and therefore it was assumed to be appropriate. So experimentalists kept trying progressively earlier ages for solids introduction, until by 1960 it was common practice to offer cereals within two weeks to a month of birth, or even at birth, and other foods in rapid succession soon afterward.

The baby food market boomed, providing in convenient form the semi-liquid, super-smooth foods that the immature infant needed for swallowing without strangling. Instructions for introducing solids stressed thinning to a watery consistency, and putting the spoonful far back on the baby's tongue so she wouldn't just spit it back out. That was only logical, as the young infant's mouth is adapted to sucking, which forces the tongue up and against the roof of the mouth and propels anything not fed by nipple right back out. This mouth pattern is called the *extrusion* reflex. Once you get food far enough back on the tongue, it activates swallowing, so it goes down whether the infant wants it or not.

It appeared that infants naturally tolerated solid foods early in life, so it became common practice to give them, despite the fact that there was no evidence that early introduction was advantageous. Early feeding of solids was more costly and complicated, but people did it because they thought it was best for their babies.

Along with early progression to solid foods came early switching to pasteurized milk, most commonly 2% milk. This was presumably easier and cheaper than prolonged feeding of formula, which

11

was said to be old-fashioned, and no longer necessary. Two percent milk was supposed to be helpful in preventing obesity, because it had fewer calories per ounce than formula. (This turned out to be an honest mistake resulting from ignorance, when it was shown in the late sixties[2] that babies over six weeks of age regulate food intake on the basis of calories consumed rather than on the basis of volume. Babies over six weeks had simply been drinking more of the 2% milk and gaining just as much weight.)

It was in this latter stage—of early addition of solid foods combined with switching to 2% milk—that the rational basis for infant feeding broke down. Feeding theory no longer matched infant needs. Babies still were more vulnerable than adults to contaminated food, and needed to be protected; they still had more immature stomachs and intestines that couldn't adequately digest a big, solid milk curd formed by pasteurized milk; their kidneys still didn't have the capacity to handle the overload of protein, calcium, phosphorus and sodium in 2% milk; and even after all those years of being dosed early on with solid foods, they still hadn't learned to get down a spoonful of runny cereal without pushing it out on their chins.

For twenty years health professionals were recommending feeding babies as if they knew nothing at all about nutrition and physiology.

It is only recently that nutritionists, physicians, nurses and other health professionals have been putting together what they know about babies, and coming up with recommendations for feeding babies that again make sense. I am perhaps too optimistic, but I don't think the trend will go back the other way. Developmental patterns of infants don't change, and nutritional requirements remain the same. Now that we are beginning to feed in a logical fashion in response to those considerations, I would hope that we have enough sense to continue to do so.

Right now, we have a particular problem, as we are at the transition between the old and the new. People I see in my practice have often been exposed to conflicting opinions and bits of information about feeding and are unsure of how to proceed. Some health workers still give strange and questionable feeding advice and parents are confused.

Social Perspective on Infant Feeding

Having taken this look back at some of those feeding practices from a nutritional and scientific perspective, I am struck with how many of the practices seem objectionable or even crazy. But when I stand back a little further and take a look at the feeding practices in the light of their social context, it begins to make sense why people did what they did. (It usually does, you know, if you can just get yourself adjusted to look at things in the proper perspective.) So let's establish a social perspective for that same period of time—the early part of the century.

The role of the family and the attitudes toward children have changed markedly since that time. In the early 1900's most women and children were involved in some concrete way with the family's means of making a living. The major occupations were the family farm or the small business or trade. Both parents were generally involved in those cooperative ventures, and child-raising had to be a part of other responsibilities. Children were expected to contribute economically from an early age, either by doing small essential tasks, or by taking care of younger children. The individual's well-being was assumed to be the result of the status of the whole family. Therefore, the welfare of the individual was less important than the maintenance of the physical, economic and social welfare of the family as a whole. At the same time, children were valued for the economic contribution that they could make to the family.

The attitude toward infants and children was that the will of the young child had to be tamed. "The right of the parent is to command, the duty of the child is to obey." Infant feeding times were regulated; parents were hesitant to respond to childrens' demands, lest their child become self-centered as an adult.

With the trend toward industrialization came a different pattern of family life. Now one or both parents, and often the older children as well, were working outside the home. Child care was delegated to a particular person in the family: the mother, older children, grandparents. Since most people working in industry had lower incomes, there simply wasn't enough money available to spare an employable family member for the express purpose of raising children. Families often lived in communities with relatives or close friends, so the community continued to act as a social network for the family, supervising and supporting the children. For the first time the family began to be somewhat isolated from the work place.

The attitudes toward children changed drastically with the industrial revolution. Industrial technology made intelligence the main skill for survival. So rather than continue to equip the child to live as part of a family, clan, ethnic group, religious group, or community, the family was called upon to equip the child to compete for a place as an *individual* in the larger society. Spontaneity and independence from the family became desirable traits. Parents were told by an emerging group of child care experts that emotional expressiveness and autonomy toward others were important for the individual who was to achieve independence as an adult. Independence was seen as the individual serving society. The person was being equipped to live as part of a technological, capitalist society.

By now pediatricians, too, were in the business of telling parents what to do about feeding their children. They had access to the unfolding body of information about nutrition. Since safe formula preparation was possible for families, the pediatrician had become able to control something he had never been able to control when babies were being breastfed: quantity and quality of their feeding. Parents were charging the pediatrician with the responsibility for taking care of children, so it seemed right that he should take charge of the important area of feeding as well.

The preoccupation with regularity in feeding had been around a long time; during those years it appeared to become a real obsession. It began to seem important to equip children from an early age with habits of regularity and punctuality, which would serve them in an increasingly technological age. Also, there was an increasing emphasis on the intellect; "experts" were coming into vogue, and the judgment of the pediatrician fit this new desire for expert opinion. The information coming from the child was less important. It was a matter of mind-over-body.

Therefore, although the emphasis was on the individual, the information that came from the child was less important than what was coming from the outside. The theme was to mold the individual from an early age, to fit into a certain pattern of society.

Along with the rigid formula routines came introduction of solid foods at earlier ages. The popular school of thought at that time, which went along with the increasing value placed on intelligence, was that the infant who could or would do something early, was displaying intellectual ability that would show up in all future activities. Thus, the willingness to swallow solid foods, or sit up, or walk at an early age predicted success later in adulthood.

Now we know that individual developmental differences in infancy are not preserved for very long. But parents were convinced of it then (probably by professionals), and acted out of genuine concern for the best interests of their children.

The separation between family life and community life which had started with the industrial revolution, became even greater after World War II. Families began moving to the suburbs, which isolated them not only from the work place, but also from their traditional social networks of kinship, and ethnic and religious groups. Since the people making this move were generally of the middle income or

15

above, they had the means to support someone in the family for the business of child care. So raising children became, for the first time anywhere, the focus of women's full-time commitment and work— and the test of mothers' worth. In fact, it became a test of a woman's worth as a person, because the primary role of women was seen to be marrying and having children.

At the same time, the status and role of the children was dramatically changed. Having been removed geographically from day-to-day contact with the breadwinner, and having the mother in the full-time role of homemaker and child-care provider, essentially changed their economic status. For the first time children became a clear economic liability rather than an asset.

The child's task became to grow up in such a way that he could take his economic place in the outside world. Children were fed in a way that reflected the pressures being put on their mothers. Women were expected, or expected themselves, to do the best with their families—to provide for them and serve them. Children who "ate well" and "grew well" reflected well on their mothering. This put pressure on the feeding relationship that made it hard for mothers to be aware of children's innate needs and potential.

We are now at a point where once again, the family is changing. Increasingly mothers as well as fathers are going off to paid employment. Child care functions are being delegated to other people and organizations. Parenthood is seen as an option rather than an obligation, as more and more couples are choosing to remain childless. The people who do choose to have children are doing so deliberately and thoughtfully, accepting what they see as a considerable economic and social responsibility. An important part of making the decision is the struggle with the question of how to provide children with a nurturant, socializing environment, and still allow all family members what they see as appropriate opportunity and autonomy.

The attitude of society toward the individual is also changing. Rather than viewing the individual as responsible and subservient to

16

society, it seems the other way around: society exists for service to the individual. Some alarmed critics have labeled the current mental set as narcissistic. Other more optimistic observers have called it an appropriate valuation of self. In any event, parents are responding by attempting to instill in their children a sense of personal competency and respect for their own and others' individuality. They seek to develop the capacity for flexible and responsible interactions with others and with the environment.

With respect to the feeding relationship, this has meant that parents are more willing than before to accept information coming from their children. They are attempting less to impose on their children external standards of schedule, quantity or food selection. They are beginning to feed their babies in a way that they see as being more functional, and responsive to the babies themselves. Breast-feeding is on the upswing, as mothers work out ways to continue the breastfeeding relationship even when going back to work.

Now, in addition to growing up to take her economic place in the world, the child must somehow do this in a way that allows her to maintain harmony with a *changing* world. Furthermore, given the optional nature of parenting, her "growing up well" becomes even more important to parents. Producing a good child validates their decision to have a child. How today's child manages to do all this represents a more complicated task than ever before. The purpose of this book is to be helpful to you as you find ways of supporting that growth.

Selected References

1. Cone, Thomas E. 200 Years of Feeding Infants in America. Ross Laboratories. 1976.
2. Fomon, Samuel J. Recent history and current trends. IN Infant Nutrition. W. B. Saunders, Philadelphia. 1974.

3. Greenleaf, B. K. Children Through the Ages: A History of Childhood. McGraw-Hill, New York. 1978.
4. Kagan, J. Overview: Perspectives on human infancy. IN The Handbook of Infant Development. J. D. Osofsky, (Ed). Wiley, New York. 1979.

2
Nutrition
for
Pregnancy

During pregnancy you are eating for two. Your need for all nutrients increases, both for maintaining the health and stamina of your own body and for providing for the growth of your baby. You need an additional 300 calories per day, your iron and folic acid requirements double, and your requirement for other vitamins and minerals increases by 25 to 50%. With the exception of iron and folic acid, you can get all the nutrients you need from a well-selected diet of ordinary foods.

Of all the nutritional considerations, however, the most critical is that of eating enough calories to maintain a slow and steady weight gain throughout pregnancy. This becomes difficult, but no less important, if you are nauseated and vomiting or have a poor appetite for any reason. At times it may become necessary to concentrate only on maintaining calorie intake—from whatever food source is tolerated.

People have always been fascinated by pregnancy and child-birth, and often have attempted to influence the outcome with dietary manipulations. In earlier times, when there was little information about nutrient composition of foods, dietary advice was influenced by the belief that obvious physical properties of different foods could produce specific effects on the mother and child. Pregnant women were sometimes forbidden to eat salty, acid, or sour foods for fear the infant would be born with a "sour" disposition. Eggs were sometimes restricted because of their association with the reproductive function.

On the other hand, certain foods were encouraged for their presumed beneficial effects. Pregnant women were often advised to eat broths, warm milk and ripe fruits, to soothe the fetus and ease the birth process.

Dietary recommendations for pregnancy were also influenced by current problems in obstetrical practice. In the early days of the Industrial Revolution, children in Europe had poor diets and worked long hours in dark factories. Rickets was a common nutritional disorder that impaired normal bone formation during the growing years; so when women became pregnant, contracted pelvis bones presented a major obstetrical risk. Physicians were unable to do cesarian sections or even use forceps delivery, and mortality of both mother and child during childbirth was very high.

Experience with his own patients in the 1880's led a German physician to advocate a fluid-restricted, low-carbohydrate, high-protein diet for women with contracted pelvis, to be followed for six weeks prior to birth. Women using such a diet produced smaller infants who were easier to deliver.[14] The diet may have had some justification in the 1880's, but it later gained in popularity and became a standard recommendation for women throughout pregnancy, even when the original rationale for it no longer applied.

This practice was consistent with the common view of the fetus as a parasite, bent on robbing from the mother the nutrients it needed for growth and development. "Responsible" nutritional practice was aimed at limiting maternal weight gain to that clearly needed by the fetus and its support systems, and did not allow for any accumulation in the mother's fat stores or tissue fluid. Eighteen pounds was the limit; anything over that was viewed as contributing to obesity in the mother.

In fact, an obstetrician who attended me during my first pregnancy and delivery adhered to this philosophy and practice. He insisted that a low-calorie, high-protein diet was necessary to prevent toxemia, or preeclampsia*. He also added sodium (salt) to the restricted list.

His reasoning was naive, similar to that of the early diets for pregnancy. A major symptom of preeclampsia, or toxemia, is fluid retention, which causes a sudden weight gain, usually about the 20th week of gestation. Since preeclampsia produced a weight gain, if you held down the weight gain and the salt intake, you would prevent the toxemia.

It didn't seem to affect his logic that the compositions of the two gains were not the same. Normal weight gain in pregnancy is made up of maternal and fetal tissue as well as some normal fluid retention. The weight gain of toxemia is water.

That obstetrician had the courage of his convictions—and was willing to get tough to enforce adherence to them. He put women on strict weight-control regimens, and set target weight gains, ranging from a high of 17 pounds to a low of no weight gain or even weight loss for the obese woman. And he used real strong-arm tactics, from an old-fashioned chewing-out, to threats not to deliver his patient. He wasn't alone in his goal of limiting weight gain. He was following

---

*Preeclampsia is a disorder found only in pregnancy, that can be dangerous to both mother and baby. To be identified as preeclampsia there must be three symptoms: Tissue fluid accumulation greater than that normal for pregnancy, elevated blood pressure, and protein in the urine.

common obstetrical practice, and the advice in standard obstetrical textbooks.

As a nutritionist, I questioned his logic, and certainly didn't like the looks of his rigid and boring diet. I knew women starved themselves for his appointments. But all he had to do to shut me up was to refer to his years of experience and superior knowledge about real-life practice.

It took another group of obstetricians, with further years of experience and better clinical information, to combat successfully his thinking and that of others like him. In 1970, a panel of respected obstetricians and nutritionists published a major reexamination of nutritional practices during pregnancy, *Maternal Nutrition and the Course of Pregnancy*.[3] Their consensus was that these routine weight, calorie and sodium restrictions during pregnancy were not only outmoded but potentially dangerous. They encouraged eating to appetite of a nutritious diet, aiming for an average weight gain of around 25 pounds, and <u>no</u> routine sodium limitations.

The Committee contradicted the parasite theory. They found that women with good diets tended to have superior infants and better obstetrical performance, and those with poor diets tended to have inferior infants and poorer obstetrical performance. "Superior" infants were healthy, robust babies with birthweights somewhere between six pounds ten ounces and eight pounds 14 ounces. (The generally accepted single figure of optimum birthweight is about seven and a half pounds.)

Our patients after 1970 were treated much differently than patients before that time. We began instructing them in normal nutrition, encouraging and supporting optimal weight gain (with the exception of one loyal nurse who persisted in sucking in her breath when patients gained well, and praising them when they gained poorly).

Three years later, we invited a graduate student in nutrition, Janet Valentine, to compare obstetrical performance before and after 1970.[5] She found that patients before 1970 gained, on the average, eight pounds less than those after 1970, 15.9 versus 24.2 pounds. She also found that the babies born to mothers who gained more were heavier by 159 grams—over five ounces. There were six mothers in the earlier study who gained less than ten pounds, and their babies were quite small—over 11 ounces less than the average babies. Women before 1970 reported for their 6 week postpartum check at about the same weight as before pregnancy. Those after 1970 were about five pounds heavier.

The five-ounce weight difference between the pre-1970 and post-1970 babies doesn't sound like much, and neither group had low birth weights. But it can be significant. For instance, babies from certain economically disadvantaged groups, on the average, weigh only ½ pound less at birth than babies from more prosperous groups; yet infant mortality in the poorer groups is two to three times that of the richer. You could blame this difference on factors other than nutrition, such as living conditions, until you realize that when poorer babies of adequate birth size are sorted out from the others, they do just as well as the more advantaged babies.[13]

To have a good diet during pregnancy you must have both good quantity and quality. You must have enough food, and it must meet your nutritional needs. The remainder of this chapter will deal with these issues.

However, as we do that, we must keep in mind that not every problem of pregnancy has a nutritional cause. It is likely that there are some circumstances in which nutrition plays a direct and critical role. But it is also probable that for some conditions, nutrition has little or no influence at all. In striving for good nutrition during pregnancy you are taking responsibility for those factors which you can control.

Weight Gain During Pregnancy

Everyone knows someone who has gained little weight during pregnancy, produced a seemingly healthy baby, and gone home from the hospital wearing her size-nine designer jeans. In our thinness-oriented society, that may seem like an admirable thing. But from the point of view of risk for the baby, it is anything but admirable. You have a slim chance of having good nutrition during pregnancy unless you eat enough calories and gain enough weight. Certainly, women have produced healthy, normal babies even though they have gained little weight, or perhaps even lost, but they have taken a risk.

During pregnancy you are in a state of growth. During growth, unless you are accumulating nutrients and putting on body weight, you are, essentially, starving. That starvation state carries two very real dangers for you and your baby. First, as long as you are not eating enough calories it will be very difficult for you to provide protein for your baby's needs. When calories in your diet are too low, dietary protein will simply be broken down and used for energy.

Second, if you are not eating enough calories, it will be easier for you to go into *ketosis*, a condition that is dangerous for your baby. Ketosis is an accumulation in the blood of the waste products of fat breakdown. It is caused by eating 1) a diet that is too high in fat, or 2) too low in carbohydrate, or 3) both, or 4) by not eating enough to maintain weight gain. When you are in a starvation state, your body starts to break down stored fat for energy. If there is too much fat breakdown, eventually the waste products start to accumulate, and you go into ketosis.*

Although there are some variations that we will discuss a little later, on the average women do best in pregnancy, and produce the best babies, when they gain about 22 to 28 pounds. You may shudder at this figure, especially if you are in that pre-maternity-clothes phase when your zippers won't zip, your blouses won't button, and you don't feel pregnant—just fat.

---

*Ketosis shows up in the urine. Your doctor is probably checking for ketosis by using a special dipstick in urine samples. If you are worried about undereating and developing ketosis, you can ask for your urine to be checked.

Dress yourself comfortably during this stage. Provide room for your hips, breasts and upper arms to expand as well as your abdomen. You'll be grateful for the clothes after you deliver, because you will have a good chance of being about the same size then that you were at three or four months gestation.

If you gain about 25 pounds during pregnancy, you will probably go back for your postpartum check at about six weeks within four or five pounds of your pre-pregnancy weight. Beyond that, it's hard to predict how quickly you'll lose after delivery. Some women lose promptly, others more slowly, still others seemingly hang on to much of their excess weight throughout breastfeeding. Continue with your moderate weight-control tactics of pregnancy (see pp. 34 and 50), dress attractively, and respect your own tempo. Eventually, it will come off.

Optimum Weight Gain. Whenever we start recommending optimum weight gains, there is a real danger that we will begin interfering with the normal process of food regulation during pregnancy. About the best we can do with weight gain recommendations is to give you an idea of what is "normal" and desirable.

You don't have to force weight gain. Starting in the second trimester you will be hungrier and, if you are willing to eat as much as your appetite indicates of generally nutritious food, you will gain weight appropriately, and the gain will be of healthy body tissue. Your body has its own wisdom about regulating your food intake and weight gain during pregnancy, and you should listen to it.

Weight Gain and Maternal Body Size. The best weight gain for you during pregnancy will depend on whether you are of normal weight or underweight or overweight. The best weight gain is that which produces the best fetus. Outcome of pregnancy is studied in two major ways: Birthweight and infant mortality. The two studies described below used the two different definitions of pregnancy outcome, but reached roughly the same conclusions about optimum weight gain.

At our clinic, we found what everyone else has found, that larger women tended to deliver bigger babies in all weight gain categories and that women who had a higher pre-pregnancy weight gain didn't have to gain as much weight for their fetus to be of adequate size. Conversely, women with low pre-pregnancy weights tended to have smaller babies, and had to gain more weight during pregnancy to allow their babies to achieve optimum size. In fact, if women achieved the "optimum" weight gains of the study below, their babies were of adequate size. (We defined women as overweight if they were 20% or more above normal, as defined in the Appendix (Table A-2), underweight if they were 10% or more below normal.)

A study of 53,518 pregnancies across the United States[8] based its outcome data on infant mortality, but also found that heavier women had to gain less weight to maintain a live birth average than did thinner women. This study defined overweight and underweight at 35%-above and 10%-below levels, respectively.

Figure 2-1. Optimum Weight Gain in Pregnancy.

Weight status at conception	Weight gain for lowest infant mortality
Normal weight	27 lb.
Underweight	30 lb.
Overweight	15 lb.

It is important to note, however, that in both studies, the overweight women's gain of less weight than optimum for her weight status appeared to have a marked effect on the fetus. Infant mortality in the national study doubled in overweight women who gained less than 15 pounds, and birthweights in our study of this same group fell off markedly. In other words, for the overweight woman it appears important to gain at least this minimum amount of weight.

Moreover, it is important for the overweight woman to avoid dieting during pregnancy as a way of regulating her weight. The many popular weight reduction diets that are high in protein and fat and low in carbohydrate increase the chances of developing ketosis. For all weight categories, but particularly for obese women, if weight gain is slow, the diet must be very carefully selected. It must be adequate in all essential nutrients, liberal in carbohydrate (preferably in the form of starch), and not excessive in fat.

Pattern of Weight Gain. Pregnancy brings little change in terms of calorie requirement and weight gain for the first 12 weeks. Then, beginning with the second trimester, calorie requirement increases by about 300 calories per day and weight begins to increase at the rate of almost a pound per week.

The graph on the next page shows distribution of "average" weight gain during pregnancy.

You are not very likely to gain in the nice, smooth pattern shown on this chart. Your weight gain from month to month will probably vary over and under the standard line. I found in my pregnancies that I lost two or three pounds immediately when I became pregnant, probably because of a shift in water balance, then gained seven pounds in each of the fourth and fifth months. I blamed that on a shift in body fluid as well, because I knew I wasn't overeating, at least to that extent. I kept my fingers crossed and tried not to do any mathematics in my head (you know, the type where you say "seven pounds times four more months is—"), and just kept on eating. Sure enough, by the sixth month the monthly gain had leveled off to a nicely respectable three pounds, and it actually dropped during the last trimester to only about two pounds per month. When it was graphed, my weight gain looked like the pattern in Figure 2-3—not really such an alarming picture, after all.

Women often will have a particular time in their pregnancies when they gain more than average or less than average. If your

27

Figure 2-2. Maternal Weight Gain in Pregnancy.

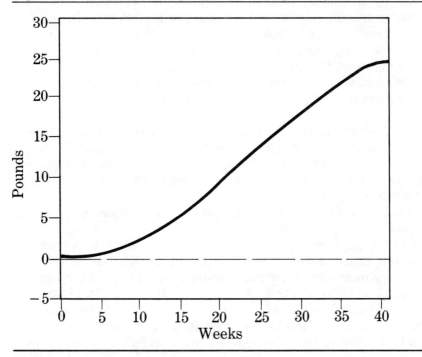

weight gain is generally varying over and under the standard line, don't worry about it. It is only when you go considerably above or considerably below the average that you may want to give some attention to your eating to see if you need to make some adjustments.

First Trimester. While growth of the developing fetus is small in actual size, its importance is very great. The beginning of all the baby's organ systems is being laid down at this stage, and the mother's body is preparing for pregnancy. Serum volume and blood

Figure 2-3. Weight gain in pregnancy: E.S.

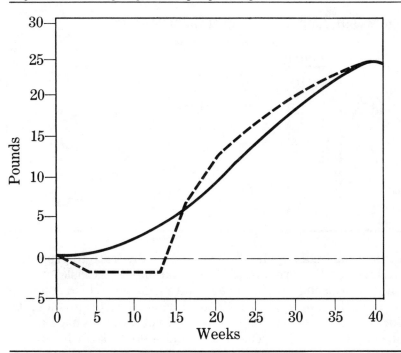

flow to the uterus both increase, there are changes in her breathing and digestive patterns, and adjustment in her pattern of carrying nutrients in the blood.

Because it is the time when the baby is basically being formed, any hazardous chemicals or severe infections are the most dangerous at this time. But because the absolute needs for nutrients is so small, any nutritional deficiencies won't have an impact unless they are particularly severe. It is primarily important during this stage to get

Figure 2-4. Components of Weight Gain.

This average weight gain is made up of the following:

	Pounds
Fetus	7.0
Placenta	1.4
Amnionic fluid	1.8
Uterus	2.0
Breasts	.9
Blood	2.7
Fat	8.0
Unaccounted	3.0
	26.8

enough calories, particularly in the form of carbohydrate to protect your body tissues and to prevent ketosis. You may be at risk for ketosis from undereating due to nausea and vomiting, which could be bad for the baby. If your appetite is poor during early pregnancy, it is important to eat whatever you can, even if you can't manage a well-balanced diet. We will discuss this in more detail later in this chapter.

Second Trimester. The second three months of pregnancy are the most important with respect to the changes in the mother's body that will support the pregnancy.

Blood volume increases by about four pints, to a total of around eight pints. Because the liquid fraction, or serum, increases in volume faster than the red blood cells are manufactured, you frequently see a drop in red blood cell count during this time. This isn't necessarily a sign of anemia. We will discuss this more in the section on iron.

Uterus and breasts grow and increase in size. It is important at this stage to have calories available to lay the groundwork for successful lactation. Placental growth during this stage is a vital part of a successful pregnancy; it is closely related to the size of the fetus.

Fat storage, to the regret of many women, is a normal and inevitable part of pregnancy. In fact a mother who is inadquately nourished will continue to deposit fat even though fetal growth is slowed.[14] This fat storage is insurance for the high energy costs of fetal growth in the last weeks of pregnancy, for labor and birth, and for lactation. In fact, it appears that depositing these energy stores during pregnancy is a very important part of assuring good lactation.

Third Trimester. The last three months of pregnancy is the time of maximum growth in the fetus and the placenta. If mothers undereat during the last 10 weeks of the pregnancy, they produce babies who are smaller in total body size. And the smallness does not just represent fat (although they do accumulate less). Babies who are underfed during the last 10 weeks of gestation have small organ systems; their heart, liver, kidneys, brains and other organs are smaller than in babies who have had access to more calories during that time.

In summary then, poor nutrition in the latter part of pregnancy affects fetal growth, whereas poor nutrition in the early months affects development of the embryo and its capacity to survive. Statistics on reproductive performance during the famine caused by the Nazi blockade of Rotterdam show this dramatically. Mothers going into the famine were generally well nourished, but once the blockade was imposed, average calorie intake dropped to less than 1000 calories per day, and protein was limited to 30 to 40 grams. Since the blockade lasted six months, babies were exposed to the famine for only part of their gestation; some pregnancies came to term during the blockade, some began.

Stillbirths and congenital malformations were highest for infants conceived during the famine. On the average, birth weights of infants exposed to the famine were reduced by 200 grams, or almost

½ pound. Weights were lowest for babies exposed to the famine during the entire last half of pregnancy.

Your Daily Food Guide

We'll begin by summarizing, in table form, the foods that are recommended for you to eat each day from the four major food categories.

There are separate outlines for adequate diets, (1) for pre-pregnancy and the first trimester (nutritional needs increase only slightly during the first trimester), (2) during the last two trimesters of pregnancy, and (3) during lactation.

The amounts are minimums—they are IN NO WAY IN-TENDED to dictate the total quantity of food that you eat.

In all of our discussion of nutrition, we will be talking about two major classes of nutrients: The macronutrients (nutrients needed in large amounts) and micronutrients (nutrients needed in small amounts). All foods contain both. The macronutrients, protein, fat, carbohydrate (and alcohol) make up most of the bulk of what we eat and are the calorie-contributers in our diet.* The micronutrients, the vitamins and minerals, are present in minute quantities and contribute no calories.

Unless you use alcohol, protein, fat and carbohydrate interact in providing all the calories in your diet. Generally, protein intake is fairly stable, with fat and carbohydrate varying in the proportion of calories they contribute to the diet.

Meal Planning; Food Distribution. Every meal should have a source of protein, some carbohydrate, preferably a starch (although sugar may also be included), and some fat. As we will discuss in more detail in the chapter on *Regulation of Food Intake*, these three sources of calories in combination will tend to be satisfying and

---

*The rest of the bulk comes from water and indigestible residue.

Figure 2-5. Your Daily Food Guide.

When Not Pregnant and During First Trimester	During Last Two Trimesters of Pregnancy	When Nursing
Milk or Milk Products		
2 cups Teenagers 4 cups*	4 cups Teenagers 6 cups*	4 cups Teenagers 6 cups*
Meat and Other Major Protein Sources		
2 servings, total of 4 ounces	3 servings, total of 6 ounces	2 servings, total of 4 ounces
Fruits & Vegetables		
4 servings vitamin C source daily	4 servings vitamin C source daily	4 servings vitamin C source daily
Vitamin A source every other day.	Vitamin A source every other day.	Vitamin A source every other day.
Breads & Cereals		
4 servings (enriched, fortified, or whole grain)	4 servings (enriched, fortified, or whole grain)	4 servings (enriched, fortified, or whole grain)

*See p. 37 for special requirements of very young teen-age mothers.

filling, and should stay with you long enough to keep you comfortable.

It is best to spread your calories and other nutrients fairly evenly throughout the day. Certainly breakfast for most people will be smaller, but don't let it be too small. In the morning you are likely to be coming off a 10 to 12-hour fast, and facing one of the high-energy-demanding periods of the day. Ideally, breakfast should account for a least 25% of your day's calorie intake, and provide at least one serving of a high-protein food, like milk or a meat group choice, along with two breads, some fat, and probably some fruit.

Protein is best utilized if it is distributed over several feedings. It is better, for example, to have an egg for breakfast, a meat and cheese sandwich for lunch and three-ounce steak for dinner, than it is to save up and have a six-ounce steak for dinner. Not only do you need those protein building materials throughout the day, but your body may have a limit as to how much protein it can use at one time.

Caloric Adequacy. If you follow the food guide on p. 33, the protein, vitamins and mineral levels in your diet should be adequate. It will not, however, be a truly adequate diet, because it will not contain enough calories.

The basic diet as outlined, even if you have four or five fat servings a day, will give you only about 1400 calories (1300 calories if you drink skim rather than 2% milk). While it is extremely difficult to estimate calorie requirement, we can guess that most women of childbearing age will require between 1600 and 3000 calories per day simply to maintain weight, and probably an additional 300 calories per day during the last two trimesters to achieve the appropriate growth and weight gain of pregnancy.

The best guide to how much you should be eating overall, is your feelings of hunger, appetite and satiety. Your body will regulate, if you let it, during pregnancy. Select a good well-balanced diet, provide yourself with regular meals and snacks, get a moderate amount of exercise, and trust yourself to eat the right amount of food.

Providing Adequate Calories. You can get the extra calories you need either by consuming more of the basic foods, or by consuming extra sugar and fat calories. Most people find it strange to be thinking about where the extra calories are going to come from to support a pregnancy. You may not in fact, have to think about it at all—you may simply find yourself eating a little more of everything from your basically adequate diet. That's a good way of doing it. Or you may want to be a little more deliberate about adding up your food choices. In case you do, let's discuss your options in more detail.

Eating more meat. The recommended amount of meat of four or six ounces, along with the protein in milk, will provide enough protein, but it is less than most of us generally eat. If you are accustomed to having more meat than that, by all means go ahead. Consuming more protein than you really need won't make your protein nutrition any better, but eating extra meat will help to insure that your diet will be adequate in minerals generally, and in some particularly important trace elements such as zinc.

Don't force-feed yourself with meat in hopes of helping to keep your weight down. A high-protein diet is no more slenderizing than any other type of diet. In fact, it almost inevitably will contain a lot of fat as well as protein, and its fat content makes it concentrated in calories. It is worth repeating that some of the popular high-protein, high-fat, low carbohydrate diets are absolutely inappropriate and even dangerous for pregnancy. They can send you into ketosis, and that is precisely what we <u>don't</u> want during pregnancy.

You should always have some substantial source of carbohydrate along with your meat—one or two servings of bread or fruit, to prevent ketosis and to keep the protein from being burned for energy. (Your body will fill its energy needs first, and if the only really good source of calories in a meal is the protein in meat, that will be used for energy rather than for building and repair of body tissue.)

Increasing Breads and Cereals. Once they get over their basic fear that eating starch will make them fat, many women find themselves eating two or more times the minimum number of servings from the bread group. They find starches filling and satisfying and, if anything, somewhat easier to regulate than some of the more concentrated foods such as meats.

Drinking More Milk or Higher-fat Milk. If you drink two extra glasses of whole milk per day, you will consume an extra 340 calories. It is up to you whether you want to drink more milk than that to get some of your extra calories. Unless you were calcium deficient to start with, the extra calcium probably won't do you any good.

Eating More Fruits and Vegetables. Like milk, fruit juices drunk for thirst can fool your natural sense of regulation. You will probably be safest if you avoid drinking any calorie-containing beverage, except as part of a nutritious meal or snack. That way, the calories will be consumed consciously as part of your food-regulation process, and you won't be so likely to take calories when you don't need them. Use good old-fashioned, cheap water for thirst.

Fruits and vegetables contribute moderate amounts of calories to your diet until you put extra sugar or fat on them. Apples baked in apple pie, or lettuce with roquefort dressing, are quite different in calories from their plainer counterparts. Whether you use extra sugar or extra fat will depend on how hungry you are and how your weight is responding.

Fats and sugars. Once you satisfy your requirements for *Your Daily Food Guide*, you can use sugars and fats for some of your extra calories. Sugar and fat, used to excess, can distort your diet; but used in moderation, they can enhance nutritious food and make it more appealing, and thus help you maintain the nutritional quality of your diet.

For example, you can probably afford butter on vegetables and on your bread. An oatmeal cookie has more fat and sugar than whole grain bread, but the basic vitamins and minerals of the bread group are still there. A cheese sauce may be just the thing to make the broccoli more interesting, and pumpkin pie, contributing a high-vitamin-A vegetable, milk and eggs, makes a great nutritional snack or part of a meal.

Making Up for Lost Time

You may be going into pregnancy poorly nourished. You might not have been too consistent in the past at feeding yourself well. You may have been a chronic dieter, willing to forgo nutritious food to keep your weight down. You may have had pregnancies close together and not have had time to recover nutritionally. You may have had twins.

Your nutrition before and between pregnancies has an impact on subsequent pregnancies. If you feel you have done less than well, you should make a special effort to eat nutritious foods during pregnancy. In fact, you should choose your extra calories more from the basic-foods groups, and less from the high-sugar, high-fat "extras" categories.

Teenaged Pregnancies

A girl continues to grow in height, skeletal, muscle and organ mass for about three years after she reaches menarche. If she becomes pregnant within two years of menarche, she is at particular nutritional risk, because she must provide calories and nutrients for her own growth at the same time that she must provide for her developing fetus.[1]

To get the large amounts of calcium, protein, vitamins and minerals she needs, the teenage mother should take six cups, rather than a quart of milk per day, and she should also pay particular attention to getting all of the foods in the daily food guide.

Given common teenage food preferences, this may seem unrealistic. However, being in the teenage group need not prevent a woman from enjoying nutritous foods. Assuming you are keeping

37

within healthy limits on fats and over-all calories, you can include many common snack foods which are actually very nutritious (e.g., pizza, hamburgers, milkshakes and barbeques). More food suggestions that might appeal particularly to the teenage taste are included on p. 46.

Portion Sizes, Substitutes for the Daily Food Guide

Milk and Milk Products. Many women find their dislike or intolerance of milk changes during pregnancy, so give yourself a chance to like it, even if you haven't before. It is virtually impossible to get enough calcium and vitamin D from food unless you include milk and dairy products. If you can't drink milk, you will probably have to take a calcium supplement. Depending on what form of calcium you use, to get the 1200 mg calcium per day that you need, you will probably have to take six to twelve calcium pills.* You must also keep in mind that dairy products contribute 40% of the protein in your diet. If you omit them, you must increase your daily servings of meats or non-meat alternatives by two during the first trimester, and four during the second and third trimesters.

The following foods each gives as much calcium as you would get in a cup of milk.

Figure 2-6. Substitutes for Milk Calcium.

1 cup of milk = 1 cup buttermilk or skim milk
                1 cup yogurt

---

*Avoid calcium diphosphate, as it can interfere with iron absorption. Also avoid dolomite and bone meal as calcium supplements; these contain excessive amounts of lead, as well as other toxicants.

1½ ounces cheddar-type cheese
1 cup custard or milk pudding
1½ cups ice cream
1½ cups cottage cheese
¼ cheese pizza (14 inch)

Check the *Toddler* chapter (p. 279) for a list of the calcium content of common foods. In the same section (p. 280) is a list of suggestions for including calcium in your diet.

Meat and Other Major Protein Sources. Meat and other major protein sources are good sources of protein, iron, B vitamins and trace elements. To help you estimate portion sizes, on the next page are some examples of one and three-ounce portions of cooked meat from the meat group, and also some non-meat alternatives, such as cooked dried beans and peanut butter. If you use cheese as a "meat" source, make sure you count it only once. That is, you can't count it as a milk serving and as a meat serving as well. Cheese is good for you, but it isn't that good!

Fruits and Vegetables. We depend on fruits and vegetables as the primary sources of vitamins A and C in the diet. They contain other nutrients as well, such as calcium, B vitamins, iron and trace elements, but in selecting fruits and vegetables we look particularly for the ones that are good vitamin A and C sources. If we provide those nutrients in natural foods, that is, vitamin C in orange juice rather than in a manufactured fruit drink, we can generally assume that other nutrients will be provided in adequate quantities. Here are charts to help you select fruits and vegetables. (They will be repeated in the *Toddler* chapter with different portion sizes.)

Vitamin A. During pregnancy your vitamin A requirement increases from 4000 to 5000 IU per day. A quart of milk will provide

39

Figure 2-7. Estimating Meat Portion

Meat Serving	Alternatives
1 oz. meat, poultry or fish	1 egg 1 slice (1 oz.) cheddar-type cheese ½ cup cooked dried beans, dried peas, lentils ¼ cup cottage cheese 2 Tbsp. peanut butter 2 slices (2 oz.) bologna 1 frankfurter (packed 8 per pound) ⅛ cheese pizza (14 inch) 4 slices bacon
3 oz. meat, poultry or fish—a piece of meat or fish about the size and thickness of the palm of your hand	One-fourth of a 2½ to 3-pound chicken (½ breast, or a leg and thigh) One medium loin pork chop, ¾-inch thick One lean ground beef pattie, made four to the pound*

*Meat shrinks about 25% with cooking, so a four-ounce raw patty cooks down to three ounces. Restaurants who sell "quarter pounders" are usually advertising raw weight.

you with 1000 IU, so you need to get 3000-4000 IU from fruits and vegetables. (We assume you'll be getting some vitamin A from miscellaneous sources like butter and margarine, and from fruits and vegetables not on this list.) Choose from the chart one excellent vita-

Figure 2-8. Vitamin A in Fruits and Vegetables*

Excellent Sources	Good Sources	Fair Sources
More than 4500 IU per ½ cup	1500-4000 IU per ½ cup	Less than 1000 IU per ½ cup
Apricots, dried	Apricot nectar	Apricots
Cantaloupe	Asparagus	Brussel sprouts
Carrots	Broccoli	Peaches
Mixed vegetables	Nectarine	Peach nectar
Mango	Purple plums	Prunes
Pumpkin		Prune juice
Spinach, other greens		Tomatoes
Squash		Tomato juice
Sweet potatoes		Watermelon

*U.S.D.A. Home and Garden Bulletin Number 72

min A source every day, or a combination of two good sources, or at least one good plus one fair source.

Vitamin C is easier to get than vitamin A. You need about 80 mg of vitamin C daily during pregnancy, which is about 20 mg more than the non-pregnant level. From the chart on the next page, choose one excellent source of vitamin C or two good sources per day. Almost all fruits and vegetables have some vitamin C, so if you get your four servings of fruits and vegetables a day, you can assume that you will easily get the other 20 mg.

Breads and Cereals. I said it before, I'll say it again, and I am saying it right now: breads and cereals are important in your diet. Far from being the "filler," nutritionally-marginal food that many people think they are, they are good sources of B vitamins and iron, and

Figure 2-9. Vitamin C in Fruits and Vegetables*

Excellent Sources—	Good Sources—
About 60 mg per ½ cup (One serving daily)	25 to 40 mg per ½ cup (Two servings daily)

Broccoli	Asparagus
Brussel sprouts	Bean sprouts, raw
Cabbage	Chard
Cauliflower	Honeydew melon
Cantaloupe	Potato
Grapefruit; grapefruit juice	Tangerine
Kohlrabi	Tomatoes, tomato juice
Mango	Pureed baby fruits
Oranges, orange juice	
Papaya	
Peppers	
Spinach	
Strawberries	
Vitamin-C fortified infant juices	

*U.S.D.A. Home and Garden Bulletin number 72.

they provide valuable complex carbohydrate, or starch. If they are whole grain, they also provide fiber, and contribute trace elements, such as zinc and copper.

To get fiber and trace elements, it is desirable to use whole grain breads and cereals up to about half the time. (Beyond that, it may be that the fiber starts to interfere with mineral absorption—see the discussion in the *Toddler* chapter, p. 314.)

Read labels to be sure of what you're getting. The bread or cereal should be made with "enriched" or whole grain flour. "Enriched" means that iron and the B vitamins, thiamine, niacin and riboflavin have been added to restore that lost by refining. Many delicatessen and specialty breads are not made with enriched flour, so be careful. Some enriched products, rather than indicating "enriched" flour, list the nutrients separately, as in the following example:

Ingredients: flour, water, corn syrup, yeast, partially hydrogenated soybean oil, honey, molasses, wheat bran, crushed wheat, salt, wheat gluten, cornflour, oatmeal, soya meal, mono and diglycerides, barley malt, calcium sulfate, ethoxylated mono and diglycerides, vinegar, dry honey, dry molasses, inactive dry yeast, ammonium sulfate, niacin, ferrous sulfate, potassium bromate, thiamine mononitrate, riboflavin.

To get a whole grain product, read the label to be sure the first listed ingredient is whole wheat, or oatmeal, or whole grain of some other type. "Wheat flour" is not whole grain, nor is "unbleached flour." The following grain products are roughly equivalent with respect to calories, thiamine, riboflavin and iron content, but whole grains contribute additional vitamins, trace elements and fiber:

Figure 2-10. One-serving Equivalents of Breads and Cereals

Bread	
White, Whole wheat, Rye, Raisin	1 slice
Bagel	½
Biscuit, Dinner roll	1 (2″ diam.)
Buns	
Hamburger bun	½
Hot dog bun	1
Cereal, cooked	½ cup
Cereal, dry	
Flakes or puffed	¾ cup
Bran cereals	½ cup

Figure 2-10 (continued)

Natural cereals, Granola	¼ cup
Cornbread	1½" cube
Crackers	
Graham	2 (2½" squares)
Oyster	20 (¼ cup)
Saltines (2" square)	5
Round thin (1½" diam.)	7
English muffin	½
Grits	½ cup
Muffin	1 (2" diam.)
Macaroni	½ cup cooked
Noodles	½ cup cooked
Pancake	1 (6" diam.)
Rice	½ cup cooked
Spaghetti	½ cup cooked
Taco shell	1
Tortilla	1 (6-8" diam.)
Waffle	1 (½" × 4½" × 2½")

Fats. Fats contribute calories, flavor, and satiety value to the diet, as well as modest amounts of some fat-soluble vitamins like vitamin A. Because they are so concentrated in calories,* varying the fat content of your diet is a good way of adjusting calories to influence weight gain.

The following list of fat sources in the diet may be helpful to you. The portions are adjusted so that each choice contributes about 45 calories. From this list you can get an idea of the relative calorie

*1 gm. fat = 9 calories
1 gm. carbohydrate = 4 calories
1 gm. protein = 4 calories
1 gm. alcohol = 7 calories

concentrations of different kinds of fats, as well as some ideas for varying the fats you use in your diet. Keep in mind that with fats, as with other foods in your diet, it is probably safest, most nutritious and most enjoyable to use them in moderation and to select a variety, including vegetable oils as well as animal fats. If you have a particular concern about avoiding heart disease (see p. 311, *Toddler* chapter), have your doctor test your blood cholesterol, evaluate your risk factors, and help you decide whether you should go on a therapeutic diet.

Figure 2-11. One-Serving Equivalents of Fats.

Butter or margarine	1 tsp.	French dressing	1 Tbsp.
Bacon, crisp, drained	1 slice	Mayonnaise	1 tsp.
Cream, light (half &		Nuts	6 small
half)	2 Tbsp.	Olives	5 small
Cream, heavy 40%	1 Tbsp.	Avocado	⅛ (4″ diam.)
Sour cream	1½ Tbsp.	Cooked salad	
Sour half and half	2 Tbsp.	dressing	
Cream cheese	1 Tbsp.	(Miracle Whip)	2 tsp.
Bacon drippings	1 tsp.	Salad oil	1 tsp.
Cream sauces	2 Tbsp.	Gravy	2 Tbsp.

Combination Foods. People remain somewhat puritanical about good nutrition, assuming anything that tastes good must be bad for you, particularly if you can buy it at a "fast-food" outlet. They are always surprised when I show them the following list. They make comments like "but lasagna is so starchy—I didn't know it was *good* for you" or, "it never occurred to me that tacos could be nutritious, but I guess they are." For the part of you that remains a puritan about food selection, here is a list of combination "fun foods" that can perk up your food selection. You may not have considered how many nutrient food groups are represented. Bon Appetit!

45

Figure 2-12. *"Fun Foods" that Make Nutritional Sense*

	Meat/Protein	Milk	Fruit & Veg.	Bread	Sugar Fat
Barbeque on bun	✓		✓	✓	✓
Hot dog on bun	✓			✓	✓
Corn dog	✓			✓	✓
Coney (chili dog) on bun	✓		✓	✓	✓
Hamburger delux (with lettuce and tomato)	✓		✓	✓	✓
Cheeseburger	✓	✓		✓	✓
Hero, torpedo, submarine	✓	✓	✓	✓	✓
Fish sandwich (with cheese)	✓	(✓)		✓	✓
Steak sandwich	✓			✓	✓
*Bratwurst on bun	✓			✓	✓
Gyros sandwich (a Greek specialty)	✓	✓	✓	✓	✓
Other sandwiches					
Peanut butter and jelly	✓			✓	✓
Grilled cheese or plain	✓ or ✓			✓	✓
Salami, bologna, etc.	✓			✓	✓
Tuna salad, egg salad with lettuce	✓		✓	✓	✓
Fried egg	✓			✓	✓

	Meat/ Protein	Milk	Fruit & Veg.	Bread	Sugar Fat
Ham with lettuce	✓		✓	✓	✓
Bacon, lettuce, tomato	some		✓	✓	✓
Chili	✓		✓	✓	✓
Tacos	✓	✓	✓	✓	✓
Burritos, etc.	✓		✓	✓	✓
Pizza	✓	✓	✓	✓	✓
Spaghetti—Meat balls or meat sauce	✓		✓	✓	✓
Lasagna	✓	✓	✓	✓	✓
Beans: Bean soup	✓		✓		✓
Bean salads (cheese)	✓		✓		✓
Refried beans	✓		✓		✓
Pork and beans	✓		✓		✓
Eggs: Hard, deviled, pickled	✓				✓
Pickled herring	✓				✓
Sardines and crackers	✓			✓	

*You may have to come to Wisconsin for this one!

Miscellaneous Foods. What about "junk foods?" Nutritionists are fond of saying, "there are really no junk foods, only junk diets." Translated, that means that there are really no good or bad foods, it all depends on the context.

Say you still need more calories, you have satisfied all of your other nutritional requirements for the day and you get a yen for potato chips. Those chips will provide you with calories you need and not replace any needed sources of nutrients. Thus, potato chips in that instance are not "junk foods." In fact, if your diet is lacking only in calories, the chips would be better for you than something like carrots because the chips would give more calories. If, on the other hand, you have had nothing to eat all day but coke and candy bars, those potato chips would definitely fall into the junk (or, more junk) category.

Keep in mind that incidence of tooth decay increases with your frequency of eating sugar. Also keep in mind that a very high fat diet is a distorted and potentially unhealthy diet. Because you want your diet to be as good as possible during pregnancy, for the most part, it is better if you choose fairly nutritious food for your meals and snacks.

Enriched snack crackers or chex snack mix are more nutritious than potato chips and give you the same salty crunch. An oatmeal cookie or some raisin spice cake (perhaps made in part with whole-grain flour) provide more nutrients than a sweet like a snack cake (like Twinkies®, for instance). A whole grain coffee cake with nuts is more nutritious than a doughnut. But, if it's potato chips or snack cakes you love, you had better allow yourself a treat now and then, if only to keep from being obsessed with them (and ending up on truly stressful eating binges). Only you know how often that is!

Selected Nutrients in Detail

The need for all nutrients is increased during pregnancy. As a new cell is formed in your baby's body, all the nutrients must be there to build the cell and allow it to function biochemically. You have to have the structural nutrients like protein (and calcium for bone cells) to build the framework of the cell. Then you have to have the functional nutrients, like vitamins and minerals, to provide for the chemical reactions that take place within the cell and give it life.

In all there are over forty nutrients that we know to be essential for good health. Of those forty nutrients, there are a few that we single out for particular attention during pregnancy and that we will be discussing in this section. Some nutrients, like iron and folic acid, are selected for "special attention" because they are difficult to get in adequate quantities in the American food supply. Others, like fluoride and B_6 are controversial, and you may have questions about them. Still other nutrients like protein, and also calories, are not that difficult to get, but bear discussion because they occupy such a centrally important role in the healthy pregnancy.

Some nutrients, like calcium and iron, are more immediately important for mother than baby. Zinc and other trace elements are included because of the problem of nutrient interaction. Fiber is discussed along with the nutrients, because of the common problem of constipation during pregnancy.

Calories. As we said earlier, it is difficult to predict the calorie requirement for a healthy pregnancy. Not only do women (like people generally) vary a great deal in their ordinary energy requirements, but in addition their bodies change during pregnancy in ways that influence energy needs. During the last half of pregnancy, the basal metabolic rate increases, using energy at a faster rate. At the same time, the intestine slows down, increasing the efficiency with which it extracts energy and other nutrients. In normal digestion, a certain percentage of available calories, and of nutrients in the diet "slip through." That percentage drops during pregnancy.

Women's activity levels vary. Some women react to pregnancy with increased energy and activity. Others, particularly during the last trimester, are tired, feel heavy and don't move around as much.

Some people try to calculate calorie requirement during pregnancy and prescribe a calorie requirement. In view of what I have just said, it is pretty obvious that this is not only difficult but perhaps foolhardy. About the only safe way to regulate food intake during pregnancy is with a healthy and well-functioning appetite. The only reasonable way to assess adequacy of calorie intake is by measuring weight gain.

As I've said repeatedly, you mustn't diet during pregnancy. Instead you should help yourself to regulate well. You can do this by:

1. Providing yourself with regular and satisfying meals, and devoting time and attention to eating them.
2. Providing snacks, if you are hungry for them, making them significant by choosing good food, and taking your time with it.
3. Getting moderate and regular exercise. Your body regulates better if you aren't too sedentary.
4. Paying careful attention to your body's signals of self regulation; that is, hunger, appetite and satiety. (Satiety is the feeling of fullness and well-being you get after a filling and tasty meal or snack.)
5. Varying the caloric density of your foods. If you must attempt to slow weight gain, you can increase your proportion of bulky and relatively low-calorie foods, like fruits and vegetables, breads and cereals and broth soups. To increase weight gain, do the opposite: hold down the low caloric density foods and eat more high caloric density (like fatty and sugary) foods. (Nutritious foods that are high in calories include ice cream, peanut better, sweetened yogurt, cheese, fruit and custard pies, etc.)

Protein. Protein provides the basic structure for all cells in the body. You need extra protein for the changes taking place in your own body (increase in blood volume, breasts, uterus, nutrient storage), plus protein to build your baby's body.

Protein requirement. In the *Toddler* chapter (p. 276) there is a table summarizing the protein content of different foods. Seventy-four to seventy-six grams of protein per day is recommended during pregnancy at any age.[2] Most people in this country eat about 100 grams per day, which probably shouldn't be discouraged. While the excess protein won't do any good, high-protein foods are important for other reasons: they are good sources of B vitamins and trace elements. As we said earlier, however, don't go overboard on the protein.

Protein and calories. Protein nutrition depends on calorie intake. If calorie levels in the diet are insufficient to support the growth of pregnancy, the protein will be sacrificed to provide energy.

In a study in Guatamala with a group of women whose diets appeared to be poor in all nutrients,[9] supplemental calories from non-protein sources produced as much of an improvement in the outcome of pregnancy as did calories plus protein. It appeared that the mothers could get by on relatively low amounts of protein in their diets as long as they were getting enough calories.

It may be, although this is not proven as yet, that those Guatamalan mothers who didn't get the extra protein were depleting their own muscle and organ tissue to provide for their babies' protein needs. That certainly isn't desirable for the mothers, particularly when they are facing the stress of lactation. However, it appeared that as long as the calorie levels were adequate, their babies came through the pregnancy in good shape.

Non-meat Protein. The non-meat sources of protein we referred to earlier, cooked dried beans, peas, lentils and peanut butter, all give fairly concentrated amounts of protein. However, these proteins are "incomplete." They must be properly planned into meals to make them good protein sources for you, because with incomplete protein you must match foods, compensating with one food for the protein deficiencies of another.

If you plan to eat a vegetarian diet, you should study the subject in detail. (The *Toddler* chapter, p. 312 discusses the subject a little more thoroughly.) It might be a good idea to consult with a good dietitian about the quality of your diet. However, to briefly

summarize, there are two ways you can utilize plant protein so it will supply your protein needs:
1. Consume plant with animal protein, at the same meal or within about two hours of each other (e.g., chili with ground beef or navy bean soup with bits of ham).
2. Eat grains and legumes or grains and nuts at the same meal (e.g., lentils and rice or peanut butter on bread).

Iron. Iron is essential for the formation of hemoglobin, the red substance in blood which carries oxygen from the lungs to the body tissues. During pregnancy, your iron requirement increases markedly, as you make up to four pints of additional blood, provide iron for your baby's iron reserve, and fortify yourself against blood losses during delivery.

Iron is one of the few nutrients in which the fetus acts as a parasite—it assures its own availability of iron by drawing from the mother. If you don't have enough iron during pregnancy, you could become anemic, but it is unlikely that your baby will be anemic. The most common cause of iron deficiency anemia in the infant is prematurity. The infant who has a short gestation misses out on at least part of the time when most nutrient storage takes place.

Providing iron for pregnancy. You can use a combination of strategies to provide for the considerable iron demand of pregnancy:
• Make sure you have good iron stores going into pregnancy. Eat a nutritious diet (following the suggestions below). Give yourself two years between pregnancies to get your iron storage up to normal.
• Keep your diet adequate in all essential nutrients. You can't build red cells with iron alone; you have to have enough food energy (calories), protein, vitamins, and minerals.
• Eat meat, poultry and fish. Iron from these sources is absorbed by your body several times as well as plant iron. These foods also contain something known as "meat factor," which improves iron absorption from other foods eaten at the same time.

- Eat a good vitamin-C source along with the meal. This improves iron absorption from the whole meal. Keep in mind the many vegetables and fruits that are rich in vitamin C, such as broccoli, spinach, and cantaloupe. (See the list on p. 42)
- Eat meat, poultry or fish and a vitamin C source at the same meal. Each helps iron absorption of the other. Spaghetti and meat sauce made with tomatoes is an example of an iron-containing meal with meat factor and vitamin C.
- Choose snack foods that provide some iron, such as fruits and vegetables, enriched or whole grain breads and cereals, nuts and seeds. Many times meals give adequate iron but snacks are poorly chosen.
- Take an iron supplement of 30 to 60 mg. per day.*
- Cook with cast-iron pans, to enrich your food with iron.
- When you eat, avoid consuming substances that are known to impair iron absorption, such as tea, antacids and calcium phosphate.

(Calcium diphosphate is sometimes used as a calcium supplement.) The chart in the *Toddler* chapter (p. 282) shows amounts of iron in common foods. The most iron you can reasonably expect to get from your diet is about 12 to 15 mg. per day. Liver is a rich source, but you should limit your liver consumption to twice monthly; eating too much liver will give you too much vitamin A. (Three ounces of beef liver can have about 45,000 IU of vitamin A.)

Supplementation with Iron. There is a long-standing nutritionists' and physicians' hassle about iron supplementation during pregnancy. Most accept the 30 to 60 mg. supplementation level[3] as reasonable, although a few argue that we are supplementing unnecessarily. They point out that blood levels of all nutrients tend to decrease during pregnancy. Generally, small women, those who have

---

*Most iron in supplements is combined with other elements. Common forms of supplemental iron, ferrous sulfate and ferrous fumarate, are about ⅓ iron; ferrous gluconate contains 11% iron. Ask your pharmacist to calculate the elemental iron in your supplement.

had several pregnancies, and those with multiple births show the greatest drop.[3] Most blood levels, including those of iron, can be increased if oral supplements are given, but whether these increases are normal or even desirable is the question—one that will require additional research.

Generally, it appears that this modest supplement of 30–60 mg. per day does no harm and may do some good, particularly for women who have low iron stores or iron-poor diets. But the controversy focuses on *levels* of iron—many physicians respond to dropping blood values of iron (the hematocrit and hemoglobin) by prescribing supplementation with an additional 100–200 mg. iron per day.

This practice, in my view, is unwise and not helpful. In the first place, these high levels of iron cause constipation and sometimes stomach upset. In the second place, too much iron interferes with absorption of trace elements such as zinc.[12] Thirdly, it is generally unnecessary.

Low blood values are generally caused by an increase in blood volume rather than a drop in number of red blood cells.[3] During the second trimester, blood serum production gets ahead of red cell formation and hematocrit drops. During the third trimester, with or without supplements, red cell formation catches up, and blood values approach the levels of the first trimester. And finally, the clincher is that those big doses of iron don't help anyway. They just pass through the intestine without being absorbed. Pregnant women absorb as much iron as they can and make red cells as fast as they can.[3] Additional iron can't speed up the process.

Folic Acid. The demand for folic acid doubles during pregnancy—in contrast to the requirement for other nutrients, which increases by 25 to 50%.[2] That, in combination with the low folate content of the typical American diet, leads to the standard and desirable practice of supplementing the diet with 200–400 micrograms of folic acid per day.

Folates play a central role in all cell synthesis. They provide the raw materials for DNA and RNA, the genetic messengers of the cell. Because of this central role of folic acid, a deficiency can have far-reaching consequences. The most common symptom is megaloblastic anemia, a type of anemia characterized by accumulation of large, immature red blood cells. Excellent food sources of folic acid include liver, kidney, brewer's yeast, and dark green leafy vegetables. Good sources are lean beef, veal, eggs, orange juice and whole grain cereals.

Vitamin B$_6$. Some people take vitamin B$_6$ in high doses to help control the nausea of early pregnancy. While some women who take it say it helps, there are no controlled studies to support its effectiveness.

Calcium. If you are over 18 years old, your base requirement for calcium is 800 milligrams per day. Younger women need 1200 mg. daily. For pregnancy and lactation you need to add 400 mg. per day. You need calcium during pregnancy to keep your bones strong and to build your baby's bones and teeth. You also need calcium circulating in your blood to allow normal blood clotting and muscle contraction.

The Baby's Need for Calcium. The fetus needs most of its calcium during the last trimester, when skeletal growth is maximum and the teeth are being formed. During that time the infant requires about 250 to 300 mg. calcium per day from the maternal blood supply. As with iron, the fetus appears to act like a parasite with respect to calcium. If you do not provide calcium from your diet, your bones will be robbed to provide calcium for your baby. (The saying, "a tooth for every child" accurately describes the process, though not the source.) The fairly common increase in dental caries during pregnancy probably has more to do with a slight increase in mouth acidity[11] (which gives a good reason for cautioning against too-frequent sugar consumption and for encouraging regular toothbrushing and flossing).

The Mother's Need for Calcium. Although the fetus is protected, this process of "robbing mother's bones" could have severe consequences for your own bone health. Maintaining strong bones is particularly hard for women. Women over age thirty gradually begin losing calcium, and in older life, many women have thin, weak, demineralized bones—a condition called osteoporosis. It appears that consuming adequate calcium and vitamin D throughout early life establishes good calcium stores prior to age thirty, and protects them after that time (though it isn't clear right now whether the process of bone demineralization can be stopped completely by good calcium nutrition).

Calcium and Leg Cramps. Many people think milk consumption has something to do with the muscle spasms and leg cramps that often appear during the last trimester. The problem seems to be that pregnant women have trouble maintaining serum calcium, which can make muscles more irritable. This problem can be worsened by exceptionally high intakes of phosphorus in the diet, because too much phosphorus can interfere with calcium absorption. Because milk is a source of phosphorus as well as calcium, some clinicians reason that the way to prevent cramps is to omit milk and substitute calcium pills. However, it does not appear that milk intake is the culprit, nor can leg cramps be prevented if milk drinking is curtailed. It is better to limit high phosphorus foods such as processed meats, snack foods and cola drinks.[14]

Sodium. Along with the strict limitations on calories, for many years sodium restriction was a part of the routine dietary management of pregnancy. That practice has pretty well been eliminated. More and more clinicians are realizing that sodium, like any other nutrient, is necessary during pregnancy.

A mild degree of fluid retention is a normal part of pregnancy. At times, however, the fluid retention becomes more marked, blood pressure goes up and there may even be protein in the urine. These are all the symptoms of preeclampsia, which we mentioned earlier. The treatment of choice for such marked edema and other symptoms, is bed rest—not diuretics, or sodium restriction.[10]

However, on the general principle that any nutrient used to excess can be harmful, sodium can be abused. In particular, high sodium intake is associated in some people with elevated blood pressure.

Fluoride. The estimated safe and adequate intake of fluoride for adults is 1.5–4.0 mg. per day. Fluoride in drinking water may be helpful in maintaining strong teeth and bones in adults. It is certainly beneficial in children for developing strong, caries-resistant tooth enamel. Municipal water supplies are generally fluoridated to the level of one part per million or 1 mg. per liter. Check with your health department to ascertain your local levels.

There are a very few studies of fluoride supplementation in pregnancy above that found in drinking water. One study showed prenatal exposure to 2.5 mg. supplemental fluoride per day to be helpful in reducing decay in the child's permanent teeth. Children of fluoride-supplemented pregnancies had thicker, more caries-resistant tooth enamel, with less pitting and ridges.[4] Because of the limited studies it's hard to tell if prenatal fluoride supplementation helps children's tooth enamel without doing any harm.

Fluorine, like other trace elements, is toxic if you take too much of it. The first symptom of excess intake is mottling (white, opaque spotting) of the tooth enamel in children. True toxicity in adults doesn't show up until you take 10 to 40 times the usual supplementation amounts for several years. In the few current studies of standard supplementation, there have been no signs of toxicity in either mother or infant.[4]

You certainly should drink plenty of fluoridated water during pregnancy and, if your local water is *not* supplemented, it could conceivably help your baby's teeth if you take a supplement, probably no larger than 1 mg. per day (2.2 mg. sodium fluoride).

Fiber. Making sure you get enough fiber will be helpful for preventing the constipation that often accompanies pregnancy. As we said earlier, the speed with which food moves through the gastrointestinal tract decreases during pregnancy. At the same time, the fetus grows and causes crowding in the abdomen. Both these factors appear to contribute to constipation.

Good sources of fiber in the diet are plant foods—whole grain breads and cereals, bran, dry beans and peas, nuts, fruits and vegetables. Of these, the whole grains appear to help the most. If you decide to increase the fiber in your diet, however, you should do so gradually, because you can cause diarrhea if you overdo it. Add on one serving of whole grain at a time until you find your bowel function is improved.

Generally, we call it good bowel function when you have a formed stool that you can pass without excessive straining or discomfort. You don't have to go daily—every two, three or even four days is OK. Stop your whole grain intake at 3 or 4 servings, or about half of your total bread and cereal intake. After that, if your bowel function is still not what you want, you can add a couple tablespoons of bran to your diet. The miller's bran that you get in the health food store is a good choice, as are bran cereals.

Zinc and Other Trace Elements. We have mentioned zinc in connection with several other nutrients, notably protein, iron and fiber. In every case, zinc absorption and utilization is affected by intakes of the other nutrients. These nutrient interactions are typical of nutrition in general and of trace element nutrition, in particular—an excess of one nutrient can interfere or even prevent the absorption of another. Zinc is also typical of other trace elements such as copper, fluoride and selenium, in that a certain small amount is necessary for good nutrition, but an excess amount can be toxic. And the difference between a safe dose and a toxic dose is, for the most part, very small.

Because overdosing is so easy and so dangerous, your best bet, with zinc as with other trace elements, is to count on a wide variety of foods to provide them in your diet.

The people in danger of developing trace element deficiencies are those at the dietary extremes—on extremely high fiber diets, or on limited and extremely refined diets. People who exist on low meat diets and eat primarily white bread, snack cakes, toaster pops, breakfast drinks, space food sticks and the like are in the greatest danger of developing trace element deficiencies. Most fabricated foods like these are enriched, or supplemented with only a few nutrients, leaving trace element nutrition untouched.

Supplements. There are something over 40 nutrients known to be essential for humans. Of those, a maximum of about 15 are provided in an "all-purpose" vitamin-mineral supplement, even in the wide-range supplements that are sometimes prescribed during pregnancy. To repeat, with the exception of iron and folic acid, which are probably desirable as supplements during pregnancy, your best bet for getting a nutritionally adequate diet is in consuming a wide variety of food—ordinary food from the ordinary grocery store.

The so-called "natural" vitamin and mineral supplements are very expensive and no more effective than the synthetic preparations. In fact, "natural" supplements frequently are mixtures of synthetic and natural substances, a step necessary to guarantee potency, since natural food substances vary widely in their nutrient density.

If you must take nutritional supplements during pregnancy, keep the total level of supplementation down to that of the Recommended Daily Allowances in the appendix. You should consult with a dietitian if you need help with your figuring. (While you're there, have her evaluate your diet.) REMEMBER: A LITTLE BIT IS

GOOD, BUT A WHOLE LOT MORE CAN BE HARMFUL, ESPE-
CIALLY IN PREGNANCY.

To repeat, taking excessive quantities of some nutrients can
be harmful. This is particularly true for the fat-soluble vitamins A
and D. Both are toxic in high amounts, and both can produce fetal
deformities, including urinary tract anomolies, abnormal skull development, and calcium deposits in the arteries.

High doses of water-soluble vitamins are not toxic, since the
fetus can excrete unneeded amounts, but high doses given to the
mother may have other undesirable consequences. Too much of any
nutrient can take up more than its share of the carrier system that
transports nutrients across the placenta, and thus cause a deficiency
of another nutrient. Excessive vitamin intake can also promote a
higher-than-normal requirement for the vitamin in both mother and
baby. An infant born of a mother on high vitamin C doses can temporarily show deficiency symptoms on otherwise adequate amounts,
until he adjusts to the more normal intake. The bodies of people on
vitamin C supplements become so accustomed to wasting the excess
vitamin C that they continue to do so for a time after the supplement
is discontinued.

Food-related Problems in Pregnancy

Nausea and Vomiting. "Morning sickness is a myth . . ." The face of
one knowing husband lighted up during a counseling session when I
pointed this out to his suffering wife. But his face fell when I went on
to add, ". . . Actually, it lasts all day." His wife, however, was de-
lighted.

As far as she was concerned, I had tweaked him, however
unwittingly, in exactly the right place. She had been getting little
sympathy for her struggle with the very common discomfort of early
pregnancy: the moderate, but (if you have it) always-present nausea
and stomach uneasiness.

It seems that this nausea is relieved by eating, but often only while you are eating and immediately afterward. About the only things that really seem to help are sleeping and getting your mind off it. Some women are sick in the morning and get it over with; others don't get sick at all.

Some women have a marked nausea almost all the time, and may vomit seemingly every time they eat. One woman reported that it made her so mad that she went right back to the table and ate again. That was probably not such a bad tactic, unless it aggravated the vomiting. The digestive process appears to be pretty quick and resourceful about capturing nutrients even under such adverse conditions. To use a macabre example, women who vomit intentionally as a way of losing weight usually don't, even though to all outward appearances they are getting rid of all the calories they consume. Their digestive systems manage to extract the calories even though much of the food bulk is forcefully ejected.

If your problem is severe nausea, remember that your major nutritional concern during that first trimester is to prevent ketosis. Small, regular, high-carbohydrate meals will keep you from falling back on your fat stores as a source of calories. Breads and cereals and fruits are good sources of carbohydrate, as are soda pop and candy. Some few women can't eat at all, and have to depend on constantly sucking on hard candy and popsickles and sipping Seven-Up to get their calories. If that is all you can manage, you had better go with it. The alternative may be hospitalization and intravenous feeding.

Many women worry because they lose their interest in meats and vegetables during the early months. This is really less of a concern than maintaining carbohydrate intake; most people have plenty of nutrients stored in their bodies to provide for the small early demands of the fetus.

But there are some tactics that seem to help maintain nutritional balance. It seems that meats and vegetables are more acceptable if they are laced liberally with starchy foods. Many times a casserole or sandwich will taste good, and can give the same nutrients as plain meat and vegetable. Surprisingly, even people who are nauseated can sometimes enjoy spicy foods such as pizza or chili. Beyond keeping the carbohydrate intake up, there are really no rules about what you should eat. You simply have to respect your appetite.

Many women say the smell of cooking bothers them, and that they can eat better if they don't have to do the cooking. And many men, in contrast to our earlier example, are very understanding and supportive about taking over the cooking for a time. You may feel better if you eat very small, regular meals. It might also help to eat meals dry, that is, without any beverage, and drink your fluids in between meals.

Gas, Bloating and Indigestion. Gas, bloating and indigestion increase in frequency during the last months of pregnancy when the baby begins to compete for space in the abdomen.

Heartburn. Many women complain of heartburn, which is an irritation caused by the stomach contents rising into the lower esophagus. During pregnancy the regulatory valves, or sphincters, relax in your digestive tract, including the one at the junction between your esophagus and stomach. This allows the acidic stomach contents to back up into the esophagus and cause irritation.

You may be able to control this problem chemically and mechanically. In the first place, avoid stimulating excess acid formation by avoiding caffeine and excluding stomach irritants like aspirin, pepper and nutmeg. Drinking milk and eating other protein and fat sources may help control stomach acid. Relax at meals and chew your food thoroughly. Avoid filling your stomach too full; eat small frequent meals and limit fluids at meals. Don't bend over or lie down after you eat, or do anything that will allow the stomach contents to flow up your esophagus.

It may be, however sadly, that nothing will help your heartburn (except for delivery). Even the antacids that are often prescribed to control the problem may not help (and some kinds of antacids may combine with calcium to make it less available to the body). An occasional use to allow you to sleep or to reduce a marked discomfort may be all right, but don't get in the habit of taking them regularly.

Gas. Stomach and intestinal gas are generally more of a social than a physical problem. For you, it might not even be a problem. If you would like to control belching and flatus with diet, it might help you to avoid certain foods that are generally thought to be gas-forming.

Figure 2-13. Foods That May Be Gas-forming

Raw apples
Melons
Onions, garlic
Cabbage
Cucumbers
Dried beans, split peas, baked beans, etc.
Spiced luncheon meat items
Chili, Mexican food
Italian food, pizza
"Hot" spices

Also keep in mind that much gas in the gastrointestinal tract comes from swallowed air. Make sure you relax when you eat and don't gulp your food.

Loss of Appetite. There are a few times in pregnancy when your appetite is not an appropriate guide to food intake. This will show up in a weight gain that is too low. Typically, women have problems with poor appetite when they are: 1) just getting over nausea from the first trimester; 2) have been ill and not eating well; 3) are in the third trimester and finding that the physical size of the fetus is affecting their appetite.

Start out by cutting down on bulky low-calorie foods. Filling up on broth soups or salads will interfere with your ability to consume more-concentrated foods. Another approach would be to eat somewhat more often. This is especially helpful during the last trimester when your stomach capacity is lower. Sometimes it is necessary to deliberately eat more than you really want to for a while to stimulate your appetite. Women report that after a week or two of "overeating" their appetite improves and they can again regulate their eating automatically.

Constipation. See the discussion on fiber (p. 314).

Excessive Weight Gain. It is very difficult to make general statements about what constitutes excessive weight gain in pregnancy as far as the *mother* is concerned. (The earlier discussion was from the infant's perspective—how much weight gain does it take to produce a healthy *infant*.) Some women have told me they gained forty pounds in a pregnancy and had absolutely no difficulty getting it off. These tend to be women who are good regulators when they aren't pregnant—who seemingly can eat to appetite and maintain a stable body weight. Others report gaining modest amounts of weight and having terrific problems getting it off afterwards. These are often women who generally struggle with their weight, supervise every bite and every ounce they gain, and gain at or below the bare minimum. I have often suspected, but can't prove it, that the pregnant metabolism simply becomes very efficient under these circumstances and squeezes all the juice it can out of every single calorie.

Still other women clearly overgain. They put on weight very rapidly during pregnancy and have a great deal of difficulty getting it off afterwards. These tend to be women who are chronic dieters, who are used to depriving themselves and supervising their weight very carefully—when they get advice to stop dieting and gain weight during pregnancy, they really don't know how to go about it, and overdo it.

If you're in the easy gain-easy loss group, you probably don't need to worry. Your body seems to have a great deal of reliable wisdom and I prefer not to disrupt that. If you're in the modest gain-difficult loss group, you may benefit from relaxing your standards a bit, allowing more food and more weight gain. In the long run I would hope that your body would come through pregnancy not quite so conserving and somewhat better at being able to let go of the extra weight.

The group I think that should give careful attention to food regulation during pregnancy is the third group, the chronic dieters. If you are in this group, you may be malnourished going into pregnancy, because of the frequent dieting and chronic struggles with weight. If you are, the excessive weight gain may not be all bad, because it at least helps to restore depleted nutritional stores. However, coping with major weight gain after pregnancy can be a real burden, especially to the women who depend too much on skininess to feel good about themselves.

Generally, if you are a chronic dieter and are constantly working against your body's natural tendencies of appetite and weight, it is probably wise to gain on the high side of average—more in the area of the high than the low twenties. (This is particularly true if you are underweight going into pregnancy.) However, you should also be wary of finding yourself on the way to super gains of forty and fifty pounds. And in control lies the rub.

From the "bad old days" of strict weight control during pregnancy we found out what women do when they are trying to hold down on weight. They starve themselves for three days before they go to the doctor, and then after their appointment they go out for french fries. Or they cut themselves down so low at meals they are starving, and then knuckle under at break time and raid the candy machine. That is precisely the kind of behavior we don't want to touch off by prescribing weight control.

During pregnancy is a good time for you to learn to eat normally, and to find out what happens with your weight when you do that. You need to know that your body will regulate if you let it—and give it *reasonable* help. You need to learn what it is like to sit down to the table hungry and eat slowly until you are satisfied. And you need to learn to manage, appropriately, foods that you have long denied yourself permission to eat, such as bread, potatoes, or even sweets.

You can get some clues about how to go about helping yourself to learn this process by reading the sections in this book on food regulation and obesity. In some ways you may have to treat yourself like a child as you learn, or relearn the whole process of tuning in on, and trusting, your body's cues of self regulation.

And don't forget to get enough exercise (if there is no physical problem which rules out exercise). Regular exercise will make your appetite a more trustworthy guide to how much you should be eating, will burn off excess calories, and will enhance your feelings of well being so you may be less dependent on food for emotional reasons.

A Few Cautions

Saccharine. If you give mice enough saccharine, they will develop cancer in their bladders. We don't know whether malignancies will develop in humans (and don't experiment by force feeding them the substance). However, it is important to keep in mind that a potentially carcinoginic substance is most dangerous during cell division, when its presence can distort and disrupt the division process—in other words, its danger is greatest during the growth of the fetus and in young children. While there are no studies available relating saccharine-related injury to this group, it still seems wise to avoid saccharine during pregnancy and during the rapid growth of childhood. Diet soft drinks are the primary source of saccharine in the American diet.

Caffeine. Any substance consumed by a pregnant woman will appear in some form in her fetus. Caffeine appears to be transported particularly well, and achieves the same concentration in the baby's bloodstream as in the mother's. That gives reason for pause. It is unclear what harm, if any, caffeine does to the fetus. A recent study in mice, that found birth defects in fetuses of mothers receiving 600 mg. caffeine per day, has been reinterpreted to indicate no damage to the fetus. Human studies show no association between caffeine intake in pregnancy and fetal abnormalities.[6, 11]

We do know, however, that caffeine can cause a variety of problems, from agitation and sleeplessness to excess stomach acidity. It is probably wise to avoid overdosing yourself, and your baby, with what is really quite a powerful drug. The following list shows major caffeine-containing foods and their approximate caffeine content.

Figure 2-14. Caffeine Content of Foods and Beverages

Food Source	Amount	Caffeine Content
Regular Coffee	8 oz.	100-500 mg.
Instant Coffee	8 oz.	80-100 mg.
Decaf. Coffee	8 oz.	3-5 mg.
Tea	8 oz.	60-65 mg.
Regular Cola	6 oz.	36 mg.
Diet Cola	6 oz.	18 mg.
Chocolate Bar	1 oz.	20 mg.

Read the fine print on the labels for the caffeine content of other soft drinks, such as Mountain Dew, Dr. Pepper, etc.

Nicotine. A discussion of smoking may seem out of place to you in this book. Perhaps it is. Nicotine consumption, however, can negate the effects of a careful and nutritious diet. Infants are smaller if their mother smokes during pregnancy. Smoking is also associated with increased frequency of stillbirth, and mortality during the newborn period.[14] DON'T SMOKE during pregnancy, and while you're about it, stay off it after your baby is born. The evidence is accumulating that non-smokers subjected to tobacco smoke suffer many of the same ill effects as smokers.

Alcohol. If a pregnant woman drinks alcohol in large and regular amounts, it is likely to cause birth defects in her baby. Fetal Alcohol Syndrome (FAS) is a well-known pattern of physical, mental and behavorial problems found in infants of drinking mothers. In addition, there is accumulating evidence that even moderate alcohol intake during pregnancy can be harmful: it can lower birth weight and increase the number of birth defects.

It is hard to say what constitutes "moderate" intake. It appears that regular daily use of as little as one or two ounces of absolute alcohol (equivalent to two to four ounces of hard liquor, two to four bottles of beer or the same number of three-ounce glasses of wine) can be harmful.[14] It also appears that saving up the alcohol for an occasional binge is worse than regular moderate intake.

Clearly, the safest course during pregnancy is to avoid alcohol altogether. A daily or occasional glass of wine or other alcohol-containing beverage will probably do no harm. However, there is a disturbingly small difference between a safe and a toxic dose.

Medications, Drugs. Don't take any medications or drugs without the approval of your doctor. This includes over-the-counter preparations such as antacids, headache remedies, and laxatives as well as prescription or non-prescription diet pills and diuretics.

PCB's. The toxic industrial chemical, polychlorinated biphenyl (PCB), accumulates in the fat of fish living in waters which have received discharges of waste containing PCB. Pregnant women, nursing mothers, and children under six should not eat fish from areas known to be contaminated with PCB. Since these are inland waters and streams, these fish would not generally be found in commercial trade. You would only be exposed to them if you are eating the catch of a hobby fisherman. The Wisconsin fishing license booklet has a listing of rivers and streams known to be contaminated with PCBs. Your local fishing booklet may have the same, or you might check with your department of natural resources or state health department.

If you have been heavily exposed to PCB, your breast milk may be sufficiently contaminated to discourage your breastfeeding. If you suspect you have been heavily exposed, it is wise to have your milk tested.

There is a great deal of basic nutrition information tucked away in this chapter, so I hope you won't put it away when you get through your pregnancy. I also hope you don't put away your emphasis on feeding yourself well, once you get through pregnancy.

If you are planning to breastfeed, you will need a good diet to support that. But more than that you, personally, need a good diet to remain strong and well. Don't turn all of your attention to nourishing your child. Remember to nourish yourself.

Selected References

1. Beal, V. A. Assessment of nutritional status in pregnancy—II. The American Journal of Clinical Nutrition. 34:691–696. 1981.
2. Committee on Dietary Allowances, Food and Nutrition Board, National Research Council, National Academy of Sciences, Rec-

ommended dietary allowances. U.S. Government Printing Office. 1980.

3. Committee on Maternal Nutrition, Food and Nutrition Board, National Research Council, National Academy of Sciences: Maternal nutrition and the course of pregnancy. Washington, D.C. 1970. U.S. Government Printing Office. 1970.

4. Glenn. Immunity conveyed by sodium fluoride supplements during pregnancy—II. Journal of Dentistry for Children. January–February 1979. p. 17.

5. Gormician, A., J. Valentine and E. Satter. Relationships of maternal weight gain, prepregnancy weight, and infant birthweight. Journal of the American Dietetic Association. 77: 662–667. 1980.

6. Linn, S., S. C. Shoenbaum, R. R. Monson, B. Rosner, P. G. Stubblefield and K. J. Ryan. No association between coffee consumption and adverse outcomes of pregnancy. The New England Journal of Medicine. 306:141–145. 1982.

7. Monson, E. R., et al. Estimation of available dietary iron. The American Journal of Clinical Nutrition. 31:134–141. 1978.

8. Naeye, R. L. Weight gain and the outcome of pregnancy. American Journal of Obstetrics and Gynecology. 135:3. 1979.

9. Naismith, D. J. Maternal nutrition and the outcome of pregnancy—a critical appraisal. Proceedings of the Nutrition Society. 39:1–15. 1980.

10. Pike, R. L. and D. S. Gursky. Further evidence of deleterious effects produced by sodium restriction during pregnancy. The American Journal of Clinical Nutrition. 23:833. 1970.

11. Rosenberg, L., A. A. Mitchell, S. Shapiro, D. Slone. Selected birth defects in relation to caffeine-containing beverages. Journal of the American Medical Association. 247:1429–1431. 1982.

12. Solomons, N. W. and R. A. Jacob. Studies on the bioavailability of zinc in humans: effects of heme and nonheme iron on the ab-

sorption of zinc. The American Journal of Clinical Nutrition. 34:249–258. 1981.

13. Winick, Myron. Growing Up Healthy. William Morrow. New York. 1982.

14. Worthington-Roberts, B. S., J. Vermeersch and S. R. Williams. Nutrition in Pregnancy and Lactation. C. V. Mosby. St. Louis. 1981.

3
Breastfeeding Versus Bottle Feeding.

Breastfeeding is better than infant formula for most babies. But formula feeding, appropriately conducted, is a highly acceptable substitute. Babies fed both ways can be appropriately fed—or overfed—or underfed. Breastmilk is undeniably more sophisticated nutritionally, and will continue to be because it is a living substance. Babies appear to have less stomach and intestinal upsets on breastmilk than they do on other kinds of feeding. Other arguments can support either breastmilk or formula— these include considerations of convenience, immunity to disease, working, economy, appearance and sexuality.

Your first task in feeding your infant is to decide which kind of a milk feeding you will use. I will be discussing the nutrition of the milk feeding in a later chapter. For now it is enough to say that the only food that an infant needs for the first five to six months of life is a properly-constituted milk-based feed, either breast milk or a formula.

I want you to know my bias right from the beginning, and that is that if at all possible I would like to have you breastfeed your infant. Breastmilk has some characteristics that cannot be duplicated by even the most sophisticated formula. But formula feeding, appropriately conducted, is a highly acceptable substitute.

In this country, as in other technologically advantaged countries, we have access to refrigeration and are generally able to maintain adequate standards of sanitation. Most people can read and follow directions and are able to afford enough formula for their babies.* All these factors have allowed successful artificial feeding. Breastfeeding is not the life-or-death matter it is in some developing countries.

Right now it is in vogue to strongly encourage breastfeeding. To listen in on some circles of nutritionists and pediatricians you would think breastfeeding was right there next to godliness. While this is all very nice for people who want to and can breastfeed their baby, it can represent nothing but a big guilt trip for people who can't. Forget about that. You will have plenty of opportunities to feel guilty as a parent without feeling guilty about *that,* too.

However you decide to feed your baby, give yourself the credit of having reached a carefully-considered decision that is best for you and your family. You can feed your infant well (or poorly) either way. You can have a warm, close feeding relationship either way.

My task, then, becomes one of helping you make a decision, based on your knowledge of the needs of your family.

---

*For families who are economically limited and at nutritional risk, the Women, Infants and Children program (WIC) provides food for breastfeeding women or formula for infants.

Producing an Adequate Amount of Breastmilk

One of the very common reasons women give for deciding to bottle feed is that they think breastfeeding is hard. They think it is difficult to provide enough milk for the baby, and they don't know if they can do it or not. Often they have heard stories of someone whose milk supply was inadequate, or who simply "dried up" and was forced to wean her infant from breast to bottle. And that can be a realistic picture. In some cases breastfeeding isn't successful—but usually not for physical or physiological reasons.

There seem to be a couple of major factors involved in breastfeeding failure. The most important one is lack of knowledge. Breastfeeding is not difficult, but there are a few basic principles that you do have to know. Let's look at them in general terms. (I'll discuss these principles in more detail in Chapter 6.)

Breastfeeding is not entirely instinctive. Primates as well as people learn how to breastfeed by observing the process in others. We have had little such opportunity in our society. Most of our mothers and even grandmothers did not know how to breastfeed. When they were having their babies, bottle feeding was popular and breastfeeding was considered slightly disgusting and/or too difficult. If they did try to breastfeed, failure rate was high, partly because it was just too easy to supplement with a bottle. They had seen their siblings and cousins being bottle fed, so they knew how to do that.

They also had little confidence in their physical ability to provide enough milk for the baby—which brings us to the other major factor in breastfeeding failure, and that is self doubt. If parents are overly hesitant about the mother's ability to breastfeed, it can impair her breastmilk supply and bring about a failure.

That's because breastmilk is produced according to a law of supply and demand. Emptying of the breasts stimulates them to produce more breastmilk. If a mother is <u>too</u> anxious (most beginners are <u>somewhat</u> anxious), it can impair letdown of breastmilk, the mechanism that gets the milk from the production to the delivery area in

74

the breasts. The milk is there, at least initially, but anxiety, suspicion and self doubt make the mother tense, and impair its delivery to the infant. The milk stays in the breasts, the biological message is relayed to the mammary tissue to make less, not more milk, and milk supply does, indeed, decrease.

It is also important to have reassurance that the ability to produce breastmilk has nothing to do with the apparent size of the breasts. It appears that there is no correlation between breast size and amount of glandular (milk-producing) tissue in the breasts. Larger breasts contain more fat and fibrous tissue than smaller breasts, but not necessarily any more glandular tissue.

The breastfeeding mother needs two important things: information and support. Most women *can* breastfeed their infants. Some of our best statistics on this come from the developing countries, where twenty years ago even under conditions of poverty, over 90% of mothers were successfully breastfeeding their infants.[4] I say *were,* because with the advent of western ideas and customs, and planting of the seed of doubt, breastfeeding "failure" is on the increase, as is bottle feeding. There are other factors involved, such as movement away from family support, and imitation of western patterns of infant feeding, but the basic fact remains that before these intrusions, a very high percentage of women were breastfeeding successfully.

Now that women are receiving support and information from each other, from well-informed health professionals and from well-written books, the success rate in this country is again rising. If you want to breastfeed, chances are very good that you will be able to do it.

Nutritional Desirability

We are sophisticated enough to admit that we don't know all there is to know about nutrition. Attempts of nutritionists and formula manufacturers to duplicate nature, i.e., breastmilk with formula, are constantly improving, but all must still acknowledge that there is more to be known. Research on breastmilk components continues to turn up remarkably sophisticated and intricate interactions between infant need and nutritional provision. For example, colostrum (the yellowish fluid produced before breastmilk) and early breastmilk are relatively high in zinc.[3] This high level is provided at a time when the "still-unfinished" newborn has special needs for zinc—while rapidly synthesizing zinc-containing enzymes. (Nutritionists are still debating optimum levels of zinc in formulas.) In addition, colostrum and early breastmilk contain proteins which give the baby immunity from organisms that enter through the intestine.*

Breastmilk also contains lipase, an enzyme that helps the infant's immature intestine digest other fats. Breastmilk is living, and those immunoglobulins and the lipase can be destroyed by heating. So taking it unpasteurized, directly from the breast, is a benefit formula can't duplicate.

Breastmilk is constantly changing: Breastmilk for the newborn is different in some ways than that for the child a few months old; a specific example would be the variation in zinc levels. Also, within each breastfeeding, the first milk is quite low in fat and looks thin and bluish. Then as the feeding progresses it contains more and more fat, until most of the fat is produced in the last minute of nursing. The infant then stops nursing and will only resume with the lower-fat milk from the other breast. This may have something to do with signaling the infant to stop nursing, and could have an impact on food and weight regulation.[2]

---

*As a matter of fact, factors in breastmilk that appear to confer immunity from viruses and bacteria are amazingly diverse. One that appears particularly interesting is the form of fat in the breastmilk (monoglycerides and free fatty acids of a particular chain length[6]). This appears to destroy certain viruses and bacteria by dissolving the fatty sheath around them.

Breastmilk is nutritionally very nearly complete: it needs only to be supplemented with vitamin D and fluoride to make it nutritionally complete for the full-term newborn infant.

Commercial proprietary formulas are good imitations of breastmilk. They are digestible, we can generally keep them sanitary, and we are able to give them to our infants in adequate amounts to allow appropriate growth. Their nutritional adequacy is demonstrated by the healthy and robust babies they produce. Commercial formulas are complete to the limits of present knowledge—no supplements are necessary. Formula manufacturers respond to research on breastmilk by duplicating insofar as possible breastmilk components.

The "old fashioned" evaporated milk formula is still a good substitute for breastmilk and is a good feeding choice for many families who need to control costs. If it is made with vitamin D-fortified evaporated milk, it needs only to be supplemented with vitamin C to be nutritionally complete.

We could debate endlessly on the convenience-breast-versus-bottle topic. It's handy to take the breastfed baby and disposable diaper and be all set for an outing. For long trips it's even better. However, if you leave the baby at home with a sitter, the bottle-fed baby may give you more flexibility for coming and going.

Convenience

There is also the consideration of *where* you can breastfeed your baby. Social custom allows you to bottle feed a baby in a restaurant, a waiting room, or any public place. It is ironic that social custom is not as free in defining acceptable locations for breastfeeding. You may be adroit enough or uninhibited enough to feel comfortable about feeding your infant almost anywhere, and I say, "Good for you!" But the fact remains that at some times and in some places, some people will frown at your breastfeeding your infant. And <u>that</u> also has something to do with convenience.

Is it more difficult to prepare bottles or to learn how to breast feed? You'll need to pamper yourself a bit to help establish and maintain a breastfeeding relationship. A matter of individual judgment and preference, don't you think?

Working

Since about 50% of women with children under six years of age are now working, this has a major impact on the decision as to whether to breast or bottle feed. Many women are able to breastfeed even if they are working full time. It takes a cooperative baby, however, and sometimes babies wean themselves abruptly to the bottle. It appears to be most successful if Mom can have a pregnancy leave of at least a month to six weeks when she breastfeeds totally, to get her breastmilk supply well established. Then when she goes back to work her supply has a better chance of maintaining itself with the nursing during the times she's at home. (I will discuss working and breastfeeding in more detail in the *Breastfeeding* chapter, p. 204)

Working women who bottle feed feel bottles are more desirable because their baby won't have to make a transition in feeding. They think they would end up bottle feeding anyway, and don't think it's worth the trouble to get their breast milk established. Both groups include parents who are concerned about their babies and come to thoughtful and considered decisions about the feeding style that is best for their family.

Weight Gain in Infants

A common argument is that breastfed babies are leaner than bottle-fed babies, which supposedly confers an advantage in terms of potential obesity in adult life. Some large and well-conducted studies done in the early 1970's have supported that, others have not.[1] A possible explanation for the discrepancy is the wide variation in the way breastfeeding is conducted. A child who is fed casually on demand is going to have quite a different breastfeeding experience than the one whose parents are very insistent on adhering to something that resembles a schedule.

Early in the '70's, many parents and professionals didn't know much about breastfeeding, and the tendency was to be more rigid. As parents have become more knowledgeable on how-to-breastfeed, they have become more casual about scheduling. More have been having a successful breastfeeding experience because breastfeeding depends on frequent stimulation.

Growth rates have improved as people have become more knowledgeable and successful. From my observation of my own children and those of friends, this has certainly been the case. We have all produced chubby little breastfed babies who later slimmed down into just-right toddlers and preschoolers. Pediatricians and nurse practitioners, too, have commented on the chubby-appearing (though weight-appropriate) breast babies thay have been seeing, and have observed informally that those babies pretty consistently slim down by the time they are three or four.

You will note that I am speaking of my observations. That has a value, particularly when one has had considerable experience and there is a scarcity of evidence from solid scientific research. I have not done a controlled study of a large group of breastfed babies who were being well and generously fed in response to demand, and followed them through their growing-up years to see what happens to them, weight-wise. Until I do, or unless I cite the scientific findings of others, you should be aware that I am giving you my opinion only. You should also keep this in mind the next time you get advice from someone based on their "long experience." In most cases what we're all talking about is a preconceived idea, supported by years of selected observations!

Economy

Evaporated milk formulas are least expensive, followed by breast-feeding, then commercial formulas. It costs more for you to eat when you are breastfeeding. It costs ⅓ to ½ more than breastfeeding to buy commercial formula—the lesser amount if you are purchasing it in powdered form, the greater if you are buying the liquid ready-to-feed. Cost of liquid concentrate formulas, which you mix with equal parts of water before feeding, is in between. (I will go into all of this in more detail in Chapter 5.)

Sexuality

One thing that you and your mate definitely need to discuss is your thoughts and feelings about how breastfeeding is going to affect your personal and sexual relationship. There is no denying that the infant-mother breastfeeding relationship represents a unity that can be seen in some ways as excluding the father. The mother may be giving the infant time, attention and emotional involvement that would have been previously reserved for her mate. It's important for the father to be able to talk about how he reacts to this. There may be little that can be done about changing the situation, but talking and sharing feelings can help a great deal to relieve anxiety and help keep you close.

Both men and women fear that breastfeeding will be an intrusion on the sexual relationship. Men think that a woman who is breastfeeding won't be as interested in sex. Also at times it is disturbing to them to see their mate's breasts, which they consider to be a sexual organ reserved for their erotic pleasure, used in a fashion which seems to be divorced from sexuality.

The truth of the matter is that breastfeeding is not divorced from sexuality, either emotionally or physiologically. Masters and Johnson[8] found that post partum women who breast fed had more rapid return to nonpregnant levels of sexual interest. Some also reported significantly higher levels of sexual tension than in the non-pregnant state.

This breastfeeding-sexual association can be a cause for concern. Some women experience sexual arousal from nursing, some don't. Those who do may worry that they are somehow abnormal. They aren't. All women, with the initiation of suckling, release certain hormones from the pituitary gland. These hormones cause uterine contractions that go on during the feeding and for about 20 minutes after the feeding. (This is one of the advantages of breastfeeding, as it enhances the return of the uterus to a more nearly pre-pregnant size.) Some women experience sensations from the contractions as sexual, some do not, others are not even aware that there are contractions. All are normal perceptions.[9]

The breastfeeding-sexual association can go the other way as well. Sexual arousal and orgasm frequently are accompanied by milk dripping from the breasts. That is because breastfeeding and sexual arousal use the same nerve pathways and hormones. The hormones prolactin and oxytocin are secreted in response to suckling, and allow milk secretion and milk let-down by the breast. The same hormones are released in response to sexual arousal.

The possibility of having nursing stimulate you erotically may be perfectly logical and acceptable to you. On the other hand, it may be alarming and even disgusting. Having milk drip from your breasts while you are making love may be a real turn-on for you—or a real turn-off. It's hard to know how you *will* react. It may be better just to take a wait-and-see attitude: try out breastfeeding, let yourselves feel what you feel, and then discuss it.

Personal Preference

Some people get a real emotional and physical high from breastfeeding. Others see it as all in a day's work. Some people think it's disgusting and can't imagine doing it.

It's important to consider and respect your own feelings in making your choice of infant feeding. A good feeding relationship with your infant is all-important, and if you hate it, you won't be able to hide it from yourself, your baby, or anyone else. Even the sophisticated components of breast milk can't make up for that.

As I said earlier, the father's feelings come into play here, too. Some fathers feel breastfeeding is just great, and encourage it strongly. Others have reservations. They might see breastfeeding as being too much of a burden for the mother. Perhaps they would like to feed the infant themselves, and feel left out. Or, as I have discussed, they may feel that breastfeeding is an intrusion on the sexual relationship. Possibly they would like to have a little more social freedom, and dislike the thought of being tied down to a feeding schedule. These feelings all need to be considered in making the choice of feeding.

Particularly if this is your first child, you can't really anticipate how you and your mate will react to feeding your infant. You might become so involved that you won't even want to leave her. On the other hand, you may feel hemmed in, and really feel you need some time to get out.

Your baby will have a lot to do with your feelings about needing to get away, as well as your feelings about the feeding relationship. Your baby may be so placid and well-mannered that you can take her anywhere; being around her may be so easy that you won't feel tied down. On the other hand she might be a dissatisfied little barracuda who makes her presence known at all the worst times. Having an opportunity for a breather from a difficult child can be wonderful. (A hasty word of encouragement: children change.)

If you remain undecided, you might consider trying out breastfeeding right after you deliver. If you decide you don't like it or it's not working out, it's much easier to switch to the bottle than vice versa. In some maternity wards well over 50% of infants are now being breastfed. Health professionals are now more supportive of breastfeeding, and better at helping you get started.

Appearance

Most women are concerned about their figures. They are eager to return as quickly as possible to their prepregnant weight and shape, and wonder how breastfeeding will affect that. Some have heard that they have to gain weight to breastfeed.

Breastfeeding allows you a normal physiological process of using calories in breastmilk production to help you lose the weight. It also forces you to be patient in your attempts to regain your figure. One of the ways that your body apparently prepared for lactation is by fat deposition during pregnancy. About eight pounds of the average 25-pound weight gain during pregnancy is fat, which represents a calorie store of roughly 28,000 calories. Breastfeeding allows you to utilize this calorie store in providing some of the calorie demands of lactation, which for the newborn can range from 400 to 700 calories per day. As you draw on this calorie store you will lose weight gradually.

Breastfeeding, however, makes it important not to lose weight too fast, as that can impair your breast milk supply. Generally, we recommend a weight loss of no more than one pound per week. That should enable you to eat enough to maintain both your energy level and your breastmilk supply.

From a physiological standpoint, you don't have to be as patient in waiting to diet when you are bottle feeding. But I still have my reservations about your dieting right after delivery. Physically and emotionally I doubt that it is generally wise to be cutting down on food intake at a time when you have so many new demands on you. But in any event, dieting while bottle feeding won't impair the baby's milk supply.

Mother-infant Bonding

It appears that formation of intense attachment between mother and infant, and father and infant, occurs readily during a sensitive period in the first 24 hours of life,[7] and in the early days after birth. The beginning of this bonding may have a long-term impact on the relationship between parent and child.

Certainly bottle feeding as well as breastfeeding parents can insist on extensive contact with their infant during this important time. Whether breastfeeding increases the intensity of the attachment is not really known. Because breastfeeding forces a close contact and interdependence of mother and child, however, the mechanics do promote proximity. In cases where there is a high risk of "disorders of mothering," health professionals in pediatrics are particularly likely to encourage breastfeeding to promote this contact and interdependency.

Safety

A certain very small and variable percentage of every drug taken by the mother will show up in the breastmilk. For that reason caution in drug selection and consumption during breastfeeding is extremely important. Certain of the antacids, anticoagulants, hormones, anticonvulsants, laxatives and other drugs are absolutely contraindicated for use while breastfeeding. Indeed, any drug, over-the-counter or otherwise, should be carefully checked before use by the breastfeeding mother. There are also a few foods, such as rhubarb and chocolate, that are inadvisable during breastfeeding because they contain an active ingredient that is laxative.[1]

Environmental contaminants are another major consideration for the breastfeeding mother. Certain chemical pollutants in the food chain are excreted in the fat of breast milk. The insecticide DDT was banned from general use years ago but is still present in breast milk. It appears, however, that the maximum likely to be ingested is several hundred times less than that known to cause acute intoxication in humans.

Additionally, it is somewhat cold comfort to know that the newborn already has more insecticide stored in body fat from intrauterine exposure than he is likely to acquire if suckled. In other words, the exposure is unavoidable, and it is unlikely that you will exacerbate the problem by breastfeeding.

More recent has been the concern about polychlorinated biphenyls (PCB's) and polybrominated biphenyls (PBB's). The first is a heat-transfer agent, the latter a fire retardant. They are present in the food supply purely by accident, sometimes as a waste discharged into water from factories. These, too, are carried in body fat and transferred to the fetus and to breast milk. Currently most health authorities, on the basis of absence of evidence of harm to infants from present levels of PCB's and PBB's in breastmilk, are recommending no change in current nursing practice. However, they are recommending that young women, especially if they are pregnant or lactating, limit their consumption of game fish from PCB-containing waters. Further, they are recommending that if a woman has been exposed to known contaminated areas that she get her breastmilk analyzed and decide on an individual basis whether or not to continue breastfeeding.[10]

Cows' milk contaminated with PCB is simply not allowed on the market. Further, these substances are stored in fat, and milk fat is replaced with vegetable fat in formulas, eliminating a substantial source of these contaminants.

Commercial formulas, however, are not without their dangers. Unless handled properly, they can be contaminated bacterially. Also, unless mixed properly they can be diluted too much and cause retarded growth or, at the other extreme, diluted too little and cause dehydration of the infant.

There have been mistakes over the years in proprietary formula production. Nutrients have been present in inappropriate amounts. When this has happened, babies have not done well, and the error tracked down and corrected.

In summary, then, there are three major factors to be considered in making the decision about breast or bottle feeding for your infant:

1. Your home and work demands.
2. Nutritional and physiological considerations for you and the baby.
3. Your feelings.

All three are important. But because it is sometimes harder for people to pay attention to their feelings, I would like to close by emphasizing those.

All your logic may tell you that breastfeeding is the most desirable alternative. But your feelings may say you don't <u>want</u> to. <u>Don't</u> let anyone (not even yourself) tell you you <u>shouldn't</u> be feeling that way. They are your feelings and they are valid.

If you would like to change your feelings, that's another matter. Think about how you feel, and talk about it with your mate. Really explore your feelings and see if you can find out where they come from. Step back and try to get a broader perspective on the matter. Your feelings may have something to do with the way you see yourself in relation to each other or in relation to the world in general.

Find out how your partner is feeling. Keep in mind as you listen to him that there is room for you each to have *different* feelings. You can only acknowledge and accept. You can't persuade or argue someone out of their feelings. Nor need you somehow change things to make the feelings go away. (Sometimes that's possible, but often it's not.) If you feel that you are really struggling or reacting in a way that puzzles or distresses you, you might want to get professional help.

Spending some time exploring in this fashion *before* the baby comes, as you both decide on a milk feeding, is good preparation for *after* the baby comes. Then you may have ambivalence about many things, and you certainly will have feelings and reactions to your changed status. To keep you together at that time it is important to keep you talking to one another. A major key in caring for your child is caring for your relationship.

Selected References

1. Fomon, Samuel J. Infant Nutrition. 2nd ed. W. B. Saunders. 1974.
2. Hall, B. Changing composition of human milk and early development of an appetite control. Lancet. April 5, 1975, 779–81.
3. Hambridge, K. Michael. The Role of Zinc and Other Trace Metals in pediatric nutrition and health. IN Pediatric Clinics of North America: Nutrition in Pediatrics. February 1977, 95.
4. Jelliffe, D. B. Infant Nutrition in the Subtropics and Tropics. 2nd ed. World Health Organ. Monograph Ser. No. 29. Geneva, 1968.
5. Jelliffe, Derrick B. and E. F. Patrice Jellifee. Breast is Best: modern meanings. New England Journal of Medicine. 297(17):912–915. 1977.
6. Kabara, Jon J. Lipids as host-resistance factors of human milk. Nutrition reviews 38(2):65–73. February 1980.
7. Lozoff, Betsy, Gary M. Brittenham, Mary Anne Trause, John H. Kennell, and Marshall H. Klaus. The mother-newborn relationship: limits of adaptability. The Journal of Pediatrics 91(2):1–12. 1977.
8. Masters, W. and V. Johnson. Human Sexual Response. Little, Brown and Company. Boston. 1966.
9. Weichert, Carol. Breast-feeding: first thoughts. Pediatrics 56(6):987–990.
10. Wisconsin Dept. of Health and Social Services. Statement on Chemical Contaminants in Breastmilk. Madison, WI 53701. October, 1977.

4
Calories
and
Normal Growth

Your child is born with a certain growth potential, and with the ability to appropriately regulate his food intake to support that growth potential. You can trust him to let you know how much he needs to eat, and you can trust him to make up for his errors in eating. He may overeat at a feeding and spit up, then go longer before he gets hungry again. He may undereat for a whole day, or several days, then make up for it by being extra-hungry for a time.

Your baby will grow by getting taller, heavier and fatter. It is generally safe to let that process take care of itself—to feed him and see how he grows. However, growth charts are generally used in the doctor's office as a way of evaluating normal progress in height and weight. Understanding how to read and interpret them can be helpful and interesting for you. However, to be useful, and not harmful, they must be based on accurate height and weight measurements. It is also helpful to maintain a somewhat detached attitude in following your child's growth, and not to overreact to normal variations in growth patterns.

Nourishing a young infant presents very specialized nutritional considerations. A newborn has an extremely high nutrient requirement per unit of body mass. Due to his rapid growth rate, the newborn has relatively higher requirements for calories and for all nutrients, including water, than at any other time in his life. At the same time, excesses in total food, or in any one of the nutrients, can be harmful and even dangerous. Not only do there have to be enough nutrients in the baby's diet, but they have to be there in the right quantities and in the right balance to each other. Managing all that can be complicated, given the day-to-day fluctuation in food intake of a normal infant AND the gradual increase in nutrient needs as the child grows.

Given the complexity of the nutritional puzzle, the solution is remarkably simple. Your infant regulates his total calorie intake, using his hunger and satiety. And if his food is appropriate, as with breastmilk or a carefully-balanced infant formula, he will be getting the right relative amounts of each of the necessary nutrients with each calorie of food. At the same time that he takes enough calories to satisfy his hunger he will automatically be taking enough of all the nutrients necessary for growth. As he gradually gets bigger and needs increasing amounts of nutrients for growth and development, his hunger will increase and he will get those nutrients. Again, the nutrients will be in proper quantities and in proper balance to one another.

As we pointed out in previous chapters, for the first few months, either breastmilk (with supplemental fluoride and vitamin D) or a properly-constituted commercial formula will provide all required nutrients in the proper balance for the growth and health of your infant. So, having made that important decision early on, you will need to know two things:

1. How to provide the proper amount of food to allow your baby to grow properly.
2. How to interpret his growth.

The calorie* is an important base unit of the science of nutrition. Calories are a measure of the energy that is essential for life to exist. The average calorie requirement for a newborn is about 45 to 50 calories per pound of body weight. (The adult calorie requirement is about 10 to 15 calories per pound of body weight.) Of these calories, during the first four months, about one-third go for growth; about two-thirds go for maintaining the moderate physical activity of the newborn and his physiological processes: breathing, digestion of food, circulation of blood, and the various metabolic processes necessary for life.

The Growth Process

The infant usually doubles his birthweight within four months. Most infants this age spend much of their time sleeping. Between four and twelve months the calorie requirement remains about the same: between 45 and 50 calories per pound of body weight. After four months of age the infant usually spends only about 10% of calories for growth, but uses a higher proportion of calories for physical activity.

Along with body size in general, the brain and nervous system in particular do a great deal of growing during the first 24 months of life. The most active phase of brain growth in the human infant begins during the last trimester of pregnancy, and continues until about two years of age. It would seem logical to assume that this would make the malnourished infant very vulnerable to retarded intellectual capacity.

Studies have failed to support that point of view; some apparently malnourished infants who are in socially rich and stimulating environments seem not to show tne intellectual effect of malnutri-

---

*I will use the word "calorie" in the way it is popularly understood. It actually refers to the "kilocalorie," which is a unit of scientific measurement.

tion. That was the situation during the World War II blockade of Rotterdam in 1944–45. Despite the fact that food was severely limited, to the point of famine, males born during that famine had scores on intelligence tests at age 18 similar to babies born in non-famine areas.

But usually the malnourished infant is also in a limited social environment. The malnourished infant is usually also intellectually under-stimulated and socially deprived, and develops an impaired intellectual capacity because of the combination of these factors. The undernourished infant is often in the care of an undernourished mother. Because of low energy levels caused by their lack of food, each of them fails to provide much stimulation for the other, and the environment of the infant, as well as the nutritional status, becomes limiting. So, in such cases you could say that the nutritional status does have an effect on the infant, but that it seems also to involve social and environmental factors.

Now, I am not telling you that good nutrition is unimportant for intellectual growth. It can be one of the factors, but to have a negative impact, other factors must be present as well. What I am saying is: RELAX. Children have ups and downs in food intake. It is not necessary to entertain yourself with visions of an intellectually defective child each time your infant eats poorly.

Obesity. Simple survival, and laying the basis for healthy mind and body is the vital nutritional goal in the early months. In practice sometimes I wonder if this consideration is overlooked or forgotten among all the publicity about obesity prevention.

The beginnings of adult obesity are said to be laid in infancy. Since concerned parents and professionals are eager to avoid the social, psychological and emotional consequences of obesity, I see them worrying more about overfeeding than about underfeeding their infant. They wonder how much they should be feeding their baby and

91

worry that they might be feeding too much. Sometimes I see a baby who seems to be positively underfed, and usually find I am talking to a parent who is extremely concerned about overweight.

I think, however, that many of us have begun to pull back some in our alarmist tactics about preventing obesity. There is a very low correlation between excessive fatness in infancy and overweight in older children, and possibly in adults. Not every fat baby is a fat adult, but there is some risk so some prevention seems appropriate.[10] It seems to me that in most cases this prevention can take the form of setting things up so the baby can achieve normal growth and food regulation. And, in the few cases where this normal process must be modified, the prevention must not be so vigorous that the infant simply isn't allowed to grow normally. (See the more detailed discussion of these questions in Chapter 11.)

Slow or Inadequate Growth

It is easy to get caught in a feeding struggle with a slow-growing child or with one who appears to eat poorly because of illness. My neighbor, David, had some problems with asthma when he was about a year old and his chest congestion, occasional pneumonia, and frequent ear aches would repeatedly put him "off his feed," usually just about the time his parents were feeling good about his eating and hoping he could catch up a bit on his weight.

I warned them that a major risk for them was getting too anxious about his eating and trying too hard to feed him. His mother acknowledged that already at 14 months he was getting a wicked little gleam in his eye when she would try various food tactics to get him to eat. (David, like most children, is no dummy and knows when he has the upper hand.)

Hard as it is, you have to feed a child like David the way you would any other child—present appropriate food in a supportive fashion and allow him to make the choice about eating. As we will discuss in the chapter on *Regulation* (p. 345), the more you pressure, the more poorly they will eat.

Getting the Right Amount of Calories

So it becomes a balancing act: enough calories to allow optimum growth, but not so many that the baby gets too fat. That sounds difficult enough—but we must also consider other factors: some infants eat more and grow faster than others; every infant eats more some days than others. Also, infants vary widely in their caloric requirements. If you have a big, wide awake, demanding baby who grows very rapidly, he will probably have a higher calorie need than a small, sleepy, placid baby who is growing very slowly.

In addition to variation in rate of growth and differences in personality, there seems to be a definite relationship to physical activity. A number of years ago, Rose and Mayer[3] did a research project where they strapped tiny pedometers to the arms and legs of young infants. They found consistently that the more active babies tended to be thinner and to eat more than the less active babies, who had a higher proportion of body fat and ate less. It appeared that these activity levels were the result of innate characteristics of the infants and could not be attributed to external circumstances.

There is even beginning to be some evidence that there is variation in calorie requirement between infants who appear to be the same in size, growth and activity. One infant will be comfortable, healthy and normal on food intake that is significantly less than that of another.

Variation in Calorie Requirement. The following chart gives you some idea of the variation in calorie requirement at different ages.[4] The energy requirement figures were calculated by taking standard weights at different ages and figuring 50 calories per pound of body weight. The calorie figures were converted to formula intake by figuring 20 calories per ounce of formula.

Figure 4-1. Spread of Daily Calorie Requirements During First Year (Courtesy the Gerber Company).

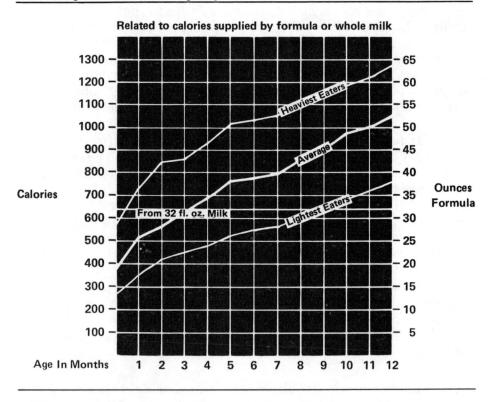

As you can see, there is a wide variation in calorie intakes among normal infants at a given age. At age three months, for example, the smallest, least-hungry baby will be consuming about 500 calories, or about 25 ounces of formula per day. If that baby is eating as few as six times per day, the average amount of formula per feeding will be a little over four ounces. By contrast, the largest, possibly most active baby will be taking almost twice as many calories, about 860 calories, and about 43 ounces of formula per day. If that hungry baby can get by on six feedings a day, he will be getting an average of over seven ounces of formula or breastmilk per feeding. If you are breastfeeding one of the big, active, hungry babies, you may need more frequent feedings to keep up with his needs.

The charts can give you an idea of the range of food intakes for different infants. How much a given infant actually eats depends on his size, activity, growth rate and metabolic rate. It can also depend on the digestibility of the food, a subject I will discuss in the *Milk Feeding* chapter. It's difficult to predict exact calorie requirements at any age, but with the infant it is particularly so.

Variation in Day-to-day Intake. Not only do infants vary from one another in food intake, but the individual infant also varies on a daily basis. Back in 1937, Arnold Geselle and Francis Ilg demonstrated that point very nicely.[5] They fed babies on demand, allowing sleeping and waking times, as well as eating times and quantities of formula to shift at the will of the infant. It became apparent from these observations that babies, like big people, are not consistently hungry from one day to the next. This chart plots the milk intake in ounces per day of baby "J," who was followed through his sixth, seventh and eighth weeks.

In day one of week six, little "J" consumed 23 ounces of formula (460 calories). On the next day he took 24 ounces (480 calories). The third day his milk intake went up to 29 ounces (580 calories), then 25, 30, 23, 28. The fluctuation in the eighth week was even greater. On the fourth, fifth, sixth and seventh days of week eight, the milk intake was 26, 21, 28 and 32 ounces, respectively. The pattern seemed to be that a hungry day was often followed by a less-hungry day, which in turn preceded another hungry day. Despite all that fluctuation, though, baby "J" grew at a consistent rate, as you can see by the following chart, which shows the body weight in pounds for those same three weeks.

Figure 4-2. Formula Intake of Baby "J" (Courtesy J. B. Lippincott)

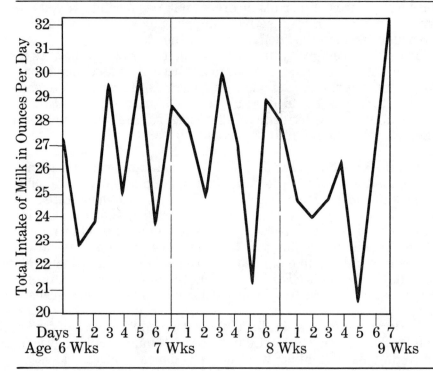

During that three-week period "J" increased his weight from 9 pounds 12 ounces to 11 pounds. He was weighed daily, and his weight fluctuated by no more than two ounces on a daily basis. Even in week eight, when his food intake fluctuated wildly, his weight increased at a steady rate.

Figure 4-3. Growth of Baby "J" (Courtesy J. B. Lippincott)

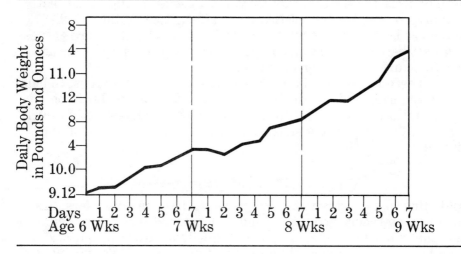

It appears not only that the child was regulating food intake on a daily basis, but also that his process of food regulation was somehow able to accommodate for daily fluctuations in food intake. His caretakers made no attempt at all to regulate the quantity of food that he took. They simply responded to his cues of hunger and satiety with a nutritious milk feeding, being sure that they gave him enough time to eat until he was satisfied, but at the same time taking care not to urge him to eat.

Feeding intervals were irregular, with some naps going longer than others. At times little "J" probably drained his bottles and wanted more, and at other times refused part of the bottle.

These studies were done in 1937, when the then "modern" physicians, using the then-perfected evaporated milk formulas, calculated "appropriate" ounces of formula on the basis of babies' weight. Babies were expected to eat that amount, no more, no less, and to take it at regular intervals and in regular amounts. Parents were expected to see to it that they did. Geselle and Ilg called that feeding process "over-sophisticated . . . if the constitutional indicators are ignored in the interests of inflexible schedule there ensues a contest between infant and adult . . . with unnecessary losses and emotional disturbances on both sides."

There had to be a better way—there was, and there is, to help babies regulate food intake. Ironically, the way was, and is to be unsophisticated, to go back to the method parents have used forever: seek-and-find, depending on the infant for the major source of information.

Origin of Food Regulation

Hilde Bruch, a psychiatrist who specializes in eating disorders, has an appealing theory about the beginnings of food regulation.[1] She says that a newborn infant is presented with a variety of sensations from his body, some pleasant and some unpleasant. He has no way of sorting out one sensation from the other or identifying a source of appropriate comfort for the feelings of uneasiness or distress. It is up to the discerning parent or caretaker to take the time with the infant to figure out what is bothering him.

If the parent is able to do this with reasonable accuracy and consistency, eventually the child, too, will come to the point where he can accurately identify what is bothering him and fulfill his needs appropriately. That is, as an older person, if he is hungry he will eat, if he is bored he will find something to do, etc. If, on the other hand, the parent consistently misidentifies the source of the infant's discomfort, the child too will learn to confuse one sensation and source of gratification with the other. If the parent offers bottle or breast in response to any signal of discomfort or distress, she will probably teach the infant that the way to fix any problem is to eat.

So the idea, then, is to correctly identify and respond to your infant's discomfort signals. With some babies it is easy; they only cry if they are hungry or wet, and sometimes not even when they are wet. Other babies are not so easy. They cry a lot and seem to complain about every little thing—boredom, gassiness, loneliness, temperature, heaven only knows what all, maybe even politics and the weather.

Soothing the Fussy Baby

The fussier infant may also want to eat fairly frequently, as his wide-awake lifestyle makes him more active and he may need more calories. For a child like that you will need more flexibility in care, comfort and entertaining tactics. Talk to friends and professionals, read books, and experiment. (My favorite tactic was to put the baby in a soft backpack with good head support and just "wear" him while I went about my work.) Don't feel you are doing something wrong if you feed a child like that quite often. Once you have burped, changed, cuddled and entertained, if your baby is still pressing, you had better go ahead and feed him, even if it seems like an unlikely time. These same babies seem to take a long time settling down to any kind of routine.

Feeding Schedules

One of the things that could sabotage your response to your baby's needs is trying too hard to follow a schedule. I have not talked to any professionals or read a book in years that recommends a feeding schedule. But, generation after generation of young parents (including me, when I was at that stage) have somehow preserved the myth of the every-four-hour feeding schedule as some kind of a standard for which they should strive. It is remarkable to me that that should be so, since it has been over 30 years since rigid schedules were professionally in vogue.

But persist it has, and it causes parents lots of unnecessary discomfort. There is nothing magic about an every-four-hour feeding schedule. Certainly it is much more convenient for parents to be able to anticipate when their child will be able to eat next, and some children adapt themselves to this very nicely. Others just don't make it. Some won't settle for *any* sort of regularity with their feeding schedule. They may, for example, manage to make it for five hours from one feeding to the next, and then demand two feedings an hour apart.

That is really all right as far as the infant is concerned. He just has some residual hunger that he needs to have satisfied. Whether or not it is all right with you is another matter. You may find this irregular feeding pattern absolutely maddening, and feel you must persist in your efforts to regulate your infant's schedule.

Most times I find the source of a lot of the parents' discomfort with eating patterns like this coming from the outside: other people are pressing subtly (or not-so-subtly) for the parent to get the child on a "regular schedule."

I see many parents who seem to be in this predicament, but I am thinking particularly about Mrs. Washburn as I write this. She and little Daniel stopped into my office one day after their pediatrician's appointment. She wanted to know what she could do to get her baby on a different feeding schedule.

Dan was a big, active, wide-awake two-month-old baby. He had gained five pounds since birth and had done it all on breastmilk. He was eating at frequent and irregular intervals and was still getting up twice a night to nurse. It was apparent that Mrs. Washburn was a conscientious and concerned young mother who enjoyed her infant, but it was also apparent that she was feeling very upset about their feeding relationship.

Before I responded to her request, I asked her, "What is there about the way he is eating that bothers you?" She looked a little startled and then became thoughtful. "I really don't mind feeding him that often," she said. "He nurses well and I am enjoying having him around. But everyone keeps talking about getting him on some sort of schedule. And the doctor asked me if he wasn't sleeping through the night yet. I just think that I must be doing something wrong."

I asked her what she did when he woke up, fussing. "At times he seems very hungry, almost frantic, so I feed him right away. Other times I cuddle him and play with him. I change him and put him in his swing for a while. Or he sits up in his infant seat and watches me while I do my work. But nothing works for very long. He just starts fussing again and doesn't seem like he is happy until I feed him. Maybe I should put him on a bottle or something to see if I can get him to be on some sort of schedule."

"Is a schedule important for you?"

"Well, it would be nice at times. But no, I can really manage without it. I just want to do the right thing for Dan."

What an easy case to solve! I was able to reassure Mrs. Washburn that she was doing exactly the right things for her baby. He was clearly an exceptionally hungry, fast-growing little guy, very bright and curious. It *was* possible to overfeed him, as he could get in the habit of using eating for entertainment, but she was forestalling that by going through the list of other possibilities before she fed him. In short, she was following a rhythm that was right on target for her particular baby.

What a shame that she was being made to feel uneasy by the subtle demands for an external schedule! How ironic that she would consider weaning him to formula in an attempt to satisfy something as unnecessary as a regular schedule!

With Mrs. Washburn it was easy, as she really didn't want a regular schedule. She needed support for doing it the way she was doing it. For others it is not so easy, as they really *are* disturbed by the irregularity and frequency of the feedings. That is, in fact, the way I was with Lucas, my second child.

Given my experience with Kjerstin, our oldest, who was a placid, compliant, regular little baby, I figured I could shape Lucas' habits into some sort of schedule right away. (Always be wary of advice from parents who have had easy babies.) So I tackled Lucas with a fair amount of vigor and self confidence.

He was an entirely different kid from his sister. In fact, he was a lot like little Daniel: hungry, curious, active. What a character he was! And could he eat! He would nurse about every two hours, on the average, then take a little catnap and be up again, wanting us to entertain him. He would wait five hours to eat and then want two feedings, one right after the other. Some days seemed like they were a hundred years long; I was either caring for him or trying to predict when I would care for him next.

I was absolutely insistent that I would get him on a schedule. Not only did I think we were doing something wrong in allowing this non-schedule, it was driving me bananas. So struggle, we did. I staved him off when he was hungry, and woke him up when I thought he should be having a feeding. Some days he would behave in a way that approximated regularity and my hopes would rise, only to be dashed by his subsequent return to his random patterns. I think, short of allowing him to scream from hunger, I was about as close to a rigid, insistent parent as you would find. And all to no avail. It was clear that my most persistent efforts were not working.

So I gave up. He wasn't about to change, so I changed. I fed him when he wanted to be fed and forgot about scheduling. And it helped! Once I stopped fuming and fussing about needing the schedule, I began to learn to be more casual.

When Curtis was born he was even bigger, hungrier and more irregular than Lucas. So I gave up from the very start. It seemed to me with three children the only answer was to HANG LOOSE—a philosophy that has yet to fail me.

I was committed enough to breastfeeding that I wasn't about to give it up on the gamble that bottle feeding would make them more "manageable." I figured that they would probably keep their same habits, and meanwhile I would be struggling with bottles as well.

Some parents choose to switch to the bottle with kids like this. Then, at least Mom can get some help with some of the feedings. Again, I think that is pretty much an individual decision, that only you can make in your own situation.

I wasn't alone in my concern about feeding intervals. A common reason that parents over-encourage their children to eat at any given feeding is they are hoping to prolong the interval between feedings—if they can get in a few more swallows, it should hold them longer. Parents do this for a variety of reasons: to make child care less time-consuming, because they think it is somehow better for the infant; or the way it "should" be done; or because they are afraid of making their infant too spoiled and demanding if they respond to his needs too often.

There is nothing to suggest that widely-spaced feeding intervals are any better for the infant physiologically, nutritionally or socially. In fact, the infant's small digestive system, her high calorie needs, and the rapid digestibility of breastmilk and formula would all seem to encourage relatively frequent feedings.

Carrying *vs* **Caching.** People evolved, in fact, as mammals that eat often. Babies have probably been carried and nursed frequently for over 99% of the human species' existence.[7] As the story goes, there are two different infant-rearing patterns in mammals: carrying and caching. The carrying kind, like the human, keeps the infant near at hand at all times, responding to and feeding the infant as his needs occur. The caching kind parks the infant somewhere and goes off to forage for food, coming back periodically to feed.

There are differences in milk composition that correspond to these differences in nurturing patterns. The milk of the carrying mother is lower in fat, so it is utilized more rapidly, causing the infant to demand to be fed more frequently. Milk of the caching mother must stay with the infant longer, so milk is relatively concentrated, especially in fat.

Since the human approach to child rearing fits the carrying pattern, you would expect to see more frequent feeding and interacting. And that is what you do see, in some infants more than others. Daniel and Lucas and Curtis, for example, insisted on being involved and cared for frequently. Others are more cooperative about allowing themselves to be cached, in bed or elsewhere, and cared for more intermittently. The former are defined as being difficult, troublesome children and the latter as better, easier babies. It seems that despite the fact that people are generally fascinated with their children, they also feel uncomfortable about giving them too-frequent attention and stimulation.

I have wondered if the myth of spoiling has something to do with that discomfort. People fear that too-close attention to infants' needs, or too-great readiness to respond to them will cause them to be "spoiled." You really can't spoil a little baby. The fear of spoiling is based on the philosophy that if you give in to a child's demands too readily and too consistently, that will cause her to be even more demanding, that somehow she will generate even more reasons to keep you coming back.

That presumes that the child is involved in some sort of struggle for dominance with his caring adults. And of course that's not true. The infant is aware only of his feelings and responses and can only communicate those. If he is calling for attention, it is because he has a real, genuine need, not a manufactured one.

104

The newborn infant and young child have a great need for closeness, warmth and nurturing. While the older child and adult have the same needs, they can be satisfied with more intermittent contact. In order for a child to make that transition, he must have his needs responded to consistently so he can feel satisfied and secure. Then he can move on to his next developmental stage, secure in having accomplished his previous tasks.

Signs of Satiety

Babies have many different ways of showing they have had enough to eat: they spit out the nipple, they doze off with milk drooling out of their mouth, they start to play with or bite on the nipple rather than suck. Many babies have an appealing little face-squeezing maneuver they make when they have had enough to eat. For some babies satiety comes abruptly and absolutely, and they quit nursing suddenly. Others taper off, eating more and more slowly as they kind of drift into satiety.

In summary, then, we can say your best tactic in feeding your infant is to tune in on and trust his signals of self regulation.

Your child's response to that feeding approach will be growth that is optimum for him. How large a person he will become depends on his genetic potential. Whether or not he grows to the limits of his genetic potential depends primarily on how he eats throughout his growing years. Your goal then, in feeding your child is to enable him to eat in such a way that he can get the body that's right for him.

Growth Curves

I am so convinced of the infant's ability to regulate his own food intake and growth that I would feel comfortable in stopping right here with our growth discussion. As long as you are giving a good milk feeding in a friendly and supportive way, you generally don't have to worry about normal growth: it will happen. But, there are a few exceptions, and there is the curiosity and fun of evaluating that

105

process as it takes place. So, in the rest of the chapter I'll be interpreting for you the method that your health professional uses in monitoring your child's growth: the use of growth curves.

Some health workers feel very strongly that parents who are not trained in interpreting normal growth should not be given growth curve charts. They fear that the parent will weigh and measure and plot their child's growth compulsively, overreacting to every little variation. So, don't do that. Realize that there will be trends and variations over time, and that generally there isn't too much to get excited about.

Also realize that properly interpreting these growth curves is a complex process that requires schooling in growth and development, and experience with many infants. The health professional is definitely the person with whom to consult in evaluating the growth curves, AND THAT'S IMPORTANT. But they will be giving you information from the growth curves, and you will have to know some basics in order to interpret them properly to yourself. It's the basics that I propose to give you in the following discussion.

Standard growth curves are graphs of the variation in normal growth of normal children. They have been constructed by weighing and measuring large numbers of children and noting the variations in height and weight that occur in different age groups. Once the growth patterns of all these children are plotted, you come up with a series of normal curves that look like the ones on the next pages. These charts were published in 1976 by the National Center for Health Statistics.[6] They are the growth standards recommended at this time for general use.

Types of Growth Curves. There are separate graphs for heights and weights of boys and girls of different ages, as well as graphs that plot the two together. There are graphs for head circumference, as well as graphs that correlate weight and height, and special graphs for prepubertal boys and girls. For our purpose we will use about four (see Figures 4-4 through 4-7).

1. Girls: Birth to 36 months—Physical Growth
   a. Length-for-age/weight-for-age. (Figure 4-4)
   b. Head circumference/weight-for-length. (Figure 4-5)
2. Boys: Birth to 36 months—Physical Growth
   a. Length-for-age/weight-for-age. (Figure 4-6)
   b. Head circumference/weight-for-length. (Figure 4-7)

All four figures show two graphs in one, which is somewhat confusing, and I apologize. However, this is probably how you will see them in the doctor's office, so I will present them that way to you here. On Figures 4-4 and 4-6, the upper left-hand graph is the length graph (we measure children lying down until they are about three years old, when we start standing them up to be measured), and the lower right-hand graph is the weight graph.

On Figures 4-5 and 4-7, the upper left hand graph is head circumference (your doctor will take this from time to time, but we are going to overlook it) and the lower right is weight-by-length. This latter graph ignores age and plots only according to weight and length.

The small numbers within the lines at the right-hand side of the graphs refer to percentile: "5" means fifth percentile, "10" means tenth percentile, and so on.

If you want the charts for older kids, they are constructed as weight and stature charts for boys and girls from 2 to 18 years, and are available in pediatricians' offices.

Typically you will encounter these charts when you take your child in for regular checkups. He will be weighed and measured and the figures plotted on growth charts that will be inserted in his medical record. Each time you will be told his position in the percentile ratings for growth. (For example, your child might be 50th percentile for height and 60th percentile for weight.)

Reading the Growth Curve. Let's discuss this in more detail, using the chart in Figure 4-4: *Growth chart for infant girls—Length-for-age and weight-for-age.* As you look at the chart, you will notice that

Figure 4-4. Growth Chart for Infant Girls. Length-for-age and Weight-for-age (Courtesy Ross Laboratories).

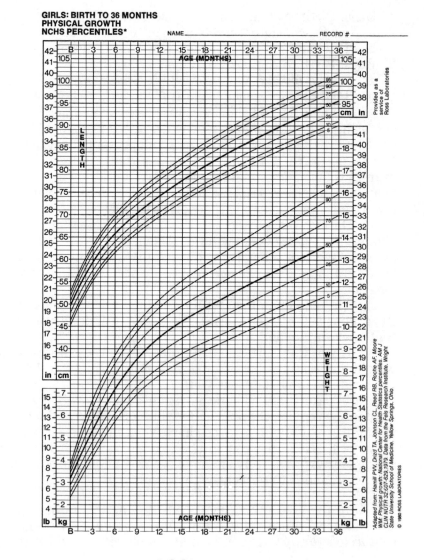

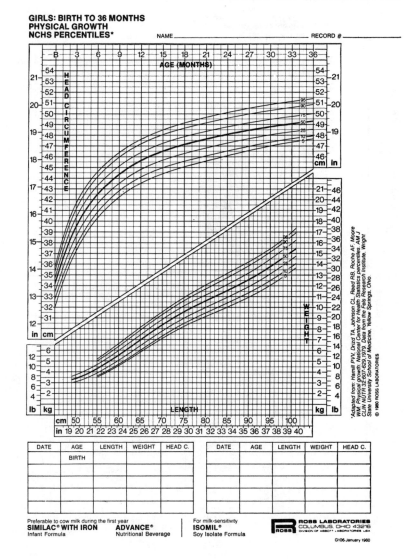

Figure 4-5. Growth Chart for Infant Girls. Head Circumference and Weight-for-length (Courtesy Ross Laboratories).

Figure 4-6. Growth Chart for Infant Boys. Length-for-age and Weight-for-age (Courtesy Ross Laboratories).

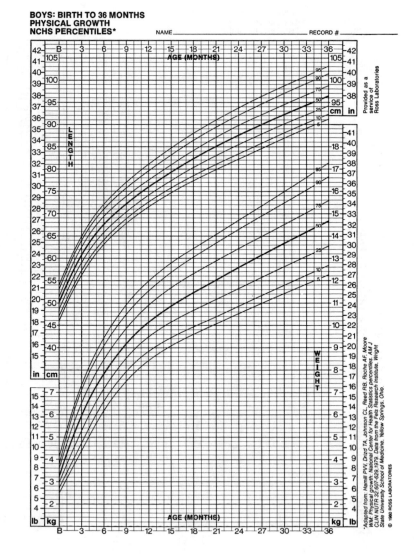

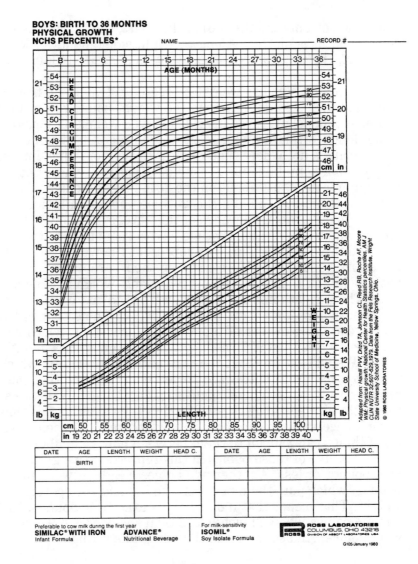

Figure 4-7. Growth Chart for Infant Boys. Head Circumference and Weight-for-length. (Courtesy Ross Laboratories).

along the bottom (and the top) of the chart, the horizontal axis, the *age* in months is plotted. Along the right side (and lower left side) of the chart, the vertical axis, the *weight* is plotted—in kilograms, and in pounds.

You plot a child's weight by reading straight up from the age point and then straight out from the weight point. For instance, if you have a little girl three months old who weighs 11 pounds, you would follow straight up along the line for age three months. You would make a dot where that vertical three-month line intersects with the horizontal line for 11 pounds. That dot, where those two lines intersect, is just about on the 25th percentile line. That means that that three-month-old girl is 25th percentile for weight.

Perhaps the significance of this categorization will be easier to understand if we imagine that we have a room filled with 100 baby girls, all three months old, who represent the weight distribution of the entire population. (Here's hoping their parents are in that room with them!) Of those 100 babies, five would weigh nine pounds or less. (The 3-month line intersects with the "5" percentile curve line at the point where it lines up, horizontally, with nine pounds.) We say they are at or below the fifth percentile for weight, which means that they weigh less than 95% of the other baby girls three months old.

We will assume that they are eating adequately, which allows us to say that these babies are perfectly normal and that they are growing well, but that their genetic potential simply dictates that this is the size and growth pattern that they show at this time. It doesn't necessarily mean that they will be small all their lives, as a lot of things can happen to them between now and puberty.

So, five of those babies in this representative group weigh nine pounds or less. Another five babies weigh between nine and ten pounds, which puts them between the 5th and 10th percentiles for weight. That means that if one weighs exactly 10 pounds, there will be nine babies who will weigh less than she does and 90 who will weigh more. And so we go up the percentile ratings.

When you get up to the one baby on the 50th percentile rating line, she will be smaller than half the babies and bigger than the rest. Fifty percent of the babies will weigh between 11 and 12.5 pounds; they will be between the 25th and 75th percentiles on the weight curve. Those babies "tend toward the average." That doesn't necessarily mean their growth is any more or less desirable than that of infants weighing more or less than those in this mid-range. It simply means that they are closer to the midpoint of weight, so they have more company in their weight range than do the infants at the outside extremes—in the 75th-and-above or in the 25th-and-below percentile ranges.

When you use the growth charts in this way—to compare an individual child's growth with that of other children—you are primarily satisfying your curiosity. Don't get caught up in treating growth curves like grades in school. A child growing at the 95th percentile isn't doing any better than the one growing at the 5th percentile. The most important aspect of the growth curve is to be able to compare each individual child to herself—to evaluate her growth as it progresses from one month to the next.

Evaluating Your Child's Growth. In most cases, once a child is established in a percentile rating of growth, she will remain in that percentile track. For instance, Jane started out in the 25th percentile range. She weighed 9½ pounds at two months of age and around 11 pounds at three months, and we predicted that she would stay in the same 25th percentile track from month to month (see Figure 4-8). However, at four months her growth rate started to slow. She weighed 11½, 12 and 12½ pounds respectively, at her fourth, fifth and sixth month checks, and her percentiles fell from the 25th to the 5th. We started looking around for causes.

Had she suddenly become more active? Was breastmilk production falling off? The change in percentile rating gave us a clue that something was going on that could be affecting her health

Figure 4-8. Inadequate Weight Gain of Jane.

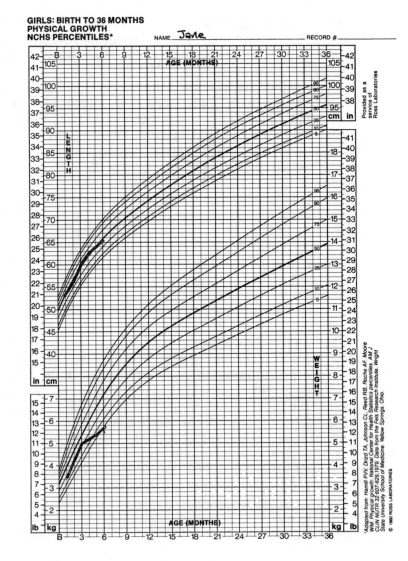

GIRLS: BIRTH TO 36 MONTHS
PHYSICAL GROWTH
NCHS PERCENTILES*

NAME _Jane_

RECORD #

status. In her case, it turned out to be the beginnings of asthma, which was causing chronic lung infections.

Jane continued to grow smoothly in height, even though her weight was falling off. Generally height increase will continue smoothly; the weight is the most immediate and reliable signal of a change in nutritional status.

Using the growth curves for height as well as for weight gives some further information. Each time your child is weighed and measured, he will be plotted on both curves, and you will be given a report that could say, for instance, 60th percentile for height and 60th percentile for weight. That would mean that your child is somewhat larger than the average child and that she also has an average body build: her height and weight percentiles are balanced.

Jane was a tall slender baby from the start. She was 50th percentile for height and 25th for weight. And, of course, as her weight dropped off, she got even more slender.

Weight-for-length graphs. The weight-for-length graphs use a single figure to give you information on your baby's relative weight and length. Figure 4-9 shows this relationship for Jane using the data plotted on Figure 4-8. If we plot Jane's length at 3 months, which was 23½ inches, against her weight, which was 10¾ pounds (both shown on Figure 4-8), she comes out (on Figure 4-9) a little below the 25th percentile, weight for height.* You can use this figure to compare Jane with other children and find out what we already know, that she is on the slender side. More importantly, you can use it to assess her growth progression and will be able to see that her weight for height dropped from a little below the 25th percentile to below the 5th percentile by the time she was six months old.

In interpreting these percentile ratings, take a look at yourself. Do you have an average body build or do you have more of a

---

*Children below the 50th percentile are relatively taller and thinner, those above are relatively blockier.

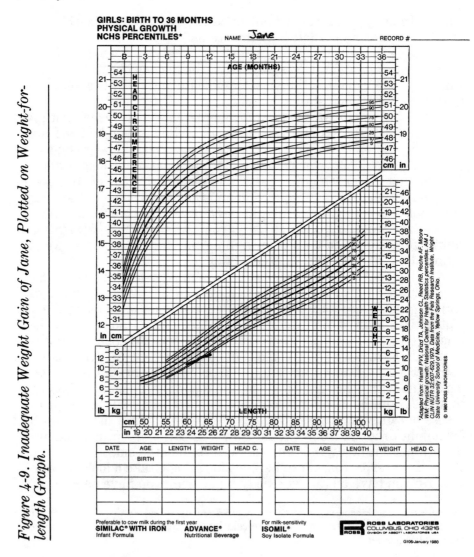

Figure 4-9. Inadequate Weight Gain of Jane, Plotted on Weight-for-length Graph.

Child of Mine

116

blocky, chunky build? Or perhaps you are tall and slender, with longer, thinner bones and longer, more slender muscles. Your child's body build may reflect your body build.

Physical vs Aesthetic Standards. One of the things that you must watch out for as you evaluate your child's growth is that you don't confuse standards of normal growth with standards of fashion. The "ideal" body, according to the dictates of fashion, is a fairly slender body. That is very nice, if you or your child happen to have a naturally slender body. But it is not so nice if you are dealing with a more blocky body build. All too often what is happening then is that someone is trying to get his child to conform to the fashionable slender standard—to get thinner. In reality, what that does is try to force that person to be thinner than is really right or natural for him.

To achieve and maintain this abnormally low weight, it will be necessary for the person to give quite a lot of attention to an otherwise automatic process: that of food regulation. The person tries to be thinner than his body is really set up to be. To accomplish this, he will have to eat less than his body tells him to eat. In other words, he will have to stop trusting his appetite and his internal cues of hunger and satiety, and will have to start regulating his food intake with his head. He (or someone making his decisions for him) will have to use some system of deciding how much food he should be having, and he will have to limit himself to that. And, he will have to adhere to that system of regulation for as long as he wants his weight to remain at what for him is a lower-than-normal level.

If you are the parent, and trying to force this slimming regimen on a child who is constitutionally more heavy, you really have your work cut out for you. You essentially will be trying to get the child to eat less than he really wants, and you will have to keep it up for a very long time.

The same kind of struggle can occur when people are trying to manipulate their weights the other way. Anyone who has tried to

117

gain weight can tell you that it can be as involving and discouraging as trying to lose. And it is just as difficult to try to adjust a natural weight upward as it is to try to adjust it downward.

It seems to me to be the more reasonable and logical approach to allow the child to achieve the growth pattern and body that is right for her. Then, the next step is to allow or encourage her to feel good about her body. You need to let her know that it is a good body, and allow her to develop an aesthetic appreciation of her body that is broader and more flexible than this crazy, rigid norm that we now glorify. You need to help her to realize that her health and physical capability are as important as the way she looks.

I am using "her" intentionally in this section, because I think that it is harder to provide this for girls than for boys. There seems to be a narrower and more rigid standard of appearance for girls. This is changing, but girls are encouraged less to participate in sports, so they get less of a sense of themselves physically and functionally than boys do.

I was reminded the other day of how difficult this is for kids when I went to an office picnic. As I played volleyball with the kids, I watched them. I was intrigued by two of the girls in particular, because their bodies (and, it seemed, their personalities) were in such a contrast to each other. The older girl, who was 13, was a tall, very slender girl. Aesthetically, she was just right. She moved somewhat slowly after the ball if it came near her and had about average coordination for a kid her age.

The other girl, age 11, was about average height and was one of the most muscular little girls I have ever seen. She had wonderful strong little legs, heavy legs, with hardly any fat on them. She had a square compact little body and arms that were well-shaped and solid-looking. She was dodging and diving for the ball and doing very well—her coordination was remarkable. It was so much fun watching her. She simply had a great body and she could handle it very well.

I was surprised after the game ended to find out that the two girls were sisters. Their mother confirmed my suspicions that the older one had primary interests other than sports, and that the little one really went for physical activities of any sort. She apparently was doing very well in gymnastics and goes out for any sport that she can. But, her mother said, the little girl gets lots of teasing from the other kids because they say she is too fat. And the gymnastics teacher keeps telling her that she should cut down on her eating because to be really good at gymnastics she should be more slender. Her mother thinks that all that emphasis on being thinner is stupid, so she's not about to pressure her daughter to slim down. Here's hoping that despite all that social pressure, the little girl can hang on to a sense of her own body as being good.

We have wandered into a considerably older age group in our discussion of growth curves. I hope you agree that the digression was valid. Parents' standards and preconceptions of appropriate growth are going to have an impact on how they feed their infant, right from the start. We will discuss this topic in more detail in chapters 10 and 11.

Improper Use of Growth Curves. But let's go back to infancy. I want to spend some time alerting you to how the growth curves can cause problems if they are used improperly. One big hazard comes from inaccurate measurements. Weights are generally measured accurately. Usually doctors' offices will use the beam-type baby scales for weighing, and that's good, though even those scales should be checked periodically for accuracy. In a very few cases you will see the spring-type scales and that is not good. Readings from those scales frequently vary considerably, depending on the vagaries of the machine.

Heights, however, are generally done poorly. Accurate length measures of babies are difficult to take, and typically are not taken in the doctors' offices. To do it right you need to have the baby resting

119

on a rigid surface, and you need two experienced people to do the measuring. One person uses both hands to hold the baby's head straight and against a vertical headboard. The other person holds the feet, knees and hips completely extended. Applying gentle traction, this latter person brings a movable footboard to rest firmly against the baby's heels. (It sounds awful, doesn't it? But it is really quite humane.) Then you get an accurate measurement that can be charted with some reliability on the percentile curves.

I have never seen it done that way. What I have seen is done by one person, who lays the baby on the paper-covered pad on the examining table. He takes a pencil and makes a mark at the top of the baby's head. Then he pulls down one of the feet and makes another mark on the paper. Finally, he moves the baby and measures between the marks. A well known authority on infant nutrition says, "measurement of length is difficult and should not be attempted unless satisfactory equipment and two trained examiners are available. In many instances, it will not be practical to measure length routinely."[3]

It is unfortunate that this is the source of the height data you will probably have available for your child, because height is the measurement that indicates long-term nutritional status. Further, these inaccuracies in height measurements make it very difficult or even futile to attempt to interpret weight-for-height measurements. For example, if we go back to our three-month-old baby girl, we will figure that at age three months she is right on the 25th percentile line for weight and height: she weighs 10.8 lb and she is almost 23 inches long.

Say when we check her three months later her weight is still on the 25th percentile line: she now weighs a little over 14½ lb. But this time, using the paper and pencil system of measuring height, she now appears to be 24½ inches tall, or right on the 10th percentile line. To be on the 25th percentile line, she would have to be 25¼ inches long, an error of only ¾ inch. That error is quite possible, given a standard squirmy baby with typically elastic legs. So now it looks like our baby, who was so well-balanced before, is doing one of two things: falling off the growth curve for height, or getting fatter. Either can be alarming for parents. Both are entirely unnecessary conclusions, based on the available evidence.

What I have seen happen, on the basis of results like this, is the parent will become alarmed about excessive weight gain and attempt to cut back on the child's food. As is absolutely predictable when the parent tries to intrude on the child's business of food regulation, a struggle ensues. Everyone becomes too preoccupied with eating, and what was an easy, natural process gets invested with all sorts of anxieties.

The maddening thing about all this is that it is so absolutely unnecessary. Measurements of height that casual, simply should not be used as a basis for any kind of recommendations. But they are used in exactly that way, and more. I was horrified to hear of a health professional advising parents that they should shoot to keep their child's weight at about 10 percentile ratings lower than the height, because it was really better to have a child who was a little leaner than a little fatter. In other words, normal growth is invalid, and one should try to modify it to fit these arbitrary standards. It is exactly that kind of advice that makes parents rigid and preoccupied with feeding, and involved in a struggle in which they are essentially encouraged to deprive their child of food.

I see harried parents who come in complaining that they are concerned about their child's weight, and reporting that they are trying to get her to eat a little less. But, they explain, their child will *not* be satisfied on smaller amounts of food. She fusses and complains until she gets as much as usual and continues to gain at her regular rate. The parents typically feel ambivalent but always guilty: guilty at not being able to restrict their child's food intake more effectively, guilty at trying to be stingy with food for a little baby.

121

At that point I would say that it is better to burn the charts than to cause that kind of crazy and unnecessary anxiety and conflict.

What I have given you is a very mixed review of growth charts. I have introduced them to you and explained how they can be used productively, and I have spent a fair amount of time pointing out the harm that can be done if they are used poorly. So what, you may ask, is the point?

The point is that they will be used. In most cases your child's growth will be plotted on these charts, and you generally will be given the percentile information. It's what you do with the information that will make all the difference.

Information on the growth curves is only one of the pieces of information you will have on your baby, and not the most important one, at that. You can do one of two things with it. You can put yourself in the position of monitoring and manipulating your child's growth, responding to apparent changes with changes in feeding. Or you can keep your fingers crossed and trust that growth will proceed appropriately, meanwhile feeding in response to your baby's demand. I would encourage the latter.

If your child seems to be demanding and getting enough to eat, and seems to grow and be reasonably happy and content, that is an important piece of information. If the weight is being accurately checked and is increasing at a fairly smooth rate, that is an important piece of information. But as long as heights are being taken improperly, you have no choice but to be very cautious in drawing any conclusions using height data.

Your Child's Appearance

In addition, of course, you will be evaluating your baby's growth the same way parents have always evaluated their infant's growth: by looking at him. He'll usually be getting longer and heavier; his body and arms and legs will be filling out. He'll develop a round stomach that sticks out, and the shape of his face will change and probably get rounder and fatter looking. In fact, compared with what he looked like as a newborn, your infant may just look fat to you. That's fine. Babies normally put on a lot of fat in the first year of life.

At birth the infant has only about 11% body fat. By age one year, the percentage of body fat has increased to 24%. (Subsequently this decreases to about 21% by age two and 18% by age three.)[2] This accumulation of body fat is normal and desirable. Fat functions importantly in the little body as a source of calories in case of illness. With the high metabolic demands and calorie requirement of a person that small, even a short-term illness could be dangerous if it weren't for that calorie store. Fat also functions to protect the baby's organs and as an insulator to help maintain normal body temperature. Fat stores in the human body are functional. It is only when the fat stores become excessive that they should be a cause for concern.

This chapter is intended to help you understand, not manage, the process of growth. Your baby is the one with the information about *his* normal growth and *his* process of food regulation. In the very great percentage of cases, your best and safest approach is to support that regulatory process with appropriate food, offered in response to the infant's signals of hunger and satiety.

Enabling your child to get the body that is right for him is your important task. The way you accomplish that task is through paying attention to information coming from him.

Selected References

1. Bruch, Hilde. Eating Disorders. Obesity, Anorexia Nervosa and the Person Within. Basic Books. New York. 1973.
2. Fomon, Samuel J. Infant Nutrition. W. B. Saunders, Philadelphia. 1974.

3. Fomon, Samuel J. Nutritional Disorders of Children. Prevention, Screening, and Followup. DHEW Publication No. (HSA) 76-5612. DHEW Rockville, Maryland. 1976.
4. Gerber. Current Practices in Infant Feeding. 1980.
5. Gesell, Arnold and Frances L. Ilg. Feeding Behavior of Infants J. B. Lippincot, Philadelphia. 1937.
6. Hamill, P. V. V. *et al.* NCHS Growth Charts. 1976. Vital and Health Statistics-Series II. Health Resources Administration, DHEW, Rockville, Maryland. 1976(a).
7. Lozoff, Betsy, *et al.* The mother-newborn relationship: limits of adaptability. The Journal of Pediatrics 91:(L) 1-12. July. 1977.
8. Rose, H. E. and J. Mayer, Activity, calorie intake, fat storage and the energy balance of infants. Pediatrics 41:18. 1968.
9. Stein, Z. A. *et al.* Famine and Human Development: The Dutch Hunger Winter of 1944–45. New York: Oxford University Press. 1975.
10. Weil, William B. Current controversies in childhood obesity. The Journal of Pediatrics. 91(2):175–187. 1977.

5
The
Milk
Feeding

The newborn infant imposes some stringent demands on his milk feeding. It must be very easily digestible, it must not disrupt the relatively fragile balance of his body chemistry, and, because it is the major, or only food for the first six months, it must be absolutely appropriate for his nutritional needs. Breastmilk, commercial formulas (both cow's milk and soy based), and evaporated milk formula all adequately fill these specifications. Other formulas, such as the hypoallergenic formulas and the premature infant formulas, are more highly specialized, to provide for infants with the special needs they are designed for.

Although modern formula feeding is convenient and safe, it is important not to become casual about the mechanics of preparation. The water supply must be clean and safe, the nursing equipment sanitary and comfortable (for both feeder and fed), and the formula prepared precisely according to directions.

125

A newborn baby has special nutritional and feeding needs. To grow and thrive, he requires more gentle and specialized handling than an older child. But at the same time, feeding behaviors are like other behaviors: as your baby grows and develops, his abilities change and his patterns of feeding change. To feed your baby appropriately at different ages you need to observe his ability to eat and you need to choose food and feeding methods that he can handle. You also need to understand nutritional requirements and to know and respect his limitations, so you can select foods that are both developmentally and nutritionally appropriate.

During his first year, your baby will pass through three fairly distinctive feeding patterns:

Feeding Periods

0–6 Months—Milk feeding	4–12 Months—Transition (beginning solids)	8 Months on—Adult-like

The ages in the chart overlap, as babies spend varying amounts of time in each of the feeding periods.

In this chapter and in the chapter on breastfeeding we will be discussing only the milk feeding. In chapter 7 we will get into the transition period, where your baby works his way into and through the beginning solid-foods stage and up to the beginning adult stage.

Feeding recommendations for the milk feeding stage are short and to the point.

The vitamins mentioned in the feeding recommendations come in liquid form. You give them to the baby with the calibrated eye-dropper that comes with the bottle. We will talk further about this in "nutritional supplementation" later in the chapter.

Figure 5-1. Feeding Recommendations for the First Six Months.

The Milk Feeding	Nutritional Supplements
Breastmilk	Vitamin D—400 IU
	Fluoride—0.25 mg
Commercial formula	Fluoride if none in water—0.25 mg
	Iron—5–10 mg—at four months*
Evaporated milk formula	Fluoride if none in water
	Vitamin C—35 mg or 3 ounces
	orange juice
	Iron—5–10 mg—at four months

Avoid pasteurized milk. This is inappropriate for infant feeding.

*The preterm baby on all feedings needs iron at two months.

Milk feeding recommendations and feeding practices for babies have changed considerably in the last few years, as you can see by the table on the next page.[10]

Breastfeeding is definitely on the increase, both in incidence and duration. Most physicians have discontinued the undesirable practice of switching young babies from formula to 2% milk, and babies are being kept on formula longer. Pasteurized milk use for the young infant is considerably below earlier figures.

Figure 5-3 summarizes infant behaviors and abilities that have an impact on feeding.

As you can see from the table, in those early months, the young infant's only feeding skill is his instinctive suckling ability. He can't sit up, or, early on, even hold his head up, and he can't control

Figure 5-2. Infant Formula and Milk Use.

	Percentage of infants receiving*			
	In Hospital		At Age 5–6 Mo.	
	1971	1979	1971	1979
Breast	24.7	51.0	5.5	23.0
Whole cows milk and evaporated milk	0.9	0.1	68.1	25.2
Total prepared formulas	77.4	54.1	28.0	57.6
Without iron	56.5	26.8	14.6	17.3
With iron	20.9	27.3	13.4	40.3

Copyright American Academy of Pediatrics, 1981.

*The figures do not add up to 100% because some babies were taking more than one type of milk feeding.

the motion of his hands. He has the digestive ability only to handle a milk feeding that is properly catered to his needs. His homeostatic ability (his ability to protect his body from dehydration and disruptions in chemical imbalance) is low, and his milk feeding has to be modified to help him.

It is clear that only a milk feeding fed by nipple is developmentally and nutritionally appropriate during this early stage. It is further clear that the newborn baby, with his special needs, imposes some very rigorous demands on the milk feeding.

Digestion

The milk feeding must set up a soft and easily-digestible curd when it is mixed with the acid in the baby's stomach. Breastmilk, formula, or milk that has been heat treated in some way (heated to boiling) sets

Figure 5-3. Developmental Patterns and Feeding Style in the First Six Months

	Birth	1 mo.	2 mo.	3 mo.	4 mo.	5 mo.	6 mo.
Mouth Pattern:	Sucking, "extrusion" pattern.				Beginning swallow pattern. Can transfer food from front of tongue to back		
						Beginning of drooling	
Hand Coordination:	Random motion of hands.				Hands beginning to go to mouth.	Palmar grasp.	
Body Control:	Prone on back. Can raise head when on stomach.				Sits supported. Loses balance when reaches.	Sits unsupported. Can balance while manipulating with hands.	
Digestive Ability:	Can digest appropriate milk.				Intestinal amylase begins to increase to allow starch digestion.		
Homeostatic Ability:	Low. Needs carefully-adapted formula.						
Nutritional Requirements:	Relatively high nutrient requirement for rapid growth.		Iron stores depleted in premature infants.			Iron stores begin to be depleted in term babies.	
Feeding Style:	Nipple-feeding by breast or bottle					Beginning spoon feeding.	
Food Selection:	Breastmilk or formula.					Beginning solids: Iron source.	

up a soft, custard-like curd that is easy to digest. In contrast, pasteurized milk, or, worse yet, raw cow's milk, sets up a tough cheesy curd that is very difficult to digest. Protein and fat absorption from non-heat-treated milk is lower. It is so low, in fact, that some babies have to consume 25 to 50% more milk than usual to satisfy their nutritional requirements. This problem persists as long as milk is the sole or primary food.

Homeostasis

The milk feeding must compensate for the young infant's limited ability to maintain homeostasis (balanced body chemistry).

A diet that gives a baby way too much protein or salt or potassium for the amount of water it contains can draw too much water out of her body and make her dehydrated.* Breastmilk and formulas (if they are properly measured and mixed) have a good balance of water to other nutrients and you won't have to worry about maintaining homeostasis.

Straying from the standard milk feeding could cause trouble, particularly if your baby is losing more water than usual in other ways (if she is sweating a lot or is vomiting or has diarrhea). Pasteurized 2% or skim cow's milk, for example, could disrupt homeostasis because it is too concentrated in both protein and sodium for the amount of calories it contains. Commercial formulas that are inadequately diluted can offer the child too much of all nutrients in relation to her fluid intake. Meats offered too early can overload her ability to get rid of nitrogen. All of these feeding practices are common, poor, and unnecessary.

---

*Excessive sodium, potassium and nitrogen are waste products that have to be carried from the cells and excreted in the urine. The young infant has a limited ability to concentrate his urine, meaning he has to put out a high fluid volume for a given amount of waste products. The older child or adult can be much stingier with the water, so doesn't run the same risk of dehydration.

Nutritional Requirements

The milk feeding must carry virtually the whole nutritional load for the infant up until age six months. Because of that, it must be absolutely appropriate for his needs and provide optimal nourishment. Breast milk and standard formulas are both balanced, so that a given volume of milk will provide the proper proportion of calories, water, protein, fat, carbohydrate, vitamins and minerals. (Tables of nutrients in breastmilk and formula are in the Appendix.) When calorie needs are high, other nutrient needs are also high, so the infant can regulate them all appropriately with his signals of hunger and satiety.

If any nutrient is too high or too low relative to all the rest, the whole balance can be disrupted.

Calories. Breastmilk and formulas each give 20 calories per ounce; the comparison with other milks is shown in the table below.

Figure 5-4. Calories per Ounce in Common Infant Feedings

Milk feeding	Caloric density (Calories per ounce)
Breast milk	20
Standard milk-based formulas	20
Soy formulas	20
Whole milk	19
2% milk	15
Advance (formula from Ross "for older children")	16
Skim milk	10

Source: Formula manufacturers; U.S.D.A. Home and Garden Bulletin #72.

The milk feedings that are lower in calories, such as overdiluted formula or 2% or skim milk, give the baby too much volume for the calories he needs, and make it harder for him to grow and gain properly.

Protein, fat and carbohydrate. Each of these three calorie sources in your baby's diet has a nutritional role to play. Since each contributes a percentage of total calories, varying one will vary another. For example, a diet that is too high in protein is likely to be too low in fat or carbohydrate, or both.

Figure 5-5. Protein, Fat and Carbohydrate in the diet.

Nutrient	Function	Too Much	Too Little
Protein	Builds body tissue	Dehydration	Nutritional inadequacy
Fat	Provides long-lasting energy Carries essential nutrients	Ketosis* Poor appetite	Unsatisfying: baby hungry soon
Carbohydrate	Provides quick energy Spares protein for building and repair Helps burn dietary fat	Diet not satisfying	Allows ketosis Energy low Protection for protein low

*We talked about ketosis in the chapter on pregnancy. It is the accumulation of waste products from the incomplete burning of fat. It is like soot from a poorly-burning fire. Carbohydrate helps the fire burn well.

All standard infant formulas have a good proportion of protein, carbohydrate and fat. However, pasteurized milk, whether it is whole, 2%, or skim, is too high in protein for this age, with the protein excess going up as the fat goes down. Whole milk contains enough fat but, as we said earlier, the baby has a hard time digesting and absorbing the fat.

To this point we have demonstrated that breastmilk or formula, and those foods alone, are appropriate in the early months for your baby's developmental and nutritional needs.

The issues remaining to discuss in the rest of the chapter are:
- Types of milk feedings
- Cost of feeding an infant
- Nutritional supplementation
- The nursing equipment
- Position, timing, temperature of feeding
- Safety, sanitation and dilution
- Promoting good feedings
- Quantity of formula
- Feeding frequency

Types of Milk Feedings

Several types of infant milk feedings and the types of protein, fat and carbohydrate they contain are listed in the table on the next page. When we discuss special nutritional needs you'll be able to see how this protein, fat and carbohydrate information is helpful.

Cow Milk Based Formulas

Commercial. Enfamil®, Similac® and SMA® are the most commonly used formulas. They are highly satisfactory for most babies. Enfamil and Similac come with or without iron.

SMA® and Similac with whey® are based on protein that has been modified, ostensibly to make it more like the protein in human

Figure 5-6. Protein, Fat and Carbohydrate in Common Infant Milk Feedings.

Milk Feeding	Protein	Fat	Carbohydrate
Breastmilk	40% casein* 60% whey	Reflects mother's diet	Lactose
Cow Milk Formulas			
Standard commercial Enfamil® and Similac®	82% casein 18% whey	Vegetable oil	Lactose
Whey-based commercial SMA® and Similac® with whey	40% casein 60% whey	Vegetable oil	Lactose
"Homemade" evaporated milk formula	82% casein 18% whey	Butterfat	Lactose/sucrose
Soy-based formulas	Soy isolate	Vegetable oil	Sucrose or corn syrup solids, or both
Predigested Formulas			
Nutramigen®	Predigested casein	Vegetable oil	Modified tapioca starch and sucrose
Pregestimil®	Predigested casein and amino acids	Corn oil and medium chain triglycerides	Corn syrup solids and modified tapioca starch

*Casein and whey are Miss Muffett's "curds and whey." Cow milk's high casein content is responsible for the tough curd it forms unless it is heat treated.

milk, by decreasing the casein and increasing the whey. It appears the premature infants do better on high-whey formulas.[5] While manufacturers imply that these formulas, which some call "humanized," are better than the "standard" formulas for all infants, in reality term babies grow and thrive well on both types. For these babies, "humanized" seems to be really little more than a buzz word to give the impression that the unique characteristics of breastmilk can somehow be duplicated. They cannot.

Manufacturers frequently change their formulas. The information here may be out of date by the time you read it. The trend appears to be to whey-based formulas and you will likely see the standard (casein-based) formulas being changed to whey-based. You may see adjustments in the amount of iron or other nutrients.

Recipe: Evaporated Milk Formula

One 13-ounce can whole evaporated milk, fortified with vitamins A
  and D
Nineteen ounces tap water
One ounce (two tablespoons) sugar (either table sugar or corn syrup).
  Do NOT use honey.

Mix well, portion into sterilized individual bottles, cover and refrigerate. May also be refrigerated in a covered, clean bulk container.

Evaporated milk formula. Infant formula made from evaporated milk is an "old-fashioned" homemade formula that is still a good, low-cost choice for the term infant. Evaporated milk* is a canned cow's milk product that has been concentrated by removing

---

*An improved can design for evaporated milk has brought the lead content down to the acceptable level of about 0.08 parts per million. This compares with the lead content of concentrated commercial formulas of about 0.02 parts per million.

half of the water. (It is *not* the same as condensed milk, which has sugar added and is used for baking.) It is better for babies than pasteurized milk because the canning process boils it long enough to make it digestible.

Be sure that you use WHOLE evaporated milk and that it is fortified with vitamins A and D.

Since most nutrients are provided by the milk, this formula needs only to be supplemented with 35 mg. vitamin C per day. You can give this in three ounces of orange juice per day or in the form of drops.

Simple as it is, the evaporated milk formula has been calculated very carefully to give an appropriate calorie and nutrient density and to provide the proper proportions of protein, fat and carbohydrate. So if you choose to use it, you must follow the formula absolutely slavishly. Do not substitute other milks or change the proportions of milk, sugar and water. Again, do not use honey as a sugar source (much honey is contaminated with botulinum spores).

The standard proportions of milk, sugar and water are appropriate throughout the time the infant is kept on formula. In the fifties pediatricians would shift the proportions of milk, sugar and water depending on the age of the child, with the water and sugar decreasing as the child got older. That practice was probably based on the inability of health workers, and possibly parents, to tolerate simplicity in infant feeding.

Soy based formulas. Isomil®, Prosobee®, and other soy-based formulas are used for the infant who is sensitive or allergic (or potentially so) to cow milk protein, or who is having trouble digesting lactose (milk sugar). Babies may be chronically sensitive to cow's milk protein and have to stay away from it for the first several months. Or they may be sensitive only for a few days, after they have had diarrhea, and need to use soy formula just for a few days.

Babies are often put on soy formula on the assumption that they cannot digest lactose, but other sugars, such as sucrose, can be a problem as well. Usually, intolerance for these sugars is temporary and appears after an infant has diarrhea from a viral or bacterial infection.

To avoid sucrose as well as lactose you need to read the ingredients list on the label, and select a soy formula that contains corn syrup solids, and/or another carbohydrate source like modified tapioca starch, rather than sucrose.

While soy formulas are used for the infant who is allergic, or potentially allergic to cow's milk protein, it is important to know that soy protein can cause as many allergies as cow's milk. In fact, quite a few babies are allergic to both. For the infant who has allergic reactions to both cow's milk and soy milk or extreme reactions to either one, or who has a strong family history of allergies, it is probably wise to use one of the hypoallergenic, "predigested" formulas described below.

Soy formulas are safe. Many people are afraid of them because they have read about the infants taking Neo-Mull-Soy® who got sick from chloride deficiency. The manufacturer, Syntex Laboratories, had not maintained proper quality control in preparing their infant formulas, and some containing inadequate chloride were put on the market.* The Food and Drug Administration is now required by law to test formulas for proper nutrient levels.

Soy milk is not a substitute for soy formula. Nutrient density, as well as proportions of protein, fat and carbohydrate are inappropriate where used as the sole food of a young infant.

Predigested formulas. The protein, fat or carbohydrate, or all three, in predigested formulas are modified to make them more manageable to the infant with allergies or with digestive problems. The two major specialized formulas, Pregestimil® and Nutramigen®, are based on a protein that is non-allergenic and highly digestible. Pregestimil, however, goes two steps further than Nutramigen in cater-

---

*Syntex Laboratories no longer makes infant formulas.

ing to special needs, in that it modifies the fat and carbohydrate as well as the protein.

The carbohydrate in Pregestimil comes from corn syrup solids and modified tapioca starch, both of which can be handled by most babies who have trouble with other sugars. Much of the fat in Pregestimil (medium-chain triglycerides) needs no digestion and is well-absorbed by the infant who can't manage other kinds of fat, such as infants who have had part of their intestine removed, or who have cystic fibrosis, or for some unknown reason get diarrhea from other dietary fat.

To summarize, Nutramigen and Pregestimil have important, if limited, uses:

- For babies who are allergic to cow's milk and soy protein. (See p. 306 in the *Toddler* chapter for a more-detailed discussion on allergies.)
- As a supplemental feeding for breastfed babies who have a good chance of being allergic.
- For babies who have had a severe reaction to cow's milk formula—severe diarrhea, lots of mucous in the stools. These babies are also likely to react to soy protein.

Premature infant formulas. The pre-term infant must grow and gain at the same rate as if he were still in the uterus. Such babies have missed acquiring the great deal of lean and bony tissue and mineral stores which are put on during the last portion of a term pregnancy. To provide for these special needs, premature infant formulas contain more protein and minerals per calorie than standard formulas.

These formulas are only available to hospitals and are given only under careful medical supervision. They are not suitable for a term infant, and, at a certain point, the premature infant must be switched from his "special" formula to a standard formula. To give him a somewhat greater nutritional margin of error, the pre-term infant should be kept on a commercial formula for the whole first year and should not be switched to evaporated milk or pasteurized milk. In fact, if a baby has been struggling nutritionally all along, I don't think it would hurt to keep on with commerical formula, even up to 18 months.

I hope you never need most of this technical information about formulas. Ideally, you will be able to select a good formula and stick to it throughout your baby's early months. You only need to worry about the more detailed information if he develops special needs, if he has a good chance of becoming allergic, if he has a viral or bacterial infection, or if he can't tolerate the standard protein, fat or carbohydrate.

But don't be too ready to switch formulas. Not all upsets are of the sort that require special feeding. It appears that, regardless of feeding, about 40% of babies have colic, or inconsolable crying after feeding, and about 40% vomit from time to time, or even frequently, after they are fed. By age one year, studies show that 14% of babies have had at least one episode of marked vomiting and diarrhea and 16% are still waking up at night.[1] Probably in most cases these problems would have persisted despite a change in feeding.

Cost of Feeding an Infant

The cost of the milk feeding varies by as much as four-fold, depending on the type and form of feeding you choose. Formulas come in ready-to-feed liquid form, liquid concentrated form (which has to be diluted one-to-one with water), and in powdered form. They come packed in single-serving containers, including single-serving containers that are all ready for you to simply screw on the nipple and feed.

I made a survey in September of 1982 of the local grocery stores and drug stores and came up with estimates (Figure 5-7) for one quart of infant formula or milk.

These prices are going to be out-of-date by the time you read this. However, we can make some generalizations that will probably remain valid for some time.

Figure 5-7. Costs of Infant Milk Feedings—1 quart

Specialized Formulas

Powdered Pregestimil, Nutramigen	$2.76–$3.47

Standard Commercial Milk- or Soy-Based Formula

Ready-to-feed	$1.63
Concentrated	1.22
Powdered	1.32

Breastfeeding (Mother's extra food)

2 cups milk	.22	
1 fruit or vegetable	.20	
250 extra calories	.20	
	.62	
Nutritional supplement for infant	.10	
Total		.72

Evaporated Milk Formula

1 can evaporated milk	.59	
2 Tablespoons sugar	.03	
3 ounces orange juice or nutritional supplement	.10	
Total		.72

The specialized formulas are extremely expensive and something that you would probably use only if your infant was highly likely to benefit from them. Secondly, the prices vary, so it is worth shopping around. Some pharamacies are willing to sell these at a little above wholesale price, realizing what a special need they fill.

Comparing ready-to-feed formulas with concentrated formulas, you pay about 20% more for the convenience of not having to mix with water. It may be worth it to you, particularly if your water supply is unreliable. Suprisingly, the powdered formulas cost about the same as the concentrate. The price is kept high by the low demand. Our local grocery stores carried only the liquid formulas; I had to search through several drug stores before I found one that carried the powder. You might get a good price on the powdered formula if you are willing to have the druggist order and buy it by the case. But unless there is a definite price advantage, I would encourage using the liquid formula. Powdered formulas are hard to mix accurately.

Breastfeeding is not free. To produce a quart, or 600 calories of breastmilk, the mother will have to consume about 750 more calories. She will need to provide herself with more protein, calcium and all other nutrients. She will need to supplement her infant with flouride and vitamin D. The cost of these foods and supplements will vary, depending on her food choices. If the mother is taking some sort of vitamin and mineral supplement to support the breastfeeding, that will further increase the cost.

Evaporated milk formula is remarkably inexpensive—this formula, plus the nutritional supplement (which is included to provide the vitamin C lacking in evaporated milk), costs about half as much as the least expensive commercial formula. Evaporated milk formula is almost as cheap as pasteurized milk, and offers a real option to parents who have felt forced by cost to switch from commercial formula to pasteurized milk.

Nutritional Supplementation

Figure 5-1 gave recommendations about supplementing vitamins C and D, flouride and iron. You will need additional information about the needs for some of the vitamins and minerals, and may have been confused by what you have heard in the past. Among other possible

141

sources of confusion, you may have received inconsistent advice from "experts." Health workers don't agree on the timing and level of iron and fluoride supplements; they argue about vitamin D supplementation of the breastfed infant, and are confused about the need for vitamin C supplements.

I am recommending what I consider to be ideal supplementation. Others will disagree. Your doctor might disagree, and you may end up not knowing what to do. I don't want you to worry unnecessarily, if you have your baby on a pattern of supplementation other than the one I am outlining here. The disagreements show that the answers are not clear-cut. The practices you should avoid, however, are: 1) Giving too much vitamin A, vitamin D and fluoride, and 2) Failing to provide iron—much beyond age six months.

Iron. As with other nutrients, you want your baby to have the right amount of iron, neither more nor less than he needs. Giving too much iron can decrease zinc absorption. Giving iron too soon to a breastfed baby can interfere with his unique intestinal immunity. Giving too little can limit red blood cell production.

Again, the schedule for beginning iron supplementation is:[3]

Premature baby, breast or formula	2 months
Formula-fed term baby	4 months
Breast-fed term baby	6 months

Regardless of maternal iron status, term infants are born with a good supply of iron. The newborn has need for, and utilizes very little dietary iron before age four months.[4] Up until that time he gets his iron from breaking down the extra red blood cells he was born with. Breastmilk iron, although in low concentrations, is about 50% absorbed (a relatively high absorption rate), and provides some protection against iron deficiency anemia. Furthermore, breastmilk iron is carried in a form, lactoferrin, which prevents its use as a nutrient by undesirable intestinal bacteria and protects against infestation by those bacteria. Supplemental iron, on the other hand, nourishes intestinal bacteria as well as the child, and also changes the type of bacteria.

Addition of any type of solid food also changes the intestinal bacteria. Since you have to change the intestinal bacteria anyway at age six months, when you start giving solid foods, you might as well accomplish two goals at one time and make the first solid food one that is high in iron. The best choice is iron-fortified infant cereal.

In contrast to breastmilk iron, the iron in cow's milk is only about 10% absorbed.* Furthermore, the bottle-fed infant already harbors a variety of bacteria in his colon. Since he has been able to absorb little dietary iron, and since there is little to be lost (in terms of increased bacterial activity) from the addition of iron, the bottle-fed infant should be started on iron at about age four months. This can be in the form of iron-fortified formula, or as iron drops.

The amount of supplementary iron depends on the size and maturity of the child.

10-15 pounds	5 mg.
15-20 pounds	10 mg.
Premature infant	10 mg.

Iron-fortified formula has 12.8 mg. iron per liter. Generally the child will consume about the right amount of formula to give him the recommended levels of iron.** Many health workers and parents hesitate to use iron-fortified formulas because they think the iron

---

*Cow's milk feeding may actually undermine iron nutrition. Some young infants (up to 140-days-old) who consume large amounts of pasteurized milk bleed a little from the intestine. Although the amount is small (about 3 ml per day in some cases—less than a teaspoon—which means the loss of 0.9 milligram iron per day), it could cause anemia.

**There is some talk of reducing the level of supplemental iron in fortified formula to 6 or 7 mg per liter. This is probably desirable, as the lower level of iron reduces the potential interference with trace element nutrition. The amount of iron absorbed at this lower level of fortification is almost as high as that from the more-heavily fortified formula.

causes stomach aches and intestinal problems. Apparently this is not the case: all infants experience these problems, those on iron-fortified formula to no greater extent than those on regular formula.[11]

Give the amount of iron your baby needs, but no more than that. Again, if you give too much supplemental iron, it may interfere with absorption of zinc[15] and possibly of other trace elements. Although you should always read the label on your particular package, generally iron drops have 10 mg. iron per milliliter, the amount that you administer from the little dropper that comes in the package. If your child needs only 5 mg. iron, you will have to eyeball the dose by filling the dropper only halfway.

Iron-fortified baby cereal provides 7 mg. iron per four-tablespoon serving (three level tablespoons of dry cereal mixed with milk or formula).

Once a child is well established on iron-fortified cereal he will be getting adequate iron for his needs and should be taken off the iron-fortified formula or the iron drops.

A good source of iron should be continued until the child is about 18 months old or gets through the high-risk period for iron-deficiency anemia.

Vitamin D. Vitamin D is necessary for the proper absorption of calcium and phosphorus, in the formation of teeth and bones. We get vitamin D in commercial formulas, evaporated milk and vitamin-D-fortified pasteurized milk, and in egg yolks. Our grandmothers dosed their children with cod-liver oil as a source of vitamin D, and our skin can make vitamin D if exposed to sunlight. A deficiency of vitamin D causes rickets, a softening and malformation of the bones. Bones that aren't properly mineralized with calcium and phosphorus can become deformed, causing the bow legs and beaded ribs of the child with rickets.

Health workers are too casual about vitamin D supplementation, particularly for the breastfed infant. Breastfed babies can, and do, get rickets, particularly if their skin is dark and if they are exposed to very little sunlight. For a while we thought there was significant vitamin D activity in breastmilk, but it turns out there is really very little—too little for a baby's needs. For the first month or two it does appear that babies can get along without vitamin D, but certainly by age three months they should be supplemented.[13] The breastfed infant needs 400 units of vitamin D per day.[6]

Rickets has also been reported in children with milk allergy, who (in lieu of the nutrients they would ordinarily have received in milk) received a calcium supplement but not additional vitamin D, and in children who receive anti-convulsant medication. Children who drink very little milk or who consume milk not fortified with vitamin D should have a supplement of 400 IU of vitamin D daily. (Farm children often get their milk out of the dairy milk cooler, and that is not fortified with vitamin D.)

You also must be careful not to give too much vitamin D. Because it is a fat-soluble vitamin, excessive amounts can be stored in the body and cause toxicity. However, do not panic. Your child will not get vitamin D toxicity the minute he exceeds 400 IU per day. (In fact, if he is taking more than a quart of formula per day he will be getting more than 400 IU.) Generally, you are safe with fat-soluble vitamins if you do not exceed twice the recommended level. I would, however, be very careful to avoid giving vitamin in concentrated drop form to an infant who is also getting it in his formula.

Vitamin C. Vitamin C is probably our most overused vitamin. Not only do we adults dose ourselves to ridiculous extremes with vitamin C, we do the same thing with our infant children. The young infant needs, roughly, 35 milligrams of vitamin C per day. The breastfeeding mother who is drinking four to six ounces of orange juice per day can easily provide that amount in her breast milk. Commercial formulas provide about 35 mg of vitamin C per quart. The only infant who really needs to be supplemented with vitamin C is the one taking an evaporated milk formula, or, heaven forbid, trying to get by on pasteurized milk. Those infants need a supplemental source of vitamin C.

There is a drop that provides vitamin C, alone, but you have to look for it and insist on it. Generally vitamin C comes in combination with vitamins A and D. Those drops are not appropriate for the infant who is already getting ample amounts of vitamins A and D in his formula or milk.

A good way of providing vitamin C for the evaporated-milk-fed baby is in three ounces of orange juice a day. Some babies, however, can get a rash or a stomach ache from orange juice. If you notice signs of sensitivity, switch your child to three ounces of the infant-pack apple juice, which is fortified with adequate vitamin C. Apple juice isn't as nutritious as orange juice, but the infant pack is well fortified with vitamin C, and most babies don't have any problems with it. Notice I specified *infant pack* apple juice. Apple juice does not naturally contain vitamin C, and most "adult" apple juices and cider are not supplemented.

Fluoride. Children who get the recommended amounts of fluoride from birth have an average of 60% to 65% fewer cavities than children who do not get the recommended amounts. Fluoride in your baby's diet must come either from fluoridated drinking water or from fluoride supplements. Breastmilk contains little fluoride, even if the mother is drinking fluoridated water. Commercial formulas and evaporated milk do not naturally contain fluoride, nor are they supplemented.

The infant who is getting no fluoride in his diet and consuming only small amounts of water (the breastfed infant or the one on ready-to-feed formula) should be supplemented with 0.25 mg. of fluoride per day.[2] Take special note of the dosage, as some drops contain double that amount—0.50 mg. That is too high, as it can cause mottling, or white opaque spotting of the tooth enamel.

If your child is taking a concentrated, powdered, or evaporated-milk formula, he may be getting enough fluoride, provided the water you use for mixing contains at least 0.3 parts per million fluoride. However, if the level is less than 0.3 ppm, you should supplement with 0.25 mg. fluoride per day.

Fluoride drops are available by prescription, either alone or in combination with vitamins A, C, and D. The latter is an appropriate choice for the breastfed infant. (Although the breastfed baby doesn't need vitamins A and C, there are no formulations with only vitamin D and fluoride.) Fluoride alone is a better choice for the child on a ready-to-feed formula. If your problem is insufficient fluoridation of your local drinking water, you can get fluoride tablets to treat your water. Call your local department of health for more information.

Water should be fluoridated to a level of somewhere between 0.3 and one part per million. Levels above this can cause mottling or staining of the teeth; levels below may not give optimum protection against decay.

The Water Supply

The ideal water for the young infant is clean, low in nitrate and sodium, and fluoridated. Most of our city water supplies and local wells are sanitary and safe. If you have any doubt at all about the bacterial content or nitrate or sodium levels in your water, you should contact your local department of health and have it tested for cleanliness and levels of nitrate, sodium and fluoride.

Excessive nitrate intake is dangerous for the young infant because his body can change it to nitrite, and nitrite can displace oxygen in the red blood cells and interfere with oxygen-carrying capacity. Boiling the water doesn't help; it only concentrates the nitrates. If the nitrate level is 10 mg. per liter or more, you will need some other source of water until your baby is on a mixed diet.[5]

The concern with sodium in drinking water relates to possible long-term effects of excessive sodium intake, such as increased blood pressure. Sodium in water may occur naturally or it may be added by the water softening process. Have your water tested if you suspect it is salty. Use only the unsoftened water to dilute formula or juice.

The Nursing Equipment

There are some gadgets that are helpful for breastfeeding that we will discuss in the next chapter. For now we will be discussing bottle feeding.

You need equipment that works well, and that you and your baby can manage well. A nipple that is comfortable in your baby's mouth, and that feeds the formula at a manageable rate, has everything to do with establishing smooth and comfortable feeding. If your baby either is working too hard to get the formula, or is getting strangled by a too-fast flow, he will repeatedly pull off the nipple and fuss. That will frustrate both of you.

There are three main types of nipples: the traditional Evenflo® type, the Playtex® nurser type, and the Nuk® type. The latter is the one that is "orthodontically" shaped, and it looks like it has been left too close to the stove. Usually, babies are pretty flexible about taking up with the nipple you offer, but occasionally you'll find an infant who has a very marked preference. Many breast-feeding parents say their baby can only manage the Nuk, which supposedly most closely duplicates the breast nipple shape in the infant's mouth.

Nipple openings are either holes or cross-cut. It doesn't matter which you use as long as the nipple flows well. When you hold the bottle upside down, the formula should come out in steady drops that follow each other closely, but not in a constant flow. If it comes out too slowly, you can enlarge the opening with a hot needle, checking it to get the proper flow. Discard the nipple if the flow is too fast. Also discard cross-cut nipples when the opening becomes flabby.

Bottles can be the traditional rigid glass or plastic types, or the sort that have a throw-away plastic liner. The liners are sterile, so with those only the nipple and nipple cover have to be boiled.

In choosing between the rigid-sided bottles, I prefer the glass because I think it is easier to clean and dries faster after it is rinsed. Glass also keeps its shape better than plastic, so it makes a more-reliable measuring tool. Although it is true that the plastic bottles won't shatter, it really takes quite a bit to break a glass bottle. Since glass holds the temperature better, a feeding stays warm longer, and a cold bottle in a diaper bag stays cold longer. Do stay away from those cutsey animal-shaped nursing bottles; all those little curves and corners are just too hard to keep clean.

During the feeding you must provide for air flow into the bottle. If the ring of a traditional rigid-sided bottle is screwed on too tightly, no air will be able to get in around the ring. The baby will be causing a vacuum as he sucks, the nipple will collapse, and he will be forced to pull away before he wants to. On the other hand, if the ring is too loose, the flow will be too fast, and he may choke or overfeed himself and spit up. Loosen the ring just enough to get a good air flow (but not so much that you get formula all down the baby's shirt-front). As the baby sucks you should be able to hear the air feeding into the bottle and see the air bubbles. Air flow isn't a problem with plastic liners, as the liners simply collapse as they empty. You don't even have to hold them upright.

The rigid-sided bottle has to be properly tilted so the nipple is well-filled with formula throughout the feeding. Otherwise the infant will suck in air, certainly become frustrated, and possibly get a stomach ache.

Position, Timing, Temperature of Feeding

Hold your baby while you feed him so his head is a little higher than the rest of his body. If he is lying too flat, the milk can come back up in his throat, get into his eustacian tube, and cause earache.

149

Don't ever prop your baby's bottle and let him feed himself in bed. Cuddling while feeding is a vital part of nurturing; also, in addition to depriving you of important contact with each other, bottle propping can cause earache, bottle mouth, and choking. Bottle mouth is rampant tooth decay, predominantly of the upper teeth, that comes from letting a child go to sleep with milk, juice, or any caloric liquid pooling in his mouth. If your baby has teeth and is dozing off with the nipple in his mouth, you should remove the nipple, then straighten him up and stimulate him a bit so he swallows before you put him down for his nap.

Babies don't seem to mind too much whether their milk feeding is warmed or cold, as long as it is consistent. If you warm his bottle you should do it immediately prior to feeding. Don't let bottles stand out of the refrigerator to come to room temperature between feedings.

Safety, Sanitation and Dilution

One of the advantages of breastmilk is its safety. It comes straight from the source, so it doesn't have a chance to get contaminated. It is always properly mixed; it is not overconcentrated or underconcentrated. On the other hand, carelessly-prepared formula can get contaminated, or it can be improperly diluted. You must take particular care to see that your baby's formula, like breastmilk, is sanitary and properly mixed.

Modern formula preparation is deceptively simple—so simple, in fact, that it is easy to become lax and inattentive, and to begin to make some serious errors. There is no way of knowing how often babies get sick from contaminated or overconcentrated formula. Most babies who are hospitalized for vomiting and diarrhea are bottle fed.[9] Part of the difference may come from the handling rather than the formula.

While we don't know how many times formulas are contaminated, we do know that in many cases formulas are improperly diluted. A check on waiting room bottles in a pediatric clinic in England[16] showed over half of the feedings to be overconcentrated, with some of them triple the proper concentration.

Overconcentrated formula can overload the infant's ability to excrete waste products, and produce varying degrees of dehydration. Underconcentrated formula can impair growth rate and, in certain susceptible children, lead to water intoxication. Water intoxication, or overloading with water, puts a burden on the circulatory system and causes a too-great dilution of the bloodstream minerals that the body needs for normal function.

When you prepare your baby's formula, you have to pay scrupulous attention to detail in measuring, mixing, sanitation and refrigeration.

Sanitation. It is worth taking some extra care to see that your baby's food is safe and clean. Babies have less immunity to bacteria in the digestive tract, and are more sensitive to irritating substances than the older person. The baby who has diarrhea or is vomiting from a food infection risks dehydration. In our clean environments there is no excuse for food infections. In this section we will be talking about the principles of preparing and handling food in a way that will make and keep it safe.

Health workers' recommendations vary as to the degree of sterilization needed in the preparation of infant formula. Some instruct parents to boil water, bottles, nipples and all equipment used in preparation of formula. Others say good dish washing and clean water supply is enough, given our generally clean home conditions.

That might be all right if parents were as scrupulous as the health workers expect them to be. I have observed, however, that people can be woefully casual about food-handling (for adults as well as children). Unless they are taught, people don't think to wash their hands before they start working with food, they don't know about proper dishwashing techniques, and they leave food standing out at room temperature.

I think you should sterilize for the first three months. That should get your infant through the time of highest incidence of gastrointestinal upsets, and allow him to develop some tolerance for bacteria before he is exposed to them in the potentially large doses common in contaminated formula. I will describe three approaches to sterilizing, and also go into some detail about good hygenic technique in food handling. If you know all this already, bear with me. In this area I would rather tell too much than too little.

The formula manufacturers provide some very nice, free booklets with instructions and pictures detailing proper formula preparation. You can get one of these booklets from your physician, or by writing to Ross Laboratories or Mead Johnson. I will summarize and highlight some of the instructions.

Bacteria need three things to grow: food, water and the proper temperature. It is our job to see to it that they are deprived of one, two, or all three. To keep food safe we must reduce bacterial numbers as low as possible, and then make the environment for those remaining as unpleasant as possible.

Infant formulas and evaporated milk are sterile as they come from the can. That is, the bacteria have been destroyed by the heating process during manufacturing. The water supply and carefully washed utensils, bottles and nipples are clean but not sterile. Boiling equipment in water sterilizes it: it reduces the number of bacteria to a very low level, and thus decreases the amount of contamination that milk gets from these sources.

You can sterilize either by using the *aseptic* method, through *terminal heating*, or by the *single bottle* method. If you use the *aseptic method*, boil everything before you assemble it: the water used in formula preparation, the bottles, the nipples and nipple covers, and the measuring and mixing equipment. Don't forget to boil the can opener. Boil the water used in the formula for five minutes, the equipment for twenty. Then, being careful not to touch or contaminate, fill the bottles either one at a time or in a batch sufficient to last a day. Cover and refrigerate any prefilled bottles and the unused liquid formula. Use within 48 hours.

If you use *terminal sterilization*, clean but do not boil the equipment and ingredients. Prepare formula to the proper dilution, fill the bottles, invert the nipples, cover with the nipple discs (or leave nipples upright and cover with dome covers), and loosely screw on the rings. Then place the whole bottle-and-formula assembly in a pot with water about three inches deep. Cover and boil 25 minutes. (You can buy a sterilizer, but any big pot with a rack and a tight lid will work.) Remove the pot from the heat and let it stand, covered, one hour. Then take out the bottles, tighten the nipple rings and refrigerate. These filled bottles should also be used within 48 hours.

Once you get the hang of it, the terminal sterilization method is easy and quite foolproof. You don't have to be so careful about handling your bottles as you fill them, plus you don't have to preboil all the components.

For the *single-bottle* method, wash the bottles, fill each bottle with enough water to properly dilute the formula for one feeding, cap loosely and terminally sterilize. When the bottles cool, tighten the rings and store for no more than three days at room temperature. When you are ready to make the feeding, put in the right amount of concentrate or powder, shake it well and feed. (You can prepare a single eight-ounce bottle of evaporated milk formula by mixing three ounces evaporated milk, four and one-half ounces of water, and two teaspoons corn syrup or sugar.)

Of the three methods, the single bottle method is the best and easiest. You decrease the risk of bacterial contamination because you don't handle the equipment after you sterilize it, plus the germs simply don't have a chance to grow in the milk medium before the bottle is fed to the infant.

Sterilizing does not make up for sloppy habits. Your technique and handling of equipment and formula must be consistently excellent in any event, but particularly if you choose not to sterilize. First

153

of all, your hands must be clean. To get rid of as many bacteria as possible you must wash your hands with soap. Simply rinsing them off with water doesn't do much but rearrange the bacteria. If you must dry your hands after washing, dry them on a clean towel.

Then, your sink must be clean. Take the time to scrub your sink with fresh, hot water and detergent and rinse it well with clear, hot water. Sinks can become contaminated with all sorts of undesirable bacteria. For instance, almost all raw chickens have salmonella on them, and fresh vegetables have botulinum spores on them. Any grease or food particles left in a sink will probably be kept moist by frequent tap usage, providing a perfect medium for bacterial growth.

Once you get your sink clean and rinsed, you can get started cleaning the top of the formula can, the bottles, nipples, measuring cups and spoons and stirring spoons, the can opener, and other equipment you use in formula preparation. Use a clean dishcloth. Use a bottle brush only for the baby bottles; wash and rinse it carefully after each use and put it where it can quickly dry and stay dry. Remember, any time you leave things wet you are providing a good medium for bacterial growth.

As you carefully wash the bottles and nipples, scrub the insides of the bottles and be sure to get all the milk drips from around the rims. (It's a good idea to rinse bottles and nipples with cool water right after use—this prevents formation of a milk film.) Give special attention to the nipples, wiping off the milk spots and forcing wash and rinse water through the holes in the nipples. Rinse carefully in water as hot as your hands can stand. Be sure that you get all the suds off, as dried scum from soap contains food particles and, again, provides a good medium for bacterial growth. Invert the bottles in a drying rack, put the nipples in a clean strainer, and let them air dry.

Automatic dishwashers generally do a good job of cleaning bottles and equipment. You need to be sure, however, that the water is getting up to about 140 degrees, and that the rinse cycle is doing a good job of getting off all of that caustic detergent. Check the instruction booklet on the dishwasher to be sure that you are using the correct amount of detergent, and carefully measure that amount into the machine. Use the full cycle, including the pre-rinse, when you wash the bottles. If the milk is really dried onto the bottles, soak them first and manually remove the residue.

Even if you are not planning to sterilize the other equipment, I would encourage you to boil up the nipples, let them dry, and store them in a clean, dry fruit jar.

Once the bottles are clean and dry, store them, inverted or covered, in a clean place. Again, if the bottles are not sterilized, it is probably better to fill them one at a time just before each feeding. Carefully cover any unused milk or formula and refrigerate, or, if it is powder, store in a cool, dry, place.

Keeping Formula Cool. Check your refrigerator temperature to see that it is somewhere between 35 and 40 degrees fahrenheit. Food keeps best when it is kept as cool as possible without freezing.

If you decide to warm your baby's bottle, do so only immediately prior to feeding. Generally we say that if a food is held between 40 and 140 degrees (optimum temperatures for bacterial growth) for two hours or more, it is contaminated and should be discarded.

Keep time and temperature in mind when you carry bottles in a diaper bag. Have the formula very cold when you pack it, and wrap it with a thick cloth to help keep it cold. If you are going to be away from refrigeration for a particularly long time, you might consider carrying along an ice chest or buying the single-feeding bottles or cans of formula.

I am not encouraging you to become a fanatic about cleanliness. You would be going too far if you imitate a fabled professor of mine and wash your door knobs with alcohol.

It certainly would be going too far to yell at big brother or sister about touching the baby's hands with their grubby little paws

155

or sharing their toys with him. Your baby will naturally get exposed to germs in his environment, and he will gradually develop resistance to them. As he becomes exposed, his intestine will become less sensitive and react less. With your careful handling of formula, you are keeping the bacterial level down and giving him a chance to gradually develop his ability to live with the germs in his environment.

Proper Dilution of Formula. Unless your child is under very close medical supervision, it is extremely important to accurately follow standard directions in making up infant formulas. People not only make mistakes, they even vary concentrations intentionally. Some parents want their child to grow faster so they concentrate the formula. Or they want to have longer intervals between feedings, or less wet diapers. Occasionally someone will feed concentrated infant formula full strength (the liquid that you are supposed to dilute one-to-one with water), by accident or otherwise. The results can be tragic.

DON'T EXPERIMENT. FOLLOW DIRECTIONS. Use standard measuring cups and spoons, or the equipment provided with the formula. For measuring liquids, use the clear measuring cups with the volume marked off on the sides. Get your eye down even with the mark on the side of the cup to make sure you are measuring liquid accurately. Use aluminum or plastic nesting cups for dry measures. If they give you a little scoop for measuring formula for a single bottle, use it. The diameter and depth of the scoop are carefully selected to allow you to measure as accurately as possible. If you change to another brand of formula, use the scoop that comes with the new brand, and again read the package directions. Don't assume the procedure is the same for all brands.

For making up several bottles at a time, you may have to use a measuring cup. Again, follow the instructions. Some say to pack the formula into the cup, others simply say to spoon it. If it says to spoon it, do so—don't dig the cup into the powder. After you fill the cup according to directions, level off the top with a spatula or straight-edged knife. Do not level by shaking or tapping the cup. That changes the way the formula packs and makes for inaccurate measurement.

If you are making up one bottle at a time, you may use the measurements on the baby bottle, *provided it has rigid sides*, and you follow the package directions. DO NOT measure in the baby bottles that have disposable plastic inner liners; you simply cannot get an accurate measurement.

At the same time that you are being careful not to make the formula overconcentrated, be sure that you are not underconcentrating it. While too much water in the formula is not as dangerous as too little water, it can affect your baby's growth, especially if he is under six weeks of age. The baby over six weeks simply demands a larger volume of the dilute formula to satisfy his energy needs. The disadvantage is getting the child accustomed to taking great quantities of food. (Some have speculated that this is a habit that could carry over into adult life.)

The point then: when making up baby formula, don't get it close, GET IT RIGHT.

Quantity of Formula

As we discussed in the chapter on calories and normal growth, the amount of formula that your baby takes will be an individual matter, depending on his age, growth rate, activity level, and efficiency of metabolism. He can be trusted to regulate his food intake with his own cues of hunger and satiety. Your role is to learn to detect these cues and respond to them appropriately.

For your own interest and reassurance I am going to give you some figures on typical formula intakes, ranging from the 10th to the 90th percentile.[12]

Figure 5-8. Range of Daily Formula Intake

Age*	Percentile		
	10th	50th	90th
One month	14 oz.	20 oz.	28 oz.
Two months	23 oz.	28 oz.	34 oz.
Three months	25 oz.	31 oz.	40 oz.
Four months	27 oz.	31 oz.	39 oz.
Five months	27 oz.	34 oz.	45 oz.
Six months	30 oz.	37 oz.	50 oz.

*Formula intakes are reported for only the first six months because that is generally the time that a child is kept on formula alone.

At the 10th percentile the baby is taking as much or more formula than 10% of all infants. At the 50th percentile he is about in the middle, and at the 90th percentile he is taking as much or more than 90% of infants. Don't become immediately alarmed if your infant's food intake is outside these ranges. Keep in mind that 10% of infants are consuming more even than those in the 90th percentile and 10% are consuming less than those in the 10th percentile. Also keep in mind that these intakes are weekly averages. Your baby's day-to-day intake will vary.

It is remarkable that the highest-consuming newborn eats twice as much as the lowest-consuming one. At all ages, the child at the 90th percentile takes at least half again more formula than the one at the 10th percentile.

Feeding Frequency

As with quantity, you must give your child a say in determining the frequency with which he is fed. Physicians will often ask about the number of times a child is fed in a day (some even have the audacity to dictate the number of feedings). Parents often appear startled by the inquiry and will respond with something like, "well, let me see, he wakes up in the morning and wants to be fed, that's one time, and then sometimes he wants to be fed again about 9:00, but sometimes he doesn't, and then. . ." Unless they are put to the test, they simply don't know. If you regularly prepare a batch of bottles for a day, you will have to have some general idea of the number; but, beyond that, I don't really think it is important.

Your baby will feed as often as he needs to. As he gets bigger and his stomach holds more, and his digestive process accomodates more, he will eat less frequently. By the time he is a toddler he will probably be eating about six times a day: three meals and three snacks.

I will acknowledge that once in a while baby and parents get on a too-frequent pattern. By that I mean an almost-hourly feeding pattern. I would guess that parents or baby are over-interpreting hunger, and would suggest trying some other methods of comforting or entertaining. But if the infant is truly hungry he should be fed, even if the frequency is higher than some standard, somewhere, says he should be fed.

Promoting Good Feeding

The best feeding approach is one that is controlled by the baby rather than controlled by you. You let the baby control things when you pay attention to information coming from him and try to interpret and respond in a way that will allow him to eat well. Here are some examples of infant-controlled and parent-controlled feeding behavior.

The "infant-controlled" column describes how you behave when you are paying attention, and responding appropriately, to information coming from your baby. The "parent-controlled" column describes the behavior of a parent who is running the show with feeding, and ignoring or overruling information coming from the baby.

Infant controlled	Parent controlled
Attentive to infant behavior— allows quantity to vary	Ignores infant behavior Enforces externally-determined quantity
Holds bottle still at an appropriate angle	Rotates, tilts, jiggles bottle
Feeds according to baby's times or evolves a routine	Imposes feeding routine
Poises nipple over lips and allows baby to open up	Pushes nipple in
Problem solving, using trial and error	Assigns traits for problems— "He doesn't like his bottle"
Allows pauses—gives time to decide to finish feed	Terminates feeding abruptly at pauses
Soothes fussiness—finds reason for discomfort	Interprets infant fussiness as a sign of satiety

Weaning

We have to jump ahead now, to talk about weaning from the bottle or breast, as that generally becomes a concern somewhere between age eight months and a year.

Weaning at the appropriate time is important for a couple of reasons. First, the infant approaching 12 months is usually physically ready for a changed feeding style. He can feed himself chopped or mashed food and he can drink from a cup. He may even be ready to begin awkward experimentation with holding the cup and drinking from it himself. Second, excessive and overly prolonged bottle use and breastfeeding can promote some undesirable nutritional habits. He can overdemand milk, replacing other needed nutrients in his diet. Older babies often carry their bottles around and sip along, thus keeping their teeth exposed to calorie-containing liquids that can cause tooth decay.

I would like to avoid giving any hard-and-fast rules about weaning. In some cases there is a real, pitched battle between parent and child as the parent insists on eliminating the bottle or breast and the child begs and cries to have it. It does not have to be that way. Weaning is a process of gradually replacing nipple feeding of milk with other modes of eating and sources of nourishment. It does not have to become a process of depriving a child of something she holds near and dear.

You actually begin the weaning when you introduce your child to solid foods and get her started drinking from the cup. As she eats more solids and consumes more liquid from the cup, you can often drop out the mealtime nursing and she won't even miss it. When you start juices, you should do it with a cup, not by bottle, and that will reinforce her cup-drinking skill and keep her from building any more dependency on the bottle.

Babies sometimes get ready before their parents do to give up breast or bottle. The baby takes less formula and parents become alarmed. Or the baby has a bout of teething and loses her appetite for a time. Or parents are frustrated over lack of interest because they have gotten in the habit of offering a bottle as a way of calming her down. Or, most poignant of all, parents simply don't want to give up this sign of infancy. For whatever reason, missing the naturally presented opportunity to wean increases the chances that parent and child will later get into a struggle over it.

Many times children will continue to take an early morning or late night bottle or breastfeeding past the time when they are essentially weaned the rest of the day. I don't have any problem with that (as long as they are not dozing off with the liquid still pooling in their

161

mouths). Generally, morning and evening nursings offer the equivalent of snacks and aren't replacing any meals, so they are really no problem.

Often during an illness or a bout with teething a child who is virtually weaned will want to return to nursing for a while. I think there is room for flexibility in that case; generally when the upset passes they will again lose interest in the breast or bottle.

We have worked very hard in this chapter. It worried me a bit as I finished it off, wondering if I had overloaded you with too much technical information. I reassured myself that you really needed the detail to help you deal with your advisors and make wise decisions.

However, I wasn't totally convinced until I read an article in the *American Journal of Disorders in Children*[14] about five babies in California who were suffering from kwashiorkor. Kwashiorkor is a severe malnutrition in children characterized by thin, reddening hair that falls out easily, failure to grow, irritability, sensitivity, lethargy and major swelling of the whole body. Why were these children so malnourished? They had been suspected of having a cow's milk allergy and had been taken off their formula and put instead, on *non-dairy creamer* as a substitute. The article did not identify the advisor.

In developing countries, people who know nothing about nutrition will feed babies anything that looks like milk and expect them to survive on it. In the United States, that that kind of thing should happen is absolutely astounding. With that kind of ignorance around SOMEBODY has to know what they are doing. Now you know. Defend yourself accordingly.

Don't get so buried by the technical information that you forget to establish a good feeding relationship with your baby. Start out with a good feeding, and then trust yourself to feed it—in a way that works for you and your own child.

Selected References

1. Boulton, T. J. C. and M. P. Rowley. Nutritional studies during early childhood. III. Incidental observations of temperament, habits and experiences of ill-health. Australian Paediatrics Journal 15:87–90. 1979.
2. Committee On Nutrition. Fluoride supplementation: revised dosage schedule. Pediatrics. 63:150. 1979.
3. Committee on Nutrition. Iron supplementation for infants. Pediatrics. 58:765–768. 1976.
4. Dallman, P. R., M. A. Siimes and A. Stekel. Iron deficiency in infancy and childhood. The American Journal of Clinical Nutrition. 33:86–118. 1980.
5. Fomon, S. J. Infant Nutrition. W. B. Saunders. Philadelphia. 1974.
6. Fomon, S. J., L. J. Filer, T. A. Anderson and E. E. Ziegler. Recommendations for feeding normal infants. Pediatrics. 63:52–59. 1979.
7. Fomon, S. J., E. E. Ziegler, S. E. Nelson and B. B. Edwards. Cow milk feeding in infancy: gastrointestinal blood loss and iron nutritional status. The Journal of Pediatrics. 98:540–545. 1981.
8. Johnson, G. H., G. A. Purvis, R. D. Wallace. What nutrients do our infants really get? Nutrition Today. 16(4):4–10. 1981.
9. Larsen, S. A., and D. R. Homer. Relation of breast versus bottle feeding to hospitalization for gastroenteritis in a middle-class U. S. population. The Journal of Pediatrics. :417–418. 1978.
10. Martinez, G. A. and J. P. Nalezienski. 1980 update: the recent trend in breast-feeding. Pediatrics. 67:260–263. 1981.
11. Osaki, F. A. Iron-fortified formulas and gastrointestinal symptoms in infants: a controlled study. Pediatrics. 66:168–170. 1980.
12. Owen, A. L. Feeding guide. A nutritional guide for the maturing infant. Health Learning Systems, Bloomfield, New Jersey. 1979.

163

13. Reeve, L. E., R. W. Chesney and H. F. DeLuca. Vitamin D of human milk: identification of biologically active forms. The American Journal of Clinical Nutrition 36:122–126. 1982.
14. Sinatra, R. R. and R. J. Merritt. Iatrogenic kwashiorkor in infants. American Journal of Diseases of Children. 135:21–23. 1981.
15. Solomons, N. W. and R. A. Jacob. Studies on the bioavailability of zinc in humans: effects of heme and nonheme iron on the absorption of zinc. The American Journal of Clinical Nutrition 34:475–482. 1981.
16. Taitz, L. S. and H. D. Byers. High calorie/osmolar feeding and hypertonic dehydration. Archives of Disease in Childhood. 47:257–260. 1972.

6
Breastfeeding
How-to

Breastfeeding works on a law of supply and demand. Emptying the breasts stimulates them to make more milk. A hungry infant eats more often, empties the breasts more completely and promotes more milk production. The reverse is true for the less hungry infant, who leaves milk in the breast and signals it to make less milk.

Thriving while breastfeeding depends on both maternal and infant factors. The mother must eat enough, rest enough, and condition her letdown reflex. The baby must be alert and active enough to demand to be fed. She must also have a good suck and enough strength to get the milk out of the breasts.

Problems in breastfeeding are really more "bugs in the system" than signs of impending failure. Breast problems (like engorgement and soreness) as well as infant problems (like fussiness or a poor suck) can generally be solved without resorting to weaning.

Breastfeeding doesn't just happen; it has to be learned. It is striking to me how many parents get intimately involved with the whole birthing process through classes and reading, but assume that the part of the reproductive cycle that takes place after birth—lactation—will somehow or other happen naturally or instinctively. Quite the reverse is true.

There is a whole range of understanding and behavior that makes up successful breastfeeding. In our society, we have to go to some trouble to provide ourselves with that understanding and behavior. The situation is improving, but most people haven't had a chance to see a baby being breastfed. Or, if we are lucky enough to have seen the process, most of us have not been privileged enough to really look closely at a breastfeeding couple. We are too shy or constrained to be able to know how the baby's mouth fits the mother's breast, and how the two of them behave in that very intimate feeding relationship.

There are many good breastfeeding books around, books that offer you emotional support as well as information. One of my favorites is Eiger, M. S. and Olds, S., *The Complete Book of Breastfeeding*. New York, Wodman. 1972. I like that one for its emphasis on considering your own needs in the breastfeeding relationship as well as those of the baby. Another favorite is Karen Pryor's book, *Nursing Your Baby*, New York, Simon and Schuster, 1973. Ms. Pryor talks to you like a calm, supportive, and experienced friend, giving a wealth of detailed information and problem-solving tips, both for breastfeeding and for parenting in general. Her book is, however, somewhat dated by her assumption that physicians won't be supportive of, or knowledgable about, breastfeeding. That has definitely changed in the last 10 years. Physicians now are highly committed to breastfeeding, and many are good at supporting the process. Also, the La Leche League International's newly revised *The Womanly Art of Breastfeeding* (1981) is a big (350 pages) and detailed book. You might like it for its enthusiastic parent-to-parent exchange and dedication to breastfeeding, as well as its discussion of parenting topics in general.* All three are available in paperback.

With all of this good information around, our goals in this chapter are going to be:

1. To select out and emphasize what's most important for you to know.
2. To emphasize the maternal-nutritional aspects of breastfeeding.

The main and most important thing you have to know about breastfeeding is that it works on a law of supply and demand. IF YOUR BABY NEEDS AND DEMANDS MORE MILK, HE WILL WANT TO NURSE MORE AND YOU WILL MAKE MORE.

To be able to respond to the demand, however, you have to be eating enough food so you can make milk. YOU HAVE TO FEED YOURSELF IN ORDER TO BE ABLE TO FEED YOUR BABY.

Hang on to those principles as the two to take away from this chapter. Hang on to them now as we turn to our next order of business, again diving into the detail.

A Tale of Two Babies

The stories of Janet and Martha will serve as a useful introduction to our topic. Both women were first-time mothers. Both had good pregnancies, carried their babies to term and had good normal deliveries. Both delivered in a hospital with a supportive nursing staff who helped them with the details of getting started nursing. The nurses were understanding and didn't seem to be at all surprised that Martha didn't even know how to hold her baby and that Janet had a rather difficult time knowing how to position herself comfortably.

Each woman needed the nurse's encouragement to go through the process of getting well-settled in a comfortable chair, putting a

---

*I don't agree, however, with what any of these books have to say about solid foods selection. If you compare their recommendations with my solid food discussion in chapter seven, I think you'll see why.

pillow on her lap, and settling the baby in the crook of her arm to nurse. Janet appreciated being helped to nurse while she was lying down. Both had read about these positions and preparations in books, but were surprised at how awkward and self-conscious they felt as they actually went through the motions.

They were also surprised to see their babies behaving in such predictable ways. The nurse showed them how to stroke the baby's cheek nearest the nipple to get her to turn toward the nipple, and right on cue, each did, mouth open, searching for the nipple. Martha was particularly startled when her baby latched on to the breast. It was remarkable to her to see so much of her nipple and areola disappear into that tiny mouth. And she was surprised at the strength of the pressure. In fact, the baby seemed to know all about getting properly attached to the nipple and suckling.

Janet's baby was not quite as quick getting going. She seemed to be satisfied to take just the very end of the nipple in her mouth, and Janet had to pull her back off again, and flatten out her nipple and areola to fit better into her baby's mouth. It also seemed to help if she extended the baby's neck and tipped her head back a bit.

They were both surprised at their baby's willingness to nurse just to get the small amount of yellowish colostrum they had available early on. Then, when their breast milk came in, they were further interested to see that it was, indeed, thin and bluish-looking, and that the milk toward the end of the feed was creamier and more-opaque looking. The nurses confirmed what they had read about the variation in fat content between the "fore" or early milk in the feed, and the "hind" or later milk.

By the time they went home from the hospital, both babies and both mothers were doing fine with nursing. There, however, our stories diverge. Martha's baby became increasingly active, demanding, and dissatisfied. She seemed to want to nurse at least every two hours all day, and was getting her mother up at least twice nightly to feed her. She was an eager nurser and had a powerful suck. She had no patience with an empty breast, and would quit nursing abruptly and start chewing energetically on the nipple until her mother switched her to the other breast; then she would also rapidly empty it, and seemingly look around for more. She would take short cat naps and be up again, demanding to be held and comforted and entertained, and, soon nursed again.

Martha was really getting worn out. Her husband and mother were complaining because her baby ate so often, and one well-meaning advisor even suggested that her milk disagreed with the baby, and that she should try giving her a bottle. But Martha persisted, even though at times she, herself, felt like she was just being stubborn and a little crazy to do so.

Janet, on the other hand, had an easier time of it. Her baby remained quiet and placid. She would wake up to lie quietly in her crib, and seldom made much of a fuss about eating. When she nursed, she did so politely, often drifting off to sleep before she even got to the second breast. She woke up only once nightly from the early days on and adjusted during the day to three or four-hour feeding intervals, occasionally even going five hours at a stretch before she asked, politely, to be fed again. Janet and her husband felt comfortable and easy with their new baby, and congratulated themselves on doing so well with her.

It was an exhausted, harrassed and insecure Martha who presented her baby for the one-month checkup. To her astonishment, she found that her baby had gained two pounds in that short time. She protested that there must be a mistake, pointing out how unsatisfied she seemed to be, and how frequently she wanted to nurse.

Janet received other news. She was sadly jarred from her confidence and sense of well-being to discover that her baby, although she had grown nicely in height, had barely regained her birth-weight. Her baby had been so placid that she had not even been demanding enough to get her calorie needs met.

Fortunately both mothers had supportive and knowledgeable health practitioners, who were able to help them get on the right track with their breastfeeding. Martha needed mostly to be reassured that things were going well. Her schedule, although it seemed hectic and demanding, was just right for her baby and was apparently helping her to thrive. Knowing that, she was able to relax and quit feeling like she was doing something wrong. As a result, the schedule, even though it didn't get any better, wasn't as wearing on her.

Janet needed some help stimulating her baby—and herself—to encourage a more frequent feeding schedule. She had been losing weight fairly rapidly, and her doctor encouraged her to eat more, rest more, and to begin waking her daughter up at frequent intervals to feed her. She had to learn some tricks to stimulate her baby, like unwrapping her feet, moving her around, jack-knifing her,* and taking advantage of any wakefulness to feed before cleaning or dressing her.

Her baby did start to eat more and to be more demanding. Her weight was better two weeks later, and by the time another month had passed, the baby had taken over demanding to be fed, although Janet still had to be careful not to let her sleep beyond four hours at a stretch during the day.

From these stories emerge the three themes about breastfeeding that we will be following in this chapter:

1. It takes two to breastfeed. To produce an adequate quantity of breastmilk depends on infant as well as maternal factors.
2. There is an important role to be filled in breastfeeding relationships, that of support and teaching.

---

*This is also called the "China doll" maneuver—you repeatedly bring your baby from a lying to a sitting position or from a sitting position to a "flopped over" position, where the baby bends over her lap.

3. In most breastfeeding relationships, as with other relationships, there will be problems while the partners work things out.

Maternal and Infant Factors in Breastfeeding

Breastfeeding takes two. Thriving while breastfeeding depends on the child's ability to stimulate the breasts and ingest, digest and assimilate the breastmilk, as well as the mother's ability to produce breastmilk and make it available to her baby. The many factors in the breastfeeding relationship are outlined on the next page, in the *Thriving Chart.*

Thriving While Breastfeeding

Before we can take a look at the specific factors in successful breastfeeding, we have to know what we mean by a thriving baby. Your baby's growth and weight gain is your most concrete way of assessing your breastfeeding regimen. (This is not, however, to say that your breastfeeding is unsuccessful if you have not provided fully for your baby's nutritional needs . . . more about this in our discussion of relactation and induced lactation.)

Like Janet's baby, breastfed infants may have inadequate weight gain or even weight loss, without showing the signs of hunger or fussiness you would expect in an underfed infant. In fact, now that breastfeeding is on the increase, while the systems for supporting it are not yet very well established, increasing numbers of babies are arriving for their first checkup with "failure to thrive."*

Part of the problem is the delay in checking. Breastfeeding babies should be weighed after two weeks, instead of waiting for the

---

*Failure to thrive is clearly inadequate growth, as distinguished from the normally slow-growing baby we will discuss later.

Figure 6-1. Thriving Chart (Modified from Laurence, R. Breastfeeding: a guide for the medical profession. St. Louis. C. V. Mosby Co. p. 178. 1980.)

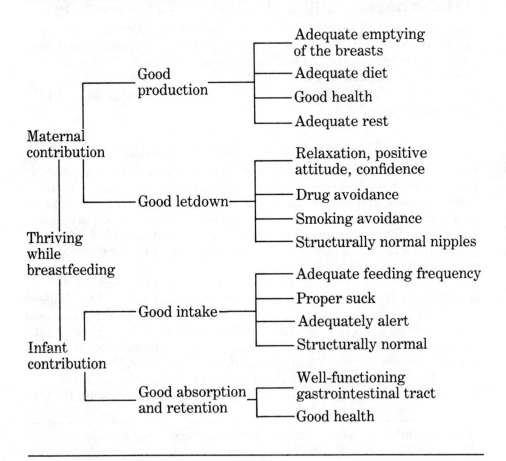

usual new-baby visit at one month. Part of the problem is that parents are not aware of risk. Babies who grow poorly are often placid babies of first-time mothers, like Janet's baby. Babies like Martha's do not grow poorly. They keep after their parents until they get enough to eat.

It is difficult to define adequate infant weight gain, especially for breastfed infants. In a study done in Iowa in 1970, at least 10% of 149 normal breastfed infants had not regained their birth weight by age 14 days. Generally, full-term babies are expected to regain their birth weight by 10 days of age and then gain about 5 to 7 ounces per week during their first month or two.[5] It can be reassuring to know that gain velocities fluctuate; the slowest growing infant one month may be the fastest growing another.

The Slow-growing Baby. However, when you assess a slow weight gain in an infant, you always have to wonder if the gain is "normal" for this particular baby. Some babies simply grow slowly but very consistently and achieve a growth that is, for them, very satisfactory.

Janet's baby was probably growing too slowly. Her infrequent feeding and low demand indicated that she was not stimulating her mother's breastmilk production enough. With other babies who are growing slowly, however, there is nothing so clearly wrong with the breastfeeding routine. They are adequately alert and show a good breastfeeding pattern. At times, these babies have been weaned to the bottle in an attempt to increase their growth rate, only to continue the very slow rate of gain.

A baby who is truly failing to thrive at the breast will show a decreased frequency of feeding, sleepiness, a weak suck, and lack of interest in feeding. If the condition is severe, he will have a lack of urination and bowel movements, his skin will be cool, and he may show some of the symptoms of dehydration.

If your baby is gaining slowly, it helps to keep a daily record of wet diapers—6 to 8 per day is a good sign. It also helps to ask an experienced person to observe a breast feeding, looking for things like infant alertness, sucking pattern and signs of milk flow. Your observer should also note your awareness of milk letdown, and involvement and relaxation with the baby. Check to make sure you are optimizing the factors important for good breastmilk production and letdown that we will be discussing soon, emphasizing frequent nursing and eating enough food.

Just as Janet's baby was running behind, so Martha's was running ahead. Fortunately, it did not occur to Martha to be concerned about overgain, but many parents do worry about that. At that early age, it is wise to concentrate on establishing the breastfeeding relationship, and let the growth take care of itself.

Martha's baby appeared to be pressing because she was hungry. The fact that she was nursing for nourishment, not entertainment, was evident from her hungry response to the breast, and lack of patience with an empty breast. Martha was wise to feed her and trust that her growth would be appropriate for her.

Let's go into more detail about the factors in adequate milk production.

Adequate Breast Stimulation. Adequate breast stimulation is essential and depends on maternal as well as infant factors. Looking at our *Thriving Chart* (p. 172), the first factor in good production is adequate emptying of the breasts. (This, in turn, depends on letdown, which we'll discuss in the next section.) As our stories have demonstrated, production also depends on infant factors, namely an infant who is alert enough to stimulate lactation by demanding a high feeding frequency.

Any rules that limit your baby's sucking and your contact with your baby will get in the way of breastfeeding. We have plenty of rules. We have prescriptions about intervals (every four hours),

174

about duration (three minutes or five or seven), about number (six in twenty-four hours), and about amount of mother-baby contact (you will spoil him).

Frequency of Breastfeeding. Parents are often concerned about the frequency with which they nurse babies, and rightly so, because the breastfeeding baby will probably need to nurse 8 to 12 times per day in the early weeks. That is tiring, especially when you combine it with all the other care required by a new baby. I once figured out that, on the better days, the feeding, changing, washing, cleaning, caring and adoring of a new baby takes about six hours.

A study in 1950[14] of 100 newborn breastfed infants on a self-demand schedule showed the average number of feedings per day throughout the first week:

Day	1	2	3	4	5	6	7
Feedings	6.2	6.9	8.1	8.6	8.5	8.3	7.0

Remember that these figures are averages, and that averaging numbers smooths out the variation. In other words, although there is an apparent variation in feeding frequency in that first week, the *actual* variation for any given baby was even greater.

It is just coincidence if the intervals between feedings show any consistency. Your baby may want to eat every two or three hours,* and then have one or two sleeping periods each day when he goes four or even five hours. Then he will want to eat right away, and then again an hour later want to make up for lost time.

Emptying the breasts stimulates them to make more milk. As your baby grows and requires more milk, he will signal his need by more thoroughly emptying your breasts and by wanting to eat more

---

*Feedings intervals are timed from the beginning of one feeding to the beginning of the next.

often. Increased emptying and sucking stimulation will increase the amount of breastmilk you make. If, on the other hand, your baby needs less milk than you are making, which is typical of that time in early lactation when breastmilk first comes in, the leftover milk in the breast will shut down manufacture, and you will make less, to match your baby's needs.

Sometimes this shutdown happens inappropriately, as it did with Janet's baby or when a baby is sick for a time. Then it is necessary to increase nursing frequency for a while to again stimulate increased production.

Hungry Days. During the weeks and months of nursing, the times when you are in balance with your baby's needs will alternate with times when his needs increase and you fall behind in breastmilk production. His growth spurts, and hungry days, may take place at fairly predictable times, such as at seven to ten days of age, five to six weeks, and at three months. Other growth spurts, however, are not so predictable. Some appear to have one hungry day a week, while others seem to be pressing all the time. It may be that Martha's baby was like that.

"A continually fretful baby" who is calmed by nursing is most likely hungry, which is good, because his hunger is a stimulus for milk production. Contrast him with Janet's too-slow-growing infant who became lethargic. That baby was not even getting enough to be demanding.

Generally you can get your milk supply up if you increase your nursing frequency for about 48 hours. Those are tough, tiring days, when your baby seems dissatisfied and unhappy and you seemingly do nothing but nurse. You may even ask yourself what you are doing to your child by persisting in the process. It appears, however, that those hungry days have a developmental as well as a nutritional function. Often you will find that after hungry days, your baby has increased the time of his quiet alert state. Being hungry and dissatisfied for a time may help stimulate his interest and awareness of the world around him.

Carrying him around in a back- or front-pack, while you do your chores, seems to help comfort him and get him through those days. Outside help with chores can be a life-saver during those times; barring that, you may need to develop the ability to let everything else go and make nursing the highest priority in your life for a couple of days.

Once you get past the newborn period,* lest you should end up spending almost all your time nursing, you should know that a hungry, vigorously-sucking baby can get most of the milk from a breast in four to five minutes. He can totally empty a breast in seven to ten, so there is really no need for you to make the feeding more than 20 minutes in length. Knowing that is a great help. Some mothers think they should nurse 45 minutes or more, and if their baby wants to be fed every two hours or so, they really spend almost all of their time nursing.

Don't overdo the ritual that goes along with feeding. Elaborate hand and nipple washing may just be wearing you out. You also might consider double diapering, especially at night, to cut down on the amount of fussing that goes along with feeding time.

The most common explanation for prematurely stopping breastfeeding is the belief that the baby is not getting enough to eat. Uninformed parents get into trouble with breastfeeding because they do not know the law of supply and demand. Then, when their baby has his first hungry days, they assume that the breastmilk is drying up and hasten to offer a bottle. The satisfied infant then fails to give stimulation to the breasts, and milk supply does, indeed, fall behind the infant's need. With each hungry day, more bottles are offered, the breasts get less stimulation, and eventually many babies begin to

---

*A newborn feeding can take an hour by the time you feed, burp, change and play.

show a preference for the bottle. The bottle delivers more milk with less effort than breastfeeding.

Meanwhile, the mother becomes increasingly frustrated and insecure with her nursing, feels a lot of conflict about the bottle, and eventually gives up altogether, feeling disappointed and like a failure. It is easy to see how lack of information about breastfeeding can make success difficult.

As your baby gets older, his nursing intervals may lengthen and his nursing times may shorten. This depends at least in part on how much food he needs. The chart, *Spread of Caloric Requirements During the First Year*, in the chapter *Calories And Normal Growth* (p. 88), shows the wide variation in infant calorie requirement. A big-eating fast-growing baby will have to provide more breast stimulation than a baby who needs less food. There is undoubtedly also a variation in the frequency of breast emptying a woman must have in order to maintain her breastmilk supply as her baby gets older. Thus, feeding frequency is a highly individual matter that can only be determined by mother and baby.

The Middle-Aged Baby. Middle-aged babies (4–6 months) nurse very fast, and get on with what they were doing. They will often come off the nipple to crane their necks and look around at any distraction, or, worse yet, try to look around without letting go. Because babies at this age can often empty a breast in five minutes or less, their mothers worry that they are not getting enough to eat. (They also miss the long, quiet intimate feedings.) But babies that age seem to be able to maintain and even increase milk supply on fewer feedings and still benefit from the intimacy, even if it is brief.

It is important to continue to keep an eye on growth rate in these middle-aged babies. At times we see an inappropriate falling-off in growth at about three months. If this happens with your baby, you may have to take the lead in resting more, nursing more frequently, and perhaps in cutting down on distractions while you nurse.

Good Letdown. In the last section, we alluded to good letdown as being important to adequate emptying of the breasts. To clearly understand that point, you have to know a bit about breast anatomy and physiology. Here is a picture of the structure of the lactating breast.[14]

Figure 6-2. Structure of the Lactating Breast (Courtesy of Worthington-Roberts[12]).

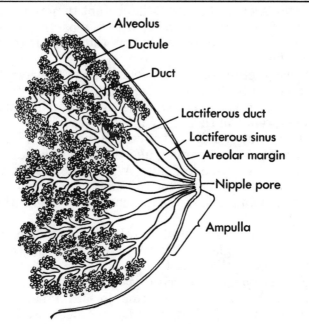

- Alveolus
- Ductule
- Duct
- Lactiferous duct
- Lactiferous sinus
- Areolar margin
- Nipple pore
- Ampulla

From Worthington-Roberts, Bonnie S.: Lactation and human milk: nutritional considerations. In Worthington-Roberts, Bonnie S., Vermeersch, Joyce, and Williams, Sue Rodwell: Nutrition in Pregnancy and Lactation, ed. 2, St. Louis, 1981, The C. V. Mosby Co.

The milk-producing parts of breasts resemble a series of bunches of grapes. The "grape" is the alveolus, which is the milk factory of the breast. The stems leading from the grapes are the ducts that carry the milk to increasingly larger "stems" or channels until each "bunch" of alveoli feeds the milk into the large lactiferous duct. Each of these channels carries its milk to a pore, or opening in the nipple. About an inch or inch and a half back from the nipple pore is an enlarged part of the lactiferous duct, called a lactiferous sinus. This bulging area in the duct is important to note for our later discussion of the infant suck. For now, we are most interested in the process that releases the breastmilk from the alveolus to the nipple: the letdown reflex.

During letdown, tiny muscles around the alveoli contract and force the milk into the duct system and eventually to the lactiferous sinuses, where it becomes available to the nursing infant. Without the letdown reflex of those tiny muscles, the infant could only get at the small amount of milk that is stored in the duct system, the breasts would not be emptied, and the feedback message would signal the breasts to make less milk. With letdown, you get a flow of milk that rapidly delivers about 50% of the milk to the baby within the first two minutes of nursing, about 80 to 90% within the first four minutes.[14]

Letdown is stimulated by release of oxytocin from the mother's pituitary gland. This release is, in turn, stimulated by the infant's sucking at the breast.

Setting up the Letdown Reflex. New mothers, particularly first-time mothers, take a little time to set up their letdown reflex.[5] Like any system in the body that has not been used before, it takes a while to get it going. And you can learn to help yourself to let down your milk.

Establishing Letdown. To begin with, you may need to take pressure off yourself by identifying, and perhaps, adjusting, your goals. Is your goal to produce a lot of breastmilk, or is it to have a warm and close breastfeeding experience? Women who have partially nursed adoptive babies, or have provided for part of the needs of an ill or uncooperative baby, seem to feel their nursing was successful, irrespective of the amounts they produced. This is not to say that you won't produce enough or that it's not a reasonable goal to produce enough. What it is saying is that you can get some pressure off yourself about achieving letdown, and can relax and enjoy the experience, by concentrating on the nursing, not on the quantity of milk.

Keeping your mind on the process itself, and not so much on the outcome, is a well-proven tactic that behaviorists have used for enhancing people's success with all kinds of pursuits, from weight loss to becoming a better golfer; and along with keeping your mind on the process goes congratulating and supporting yourself for good performance. Olympic divers, rather than berating themselves for errors, pay attention to the positive aspects of position and movement that they would like to repeat. You aren't trying to be an Olympic nurser, but the technique can be helpful.

A couple of the key behaviors we're going to emphasize in establishing letdown are a) knowing your baby, and b) relaxing yourself. When you accomplish that, give yourself some recognition. And let the letdown take care of itself.

Here are ways of setting up a routine for yourself that will condition the milk letdown, as well as make the experience more meaningful for both of you. They are listed in the order you will probably do them, not in order of importance.

1. Maintain a relaxed life style. Don't let yourself get rushed or overtired. This is particularly important early on when you are establishing the reflex. Later on the reflex can function despite some disruption, but at first you really have to protect yourself.
2. Pick up your baby; watch and hold him at times when you don't feel pressure to nurse.
3. Set up the environment. Provide yourself with a comfortable nursing spot, get something to drink, maybe something to eat.

4. Relax yourself. Take a couple of deep breaths, or use your regulated breathing exercise that you used during labor and delivery.
5. Take time to center yourself. Bring your attention to yourself, your baby and your shared activity. Be aware of the very real pleasure and satisfaction of sharing that time with your child.
6. If you're not letting down, massage your breasts as the baby nurses. Once the baby has exhausted the readily available milk supply, massage that breast gently in a circular pattern with the fingertips of your free hand, emptying first one quadrant and then another. This does externally what the letdown reflex does internally—moves the milk from the alveoli to the ducts and sinuses, where it can be readily removed. (To know when massage is necessary, you have to be able to distinguish between your baby's long, rhythmic suck and swallow when he is getting milk, and the short, choppy jaw movements when he is not. We'll talk more about this later.)
7. Take advantage of letdown that takes place at odd times. If you have leaking, you are probably having a letdown. Pick up your baby and feed her if you think she is likely to be hungry enough to cooperate.
8. Read a book or watch TV, if that helps you relax. This is contradictory to the earlier advice about focusing attention on the baby. However, it may work for you to turn your attention away in a relaxed fashion and trust your body to take care of the process by itself.

How Can You Tell if You're Having Letdown? Awareness of letdown varies. Some women have very strong physical sensations, while others have little or none. Some women are aware of a feeling of pins and needles, a kind of pain or tingling sensation, beginning shortly after nursing starts, and disappearing gradually thereafter. Sometimes women can feel uterine contractions, ranging from mild to painful. Other women get a sensation of intense thirst. With letdown you will probably get dripping or even spurting of milk from the alternate breast. And the character of the baby's sucking, as we said earlier, will change.

In the early feedings after birth, the letdown reflex may not occur for three minutes or longer after nursing begins. Later, after the learning period, the reflex usually begins within 30 seconds of starting nursing, or after hearing your baby (or someone else's baby) cry. You may find yourself letting down at odd times and not even be aware of what has stimulated it—maybe a subtle smell or sound.

We have said that frequent emptying of the breasts is essential to stimulating them to produce breastmilk, and we have discussed the importance of the letdown in releasing that milk from the breasts. Our next order of business is discussing the other major factor in breastmilk production: your consuming enough food.

Eating Well While Breastfeeding. You have to feed yourself if you are going to feed your child.[9] Feeding yourself means, most importantly in lactation, eating enough food so you can make milk and lose weight no more rapidly than one-half pound per week, *provided you have it to lose*. If you have gained insufficient amounts of weight during pregnancy, you probably should eat enough so you don't lose weight at all. Calories to support lactation come from your fat stores of pregnancy as well as from your diet. If you have stored little or no fat, you will have to make it up from your diet.

Lactation failure with low energy intake. A number of studies of lactation failure and failure to thrive in infants[3,4,8,10] have pointed to some characteristics of mothers and babies that are related to the mother's energy intake:

1. Babies of low birth weight. (Is this secondary to poor maternal weight gain in pregnancy?)
2. Mothers who were dieting to lose weight, both during pregnancy and lactation.
3. Women with poor eating habits in general.
4. Women who were very tired and seemingly experiencing some

loss of appetite associated with their fatigue.
5. Women who were "too busy to eat."
6. Women who were very concerned over what foods to avoid.

It appears that women who eat too little during lactation produce breastmilk that is lower in quantity, although quality remains the same,[8] except perhaps for fat content. If the mother's diet is low in calories, she may have a reduced total milk fat in her "hind" milk.* With poor fat content, the amount of the resulting high-water, high-protein milk that the baby must consume to satisfy his calorie requirement is tripled or even quadrupled. In such cases, regardless of whether the problem is reduction in total quantity of milk or reduction in fat content, the solution is the same: increasing the mother's calorie intake, including fat as well as protein and carbohydrate sources.

Calorie intake. Your best guides to how how much you should be eating are your own hunger and appetite, and your own and your baby's weight response. You may not even be aware of eating more than usual—most women are not. However, for the part of you that wants to run things with your head as well as with the rest of your body, the figures on estimated calorie requirements for producing breastmilk are in Figure 6-3.[13]

If you have gained adequately during pregnancy, you can probably lactate well by providing yourself with 50 to 75 percent of the extra calories necessary for producing milk, and depend on the stored fat in your body for the rest. Women seem to continue to lactate well if they lose about one-half pound per week (again, provided they have a healthy amount of fat to lose), and in some cases can even lose as much as a pound a week without problems.

However, it is important to be very cautious about accelerating weight loss when you are breastfeeding. Even women who are very well established in lactation find that if they cut down their food

---

*This is the high-fat milk secreted in the last few minutes of nursing.

intake and try to lose more weight, their babies become irritable and fussy and fail to gain weight. When they again increase the calorie, including fat content of their diets, the babies become satisfied and resume their normal weight gain patterns.

Figure 6-3. Energy cost of Producing Breastmilk

Age of baby (months)	Volume of milk taken (ml/day)	Oz/day	Energy value of milk (calories/day)	Total energy cost of producing milk assuming 90% efficiency (calories/day)
0–1	600	20	402	446
1–2	840	28	563	626
2–3	930	31	623	692
3–4	960	32	643	714
4–5	1010	34	677	752
5–6	1100	37	737	819

Fluid Intake. Be sure to consume enough liquids to quench your thirst. You do not, however, have to force yourself to drink more than that. One of the myths about breastfeeding that has been passed on in the best circles for years and years is the idea that if the mother markedly increases her fluid intake, it will increase the amount of milk she makes. Twenty years ago, two British physicians tested this theory and found that drinking water or other fluids in amounts larger than those the mother wishes to drink to quench her thirst actually impairs lactation.[6]

On the other hand, if the mother is clearly dehydrated, her milk supply will go down. Or if she is depending on fluids for calories to support her lactation, fluid intake can have an effect on lactation.

185

But simply forcing fluids in an attempt to increase lactation is apparently a tactic that backfires.

Quality of the Mother's Diet During Lactation. Choosing a good quality diet during lactation is more for your benefit than the baby's. Unless you are extremely poorly nourished and depleted in some nutrients, lactation will draw on your nutrient stores to make your breastmilk adequate in protein, vitamin and mineral content.

Accordingly, your diet during breastfeeding should protect you against depleting your own nutrient stores. You shouldn't rob your own bones of calcium to get the calcium for milk. And you shouldn't have to break down your own muscle and organ tissue to get enough protein for manufacturing breastmilk.

An optimum diet for lactation is very much like an optimum diet for pregnancy except it is higher in calories and lower in protein.

Figure 6-4. Food for lactation

Milk and milk products	4 cups (six cups for teens)
Meat and other major protein sources	2 servings (total of four ounces)
Fruits and vegetables	4 servings Vitamin C source daily Vitamin A source every other day
Breads and cereals	4 servings

This basic diet will not give you enough calories—perhaps only half of what you need for lactation. Check back to the discussion in the *Pregnancy* chapter. (p. 35) to get some suggestions for increasing your total food intake to an adequate level.

Vitamins and Minerals in Breastmilk. The mother's intake of some vitamins and minerals is reflected in breastmilk content; others appear not to be. Figure 6-5 summarizes what we know about this topic:[2]

Figure 6-5. Effect of Maternal Intake on Milk Content of Vitamins and Minerals.
(Copyright, American Academy of Pediatrics. 1981.)

Minerals	Effect of intake on milk content
Sodium	None
Calcium	None
Iron	None
Zinc	None
Copper	None
Manganese	Yes
Selenium	Unknown
Iodine	Yes
Fluoride	None

Fat-soluble Vitamins	Effect of intake on milk content
D	Unknown
K	None
A	Yes
E	Unknown

Water-soluble Vitamins	Effect of intake on milk content
Ascorbic acid	Yes
Thiamine	Yes
Riboflavin	Yes
Niacin	Yes
Panthothenic acid	Yes
Pyridoxine	Unknown
Biotin	Unknown
Folate	None
Cyanocobalamin	Yes

As you can see, the nutrients that can be affected by maternal intake are manganese and iodine, fat soluble-vitamin A and the water-soluble vitamins with the exception of folate and possibly pyridoxine and biotin. Manganese is found in whole grains and nuts. Iodine should be no problem if you use iodized salt; it is also present as a byproduct of the production of milk and commercially-baked bread.

Breastmilk is not a good source of vitamin D, so I will not recommend supplementing your diet to provide it.[11] Also, there should be no need for concern about vitamin K because it is routinely supplemented as an injection for all newborns.

Ample supplies of vitamin A and the water-soluble vitamins can be maintained with wise selection of a good quality diet as outlined in the table on p. 186. Generally vitamin and mineral supplements are not necessary for women eating a nourishing well-balanced diet.

The nutrients listed as "unknown"—selenium, vitamins D and E, pyridoxine and biotin—have not been researched enough to know whether or not the mother's intake influences breastmilk composition. All can be provided in adequate amounts from a well-selected diet.

Foods to avoid while breastfeeding. Traces of anything you eat can show up in breastmilk. If you eat a lot of onion or garlic, chances are your breastmilk will taste like onion or garlic. Most babies do not seem to mind.

Some babies, however, appear to get fussy or have some congestion when their mothers eat certain foods. Some clinicians associate the mother's consumption of cow's milk (or occasionally, of eggs) with infant colic. They have observed that the colic in babies they have tested has disappeared when cow's milk was removed from the mother's diet and reappeared when the mothers again drank milk.[7]

188

It is probably the unusual child who reacts to his mother's diet. Further, it is hard to sort out whether infant behavior is a true reaction to food or simply a coincidence, since all babies are fussy, get congested, or appear colicky at times. But if you have a fussy or colicky baby, it is probably worth a try to see if your food could be causing it. Try by removing the food from your diet, but check to make sure you are not unnecessarily limiting your food selection before you cut it out completely.* (Stop eating it a couple of times, see if symptoms disappear, then reintroduce it and see if they reappear.) Often babies will develop a tolerance for most foods by the time they are four or five months old.

Other Factors in Production and Letdown.

Being good to yourself. We have touched on adequate rest and a positive mental attitude as being factors in good breastmilk production. Babies respond to their mothers' tension and fatigue with fretting and crying. If you are getting too strung out, your baby's fussing may be telling you that you are too tense, or that you are over-working. In a sense, your baby is telling you to take better care of yourself.

Smoking and drug and alcohol abuse may also impair milk production and letdown. Some drugs in the mother's milk, such as pain-killers and tranquilizers, may sedate the baby and make him less insistent on nursing.[5]

From the physiology of the mother's milk production and letdown, we can now move to the mechanics of getting the milk into the baby. The whole process of suckling is again a topic in which infant and maternal factors are interrelated. The milk delivery system depends on an infant who can suck properly—who has a mouth that is

---

*As with all cases of allergy, if the original reaction to the food has been extreme or violent, do not challenge unless there is a physician supervising. It is highly unlikely, but I suppose not impossible to get a reaction of this magnitude to breastmilk.

189

adequate structurally, and who can learn the patterns necessary for appropriate suckling. It also depends on the mother's having a nipple that protrudes enough so the baby can grasp it and hold it in his mouth.

The Mechanics of Suckling. Breastfeeding is a three-fold action of suction, chewing and compression by the tongue and lips.[12] It is a process of suckling, which differs basically from the sucking that a baby does at a rubber nipple. The picture below demonstrates why breastfeeding is sometimes called a "pump suck."

The properly-grasped nipple is drawn into the mouth, and up against the roof of the mouth with the aid of the tongue. Suction is important, not to remove milk from the breast but to hold the nipple in place in the baby's mouth. The tongue is in the front of the mouth and strokes the bottom of the nipple.

The baby in Figure 6-6 is properly positioned on the nipple, with his lips almost completely encompassing the areola. His jaw is in a position to apply pressure on the lactiferous sinuses. As he nurses, his lower jaw squeezes the lactiferous sinuses against the roof of the mouth and forces the milk out through the pores in the nipple. The tongue, in turn, moves backward and forward in a swallowing action that is well-coordinated with the suckling.

In Figure 6-7 the baby is poorly attached to the nipple. Because his mouth is not placed far enough back on the areola, his jaws cannot compress the lactiferous sinuses, and the whole position and movement of his tongue are disrupted.

Evaluating your baby's suck. Some mothers report that the baby's ears wiggle when he is nursing appropriately. This is probably a good sign, as it lets you know he is using his jaw in an appropriate up and down motion. The temples near his upper jaw will also move in and out. Here are some additional signs that your baby is suckling properly:[12]

1. Is his lower lip out and not tucked in?
2. Are his cheeks rounded and firm? If they are drawn in too much, he may be maintaining inadequate suction.
3. Is his tongue visible when you draw his lips aside? If not, it may be curled backwards instead of being placed properly beneath the nipple.
4. Can he be easily removed from the breast? If he is properly attached, you will have to put a finger in the corner of his mouth to break the suction in order to remove him comfortably from the breast.
5. Is there a noisy "drawing" sound of milk being removed from the breast during suckling? If he is improperly positioned, you will hear a soft, clicking sound.

To correct faulty positioning, depress the baby's tongue immediately before inserting the nipple. You might squirt a little milk into his mouth to get him to open up further. Another help may be tipping his head back just a bit, to position the nipple well up against the roof of his mouth.

Another approach to teaching your baby to suck is to encourage him to use an orthodontic rubber nipple, such as the Nuk®, between breastfeedings.

Proper Nipple Shape. The most important question for you in nipple preparation is to find out whether you have properly protractile nipples. There are tiny muscles around the nipple that contract with stimulation and allow the nipple to stick out for the baby to grasp it. You probably know if your nipples become erect when they are stimulated or cold. If the nipple remains flat, or shrinks in when it is stimulated, you may have inverted nipples. The test is to pinch your nipple (where it meets your breast) with thumb and forefinger. If the nipple contracts or shrinks back, it is considered inverted. One nipple may be inverted, the other not.

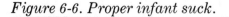

Figure 6-6. Proper infant suck.

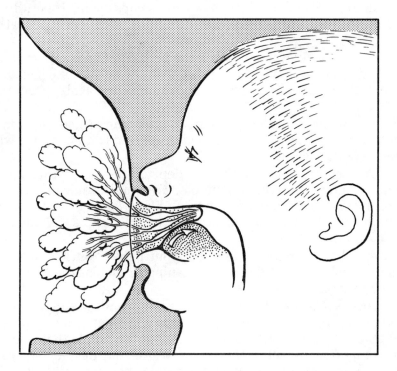

From Worthington-Roberts, Bonnie S.: Lactation and human milk: nutritional considerations. In Worthington-Roberts, Bonnie S., Vermeersch, Joyce, and Williams, Sue Rodwell: Nutrition in pregnancy and lactation, ed. 2, St. Louis, 1981, The C. V. Mosby Co.

Figure 6-7. Improper infant attachment to nipple.

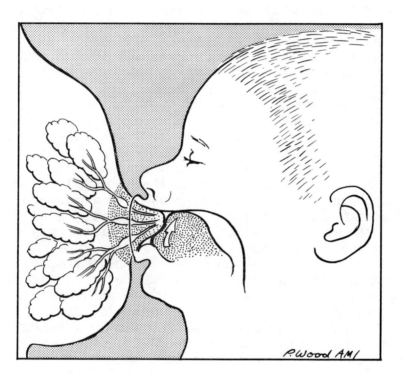

From Worthington-Roberts, Bonnie S.: Lactation and human milk: nutritional considerations. In Worthington-Roberts, Bonnie S., Vermeersch, Joyce, and Williams, Sue Rodwell: Nutrition in pregnancy and lactation, ed. 2, St. Louis, 1981, The C. V. Mosby Co.

Many times inverted nipples become protractile during pregnancy. However, if nipples are still flat or inverted during the third trimester, it will certainly be helpful and may be essential to work with them to make them more protractile. There are several techniques that are successful in making nipples more protractile. The two main approaches are, 1) A manipulation technique, called the Hoffman technique. 2) Wearing a breast shield, called the milk cup. A third technique, nipple rolling, may be added after the nipple can be grasped.[5]

The Hoffman Technique involves placing the thumbs opposite each other on either side of the base of the nipple and, pressing firmly against the breast, gently draw the thumbs away from each other. Then place the thumbs above and below the nipple and repeat. This should be done twice a day for a few minutes each time.

The milk cup is pictured below. The inner of the two concave plastic shields has a hole in the middle which, when pressed against the breast, forces the nipple to protrude. Begin wearing the cup as early as three months gestation (if it appears you have truly inverted nipples), and gradually work up to eight to ten hours per day.

Nipple rolling can be done after your nipples become protractile from using the other two methods. Pull the nipple gently but firmly outward and roll it between your thumb and forefinger. Then move the thumb and finger to another location and repeat.

Even if your nipples aren't nicely protractile by the time you deliver, it should not rule out breastfeeding. Many times a baby with a good healthy suck can bring them out.

Other Factors in Breastfeeding. Sometimes you can do everything right and breastfeeding simply will not work, for reasons that are outside of your control. If you are very sick, or your baby is very sick, it may make it impossible to breastfeed. Babies with heart defects sometimes don't have enough energy to take on the extra work of breastfeeding. Babies born with structural abnormalities, like cleft

Figure 6-8. The milk cup (Courtesy of Goldfarb and Tibbetts[5]).

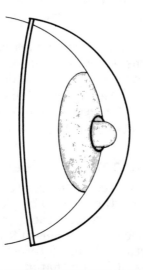

palate, have a harder time breastfeeding. If the cleft is severe and extensive, breastfeeding may even be impossible.* Tragically, some babies are born with insufficient neurological or muscular control to be able to breastfeed. And some babies have inborn errors of metabolism that demand highly specialized diets.

Sometimes babies who do poorly on breastfeeding will also do poorly on bottle feeding. Looking back at our *Thriving* table (p. 172), you will note that part of the infant contribution to breastfeeding is good absorption and retention, which, in turn, depend on a well-functioning stomach and intestine. Babies who have pyloric stenosis (nar-

---

*It may be possible for you to hand-express breastmilk and give it to your baby with a nipple especially designed for a cleft palate.

rowing of the passageway between the stomach and intestine), or who spit up excessively, may grow less rapidly than other babies, at least for a time. Often you will see catch-up growth once the problem is resolved.

Good health is an indispensible part of thriving. Babies with infections, lung problems, or with conditions requiring surgery, will not thrive in the same way as babies who do not have to struggle against such problems. These babies will likely do as well with breastfeeding as with bottle feeding. However, you must carefully evaluate this with the aid of your physician.

Support and Teaching

A second theme we extracted from our stories early on in the chapter was that there is an important role to be played in breastfeeding relationships—that of support and teaching. Breastfeeding goes better in more primitive societies. In our culture we say a baby is "born"—the child's birth shifts our interest away from mother to baby. In many cultures, it is said that at delivery a woman "becomes a mother," which keeps the emphasis on the mother.

In those cultures where breastfeeding is common and successful, there is a special system of support to help the young woman learn to mother. However, in those same cultures, with urbanization and mobility and moving away from traditional support systems, breastfeeding failure is increasing.

Dana Raphael, an anthropologist who has made a detailed study of lactation in primitive societies, calls this supportive function the *doula* role.[5] The doula is the supplier of information, the giver of physical and emotional support and the engenderer of confidence.

Unfortunately, we are too sophisticated in our society to have maintained this doula role. You may find, however, that it is worthwhile creating for yourself. You may be fortunate enough to have a mother or a special friend or a nurse, who can move in with you and provide for you for the first weeks after your baby is born. Most new parents, however, will have to draw on several resources to put together a well-functioning doula system for themselves.

Where would you find such resources?

1. Obstetrical care that informs, encourages and supports breast-feeding, both before and after delivery.
2. A hospital setting that will teach and support your early experiences with your baby and with breastfeeding.
3. A pediatric staff that is enthusiastically pro-breastfeeding, but also realistic enough about nutrition and lactation to provide careful follow-up of your breastfeeding experience.
4. A person experienced in lactation who is willing to talk with you before delivery about breastfeeding, and to stop by at frequent intervals afterwards, just to find out how things are going, and to offer information, encouragement and support.
5. Someone who is willing to point out to you over and over again how well you are doing.

Supportive Obstetrical Care. Because the whole birthing experience is such an intense one, the obstetrician, midwife, nurses, and nutritionists with whom you work before delivery become very important people in your life. If those people feel breastfeeding is important, their attitudes will provide good support for you. They are the ones who should begin to inform you about what to expect, and who should be able to help you if your nipples are flat or inverted.

Find out in detail about the routine at delivery. Breastfeeding goes better if you hold down on sedation and anesthesia, and if you have access to your baby early and often. Ask about sedation and make sure your baby can be with you in the delivery and recovery room.

Keep in mind that during labor and delivery you are likely to be very sensitive. Even a casual comment may seem to you to be serious criticism; conversely, a simple gesture of praise may be reas-

197

suring out of proportion. You are justified in looking for an obstetrician who seems supportive to you, and who is sensitive to your emotional as well as physical needs.

The Hospital Setting. Don't take anything for granted. Talk to the head nurse, the obstetrician, and the pediatrician to find out about hospital routines. Specifically, you need to find out if they encourage parents and babies to be together in the delivery room and right afterwards, whether they allow rooming in, whether they know how to instruct you in breastfeeding, and whether they refrain from giving formula to breastfed babies.

The most helpful hospital routines are the ones that encourage you to nurse according to the baby's needs, both while you are in the hospital and at home. Until about ten years ago, however, hospitals whisked the baby away immediately after birth, bathed him, and then popped him into a little warming oven to make sure his temperature was stabilized before he was returned to his parents. But routines are changing and you can likely find a hospital that encourages you to have access to your baby during that important, exciting, and extremely receptive time, right after birth.

Rooming in, as you probably already know, is having the baby in your room with you at the hospital. This is very important to you for getting comfortable with your baby and finding out you can soothe and comfort her and take care of her needs. If it is your first baby, you probably won't know the simplest tasks like diapering, holding, and burping. It may be terrifying to you to be left alone with your baby, and you may feel helpless at first about knowing what to do with a tiny baby.

You need a caring and supportive person to be there to coach you while you learn about breastfeeding and child care. This is the role that is best played by an obstetrical nurse.* About the only way

---

*Don't depend so much on the nurse that you don't really learn to do it yourself. Ask all the questions you can.

you can find out whether the attitude of the nurses is respectful and supportive is to talk with other mothers who have delivered and breastfed in the hospital. If you don't know anyone personally, ask for the names of some women who have delivered there recently, and talk with them about how they felt about their care and instruction.

Some hospitals give their nursing babies sugar (glucose) water during the time they are waiting for the breastmilk to come in, and sometimes even afterwards. The biggest problem this presents is that the rubber nipple on the glucose water bottle demands a different sucking pattern from that of the human nipple. It can be confusing to the baby. Water given from a spoon or through an eyedropper is much better.

While it may be better for the hospital to use plain water rather than glucose water, it may not be worth getting too excited about it. The five percent glucose water that is generally used has only about 20 calories in three ounces. Most babies won't take much more than half an ounce. (They seem to hold out for breastmilk, even if they get hungry before it comes in.) Using the water might help if it is reassuring to you to know that your baby is hydrated during that time, especially if your milk is somewhat slow to come in. And it certainly helps pediatricians relax.

The Pediatric Staff. The physician you choose to care for your baby is the person who will be most directly involved with your breastfeeding experience. About the only time your obstetrician will get involved, after birth, is if you have some problem with your breasts, like an infection. (If this fragmentation of professional relationships bothers you, you may find that you prefer to go to a general practitioner or a family practitioner.) The local breastfeeding grapevine will be able to tell you which physicians are knowledgeable and supportive with breastfeeding, and which ones merely tolerate it and tell you to give a bottle for every little thing that goes wrong.

Get acquainted with that person before your baby is born, discuss your plans to breastfeed, and get some of his ideas and attitudes about breastfeeding. Find out whether he is willing to do a two-week check, how he follows up on breastfeeding couples (does he call you or wait until you call him), and what he thinks about supplementing breastmilk and starting solids early.

Find out precisely <u>who</u> will be giving you the care at your doctor's office. You may spend more time in the office and on the phone with nurses or pediatric nurse practitioners or a physician's assistant than you will with the doctor. You may or may not like that. In any event you need to check out that person to make sure that you like her and find her knowledgeable and supportive. And don't hesitate to ask to speak and work with the person you want.

The Weight Check. Doctor's offices vary in their recommended frequency of well-baby exams. Around this area, it is fairly standard practice to give a baby a complete exam at age two weeks to a month, exams every two months after that until age six to seven months, then wait for the next examination until age one year. The nurse practitioners and office nurses also offer brief weight checks. These cost about one third to one half as much as the complete exam, depending on how much time the health worker spends counseling with the parent.*

While breastfed babies don't need any more well-baby exams, they may need more frequent weight checks than bottlefed babies. (Growth is, after all, your major measure of quantity of food intake.) Waiting to schedule the first well-baby exam at age one month is postponing it too long for a breastfeeding baby. You need to get in by two weeks to have your baby weighed and to get some feedback on your breastfeeding relationship.

Martha could have been helped greatly in getting through those difficult early weeks if she had come in two weeks earlier. And

---

*If you have an accurate beam (not spring) scale, you could do these in-between checks yourself at home and plot them on your own growth chart. If you feel, however, that you need support or information, it is worth the trip and the cost.

Janet could have found out her baby wasn't doing well, and adjusted her baby's breastfeeding routine, before she got so far behind. If your doctor doesn't regularly schedule a two-week weight check or well-baby exam, ask for it. It is probably also wise to get another weight check at age one month, and monthly after that until six months. As I said earlier, the three-month-old baby occasionally will fall off on weight gain. Further, the four- to six-month-old baby often changes his feeding patterns so dramatically that you will appreciate the reassurance of knowing things are actually going well.

Try to look at this weight check as an important help to you, and not as the product of a suspicious mind that thinks your breastfeeding is not going to work out. More and more physicians are becoming pro-breastfeeding. Making sure your baby is growing properly is a vital part of their role in caring for your little one. It is also an important way of assessing how well the breastfeeding is going and picking up on any problems.

Even if your pediatrician suggests a bottle at times, don't automatically assume that he is out to make your breastfeeding fail. Sometimes you just get so tired and worn out and tense and nervous that a relief bottle can help you rest and let your nerves unwind.

An Experienced Teacher and Support Person. You can do all of your studying and homework about breastfeeding, but once you get into the situation, you will still benefit from having someone to tell you what you already know. You need someone you know and trust to keep in touch with, by telephone or in person.

She should start when your baby is about a week old, when you are likely to be feeling isolated after leaving the hospital. Then she can remind you that it is normal for new babies to eat frequently, and reassure you that the decrease in the size of your breasts is not loss of milk, but only loss of the engorgement that goes along with early lactation. Or, better yet, she can listen to your concerns and allow you to figure all of that out for yourself.

It would be great if she would show up again at two to three weeks to find out about the weight check and help you deal with, or celebrate, your appointment with the doctor. Your baby is likely to be getting more alert and demanding about that time, and also you may be starting to put more demands on yourself, assuming that you are through the postpartum period. Both of these can combine to make a fussy baby, and may make you question whether breastfeeding is really worthwhile. Then it's important to have a gentle reminder to take care of yourself, and to remember that it really takes at least a good six weeks to get through that intensive new-baby learning experience.

It is also helpful to be reminded that the new-baby adjustment period is, even under the best of conditions, rather a challenging time. One woman observed that, for her, getting through that newborn time was no easier with her fifth baby than with the first. At six weeks postpartum, you can be usefully reminded that you are likely to encounter some hungry days, and be counseled about how to respond to them. You may see your breast size continue to dwindle, and appreciate the affirmation that mammary tissue is still there and functioning.

Your support person may be a good friend, a relative, a nurse or dietitian in the doctor's office, a community health nurse or nutritionist, or a member of a breastfeeding support group such as La Leche League. You may, in fact, find that going to breastfeeding support group meetings is a good way of getting the contact and reassurance that you need.

If you choose the support-group approach, it is best to get started going to the meetings before your baby is born. Generally, however, it works better during that early postpartum period if you have someone who will seek *you* out. (The support group might help provide you with this person.) You are likely to be shy and not too assertive during that early postpartum time, and perhaps a bit embarrassed about asking questions that you fear may be naive. Watch out, however, for advice and "support" from women who did not breastfeed their own babies, or who had an unsuccessful breastfeeding experience. They could be unintentionally but ever-so-subtly undermining. And feel no pressure to accept any advice you don't agree with—whether the advisor is experienced with breastfeeding or not.

If you are fortunate enough to have a helper come to the house, remember that you need someone to focus attention on *you* so you can learn to be a mother. Your helper should encourage you to relax, to nap when the baby does, and to let her take care of the house, laundry and cooking while you devote yourself to your baby's and your own well-being.

Someone to Prop You Up (Advice to Fathers). A new mother is in an emotionally and physically dependent position and needs to be mothered. This role is often played by the father, and if you are a new father, you know it is not an easy role to play. You are doing your own adjusting about that time. Your responsibilities have increased tremendously, your life and schedule have been disrupted, and in most cases you are naive about what to expect or how to cope with a new baby. At the same time, you may find your partner to be experiencing considerable psychological and physical changes, and in many cases, having difficulty adjusting to the tremendous responsibility of the new baby—and being depressed or emotionally labile.

If the baby is being breastfed, your role is even more important and difficult, because you will have to be reassuring and supportive about a process about which you probably know little.

To negotiate all of this successfully, you need to be informed about breastfeeding. You can read and talk to health professionals, to make yourself knowledgeable about the process and about what to expect. Other experienced fathers can be a good help to you if you know how to ask. Men often are not as good at this as women; they tend to joke about their difficulties, rather than seek other men's

203

help in finding their way out of them. But if you let other men know that you value their experience and sincerely want some advice in problem solving, I think they will come through for you.

You will be a big help to the breastfeeding if you offer reassurance and comfort at the tough spots. Both of you may know you are ignorant and inexperienced, but still your opinion that things appear to be going along just fine carries a lot of weight. You can help your partner gain confidence as a parent and breastfeeder. And you can also expect some help with that process for yourself.

It helps a great deal if you can just be there. Having you in the house to fall back on when things get tough is tremendously comforting and reassuring, even if you don't do anything. And of course, you can help out in a very concrete way by regulating the phone calls and the visitors, and protecting your partner from advisors who are critical of breastfeeding. You can also pay lots of attention to any older children, and see that meals are on the table, the laundry done and the house is reasonably picked up.

Breastfeeding While Working. You may be able to breastfeed your baby when you go back to work or you may not. I think it is worth making the effort. At the very least, you will be able to postpone the time when you will have to wean your baby totally from the breast. At the very most, you will be able to work full time, and provide your baby with enough breastmilk to fill all (or almost all) of his milk-feeding needs. Most likely your experience will turn out being somewhere between the extremes—you may be able to breastfeed totally, if you work less than full time, or be able to provide less than all of your baby's nutritional needs if you work full time.

You will need to think about a couple of things if you are planning to work and continue breastfeeding. First, is it your goal to provide your baby with breastmilk, only, and not use formula at all? Or is it acceptable to you to allow your baby to have formula at times when you can't be there, and maintain your breastmilk supply for the regular times when you will be with him?

Insisting on breastmilk only will mean that you must learn to hand-express your milk and to store and handle it properly for bottle or cup-feeding. Stimulating your breasts with hand expression on work days, when you are separated from your baby, will help maintain your breastmilk supply so you will be able to breastfeed totally (perhaps with some catch-up increase in frequency), on weekends and days off.* If you decide on a combination of formula and breastmilk, you will probably have to continue with the same schedule of formula substitutes and bottle feedings on days off that you follow on work days.

Keep in mind that it isn't totally going to be your decision about how you manage your working and breastfeeding. Babies respond in a variety of ways when their mothers go back to work. One will go on a virtual hunger strike during the day, seemingly refusing to eat until mom shows up, then nurse and make up for it at night. Another will begin to prefer the bottle and wean himself from the breast (this occasionally happens during the distractible four to six-month age range). But most babies will take a bottle willingly—as long as it is offered by someone other than mother—and nurse happily when they get the chance.

Managing the feeding schedule. Assuming that your breastfeedings while you are working will be more limited, it is most important that they be as calm and unhurried as possible. It is ideal if your baby is ready to eat as soon as you get home, and if you are able to sit down and relax and feed for as long as you both want to. Morning feedings should be equally unhurried. Particularly if you have older children, accomplishing that demands a cooperative partner who is willing to take on child care and food preparation at those times.

Some working mothers increase the number of evening, night and morning feedings to compensate for absences during the day.

---

*You have a better chance of eliminating bottles on days off if you are working less than full time.

205

They might take the baby to bed with them to allow more-frequent feedings during the night. While that can be effective, you might not be comfortable about having your baby in bed with you. But at least one middle-of-the-night feeding is important to help you to keep up your breastmilk supply after you return to work.

An ideal situation, of course, is to have your child-care setting close enough to your work place so you can go and nurse when your baby needs it. But even if your baby is not that handy, you still might be able to reach him over the lunch hour. Babies can be quite adaptable and patient at waiting to be breastfed at certain times, if it becomes clear to them that their only other alternative is the bottle.

In any event, you will need a cooperative and supportive child-care person to work with you; to persuade your baby to wait a little longer until you get home to breastfeed; to encourage a reluctant baby to take a bottle when he would rather be breastfed (and to reassure you through those first difficult days that "things will get better"); and perhaps to provide a quiet place for you to breastfeed.

If you are relying on frozen breastmilk, have your sitter plan to start out by thawing about four ounces of breastmilk. Most babies take somewhere around this amount, and you don't want to waste the precious stuff. If that amount is too little for your baby, he will let you know—by asking for more right away, or, by demanding to be fed again after a relatively short time.

Making the transition to work. If your goal is to manually express and provide for all of your baby's nutritional needs, study the information in the next sections. If you are planning to use formula during your working hours, select one of the formulas we discussed in the *Milk* chapter (chapter 5).

Be sure your baby knows how to take a bottle by the time you return to work—your partner will likely have to undertake that teaching project, as most babies won't take a bottle from their breastfeeding mothers. It is a good idea to start to feed your baby a bottle once or twice a week by the time he is three to four weeks old. By that time your milk supply should be established, and your baby will still be flexible about switching from breast to bottle. Some breastfed babies do better with a Nuk® nipple. Have the sitter feed breastmilk or formula on demand through most of the day, but hold off toward the end of the day so your baby will be ready to nurse soon after you get back.

When you get back to work, your breasts will feel overfull and may leak during the day, but quite soon your daytime supply will adjust to the demand, and you will be comfortable again.

Storing breastmilk. Breastmilk is extremely perishable—it must be properly handled and stored to keep it safe and nutritious for your baby. Probably the best and easiest approach is to store it in new plastic bags (these are sterile). Some people have found the disposal liners from baby bottles to be cheap and handy; others use Ziploc® or other food storage bags.

Breastmilk stored in plastic bags freezes quickly and can be thawed quickly under cold running water. New plastic bags have the advantage of being sterile, cheap and available. Some of milk's anti-infective properties will adhere to glass, but not to plastic, but that's really only a consideration for the baby who gets most of his breastmilk by bottle (e.g., an ill or premature baby).

Breastmilk may be kept unfrozen for no more than 24 hours. If you are planning to freeze it, you should do so immediately after you collect it. Freeze and store breastmilk at 0 degrees fahrenheit or lower, and keep it for no longer than a month.* If breastmilk is stored too long, the fat separates out, the protein clumps, and it gets bad-tasting. Rotate your supply of breastmilk in the freezer, using the oldest first.

---

*This storage time is recommended by Robert Bradley, Ph.D., a food scientist, on the basis of his research on freezing milk.

You may pour it into a regular bottle to feed it, or use one of the bottles intended for the disposable liner, if you have used that for storage. Discard any unused breastmilk after the feeding.

Some women can get eight ounces of breastmilk at a time when they hand express. Most express only a couple of ounces at a time and accumulate breastmilk stores gradually. You can freeze small amounts as you go along and combine them in the same container, as long as the quantity you are adding (the just-collected, liquid milk) does not exceed the amount you have frozen. Putting too much liquid milk in with the frozen milk will thaw it, impair the quality, and may even allow a small amount of bacterial growth.

You can manually remove milk from your breasts by hand expression, or you can use a breast pump. Either method starts with breast massage. For either method, express for three to five minutes on each breast at first and work up to ten to fifteen.

Milk will initially be ejected in small spurts and then will flow freely. But don't worry if nothing comes out the first few times you try—you'll soon get the knack of it.

As you express, you may find that repeating the massage briefly helps to work the milk down. You may also find it helpful to switch from one breast to another, as one breast lets down milk in response to stimulus from the other.

Breast massage. Wash your hands and expose your breasts. Stroke from the outside edge of the breast toward the nipple, applying gentle but firm pressure with the palms of your hands. Alternate your hands as you work around your breast, stroking from the shoulder down, the side in, the waist up, and the breastbone in. Massage around each breast several times before you make any attempt to manually express milk.

Hand expression. Some people feel that hand expression is faster and easier than using a breast pump, while others argue the opposite. It appears to be a matter of individual preference and capability, and is really up to you which you prefer.

Leaning over a sterile container for catching the milk, place your thumb and index finger on your areola behind the nipple, about an inch back from the nipple (this will be right over the lactiferous sinuses). *As you press gently inward toward the chest wall*, squeeze the thumb and finger together gently: push back and squeeze.

Keep that thumb and finger in the same position until no more milk comes out, then rotate to another position and repeat.

Repeat the massage on the other breast before beginning to express from that breast.

Breast pumps. All breast pumps have a funnel-shaped flange that comes in contact with your nipple. The flange is placed against the breast and the milk removed by suction. The source of power used to provide the suction may be electricity, water, or manual (using a squeeze ball, a squeeze gun, or a piston action).

Electric pumps are efficient, but expensive, so you are better off renting rather than buying. Hospitals, clinics, breastfeeding support groups and hospital supply stores often have electric breast pumps for rent. A popular new hand pump is sold both as the Happy Family® breast pump and as the Marshall® breast pump. This uses a cyclinder and piston action, and costs between $20 and $30.

To use a breast pump, first massage your breast before you start expressing milk. Moisten the flange of the pump with water or the first few drops of milk to lubricate and to allow the flange to make a better seal with your breast. Let your nipple slide along the inside of the top part of the flange of the pump. This sliding is important for contact to stimulate the letdown reflex.

Hold the flange just tightly enough against your breast to make a good seal, but not so tightly that you dig the flange into your breast and pinch off the flow of milk. Stop pumping one minute after the milk has slowed, and break the seal by pressing your finger against your breast where it contacts the flange.

After each use, make sure that you thoroughly wash all parts of the collecting apparatus that comes in contact with the milk. Rinse thoroughly, and allow to air dry.

As with breastfeeding in general, you cannot predict or force an ideal experience with breastfeeding while working. Some babies won't cooperate. Manual expression doesn't provide enough stimulation to maintain breastmilk supply in some cases, and some mothers find they don't like manual expression. But even if you have to provide less breastmilk or stop nursing earlier than you want to, remember that your baby benefits from any breastfeeding, whether it is partial or full, or continued for a day, a week or several months. Any time you have spent nursing is important and worthwhile: don't let the fact of a limited experience spoil that for you.

In all cases, the important thing is providing your baby and yourself with a positive and productive experience.

Problems With Breastfeeding

Breastfeeding is an association between two people which, like any other intimate relationship, may take some negotiating and managing if it is to work out well for both parties. The fact that problems crop up is no sign that breastfeeding is going poorly, but rather a common part of the process that you can hope to more-or-less take in stride as you work out your system.

Many women are finding they have to work out a method for breastfeeding while working. This is a "problem" that has a number of satisfactory solutions. Working or not, you may have problems with your breasts. You may have to work with your baby to encourage an optimum response to breastfeeding. You may have to use medications, or you may have to deal with relactation or inducing lactation.

Breast Problems. You may have problems with your breasts and nipples like leaking, engorgement, soreness, caking, plugging, and infections. Keep in mind that it is common to have these problems simultaneously, and that most or all of them can be related to failure to empty the breasts adequately. Inhibited letdown leads to engorgement, which, in turn, causes nipple soreness as the infant chews at the nipple to get at the milk. Many times caking and plugging, which refer to blocking of a duct with hardened milk, is caused by failure to adequately and completely empty an area of the breast.

Milk staying too long in a particular area of the breast can lead to breast infections. If, in turn, the infection is not controlled, it can get worse and cause an abscess or breakdown in breast tissue. This last condition is very serious indeed, and can be one of the few conditions that demands weaning.

To prevent most problems, nurse more frequently and for moderate lengths of time, especially early on, and use both breasts at most feedings. Most breastfeeding problems can be prevented or cured with frequent and adequate emptying of the breasts.

Leaking. Some women leak more than others, and some are more annoyed and embarrassed by it than others. To manage leaking, you can learn the tactic of putting firm pressure against your nipples to stop the leaking.* Fold your arms across your breasts and press them firmly toward the chest wall. You may also press with your thumbs and forefingers directly on the nipple. Some women use a breast cup to catch the leaks. (Don't use the cup to collect milk for feeding—it's too easy to let it become contaminated.) It is better to use absorbent pads than plastic liners to protect your clothing, but either can hold moisture on your skin and cause irritation.

Engorgement. This is the accumulation of milk in early lactation. Engorged breasts are hot, heavy and hard, with milk, but also

---

*Although this may not be such a good tactic if you are prone to plugged ducts.

211

probably more with the swelling that accompanies the beginning of lactation. This usually occurs on the first full day of milk production and lasts about 24 hours. Again, your best approach is to nurse early and often. To help your baby attach to the nipple, which may be stretched flat by the swelling, you may have to hand express some milk. You certainly will have to compress the areola just under your nipple between thumb and forefinger to help it raise up and allow the baby to grasp it well.

Sore Nipples. The parts of the nipple that get the greatest stress during nursing are: a) the points at the corners of the baby's mouth that are compressed by nursing and b) the part of the nipple and areola that is stroked by the baby's tongue. Varying the nursing position (sitting, lying, football hold*) is important to vary the points of stress. You can also lie down and put your baby upside down to nurse, that is, with his feet up toward your head. This is awkward and somewhat unsatisfying, but helps put the stress in a completely different place. You also get a closeup view of your baby's toes wiggling with the pleasure of nursing.

Also check to make sure that your baby is getting the nipple and areola well into his mouth and that he is not hanging on to the nipple.

Plugged Duct. This will show up as a red and tender area on the breast, behind the areola. To help unplug that area of the breast, take a hot shower and massage the breast from well behind the plugged area toward the nipple while the hot water flows over the breast. Nurse immediately afterward, again massaging the affected area, and the nursing will probably dislodge the plug.

Breast Infections. The first symptom of a breast infection may be like the flu: generalized aching and fatigue and elevated temperature. In fact, if you have flu-like symptoms, you should assume you

---

*Hold your baby on his back under your arm, head forward, as if he were a football.

have a breast infection until you have seen your doctor. After several hours an area of redness and soreness may develop, although this generally appears before the other symptoms.

Don't wean. The infection is best handled, and a more-serious condition more-likely prevented (such as breast abscess) if you keep the milk moving and keep on emptying your breast. In fact, some people even avoid antibiotics, and recommend the same treatment for breast infection as for a plugged duct. If you choose this approach, however, you should keep in touch with your doctor and look for improvement within 24 hours. If the infection doesn't get any better by then, you would be wise to begin taking antibiotics while continuing with the other suggestions. Again, you don't have to wean. The quantity of antibiotic that the baby will get is unlikely to cause a problem, but ask your doctor and your baby's doctor to OK the medication.

Breast Abscess. This is a pronounced infection in a local area of the breast, accompanied by flu-like symptoms and a clearly-defined, red, hot, painful area in the breast. Breast abscess is an infrequent problem that almost always follows abrupt weaning in the face of mastitis. It is a condition that is very serious indeed, and requires surgical drainage (like opening a boil) for treatment. You probably won't be able to nurse from an abscessed breast until it is completely healed.

A breast abscess is best avoided by continued frequent nursing and prompt treatment of mastitis.

Relactation. This is resumption of breastfeeding following cessation or significant decrease in milk production. To accomplish this requires time, patience and a cooperative baby. Babies under three months are generally more willing to cooperate with the required sucking than older babies.

While you wait for your mammary tissue to get started functioning again, you will have to use some system of feeding your baby formula. You may want to breastfeed, then offer a bottle afterwards. The exceptional baby may be able to take a good amount of formula from a cup. Or you may want to use the Lact-Aid® nursing trainer (see picture below). These devices are a bother to clean and fill, but they do have the advantage of nourishing the baby at the breast, eliminating prolonged feeding times, and stimulating the proper suckling reflex.

Success of Relactation. A study in Nebraska of 366 women who attempted relactation[1] showed varying degrees of success. However, most women who went through the process felt positive about it, and their good feelings really had very little to do with either the length of time they nursed their baby or with their baby's need for supplementary formula.

Most mothers stressed as important the impact that nursing had on their relationship with their baby. When the mother stressed milk production itself as a goal, she was less likely to have been satisfied with her relactation experience. In fact, striving to produce a certain amount of milk was more likely to present a barrier to her in increasing her milk supply.

Induced lactation. Most adoptive parents choose to bottlefeed their baby, and that's fine. Breastfeeding an adoptive child, without benefit of the priming of pregnancy, is a more difficult process. But given a healthy newborn with a strong sucking need, and a truly committed mother with patience and understanding, apparently it is possible to provide at least part of the baby's milk requirements through induced lactation.[5]

A Lact-Aid® nursing trainer (figure 6-9)* appears to be a very helpful part of the process, with quantities of formula adjusted to mandate a frequent nursing schedule. You can tell by the character

---

*Lact-Aid is available through the mail from Lact-Aid, Box 6861, Denver, CO 80206, or through authorized Lact-Aid representatives.

of the baby's stool when breastmilk is being produced (it gets less formed and less smelly on breastmilk), and can gradually decrease on the amount of formula, until you are providing your maximum amount of breastmilk—which may or may not satisfy all of your baby's need.

Figure 6-9. Lact-Aid® nursing trainer (Courtesy of Goldfarb and Tibbetts[5]).

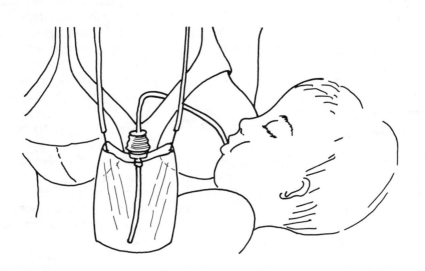

Again, don't judge your experience as a success or failure solely by the amount of breastmilk you produce. Your baby may need to get all or nearly all of his nourishment from supplementary sources, and yet still be benefitting psychologically from nursing at the breast.

Drugs. It is best to use *all* drugs as little as possible during nursing. You'll need to avoid a few drugs that present a significant risk to a breastfed baby. These are listed below in Figure 6-10. All other drugs are best consumed right after nursing, so your body has some time to clear them away before the next feeding. Still other common drugs in low doses, such as caffeine, alcohol, and oral contraceptives, deserve special consideration.

Caffeine may interfere with relaxation, both for you and the baby. Alcohol does get through to the baby, and how much is a reasonable dose? We don't know. Birth control pills, especially the higher-dosage ones, have been accused of (and defended against) decreasing breastmilk supply. Some of the hormone gets through to the baby, and we don't know what long-term effect that can have.

I think it is probably best to avoid the oral contraceptives and to be very conservative in alcohol and caffeine use. In fact, it is probably wise to limit your caffeine and alcohol use in lactation to no more than those amounts I recommended during pregnancy (pp. 67-8).

Cesarian Section. It is the passage of the infant and the placenta from the uterus, not the movement through the birth canal, that stimulates lactation. Breastfeeding after surgical birth differs from that of vaginal birth only in the amount of abdominal tenderness you are likely to experience when you hold your baby for breastfeeding. Otherwise, the breastfeeding process is the same.

Baby Problems. With breastfeeding, you have breast problems and you have baby problems. Some babies may need a little different strategy in management. For their benefit, here are a few tips you may find helpful.

The Fat Baby. As you read the chapters on *Calories and Normal Growth, Food Regulation*, and *Obesity*, you will find a consistent emphasis on not getting all excited about the baby who appears to be fat. However, some babies do seem to want a lot of sucking, and

216

Figure 6-10. Abbreviated Guide to Drug Therapy in Nursing Mothers.

Drugs viewed as safe if used in moderation

Aspirin	Most antihistamines
Antidiarrheal agents	Insulin
Most antibiotics	Epinephrine

Drugs viewed as potentially harmful if used recklessly

Sulfonamides*	Steroids
Oral contraceptives**	Diazepam (Valium)
Chloramphenicol**	Diuretics
Lithium carbonate	Nalidixic acid
Reserpine	Barbiturates
Theophylline	Phenytoin
Narcotics (including codeine)	

Drugs contraindicated for nursing mothers

Iodides	Atropine
Radioactive agents	Metronidazole (Flagyl)
Anticoagulants	Bromides
Tetracycline	Propylthiouracil
Antimetabolites	Dihydrotachysterol
Ergot preparations	Most cathartics***

From Worthington-Roberts, Bonnie S., and Taylor, Lynda E.: Guidance for lactating mothers. In Worthington-Roberts, Bonnie S., Vermeersch, Joyce, and Williams, Sue Rodwell: Nutrition in pregnancy and lactation, ed. 2, St. Louis, 1981, The C. V. Mosby Co.
*Probably contraindicated during the first month of the infant's life.
**If utilized at all, the "Minipill" is suggested, with observation of the baby for possible hormone effects.
***Milk of magnesia and nondigestible fibers are safe; mineral oil in moderation is also safe.

some do seem to fill up a lot of their spare time by demanding to be fed. With such a child, you will want to be sure that you are not overfeeding. These tactics may be helpful:

- Nurse on one breast instead of two at a feeding—if your baby will stand for it.
- Learn and use a variety of soothing and entertaining techniques for your baby between feeds.
- Before you feed, routinely sort out the other possible reasons for fussing, such as wetness or loneliness.
- Offer water between feedings.

If, however, you do all these things, and you find your baby is still hungry and pressing to be fed, go ahead and feed. You are not trying to deprive him of food with these tactics; you are simply making sure that it *is* food that he wants and not simply more sucking, more soothing or more entertaining.

The Colicky Baby. Some babies cry and appear to be in pain for part or almost all of the time they are awake. They apparently have nothing wrong with them, but they are not to be comforted, seemingly no matter what you do. Other babies are fussy, more or less all of the time. They tend to do well physically, because they often are fed in response to their fussiness.

With fussy and irritable babies, it is important to know a lot of soothing and comforting techniques, such as swaddling, rocking, short-term crying, music, noise, carrying in a baby carrier, or using a pacifier or baby swing. Search baby books, talk to health workers and other parents, and see if you can come up with some helpful techniques. Sometimes, however, the only helpful technique is giving your baby time to grow out of being a newborn and into being an older, more organized and more placid baby.

The Placid Baby. This baby, like Janet's baby, is often "so good" that she makes poor weight gain. With this child, rather than soothing, you need stimulating techniques.

Increase your contact with your baby, and try not to leave her in her crib when she is awake. Nurse frequently, even if it has to be your idea. If your baby drifts off before nursing well, stroke her under the chin, from throat to mouth, while she nurses. Interrupt the nursing with diaper changing to get her more wide awake, or give her a bath before nursing to stimulate her a little bit.

The Main Points

Once again, we are back where we started. Remember, to do well with breastfeeding,
• Nurse early and often
• Take care of yourself by eating well and resting well
• Enjoy your baby

Selected References

1. Auerback, K. G. and J. L. Avery. Relactation: a study of 366 cases. Pediatrics 65:236–242. 1980.
2. Committee on Nutrition. Nutrition and lactation. Pediatrics. 58:435–443. 1981.
3. Cunningham, A. S. Morbidity in breast fed and artificially fed infants. Journal of Pediatrics 95:685–689. 1979.
4. Gilmore, H. E. and T. W. Rowland. Critical malnutrition in breast-fed infants. American Journal of Diseases of Children 134:885–887. 1978.
5. Goldfarb, J. and E. Tibbetts. Breastfeeding Handbook. Enslow. New Jersey. 1980.
6. Illingworth, R. S. and B. Kilpatrick. Lancet. 265:1175. 1953.
7. Jakobsson, I.and T. Lindberg. Cow's milk as a cause of infantile colic in breast-fed infants. Lancet 26 August 1978.

8. Naismith, D. J. Maternal nutrition and the outcome of pregnancy—a critical appraisal. From Symposium on Nutrition of the
   Mother and Child. Proceedings of the Nutrition Society. 39:
   1980.
9. Nichols, B. L. and V. M. Nichols. Human milk: nutritional resource. In Nutrition and Child Health: Perspectives for the
   1980s. 190–246. 1981.
10. O'Connor, P.A. Failure to thrive with breast feeding. Clinical
    Pediatrics 17:833–835. 1978.
11. Reeve, Lorraine E. R. W. Chesney and H. F. DeLuca. Vitamin
    D of human milk: identification of biologically active forms. The
    American Journal of Clinical Nutrition. 36:122–126. 1982.
12. Riordan, J. and B. A. Countryman. Basics of breast-feeding
    Parts III–VI. Journal of Obstetrical and Gynecological Nursing
    9:273–282, 357–366. 1980.
13. Widdowson, Elsie M. Nutrition and lactation. In Winick, W. Nu-
    tritional Disorders of American Women. Wiley. New York. 1977.
14. Worthington-Roberts, B. S. and L. E. Taylor. Guidance for lac-
    tating mothers. In Worthington-Roberts, B. S. et al. Nutrition in
    Pregnancy and Lactation. C. V. Mosby. St. Louis. 1981.

7
Introduction of Solid Foods to the Infant Diet

The infant makes a transition in feeding, between ages 4 to 12 months, from all breastmilk or formula to table foods. Foods added during that transition period must be appropriate both nutritionally and developmentally; they must provide the needed nutrients as well as textures and consistencies that will stimulate the child to learn more mature eating styles.

Iron-fortified infant rice cereal, added at 4-7 months, is a good first solid food; it gives iron, and provides a smooth, semi-liquid texture that is helpful as a first food. Later it can be thickened up, as the child's mouth skills progress. The next addition, at 6–8 months, of cooked or soft fruits and vegetables that are mashed or chopped, offer vitamins A and C and a lumpier texture that encourages more tongue control and chewing. "Finger" breads and cereals added about the same time encourage finger dexterity and hand-mouth coordination, as well as supplementing the B vitamins and iron in the diet. The change to "table foods" at 7–10 months is a change in degree only, since the child should be increasingly encouraged to eat family fare and helped to adhere to the family eating schedule.

221

*The final transition, from breastmilk or formula to whole pas-
teurized milk, can be made once a child is eating three meals a day
(plus snacks as needed), and getting a good assortment of foods from
the basic-four food plan.*

People behave as if there were rules, carved in stone, about
feeding solid foods to infants. Each culture and age has had a pro-
tocol for guiding the nursing infant through the transition from suckling and milk-feeding to an eating style that resembles that of the
adult. And each age has had its prejudices about what is good and
bad for infants.

In the early part of this century infants were kept on breast
milk until they were about a year old.[6] People were afraid to feed
their babies solid foods: they thought the babies would get sick, or at
least not do as well on anything but breast milk. Maybe they were
right. At that time many were dependent upon an erratic food supply, and unreliable sanitation and refrigeration: depending on solid
foods was dangerous for some.

Gradually, people began to get a little more adventurous about
earlier introduction to solid food—as they looked for a substitute and
a supplement for breast feeding. Nutrition was a developing science,
bringing with it an awareness of the importance of a diversified diet.
In 1923, a German doctor published a paper describing his rearing of
12 infants on a completely milk-free diet. The infants ate well and
developed normally. There was scientific support for the new concept.[6]

During the mid-1930's people began to overcome their earlier
fear of feeding solid foods before age one year. During that period
one vitamin after another was being discovered, and the role of nutrition in deficiency illnesses began to be understood. Finally, in 1936

the American Medical Association recommended the introduction of solid foods by age four to six months to provide vitamins, iron and "possible other factors," and because of "psychological benefits on food habits."[6]

In 1943, a physician searching for ways of supplementing breastfeeding created a sensation when he successfully fed babies four to eight weeks old sardines in oil, creamed tuna fish, salmon, shrimp, and mashed peas and carrots.[6]

People didn't stop at just pushing children in their food selection; they also pushed their feeding in other ways. A 1956 article in a professional journal recommended beginning feeding of solid food on the second or third day of life, and encouraged omitting the night feeding by age 15 days. After that, the infants were to continue on three meals per day.[6]

The trend to early solids was so energetic that the *Committee on Nutrition** issued a position paper in 1958[6] cautioning against early supplementation with solid foods. They argued that feeding solids before four to six months really didn't accomplish much, and they gave three months as the earliest starting date. But even that recommendation was viewed as calling for an incredible delay. It was ignored until the 1970's, when the trend shifted in the opposite direction. Now the 1958 paper seems conservative. Pity the poor Committee that got caught in the transition.

Now the nursing and milk-feeding period is again being prolonged. Solid foods introduction is being postponed until four to six months of age, or even later. Once again, people are fearful of changing, and worried that perhaps this "new" feeding style will be wrong or bad for their babies.

---

*The Committee on Nutrition of the American Academy of Pediatrics is made up of physicians. They regularly review topics of nutritional concern and publish position papers in the journal *Pediatrics*.

Perhaps parents are looking for what they simply can't have in that age between four months and a year: predictability. In truth, the whole time from the end of the nursing period, which is signaled by the introduction of solid foods, to the establishment of the child on table foods, is one of constant transition, as you can see by the table below.

Developmental Patterns and Feeding Recommendations

During the period from six to twelve months, the baby adds mouth skills. He must first learn to transfer "prechewed" food from the front of his mouth to the back. He progresses until eventually he can take in, or even bite off, pieces of soft food and use his tongue to position the food so he can crush and pulp it with his jaw. He adds hand coordination, as he first learns to capture things by folding his fingers over his palm in a palmar grasp, and then uses his finger and thumb independently and in opposition to each other in the pincer grasp. He learns to control his body so he can sit to be fed and eventually feed himself. His digestive ability and homeostatic ability become more flexible and less prone to disruption. And as the result of all these developmental changes, he adds eating styles, as he struggles with accommodating to spoon feeding by someone else, and, eventually, to being able to feed himself.

The infant in transition changes his feeding schedule from one that caters to his hunger rhythm to one that interacts with and is affected by the family eating schedule. And his eating progression reflects his growth in other ways. Eating becomes more of a social event, and the baby's attention broadens out from his primary caretaker to other members of the family and other aspects of his environment. He becomes aware of the texture of the food, the splash it makes when it drops on the floor, the way the dog darts after it, and the way his parents jump up and run for a cloth.

Figure 7-1. Developmental Patterns and Feeding Recommendations

	6 mo.	7 mo.	8 mo.	9 mo.	10 mo.	11 mo.	12 mo.	13 mo.	14 mo.	15 mo.	16 mo.
Mouth Pattern:	Beginning swallow pattern. Can transfer food from front of tongue to back.		Beginning chewing pattern; side-to-side motion of tongue and mashing food with jaws.				Continuing maturation of biting, chewing, swallowing.				
Hand Coordination:		Palmar grasp.	Pincer grasp beginning.	Grabs spoon	Can get spoon in mouth but generally turns it over.		Beginning mastery of spoon—still spilling most times.			Spoon to mouth—with load intact!	

Urge to put anything in mouth continues until about age three. Increases risk for poisoning throughout this time.

	6 mo.	7 mo.	8 mo.	9 mo.	10 mo.	11 mo.	12 mo.	13 mo.	14 mo.	15 mo.	16 mo.
Body Control:	Sits unsupported. Can balance while manipulating with hands.		Continuing improvement in balance while sitting.								
			Begins to stand. Can pull self to feet and move around.				Beginning and increasing mastery of walking				
Digestive:			Gastric acid volume begins to increase.		Can handle balanced amounts of all reasonably soft, moderately-seasoned family food.						
Homeostatic Ability:			Increasing ability to maintain hydration and chemical balance.								
Nutritional Requirements:	Iron stores begin to be depleted in term babies.		Gradually increasing proportion of adequate diet offered by foods other than milk feeding.							All daily nutritional requirements provided by a mixed table food diet: Primary source of nutrients and calories is table food and cup.	
Feeding Style:	Spoon feeding.		Introduce cup at meals.		Begin self-feeding with cup. Beginning proficiency with spoon.					Reasonably adept with spoon and cup. Can feed self with spoon, drink from cup. Weaned from bottle. Continuance of breast-feeding up to baby and parents.	
Food Selection:	Semi-solid foods		Increase texture, stiffness of solids		Pieces of soft, cooked foods						

The remarkable thing about all of this changing is that he does it in such a short time. The four-to-six month old is still being cuddled for nursing. He may be wolfing down his feeding, or periodically jerking his mouth off the nipple and craning his neck so he won't miss out on what is going on, but he is still, essentially, being suckled. However, by the time he is 10 months old, or even eight months old, he is probably sitting up at the table with the rest of the family, eating what they eat, and quite possibly even feeding himself.

When we encounter feeding problems during this stage, it is often because parents aren't aware of the transitory nature of it all. They allow themselves to get into a feeding routine, and fail to progress when their child is ready. You simply must not allow yourself to settle down to any feeding routine during this stage. The only thing you can plan on is change.

Let's get to work. We are going to discuss when, what and how: *When* to start and progress with solid foods and feeding styles; *what* are appropriate food choices to satisfy nutritional and developmental needs; and *how* you go about starting and progressing with solid foods. Again, to give you a road map so you don't get lost in the detail, here is a feeding chart that summarizes the basic recommendations.

Solid Foods Addition in Brief

You can get through the transition period with a minimum of hassle if you start solid foods late and progress quickly to table food. It is only when you start early—say before five months of age—that you have to struggle with feeding spoons and baby-food warmers, little jars of baby food, and pureeing your own.

It's a lot easier on you, and better for your baby, if you wait to start solid foods until she is ready for them. Somewhere between four and seven months of age your baby will be sitting up, drooling, and opening her mouth when she sees something approaching. Those

Figure 7-2. Feeding Schedule: Six to Twelve Months

	4–7 months*	6–8 months	7–10 months	10–12 months
Milk Feeding	Breastmilk or Formula	Breastmilk or Formula	Breastmilk or Formula	Breastmilk or formula Evaporated milk diluted 1:1 with water Whole pasteurized milk OR COMBINATION
Cereal and bread	Begin iron—fortified baby cereal mixed with milk feeding	Continue baby cereal. Begin other breads and cereals	Continue baby cereal. Other breads and cereals from table	Continue baby cereal until 18 months. Total of four servings bread and cereal from table
Fruit and vegetables (including juice)	None	Begin juice from cup: 3 ounces vitamin C source Begin fork-mashed, soft fruits & vegetables	3 ounces juice Pieces of soft & cooked fruits & vegetables from table	Table-food diet to allow 4 servings/day, including juice
Meat and other protein sources	None	None	Gradually begin milled or finely-cut meat. Casseroles, ground beef, eggs, fish, peanut butter, legumes, cheese	Two servings daily; one ounce total, meat or equivalent

*ages overlap and are given as ranges because of variations in rate of infant development.

are all signals for a change in eating style: a progression to solid foods.

Start out with one of those little long-handled demitasse baby-feeding spoons so you can both handle it well. You might have to hold her while you introduce solid foods, to reassure her that it is really all right. Later on you can go to a comfortable high chair that supports her feet.

Introduce one new food at a time, trying it out for perhaps two or three days, and checking for reactions like stomach aches and diarrhea, skin rashes, or wheezing. Then go on the next food. If she dislikes or rejects something, take no for an answer for a while, and try it a bit later. If she still says no, take her word for it; everyone is entitled to some food dislikes. You can still check out occasionally to see if she feels the same way about it.

The best first food is iron-fortified infant rice cereal mixed with milk or formula. This provides a good source of iron, as well as a good distribution of calories among protein, fat and carbohydrate. Rice cereal is the least likely of the grains to cause an allergic reaction. Start out with one cereal feeding daily and work up until she is taking two meals daily and getting a daily total of ⅓ to ½ cup. By that time she may be somewhere between six and eight months old and capable of eating even stiffer and lumpier cereal.

The next step is to begin to offer fruits, fruit juices and vegetables, as sources of vitamins C and A in preparation for the day when formula consumption will drop too low to provide these nutrients. There is no rush about this, nor is any particular order better than any other.

Given the stimulation of the thicker cereal, your baby will start to show some up-and-down chewing motions of her jaw, and will start manipulating her tongue to guide the food. If that's the case, it is probably a good idea to give her a little more to work on: fork-mashed cooked, or even diced fruits and vegetables. Baby foods are all right nutritionally, but they don't teach chewing skills.

During the fruits-and-vegetables stage it is also a good idea to start offering dry cereals, bread and crackers. Your baby will enjoy manipulating them and to the extent she gets it down, she will take in a few nutrients.

Cereal made with milk and fruits and vegetables, along with breastmilk or formula, really provide an adequate diet. You can start shaping these foods into meals, offering cereal and fruit for one meal, cereal and vegetable for another.

Since your child has no nutritional need for more protein, you really don't have to worry about introducing meat until she is ready to go on to table food. It is generally at that point that babies start eating considerably more solid foods, their milk consumption drops, and they need that meat protein to keep their diet adequate.

By the time you have worked your way through a series of fruits, fruit juices and vegetables, your child may begin to show an interest in what is going on at the table. He may be grabbing the spoon from you and clamming up when you try to feed him. He is giving you a clear message that it is really time to let him do it himself.

You'd better let him. Mash up his food, thicken it so it will hang together, put it on the high chair tray, get out of the way and let him go after it. He may not even need his food mashed if he is able to handle pieces of cooked vegetables and fruits, breads, or noodles and macaroni. Meat, however, is one food that cannot be gummed well. It doesn't soften up in the mouth. Meat needs to be chopped or cut up very fine, and may still need to be moistened a bit with meat or vegetable juice to make it palatable for your baby.

You can begin offering a milk beverage from the cup any time during the transitional period. In fact, many breast-fed babies learn to take a cup early on, rather than an artificial nipple, as a way of getting relief feedings.

By the time he is between ten and twelve months, and perhaps even earlier, he should be sitting in a high chair eating family-food meals and drinking a milk beverage from a cup. Satisfying his hunger and thirst at the table will allow him to omit the nursing at that feeding. From then on he will increasingly resemble an older child in his eating style, as he takes his meals and snacks "just like the rest of the family."

Babies progress at different rates and in different styles through these feeding stages. One young friend of mine took to cereal so enthusiastically at his very first solid feeding (at five months) that he set up a terrific howl between bites, complaining because his mother wasn't getting the food there fast enough. Another, at age six months, did not approve at all, pursed his lips and would on no account open up. It took his mother two weeks of gentle persistence before she could persuade and teach him to eat solids. She *was* persistent, because his growth on breastfeeding seemed to be falling off. Otherwise she could have dropped the subject and tried again later.

That is what another mother ended up doing with her son—he never would try out solid foods until one day she let him do it himself. She set him up to the table and he ate everything he could get his hands on. He was so insistent on eating that she had to throw caution to winds and simply feed him all his new foods at one time.

Each of them had a different experience on their way to achieving their feeding goal: Making the transition from nursing to table food.

It all sounds very simple, doesn't it? Well, it is and it isn't. Starting solids later simplifies things. But children vary widely, and feeding information varies from one doctor's office to another and from one social group to another. Your child care worker may have a different idea about feeding solids than you do. There are many ideas, myths and persuasions about solid foods introduction. That makes it confusing and hard, and the synopsis I've just given you won't seem to cover some of your day-by-day questions. To help you cope with it all, we again have to go into more detail.

Before we can get into our sequence of when to do what and how to go about it, however, we have to lay to rest the issue of <u>when</u> to get started. That is a very hotly-debated topic.

When To Start Solid Foods

The most reasonable and logical time to begin introducing solid foods into your baby's diet is when he needs them and is ready for them. (That reasoning and logic, unfortunately, is not always applied.) Babies generally get ready for solids somewhere between four and six months of age.

Breastmilk or formula, with appropriate vitamin supplementation, is nutritionally complete for your baby until four to six months. If he eats anything else, he will consume less of his milk feeding: he will replace it with food that is for him, at that time, nutritionally inferior.

As I described earlier, somewhere between four and six months your baby will probably begin to show developmental patterns that indicate he is ready for solids. If you are unsure about what you are seeing, or think your baby is developing skills faster than average, you can try some test feedings. Other than possibly compromising the intestinal immunity of totally breastfed infants (by changing the type of bacteria in their intestines), there is probably nothing wrong with experimenting with small amounts of cereal by age four months. If you give the milk feeding first, and offer the cereal feeding afterwards, your baby can indicate his own readiness for cereal introduction. He might not eat much at most of those earlier sessions, but they are still good practice.

But even as his calorie needs and hunger levels increase at about this time, you should still continue to depend primarily on greater quantities of breastmilk or formula. Up until your baby is well-established on table foods it is too early to allow calories from solids to replace too many milk feeding calories.

Once in a while we start a baby somewhat early on solids because he has to depend on them to give him enough to eat. His growth rate on breastfeeding may be falling off, or he may be bottle-fed and simply not take his bottle very well. After an initial learning period, that baby will probably take to solids pretty well. Then it is particularly important to choose solids that provide well for his nutritional needs.*

The 32 Ounce Rule. Some physicians automatically use the rule-of-thumb of putting a baby on solid foods when he is taking more than a quart of formula per day. (More recently, it has become the "one liter" recommendation, which is 1.06 quarts.) I don't know where that idea originally came from. I suspect, in my darker moments, that it was based on the evaporated milk formula, which made up to 33 ounces: If your baby took more than that amount, you had to make another batch. Now that old recommendation is being kept alive by, among other people, the Gerber baby food company, in advertisements to parents and in informational material for health workers.[8] (If you review Figure 5-8 in the *Formula* chapter, you will see that infants reach the 32-ounce level of formula consumption at widely differing ages. The infant in the 90th percentile for formula consumption could manage 32 ounces some time before he was two months old, whereas the one in the 10th percentile could not even at six months.)

The Committee on Nutrition has recommended that milk or formula consumption be limited to one quart per day FOR THE INFANT OVER AGE SIX MONTHS.** That's logical. The high-consuming baby probably won't drop back to a quart right <u>at</u> six months,

---

*I would be sure to offer cereal two, or even three times a day, and hold off on fruits and vegetables.

**The Gerber company cites this recommendation but neglects to mention the reference to age.

but by the end of the first year he should have replaced most of his formula calories with solid foods. Using one quart as the milestone for solid foods won't have anything to do with a baby's developmental or nutritional needs—except coincidentally. But it surely sells baby food.

Sleeping Through The Night. Parents think about starting solid foods because they have heard that solids will make their baby feel "more satisfied" (perhaps meaning sleep longer, or maybe be less fussy and demanding). I won't argue with your desire to make a demanding infant a little less demanding, or to get a good night's sleep. But studies don't give much cause for hope.[9, 12] Your baby will sleep or be content for longer periods only when his stomach can hold more and his nutritional needs aren't so pressing.

Despite those wretched stories by proud parents who boast that their baby slept through the first night she came home from the hospital, most babies don't get to the point where they can sleep six or seven hours at a stretch until 12 to 16 weeks.[12] That coincides with a drop-off in their very-rapid growth rate, and the decrease in the total calories they need for growth. Most new parents will need to get up to feed babies twice a night in the early weeks. If you find that hard, it's because it _is_ hard.

There will come a time, however, when feeding solids does have something to do with contentment, particularly for the breastfed baby. Increases in appetite in the younger breastfed baby can generally be met by stepping up the nursing frequency to stimulate increased breastmilk supply. However, as the child approaches six months, it is likely that he will continue to be hungry despite increased nursing frequency, and he should be started on solid foods. (If those persistent hungry days appear considerably before six months, and particularly before four months, it is better nutritionally to give supplemental formula.)

Feeding Frequency. Some guidelines say solid foods should be introduced when the baby regularly eats more often than every three hours. I don't think that's right. Some babies, especially breastfed ones, regularly eat every two hours. I think, however, that if a baby is eating more than every two hours, *or* if his growth starts to fall off on ANY feeding frequency, that you had better do some problem-solving.* He may not be getting enough to eat or be properly utilizing his food.

"Opinionated" Babies. Back when I was young and naive, one of the ways a doctor persuaded me to start solid foods early was by warning me that if I waited too long, my daughter would get opinionated and hooked on breastfeeding, and wouldn't eat anything else. My doctor said she "knew" what she was talking about because she had seen it happen in her practice.

However, when the question was subjected to careful scientific inquiry, it appeared that my doctor's perception and what actually happened were two different things. A public health nurse[1] observed many infants over a ten-year period from 1940 to 1950 and found that babies under three or four months old really didn't seem to want much to do with solid foods. In fact, they and their mothers were getting into some real hassles over solid food introduction and, despite earlier struggles, the babies first really cheerfully accepted solid foods at around four months.

Solid Foods In The Bottle. Some people get around the acceptance problem by putting solid foods in the bottle. They mix a thin gruel of cereal, widen the hole in the nipple, and get the "solids" in that way.

The tactic is nothing more or less than forcefeeding and should be avoided. The cereal will increase the caloric density of the for-

---

*Even this suggestion is too rigid for some cultures, where babies are given breast-feeding "snacks" at very frequent intervals.

mula, and could force the baby to take too many calories in his attempt to get his water needs satisfied.

Then there is the syringe-action nipple feeder for young infants; I haven't seen these around lately, so I hope they've gone away. These gadgets have no value for the child with normal mouth patterns. The child who is not developmentally ready to eat from a spoon is unlikely to need solid foods.

Safety. We can also cite food safety as an argument for postponing solid foods. Some people are starting to question the safety of common food components such as salt, sugar, nitrate and various stabilisers and emulsifiers. Without taking sides on the issue, I can point out that the younger the child, the greater the vulnerability to questionable dietary components. An older infant will be better able to metabolize and get rid of toxicants in foods.

A good example is salt, which can be toxic, especially for infants, if you get the levels high enough. Some solid foods that I occasionally see parents choosing for their children, like hot dogs, canned spaghetti dinners and canned soups, put an additional load on the baby's kidneys, because of their high salt content.[17] The older child can handle additional salt better than the younger one, because his kidneys are more mature and capable of concentrating his urine more. An older child is also better at letting you know when he is actually thirsty, and can refuse milk when he really wants water.

Some parents simply like the idea of feeding their baby solid foods, and get a lot of satisfaction out of spoon-feeding. Others feel proud if their children are advanced in any way, and are prone to push up all schedules. In any event, try to control your impulse until your baby is at least four months old. Then, as I said earlier, be particularly careful to start out on infant rice cereal, mixed with formula or milk, and offer it only <u>after</u> you give the milk feeding.

Allergy. Estimates of the percentage of infants subject to allergic reactions to foods range from 0.3 to 55%, depending on who is being studied and how you define an allergic reaction.[13] Incidence of food allergies is greatest during infancy. Children whose parents have allergic reactions to food are at a greater risk of having food allergies than are others.

If you are particularly concerned about avoiding allergic reactions, it is probably better to wait a little longer to introduce solid foods. Any new food is a potential allergen. The younger baby is more likely to react allergically, before his immune system is fully operational.* If you keep him away from highly-allergenic foods, such as wheat, egg white, citrus and cow's milk, until 7–9 months, you may be avoiding some problems. This won't prevent you from introducing solid foods, starting with rice cereal diluted with whatever milk or formula you are using, or with one of the hypoallergenic formulas we discussed in the *Milk Feeding* chapter.

Some people argue that six months is too *early* for starting solid foods. They point to potential allergic reactions, not realizing that they can get around that by careful food selection. Or they are convinced that solids introduction will make the baby gain faster and increase the chances that he will get too fat. I don't think that's really a valid concern. Unless babies are really being force-fed with solids, it is likely that they will simply compensate for solids by taking less milk and gain at about the same rate.

As with most everything, however, there can be too much of a good thing. Now that the trend to later introduction of solid foods is becoming pretty well established, we are finding some parents and babies so comfortable with nursing that they are postponing solids introduction too long. Once your child is six months old, I would start practicing regularly with solid foods, even if he doesn't seem too taken with it. Don't get panicky or desperate, just be gently persis-

---

*The intestine develops resistance to large protein molecules as your baby gets older. Resistance significantly improves by seven to nine months, and continues to improve until up to 12 to 24 months of age.

tent. Somewhere between four to seven or eight months he is going to become developmentally ready for solid foods, and you don't want to miss it. If you do, you are going to have a child who is really hooked on nursing and doesn't want any part of any other form of getting nourishment.

When and What To Feed
and How To Go About It

If you haven't figured this out already, as you begin giving your baby solid food, I think you will become aware that if you're going to get into conflict with relatives or child care workers, it will be about food. Keep in mind that you are the parent, and while you will benefit from feedback and constructive criticism from other people, the final decisions, and the responsibility for making them, rest with you. You are the one who should first introduce your child to new foods and changes in feeding routines. You are the one to decide and determine how your child will be fed.

You are introducing solid foods for two reasons: 1) To provide for your infant nutritionally; and 2) To encourage and support developmental changes. The following sequence generally satisfies both requirements.

Figure 7-3. Food Additions During the Transition Period

4–7 months	6–8 months	7–10 months	9–12 months
Infant cereal	Fruits and vegetables. Juices	Table foods Meats	Weanling milk
	"Finger" breads and cereals.		

Once again, the times vary and overlap as infants move through these stages at different rates.

This little table is a rearrangement and condensation of the one we looked at before (Figure 7-2). You can refer to it as an outline for the rest of this chapter. The whole transition period is such an eventful time that it helps to have a clear overview of where we are and what we're doing.

Iron-fortified Baby Cereal. Iron fortified rice or barley baby cereal, mixed with formula or milk, is the best first solid food, both developmentally and nutritionally. Its texture can be varied to fit the mouth skills of the baby. (Some babies do better with it very thin, others manage it better if it's thicker.) The infant cereals contain a good amount of iron that is well absorbed by the baby. In addition the high-carbohydrate cereal, mixed with milk, gives a good proportion of protein, fat, and carbohydrate that won't disrupt the balance of the diet. Finally, rice and barley are the grains which are least likely to cause allergic reactions.

Other first solid foods have shortcomings. Some that are fine developmentally, like yogurt, cottage cheese, pureed meat, egg yolks and pureed fruits and vegetables, are all wrong nutritionally. Yogurt and cottage cheese are low in iron and simply give more of the same milk nutrients that the baby has been getting all along. Pureed meat is a pretty good source of iron, but it is so high in protein that it can imbalance the diet. Egg yolk gives way too much fat and the iron isn't absorbed well. Vegetables and fruits offer most of their calories as carbohydrate and can push dietary carbohydrate up too high, and, while they give a little iron, it really isn't enough.

We'll be making reference as we go along to keeping an eye on the protein, fat and carbohydrate in the solid foods so you don't imbalance the diet. As we said in the *Milk Feeding* chapter, excesses or deficiencies in any of these calorie-contributing nutrients can have a variety of undesirable consequences (see Figure 5-5).

To help you know what we're talking about, here is a chart that shows concentrations of protein, fat and carbohydrate in the various food groups.

Figure 7-4. Protein, Fat and Carbohydrate in Foods

	Protein	Fat	Carbohydrate	
			Starch	Sugar
Milk	✓	✓*		✓
Vegetables			✓	
Fruit and fruit juice				✓
Breads and cereals			✓	
Meat, fish, poultry, eggs, cheese, peanut butter	✓	✓		
Cooked dried beans	✓		✓	
Butter, margarine, salad dressing, cooking oils		✓		
Sweets, pop, fruit drinks				✓

*Unless it's skim milk

Once your baby is regularly on baby cereal, gradually work up from one feeding to two, until she is taking a total of about ½ cup per day—that will give her the 7 mg. of iron that she needs daily. At that point make sure you take her off any other iron supplementation because that will push her iron intake up too high. Continue to give a good iron source until your baby is about 18 months old, to get her through the high-risk period of iron deficiency anemia.

Iron in the Diet. People argue about food sources of iron in the baby's diet, and use a variety of foods that they think will give iron. Iron-fortified baby cereal is the only adequate food source of iron for the young infant. However, so you don't just have to take my word

Figure 7-5. Iron Content of Selected Infant Foods

Food	mg. Iron/3 ounces Food
Milk and Formula	
Human milk-cow milk formula unfortified with iron	.05
Iron—fortified formula	1.3
Cereals	
Iron fortified (dry) mixed with milk	7
Bottled pre-prepared cereal—fruit	5
Malto-meal, Cream of Wheat, cooked	2–3
Strained and Junior Foods	
Meats, poultry	1–2
Liver	4–6
Egg yolks	3
High meat dinner	less than 1
Vegetables, fruits	
Vegetables	less than 0.5
Fruits	less than 0.5
Standard Meat Cuts	
Beef, pork, lamb	2–3
Poultry	1.5
Beef liver, chicken liver	8.5
Calf liver	14.2
Pork liver	24.7

Source: U.S.D.A. Home and Garden Bulletin #72

for it, the amounts of iron in common infant foods are shown in Figure 7-5.

Iron in dry-packed infant cereals is in the form of very fine iron particles, and the iron in the bottled, pre-prepared cereals is in the form of ferrous sulfate. They have five and seven milligrams of iron per three-ounce serving, respectively. About 10% of each of these forms of iron is absorbed, which is a satisfactory amount.[4] In contrast, "adult" cereals that recommend themselves as good sources of iron for babies, Maltomeal and Cream of Wheat, have only two or three milligrams of iron per three-ounce serving. Furthermore, it is in the form of iron phosphate, which is only about 1% absorbed. In reality, that iron is there more for the label than for nutrition.

Meat and liver are good sources of iron. Even though the concentration of meat iron is relatively low, it is about 20% absorbed.[4] What is more, meat mixed with a meal helps absorption of all iron from that meal. However, there is the factor of calorie distribution: that amount of meat would contribute too much protein and make the overall diet too high in protein. Liver is very high in iron, but a daily serving of liver would provide too much vitamin A.*

Egg yolks traditionally have been added to babies' diets as a source of iron. However, we now discover that the iron in egg yolk is very poorly absorbed unless you take a good source of vitamin C at the same time. Without the vitamin C, egg yolk mixed with a meal that has other sources of iron will actually decrease the absorption of other food iron. In addition, egg yolks are too high in calories and too high in fat.**

---

*Not too long ago, there was a report in the *Journal of Pediatrics* about twin seven-month-olds who got vitamin A intoxication from eating chicken liver every day for three months.[10]

**Unless his diet is very low in fat. If a parent is determined to feed skim milk I may try to get her to feed egg yolks as a fat source. However, in general it is better to wait with egg yolk until the child is ready to eat the whole egg. Because egg white is a common allergen, we delay that until age nine months.

The Milk for Mixing Cereal. I have said, repeatedly, that the cereal should be mixed with milk or formula. Cereal mixed with water will provide carbohydrate only. The same is true, in spades, if you follow the recommendation of the Gerber company and mix your baby food with (Gerber) apple juice. The juice gives even more carbohydrate and no protein or fat.

Finding a milk for mixing the cereal is no problem for the formula-fed baby: just use whatever you are putting in his bottle. However, it is a little more complicated for the breastfed baby. For him, you can mix the cereal with hand-expressed breast milk, with pasteurized whole milk, with formula (either regular or hypoallergenic), or with diluted evaporated milk.

For some women, who are good enough at hand-expressing and have enough breastmilk, the first alternative works well. From the standpoint of preventing food reactions, that is certainly a good choice, particularly for the child with a strong family history of allergies. If allergies are less of a concern, one of the cow-milk-based approaches might work as well.

If you use formula, you will have to keep in mind that you will be using only a few ounces a day for diluting cereal so you will need to open, or prepare only a small amount at a time. (You could buy the powdered formula or the small individual-serving size of the liquid formula.) Use any liquid formula within one or two days. Pasteurized whole milk is probably not such a bad choice if you keep the quantities to below eight ounces a day (poor digestibility of pasteurized milk is not as much of a problem if it is well-diluted with other foods), and as long as you are not starting too early with cereal feeding. (Some infants under age six months lose small amounts of blood in their intestine when they take pasteurized milk.)

In general, I think the best choice is evaporated milk, diluted one-to-one with water. It is heat-treated, so it is very digestible and won't cause intestinal bleeding. You can buy it in five-ounce cans, so once you dilute it you only have ten ounces.

Alternatives to Infant Cereals. For a while, people were hesitating to use infant cereals because they contained salt, modified food starch, and a whole list of stabilisers and emulsifiers that combined to produce a rather ominous-looking label. Now, however, as with many commercial baby foods, the formulation has been changed. Baby cereals contain primarily the cereal flour, an emulsifier (soy lecithin), and a source of calcium. The salt has been taken out, as have the other emulsifiers and stabilisers.

If, however, "baby foods" are objectionable to you on general principles, there is an alternative. Use Malt-O-Meal or Cream of Wheat or, better yet, Cream of Rice that you have made with formula or whole milk (the cooking will boil it). Then provide the iron either with iron drops or iron-fortified formula.

Fruits and Vegetables. Somewhere in the range of six to eight months, once you get your baby well-established on iron-fortified baby cereal, you should start to work on adding fruits and vegetables to her diet. Your nutritional goal in adding fruits and vegetables is to get your baby accustomed to taking good sources of vitamins A and C in preparation for the time when her formula or breastmilk consumption drops too low to provide them in adequate amounts. Fruits and vegetables also give other vitamins and minerals, which may or may not be needed by this time. Diversifying the diet increases our chances of giving the baby everything she needs.

Your developmental goal is to introduce her to lumpier foods and foods of a different texture and flavor and to work her up, when she is ready, to finger-feeding herself chunks of soft and cooked fruits and vegetables.

Fruits and vegetables are primarily sources of carbohydrates, and are relatively low in caloric density (calories per ounce). They make good next additions to the diet after infant cereal, which is relatively high in caloric density, high in protein and low in carbohydrate.

Don't overdo it with fruits and vegetables, however, or you could dilute out the caloric density of the diet or distort the relative protein, fat and carbohydrate distribution. Three ounces of juice a day, or one or two two-tablespoon servings of fruit or vegetable is enough. Overfeeding with juice is an extremely common error. I often see mothers in the waiting room giving their babies eight-ounce bottles of juice. They shouldn't do it! Babies don't need the juice—it spoils their appetite, and sipping along on juice from a bottle can also spoil their teeth. Children who eat poorly often are filling up by drinking juice between meals. DON'T OVERDO THE JUICE. Three ounces per day is enough.

Caloric Density. Since we'll be making further references to caloric density as we go along, the chart below will be helpful to you in getting an idea of how the calories in fruits and vegetables compare with those in other common infant foods.

Figure 7-6. Caloric Density of Standard Infant Foods

Category	Calories per Three Ounces
Formulas and breast milk	60
Infant cereal made with whole milk or formula (1:6)	110
Baby cereals in jars	55–70
Infant cereal made with water (1:6)	50
Infant cereal made with juice (1:6)	85
Fruits and juices	40–80
Vegetables; plain, buttered, creamed	25–70
Meats	90–135
High-meat dinners	75–105
Egg yolks	195
Infant desserts	60–95

Source: Gerber Products Company, U.S.D.A. Home and Garden Bulletin #72.

Egg yolks have roughly eight times the calories of plain vegetables. Theoretically, a baby should be able to accommodate by simply eating less egg yolks and/or more vegetables. However, life is not theoretical, and you will want to know what you are doing with calorie concentrations in case your baby has special needs.

If your baby is a slow gainer, you want to go easy on the vegetables. If his rate of gain seems a little rapid, you would want to avoid egg yolks. (Actually, you should avoid them anyway, for reasons I will get to later.) Fruits and vegetables are quite interchangeable nutritionally and developmentally, so if you have a baby who refuses to take one or the other, you can be flexible. Furthermore, the order in which you introduce them really doesn't matter. People make up elaborate arguments for starting with one or the other, but don't worry about it.

Give Fruits and Juices in Moderation. To get a nutritionally-adequate serving, ⅓ cup of vitamin C-rich fruit or juice will do the trick very nicely. One or two tablespoons of other fruits is a nutritionally adequate serving, although children are generally willing to eat more than that because they like them so much. However, I would put an upper limit on fruit and fruit juice of about ¼ cup per serving (except for the C-rich fruit or juice) for the child under age one, because overdoing it can cause stomach ache or diarrhea. If he wants more juice than that, dilute it with water to make the small amount go farther.

Sources of Vitamin A. Infants and children ages six months to three years need about 2000 International Units (400 Retinol Equivalents) of vitamin A per day. A quart of formula or breastmilk contributes about 2000 to 2600 IU vitamin A, a quart of cow's milk about 1000 IU. The greatest need for non-milk sources of vitamin A will come after we make the transition to cow's milk, and milk consumption drops to two to three cups per day. Then your child will be getting only about 500 to 750 IU of vitamin A in milk, and we'll have to depend on vegetables and fruits to provide the other 1250 to 1500 IU.

Vitamin A is found in varying concentrations in a variety of fruits and vegetables.

Figure 7-7. Vitamin A in Fruits and Vegetables

Excellent Sources (More than 3500 IU per 3 ounces)	Good Sources (1000–3000 IU per 3 ounces)	Fair Sources (Less than 1000 IU per 3 ounces)
Apricots, dried	Apricot nectar	Apricots
Cantaloupe	Asparagus	Brussel sprouts
Carrots	Broccoli	Peaches
Mixed vegetables	Nectarine	Peach nectar
Mango	Purple plums	Prunes
Pumpkin		Prune juice
Spinach, other greens		Tomatoes
Squash		Tomato juice
Sweet potatoes		Watermelon

Source: U.S.D.A. Home and Garden Bulletin #72

The excellent sources would need to be given only every other day. (That works because vitamin A is a fat-soluble vitamin and is stored in the body.) To get enough vitamin A from the "good" sources you will have to use them every day. The "fair" sources have enough vitamin A to contribute significantly to the diet, but shouldn't be depended on as the sole sources.

If you give too many dark green and deep yellow vegetables, like broccoli, sweet potatoes, carrots and squash, your baby might turn yellow. This is a condition called carotenemia, caused by accumulation of the yellow coloring that the body converts to vitamin A. Carotenemia doesn't hurt him and it goes away if you take him off so much carotene. But there is really no reason why you should let your beautiful baby turn all yellow, so try not to give high-carotene vegetables and fruits more than every other day.

Limit potentially high-nitrate vegetables, like beets, carrots and spinach, to one or two tablespoons per feeding. Because of low stomach acidity, the young infant may convert nitrate to nitrite, which can displace oxygen in hemoglobin. The rapid breathing, lethargy and shortage of oxygen that results is called methemo-globinemia (and can actually be fatal if the dose of nitrate is very large). A while back there was a report of twin boys who were fed bottles of homemade carrot juice made from a batch of carrots that happened to be very high in nitrate. One of the babies refused the bottle, but the other took a large serving of high-nitrate carrots and became very ill from methemoglobinemia.

By age six months stomach acidity increases and nitrate over-load is less of a problem, but I still wouldn't take chances with carrot juice.

Sources of Vitamin C. In contrast to vitamin A, vitamin C is a water-soluble vitamin that is not stored well in the body. You need to provide either one "excellent" or two "good" vitamin C sources every day. The infant up to one year needs about 35 mg of vitamin C per day, and from one to three years about 45 mg.

Many, if not most fruits and vegetables supply small amounts of vitamin C—on the order of five or ten milligrams per serving. We will call these the "fair" sources and it is reassuring to know they are there as a back stop if you miss with your primary sources; but do not depend on their vitamin C contribution to the diet.

Some very tasty fruits and vegetables did not appear on our vitamin A and C lists, for example, peas, beets, bananas and apples. As I said, these and other fruits and vegetables generally have vita-mins A and C but in quantities too low to be considered "good" or "fair" sources. In addition, like the foods listed, they contribute other nutrients to the diet. For example, bananas have folic acid, and fruits

247

Figure 7-8. Vitamin C in Fruits and Vegetables

Excellent Sources (More than 35 mg per three ounces, one serving daily)	Good Sources (20 to 30 mg per three ounces, two servings daily)
Broccoli	Asparagus
Brussels sprouts	Bean sprouts, raw
Cabbage	Chard
Cauliflower	Honeydew melon
Cantaloupe	Potato
Grapefruit; grapefruit juice	Tangerine
Kohlrabi	Tomatoes, tomato juice
Mango	Pureed baby fruits
Oranges, orange juice	
Papaya	
Peppers	
Spinach	
Strawberries	
Vitamin-C fortified infant juices	

Source: U.S.D.A. Home and Garden Bulletin #72

and vegetables in general are good sources of potassium. Most will give some trace elements like zinc and copper. All have some plant fiber. They contribute to the diet, and, once the requirements for vitamins A and C are satisfied, make worthwhile choices to fill out the two or three servings a day your child will be working up to.

Don't get panicky if your child doesn't consume optimum amounts of vitamin C and A-rich foods. The recommended nutrient intake allows him to provide for his daily need as well as to store some nutrient in his body. If he doesn't drink his orange juice today, he can fall back on the vitamin C he stored yesterday.

Digesting and Ingesting Fruits and Vegetables. Don't get excited when pieces of fruits and vegetables and the stains from beets and other foods start to come through in your baby's diaper. Unless someone chews very thoroughly, those are the waste products of normal digestion. Stools of older children and adults look the same way; we just don't pay so much attention to them.

Once you get to the point of introducing fruits and vegetables, your baby is probably going to be able to digest any reasonably-bland food that he can gum well. In fact, chewing and swallowing probably represent the major limitation in his digestive system. Again, your developmental goal in introducing fruits and vegetables is to introduce him to different textures and flavors, and to get him used to the idea of handling the pieces of food you get when you mash or dice cooked fruits and vegetables or offer a chunk of banana or apple. You can use the bottled baby foods if you want, but they are really too thin and smooth to provide much developmental stimulus.

Selection of Fruits and Vegetables. Depending on your baby's oral ability and hand coordination, you may need to fork-mash fruits and vegetables such as carrots or bananas, and feed them to her. Or you may simply give her a chunk of banana to bite off and gum. If she has developed a pincer grasp, she may delight in picking up whole peas and gumming them. Any tender, cooked vegetable is appropriate at this age. Fruits canned in juice, water, or light syrup and then drained and mashed, chopped or chunked are fine. Many fresh fruits, such as peaches, pears, and plums (all with skins removed) are also good choices. You can mash, dice or chunk, depending on your child's ability. Many babies are good at sucking on an orange or grapefruit section and, surprisingly, really seem to love the sour taste. Some can gum a peeled apple wedge or a carrot, while others haven't gotten the hang of it and bite off too-big pieces.

If your baby can't handle apples, make scrapings: using a carrot peeler, remove and discard the peeling; then keep right on peeling until you have a little pile of scrapings. Cut them up, as some of the strips may be long, and let your child eat them with her fingers. Or feed them by spoon.

Try to give your baby the vegetable you are having at the family dinner table. Prepare frozen or fresh vegetables without added salt and give part to the baby. She can handle diced or mashed peas, cooked cauliflower, broccoli flowerettes, corn, mixed vegetables, etc. It's better to stay away from canned vegetables, as they really are quite high in salt.

If your baby is having trouble with pieces of food, you might consider buying a little hand baby-food grinder. You can take this right to the table and quickly reduce the family fare to a thick pulp that your baby will find delectable.

Baby Foods. Once we get into the fruits and vegetables stage we have to resolve the question of whether or not to use baby food. Actually it is probably already resolved: by starting solids late and progressing rapidly to table food, you really side-step the whole issue of baby food, and whether to make it or buy it, because the baby doesn't need it.

Making Your Own Baby Food. Generally, when people inquire about making their own baby food, they are thinking about pureeing and freezing. Whole books deal with recipes for baby, the art of blending, and freezing the puree in ice cube trays to provide "convenient" blocks of foods that can be simply thawed and fed.

Frankly, I view that as a lot of unnecessary work, a potential source of contamination, and as accomplishing very little. The infant who still needs the pureeing doesn't need the fruits and vegetables. And the infant who is ready for the fruits and vegetables doesn't need the pureeing.

The sooner you get your baby to the point where you perceive him as a participant in the family eating style, the better it is for all of you. He needs and wants to be able to imitate your eating habits;

you won't be able for long to get away with feeding your baby one way and yourself another.

Bottled Baby Foods. As I said, if your baby is old enough to take fruits and vegetables, he won't get much developmental benefit from bottled baby foods. Using the somewhat-lumpier "junior foods" helps a little, but they are still pretty thin and smooth compared to table food.

Nevertheless, there are a few times I see a need for bottled baby food. For parents who insist on starting early, the child under six months taking fruits and vegetables may need a silky-smooth texture to avoid choking. He also may need protection against botulinum spores.* Occasionally we see a developmentally delayed child who, due to a problem with muscle control, needs to be worked up through pureed food and introduced very gradually to thicker, lumpier food. Also, baby foods come in handy when you are traveling and having a hard time getting access to other appropriate foods. And then there is the occasional meal, like salad, that just doesn't work for the baby.

And of course there is the problem of the meals in the child-care setting when you are working. At times, especially in the early solid foods stage, you may find it easier to send a jar of baby food. Then, as you introduce appropriate foods at home, like hard-cooked eggs, crackers, and sandwiches, you can pack a lunch more like one you would use for an older child. (I think you should be the one to introduce new foods, not the sitter. You are the parent and you are entitled to share your child's new experiences—first.)

Bottled baby foods are safe and nutritious. They are sanitary, carefully handled to preserve nutritional quality, and they are low in

---

*Any fresh or frozen fruit or vegetable—indeed, anything that has come in contact with the ground—is potentially contaminated with botulinum spores. These can only be destroyed by pressure canning. Since "adult" canned vegetables are too high in salt, baby foods are the other alternative.

salt and sugar. The manufacturers claim that they are equal to or lower in cost than the ones you prepare yourself by pureeing. Plus, you get all those nice little jars. If you use bottled baby foods, make sure the jars are sealed. The dome on the cover should be pulled down by the vacuum inside the jar and you should hear a pop when you open it. (Incredible as it seems, shoppers will open jars, smell or taste, and then close them and put them back on the shelves.)

The Meal Pattern. As you work with adding fruits and vegetables to your baby's diet, you will be working toward a two-meal-a-day pattern. It's a good idea to continue giving cereal morning and night, or any two times when it seems like a meal-type feeding fits in well. Then, as you introduce fruit and vegetables you can, perhaps, give fruit or fruit juice with one cereal feeding and a vegetable with another.

Finger Breads and Cereals. Sometime during the fruit and vegetable stage and as you go into the table food stage you are going to find yourself giving your baby crackers, pieces of bread, and dry cereals to pick up and eat. In doing that you will be responding to his developmental needs, as he'll be right at the stage of practicing his pincer grasp, putting everything in his mouth and trying out his chewing skills. Those foods are also appropriate nutritionally. They provide B vitamins and iron and, if you are using whole grains, they also give some trace elements and fiber.

You have to keep in mind, however, that along with bread or crackers you may also be introducing wheat, which is one of the more common allergens. (Incidence of allergic reactions to all foods ranges from 0.3 to 10%.) If your baby is at least seven months old, wheat introduction is probably OK. However, if you, yourself, are particularly sensitive to wheat, your baby has an increased chance of having a wheat sensitivity and you may want to wait longer. To avoid wheat you can choose things like rice crackers, corn and rice chex, corn flakes and the like. Read the label and avoid anything that has wheat flour, wheat starch or wheat gluten in it. Generally, if a label just says "flour," it means *wheat* flour.

Probably by nine months it is as safe as it is going to be to begin experimenting with wheat in small quantities. Do keep a sharp eye, however, for such reactions as a skin rash, wheezing, stomach aches or diarrhea. If your child seems to react, take her off the wheat for a couple of weeks and then try again. It is easy to think she has an allergy when she really doesn't, because such symptoms are so common. You certainly don't want to burden yourself with avoiding wheat if you don't have to.

Making the Transition to Table Food. Somewhere between seven and ten months of age you will probably find your baby sitting in the high chair, showing good hand-mouth coordination, developing a pretty dextrous palmar grasp or perhaps even a pincer grasp, and beginning to show "adult" chewing patterns: side to side movements with her tongue and mashing her food with her jaws. You may have her entertaining herself with dry cereal and crackers while you eat your meal.

It is time that she joins you for dinner. She can by that time progress very nicely from semi-solid mashed or pureed food to pieces of soft food that she can feed and chew herself.

It's nice when the ability and the impulse to self-feed come along at the same time. Sometimes, however, the mind is willing, yea eager to self-feed, but the body won't cooperate yet. That is when your baby starts to refuse spoon feeding but can't quite manage to pick up or chew finger food. He gets frustrated at his failed attempts, his mother or father gets frustrated at having the spoon refused, and mealtime deteriorates. Take heart, this is only temporary. The skills will come and the situation will resolve itself. The most important thing is to avoid forceful spoon-feeding and to minimize the frustration for all of you.

If the grasp is still palmar, try giving your baby one spoon and feeding with a second spoon. Or use sticky foods (see below) and load the spoon for him to self-feed. Consider giving strips of toast, peeled apple wedges, long crackers, etc. for a short time until the pincer grasp appears. This may produce a limited diet, but it's only for a short time. Nutritionally, you must still be depending heavily on breastmilk or formula while you make this transition.

If the grasp is there but he is still gagging on pieces of food, go to thick mashed or milled foods. (Don't resort to baby foods unless there is a real chewing-swallowing problem; they will only slow his development.) Mix baby cereal thick, and break the mass apart so he can pick it up. Mash or mill fruits and vegetables and thicken with some baby cereal. Or put some potato and another vegetable through the baby food grinder and moisten it just enough to make a thick, gluey mass that can be picked up. This is wonderfully messy and dries to the high chair very much like cement.

What about messing and playing with the food? At first you will probably see quite a lot of this. The Arabs have a saying, "you taste with your fingers." I wonder if our sterile eating arrangements are depriving us of some eating satisfaction! In any event, the infant has a real need to feel, see and smell the food before deciding to eat it. In fact, the concept of eating that strange-looking stuff is one that is learned gradually. It's wonderful to watch the expression of amazed delight on a child's face when something tasty finally does make it into his mouth.

So at first you will see more messing and exploration than eating, but usually this stage passes quickly. The transition to table food is often abrupt and enthusiastic, particularly if the child is at the table with other family members and allowed to eat the same foods.

Meat. When your baby goes on table food (somewhere between seven and ten months), you should start adding meat to her diet. It hasn't really been necessary before then, because she has been experimenting texturally with cereal, fruit and vegetable, getting iron from cereal, and getting plenty of protein from formula or breastmilk. However, once she starts eating from the table, and works up to three meals a day, her quantity of solid foods will increase and her breastmilk or formula consumption will begin to drop. In fact it is a good idea to encourage the drop by skipping the milk feeding before the meal—or if your baby won't stand for that, giving only part of it. In other words, it is time to encourage her to replace breastmilk or formula with solid foods. At this point she will need other, non-milk sources of protein, such as meat, poultry or fish, or concentrated vegetable sources such as cooked dried beans and peanut butter.*

Introducing meat is a bit of a problem as, in some ways, your baby isn't really ready to handle it developmentally. She doesn't have the right teeth. But you can't wait until she is 18 to 24 months old to get her molars, so you will have to modify the texture of the meat to fit her capacities. Of course hamburger, in a patty or meatloaf or casserole is no problem. Neither are fish and tender poultry. The steaks and chops and roasts, however, call for some special handling.

If you have a baby food grinder, here is one place it may come in handy. You will have to cut the meat up rather finely, and moisten it a bit to get it through the grinder, but with some persistence, it will go. It also helps to mix the chunks of meat in with the mashed potatoes, and to keep stirring the mixture as you work it through the grinder. Or you can simply cut up the meat, if you cut it very fine. Using a sharp knife, cut the meat, across the grain, into about ⅛-inch fibers. Moisten it and let your baby pick it up with her fingers, or mix it in with other foods.

Your baby might take her meat and other foods better if you make her a little mixed dinner.

Treasure the recipe—it is the only baby-food recipe you will get from me. It is intended to be something you can mix up from

---

*See the discussion in the *Toddler* chapter on non-meat protein.

whatever you happen to be making for dinner. It is not intended to be multiplied and made in great vats and frozen. If you want to do that, you will have to find instructions in another book.

Recipe for Mixed Dinner

2 tablespoons chopped or ground meat, poultry, fish or grated cheese—or ½ egg
¼ cup cooked rice, noodles, macaroni, or potatoes
2 tablespoons vegetable: pieces, chopped or mashed
Liquid to moisten: broth, milk, low-fat gravy.

This works as a finger food—if you use our broader definition of a finger food as anything that sticks together long enough to get it from plate to mouth. (Or high chair tray, for that matter; most plates end up on the floor.)

If your baby has developed a palmar grasp, self-feeding will involve pushing the heel of his hand against the food and closing his fingers over it, scraping it into his palm. To eat it, he will scrape the palm of his hand against his lip. (That is, he will eat it after he enjoys squishing it a few times in his hand, letting the wonderful goo ooze out between his fingers.) It isn't pretty, but it works, and he will think he is just the smartest person ever.

Once he gets that pincer grasp going and gets interested enough in eating so he no longer experiments as much with his food, his eating will be prettier. Eventually he will even want to use a spoon, but you will probably have to wait a few months for that.

You may be surprised at the small amount of meat I recommend in the mixed dinner. It is equivalent to a ½-ounce serving, and it is really enough for a baby. If she has two ½-ounce servings of meat per day, and continues to take at least 16 ounces of formula or milk per day, that will give her enough protein. The older infant and toddler require roughly 21 grams of protein per day. An ounce of meat and a cup of formula or milk each provides seven or eight grams protein.

The following list gives protein values of common foods:

Figure 7-9. Quantity of food that gives seven to eight grams of protein

Food	Amount
Milk or formula: cow, soy	8 ounces
Egg	1
Soybeans, cooked	⅓ cup
Cooked dried beans	½ cup
Cottage cheese	¼ cup
Peanut butter	2 Tablespoons
Other nut butters	3 Tablespoons
Cheese: cheddar, American, etc.	1 ounce

Source: U.S.D.A. Home and Garden Bulletin #72.

The Three-meal-a-day Pattern. If it seems to you that we just talked about the meal pattern, you're right, we did. But once your baby starts eating from the table, it's time to change it again. She will begin to take a main meal, eating the same foods at the same time as the rest of the family. She should continue to get her ½ cup of baby cereal a day (measured after it is mixed), taking it in one or two meals or snacks. So, breakfast isn't hard to plan, and dinner isn't hard to plan, but what about lunch? That's the meal that many families find difficult.

My favorite and easiest lunch suggestion, is leftovers. Cook a bit extra the night before, put aside enough for the next day, refrigerate it promptly, and reheat it for your baby's (and your) lunch.

257

Also, by this time eggs are another possibility. Once your baby gets to seven to nine months old, he will be past the high-risk period for egg allergy and ready to eat a scrambled or soft-cooked egg. Don't forget to give him some bread or other starch with it: combine that with a fruit or vegetable and you have a nice meal. People worry about the cholesterol in eggs. Unless you have a family history of major heart disease, 3 or 4 eggs weekly should be all right for him.

Also, though it may surprise you, your baby is now ready for a peanut butter sandwich or some peanut butter on toast. You should wait a while to use lunch meats or hot dogs, and then use them only sparingly. The baby-food meat sticks are a low-salt, low-nitrate, convenient (if expensive) meat source for lunches. They give about 10 grams of protein per jar.

I will go into meal planning in more detail, and offer more food suggestions, in the *Toddler* chapter.

Keep in mind at this stage that you are helping your child make the transition from the demand feeding pattern of infancy to the meals-plus-snacks routine of the toddler. In order to allow him to fit into the family meal pattern, you may have to make some adjustments. You may find yourself eating a light breakfast and then having lunch at 11:00, so the two of you can eat together. Or you may rely on snacks as a way of tiding him over between meals. If you have a very long afternoon and late dinner, you may want to give two snacks.

At first, the snacks will be breastfeedings or bottle feedings. As your baby approaches a year, however, it is probably better to make those snacks the same that you would feed to an older child: crackers and cheese, fruit or peanut butter, apples, etc. See Figure 8-7 in the *Toddler* chapter for a list of some nutritious snacks.

Overall, you are going to have the best luck selecting food for your child at this age if you stop thinking of him as a baby and start thinking of him as a toddler. (How's that for a heart-rending state-

258

ment?) You might not be ready for him to be that grown-up: but <u>he is</u> ready, and you had better let him go. You can baby him in some other way.

The Weanling Milk. For the child who is well established on table food, including meat, there is only one transition left to make: the shift from the milk feeding of infancy to some other kind of milk. He no longer needs the extra vitamins and minerals provided by an infant milk feeding, nor does he need so much help with digestion and maintaining homeostasis.

A child is well-established on table food when he is sitting up, three times a day with the rest of the family, primarily self-feeding with his hands, and drinking, with assistance, from the cup. He should be taking at least three ounces of solid foods at each meal, with a good selection from the basic-four food plan, and his formula or breastmilk consumption should have dropped off, most noticeably through elimination of some of the nursing sessions.

Once his formula consumption drops below 32 ounces, or he has eliminated two or three of his daily breastfeedings, you may quite safely go to whole evaporated milk that has been diluted one-to-one with water. If you are switching to whole pasteurized milk, wait until the formula amount drops to between 16 and 24 ounces. Then use whole milk.

After you reach the table-food stage, you have several alternatives open to you in choosing the milk feeding for the rest of the first years.

Breastfed Infant. I think even a breastfed baby who is 10 to 12 months old should be drinking his mealtime milk from a cup. If the breast is too-freely offered at mealtime the baby won't be as hungry or as interested in table foods. That is not to say, however, that the breastfed baby that age should be completely weaned from the breast. Breastfeeding is still good for snacks and for late-night and early morning feedings.

The milk used for cup drinking can be one of the following:

Commercial Formula. The baby formula manufacturers very-energetically encourage keeping infants on formula for the whole first year. Since the product representatives from the companies are consistent and energetic teachers of physicians, this recommendation has been pretty widely accepted by health professionals and passed on to parents. However, unless there is a specific reason for staying on formula for that long I really don't think there is any need for it. By the time they are set on table foods, most babies no longer need the nutritional help that is provided by commercial formulas. Formula can cover for a variety of nutritional errors, but its use can also cut down on your motivation to teach your child to eat a variety of nutritious foods.

However, a baby who is very small or grows unusually slowly, or who has a lot of digestive upsets, should be left on his formula.

Pasteurized Whole Milk. Pasteurized milk is an acceptable choice at this point. Digestion of pasteurized milk is less of a problem for an older child, not because his stomach is older, but because he is getting a mixed diet. Dilution of milk in his stomach with other foods makes it set up a softer, more-digestible curd.

We are counting on milk to provide fat, so babies should be kept on *whole* milk until they are about two years old. Young children don't get that much other fat: they eat very little meat, they love low-fat foods like breads, cereals, and fruits, and even if their vegetables are buttered, they don't eat that many of them.

Remember that to form our well-balanced diet, we are counting on milk to provide vitamins A and D, as well as calcium and protein. Most milk that is currently on the market, even powdered milk, will give you those nutrients. Do read the label, however, because there are a few milks that are not fortified with vitamins A and D, and there are some imitation milks and milk substitutes that are simply not equivalent to milk, nutritionally.

If you use fresh milk, it must be pasteurized. There is a small risk of unpasteurized milk carrying brucellosis or tuberculosis, although dairy herds are now carefully checked for these diseases. A more-likely risk is that the milk will contain germs from undetected mastitis, or that the milk is contaminated from the barn or from the handling. There are no nutritional advantages to using raw milk.

Evaporated Milk. Particularly if your baby is still taking over 24 ounces of milk a day, you should consider using whole evaporated milk, diluted one-to-one with water, as a weanling milk. It is heat-treated, contains vitamins A and D, and is priced about the same as whole pasteurized milk. Since many families buy only 2% or skim milk for adults and older children, they will have to get a special milk for the baby anyway, and it could just as well have evaporated milk's advantage of heat treatment.

Fluoride. You can discontinue the fluoride supplement after your child is eating foods from the table and drinking water and juice, provided your water supply is fluoridated at least to the level of 0.3 p.p.m. If the water contains less than 0.3 p.p.m. fluoride, continue with the 0.25 mg supplement. Foods cooked with fluoridated water provide significant amounts of fluoride, as do juices that are mixed using fluoridated water. You should also remember to teach and encourage your child to think of water for thirst.

You should probably avoid fluoridated toothpaste for the child under age three years. Since small children generally swallow, rather than spit out toothpaste, they could ingest enough to cause fluorosis of the tooth enamel.

Fat, Sugars and Salt. I will have more to say about all of these in other chapters. For now, we'll talk about them only as they relate to the infant under a year of age.

Fat. Fat in the diet of the young infant comes mostly from milk and formula. Concern about heart disease, however, introduces a controversy about the kind of fat and amount of cholesterol in children's diets.

Breastmilk and cow's milk contain saturated fat and cholesterol. Consuming both tends to increase blood cholesterol, which may, in turn, have something to do with increasing risk of heart disease. (This is one of the points the experts debate when they argue about whether or not diet can contribute to heart disease.) Commercial formulas contain no cholesterol, have polyunsaturated fats, and tend to lower blood cholesterol.

Studies have shown that infants who are breastfed, or who get butterfat in their formulas, have higher blood cholesterols than those who are fed commercial formulas. However, infants weaned from formula or breast milk to diets that are pretty much the same have similar cholesterol concentrations at ages three and four.[13] The Committee on Nutrition, based on this evidence, has said that in view of the good growth and performance of children on current feeding regimens, there is little basis for recommending changes in fat selection before age one year, even in children who are at risk of developing heart disease.[2]

Some argue that formulas should contain cholesterol. They speculate (without clear research evidence) that babies need dietary cholesterol to properly form the fatty sheath around their nerves. Others maintain that a person's later ability to get rid of excessive cholesterol in his body can be dependent on the exposure he received to cholesterol in his early diet. The evidence of similar cholesterol levels in the 3–4 year-old preschoolers would dispute this theory.

The heart disease question aside, as your infant makes his transition to table food you will probably wonder whether you should be buttering his bread or adding fat to his vegetables. I would go by his preference. If he seems to prefer a little extra fat, then add it. He doesn't really need the fat, as long as he continues to take whole milk. If he drinks 2% or skim milk, you should see to it that he gets

Solid Foods

one teaspoon of fat (for 2%), or two teaspoons (for skim), for each eight ounces of milk that he consumes.

If your baby isn't growing or gaining as well as he should and you do add extra fat, use polyunsaturated margarine or vegetable oil rather than butter. Babies digest and absorb vegetable oils better than animal fat.

Sugar. Sugar is easy enough to avoid while your child is small, and adds nothing except calories to the diet. As long as your baby doesn't know what he is missing, you might as well keep him away from added sugar. Sooner or later someone will come along to introduce him to sweets and he will probably develop a taste for them, just like the rest of us. Until then, hold off.

There is no reason for you to sweeten his food. He may start eating his cereal sooner if it is sweetened, but it is better that he gets a chance to experience and enjoy the good taste of grain, even if it takes him longer to get going on it. (I think adding sugar to food is different from adding fat. Fat enhances food flavor; sugar disguises it.) He may like desserts and seem to go for those unnecessary little baby desserts; but he doesn't need the variety, and he will be forfeiting the pleasure of learning about other foods.

Honey. Particularly avoid honey in any form for the first year. This includes honey that has been baked into a cookie or bread, or honey for dipping a pacifier. Honey at times is contaminated with the spores of clostridium botulinum. If allowed to grow in an airtight place, these spores produce clostridium toxin, which can cause severe illness and even death. Generally this is a problem only in improperly-canned, non-acid foods, like green beans. But it can happen in the young infant's intestine, which is also an air-tight place. The spores grow, produce the toxin, and poison the infant.

The bacteria and chemicals in the intestines of older people change in some way to prevent the spores from growing. Clostridium poisoning from spores is generally found only in babies under age six

263

months, but to be on the safe side we say that honey should first be given only after age one year.

It is no great loss. The practical fact is that honey is not more nutritious than sugar. The same goes for raw sugar, and other forms of sugars that are touted as nutritious alternatives to table sugar. The amount of worthwhile nutrients in these foods is so small that if you were to consume enough to give you any significant amount of a nutrient it would give you too much sugar.

Salt. Salt should be held to a low level in the baby's diet. He won't miss it. Salt added to baby foods is there more for the feeder than for the fed: babies accept unsalted baby food just as well as salted. Breastmilk, formula and unsalted foods in their natural state have enough sodium in them to satisfy essential nutrient requirements.

It is generally agreed that there is an advantage for many people in keeping the dietary sodium low, particularly those specifically at risk for heart disease. (Life-long low sodium intakes are correlated with lower blood pressures.) However, at the same time you have to remember that sodium is an essential nutrient, and should not be eliminated completely from the diet. In fact, in some cases your doctor may even feel it is necessary to supplement with salt if, for example, your baby is feverish and perspiring a great deal or is losing sodium for some other reason. But let your doctor decide—don't do it yourself.

Baby foods no longer have added sodium. Home-prepared foods of course have varying amounts of salt, depending on the preference of the cook. Canned foods (except for fruits), pre-prepared, "convenience" soups and dinners, snack chips and crackers, lunch meats and cured meats are all generally high in sodium. To keep down on levels of sodium for your baby, avoid high-salt foods, take out the baby's portion before you salt for the family, or cook salt-free and let everyone salt to taste.

The Overview

Having worked our way through each of the additions, it is time to take an overall look at the balance of your baby's diet. Maintaining a proper diet is considerably more complicated now than when she was on just breastmilk or formula, because you have the challenge of keeping a reasonable proportion between the several food groups. I will be discussing this whole topic in more detail in the *Toddler* chapter, and I would encourage you to read that right now, even if you aren't ready to start thinking of your baby as a toddler. For the time being, I will confine my discussion to a few general observations about dietary balance.

At the end of the transition period, all of your baby's daily nutritional requirements will be provided by a mixed table food diet. The MINIMUM amount of food from each of the food groups she will need in order to have a nutritious diet are:

Milk	16–24 ounces
Fruits and vegetables	Four servings, each 1–2 Tbsp. vitamin C source: 3 ounces daily vitamin A source: 3 times weekly
Bread and cereals	Four servings daily, each about ¼ the adult serving size
Meats, poultry, fish, eggs	Two servings daily, each about ½ ounce

Your baby will vary on a day-to-day basis in the quantities she eats from each of these food groups. Generally that is no problem as long as, on a weekly average, she satisfies her minimum requirement from each of the groups. Babies will often eat disproportionately large amounts of breads and cereals, and that is fine, provided everything else is there in minimum amounts. However, if she is using a particular food group to the exclusion of the others, it can get to be a problem.

Babies will occasionally prefer to drink their meals, insisting on more and more milk and showing little interest in solid foods. If that is the case, you should impose an upper limit on the milk of three or even two cups a day, and try to get her to save some of her hunger for solid foods. The same goes for juices. If allowed to, many babies will drink so much juice that they spoil their appetite for other foods. Be sure you are regularly offering water—it may be that you just have an extra-thirsty baby.

Now you can heave a big sigh of relief. You have come through the constant changes of the transitional feeding period. From now on, your little one will be polishing his skills—getting better at drinking from the cup, chewing, finally even learning to use a spoon and fork. He'll be interested in his food and pretty accepting of a variety of foods. You can look forward to more of a regular routine as you include him in your family eating pattern. You even get a little breather before your beginning toddler starts to develop the more-limited appetite and contrariness of that age group. ENJOY!

Selected References

1. Beal, Virginia A. On the acceptance of solid foods and other food patterns of infants and children. Pediatrics 28:448–456. 1957.
2. Committee on Nutrition. Commentary on breast-feeding and infant formulas, including proposed standards for formulas. Pediatrics 57(2):278–285. 1976.
3. Committee on Nutrition. Fluoride supplementation: revised dosage schedule. Pediatrics 63:150. 1979.

4. Committee on Nutrition. Iron supplementation for infants. Pediatrics. 58:765–768. 1976.
5. Committee on Nutrition. On the feeding of supplemental foods to infants. Pediatrics 65(6):1178–1181. 1980.
6. Committee on Nutrition. On the feeding of solid foods to infants. Pediatrics 29:685–692. 1958.
7. Fomon, S. J., L. J. Filer, T. A. Anderson and E. E. Ziegler. Recommendations for feeding normal infants. Pediatrics 63:52–59. 1979.
8. Gerber Products Company. Current Practices in Infant Feeding. Freemont, Michigan. 1980.
9. Grunwaldt. Edgar, F. Bates and D. Guthrie. The onset of sleeping through the night. Pediatrics. 31:667–668. 1960.
10. Mahoney, C. P., M. T. Margolis, T. A. Knauss & R. F. Labbe. Chronic vitamin A intoxication in infants fed chicken liver. Pediatrics. 65:893–896. 1980.
11. Osaki, F. A., and S. A. Landaw. Inhibition of iron absorption from human milk by baby food. American Journal of Diseases of Children. 134:459–460. 1980.
12. Parmelee, A. H., W. H. Wenner and H. R. Schulz. Infant sleep patterns from birth to 16 weeks of age. Journal of Pediatrics. 65:839–848. 1964.
13. Pipes, Peggy L. Infant feeding and nutrition. IN Nutrition in Infancy and Childhood. C.V. Mosby Co., St. Louis. 1981.
14. Taitz, L. S. and H. D. Byers. High calorie/osmolar feeding and hypertonic dehydration. Archives of Disease of Childhood. 47:257–260. 1972.

8
Feeding
the
Toddler

It is your job as parent to avoid, whenever possible, making the inevitable battles of the toddler period battles over food. During the time from 18 months to three years, your child's rapid infant growth rate slows down, she becomes a "demon explorer," and she shows, at times, a fierce contrariness in her attempts to establish that she is a person separate from you. Her food intake decreases, and you will naturally become concerned. However, if you emphasize or enforce eating too much, you will arouse her need to exert her individuality and the battle will be on. Toddlers would rather exert their independence than eat. Successfully negotiating this tricky time demands a division of responsibility: you are responsible for what your child is presented to eat, she is responsible for what and how much she eats.

I could almost write the script for a toddler consult. When parents come to see me with a child 12 to 30 months old, they come with an all-too-familiar list of concerns and frustrations about feeding. They tell me that their child is not eating enough, especially of meat and vegetables and fruits. They complain that their child will only eat a few foods, and that he wants those foods again and again. They object to his dawdling with his food and they are concerned about milk consumption. Some worry that their child drinks too little milk; about an equal number worry that he drinks too much.

Developmental Changes

These typical food problems have everything to do with what is happening to and with the toddler socially, physically and behaviorally. To get a better feeling for that, let's first broaden our perspective and look at toddler developmental changes.

Psychological and Social Changes. The theme of this chapter is "managing toddler eating behavior." Actually, that is rather a silly theme, because NOBODY manages a toddler. There is a story about a powerful Norse god who was boasting that he could get anyone to do his bidding. A woman responded that she knew of someone whose will and strength were greater than his. She was referring to her two-year-old son. Foolish god, he didn't believe her and it was left to the son to prove the truth of her words. And, of course, he did.

That mother knew what you and I know: You can prevent a toddler from doing what you don't want him to do, but you can't force him to do what you want him to do. And you had better not try, or you'll simply have a profitless fight on your hands.

The toddler's task is to find out and prove to himself and to you that he is a separate person from you. He finds out that he is a separate person by saying "no" a lot, because whenever he resists what you want he proves to himself that he is separate from you. He has a tremendous need to be independent, to be successful, to explore, and to have limits. And he feels absolutely ambivalent about it all.

He needs to know that he is an individual, but he also needs to know that he can't dominate you. Unless you let him know clearly that the limits exist, he will become more and more provocative, until you finally move in and stop him. He also has an exuberant and unrestrained curiosity, and seems to need to make the same sort of impact on his environment that he does on you.

Dr. Spock called the child at this age a "demon explorer." He and Arnold Gesell described toddlers as demanding, assertive, mercurial, precooperative, contrary, obstinate, exasperating, imperious, balky, negativistic, bossy and over fussy. Hardly encouraging. But notice they said *precooperative*. That should give you hope.

Your role as a parent during this period is very tricky. You need to provide for exploration and independence. You need to set things up for him so he can be successful; but at the same time you have to avoid giving in to unreasonable demands. You have to keep trying to distinguish appropriate limits, and to separate them from mere reactions (although sometimes your emotional reaction is the best signal that your child is going too far).

You are also experiencing a loss. You are losing your baby and all the intense intimacy of that early period. Your child stops being a cuddly, loving, responsive person and turns into the embodiment of all those negative adjectives we strung out earlier.

With food, your child will be testing and waging a campaign for control, just like with everything else in his life. He will look to you for limits, and you must provide them without being too controlling. Your job is to strike the same balance you are struggling for elsewhere: to find the middle ground somewhere between rigidity and overpermissiveness.

Finding this middle ground is important, not only in establishing good attitudes about eating, but also in insuring a nutritionally adequate diet. Children's diets suffer when parents go to the extremes of over-rigidity or overpermissiveness.[8] Parents who criticize or manage or intrude on eating too much have children who don't eat well. Children eat poorly when parents disagree too much about how they should be managed. On the other hand, if parents ignore food selection, or leave too many decisions to children, they also eat poorly.

Physical changes. The child this age is growing more slowly than at an earlier age. In fact, as you can see from the chart on the next page, the rate of growth of the child one and two years old is only half to a third that of the infant up to age 12 months.[6]

The child this age grows in height more quickly than she gains weight, and she loses body fat, using her stored fat for part of her energy needs.

The toddler won't be as hungry, so she will eat less overall. Her appetite will be erratic and sporadic; she apparently can overwhelm any desire to eat with struggles with her parents, with excitement, and with fatigue. She is still hungry and wants to eat during this time, but she wants more to be independent.

If she is well nourished, she is likely to be troublesome, demanding and energetic. Poorly nourished children sit in the corner and don't cause anyone any problems.

Behavioral Changes. The toddler period is a thrilling, frustrating time of skill building. Your toddler will be learning to crawl, walk and run, to climb and to manipulate objects around her. She will be gaining even more control over the fine muscles in her hands and arms, so she can manipulate her food better and can learn to use eating utensils and drink from a cup. She will spill and drop a lot, won't be able to cut up her food, will have a hard time chasing and balancing peas, and won't be able to chew very tough things. She will still choke somewhat more easily than an older child, although she

Figure 8-1. Comparative weight gain of an infant during the first, second and third years of life (Courtesy Gerber Products Co.).

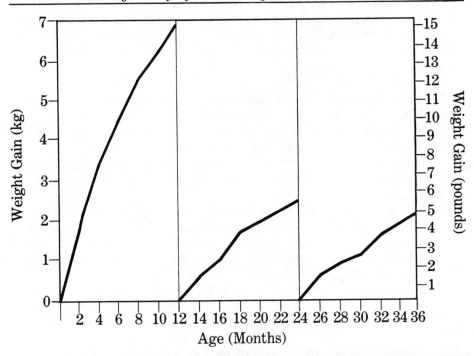

will likely take the difficult food out of her mouth, rather than allowing it to strangle her.

She needs to feel successful, and her tendency to feel embarrassed when she is not successful will show in her habit of slipping the difficult food under the edge of the plate, or sticking it in her pocket. Sympathetic food selection can help the toddler feel more competent and proud of herself. Providing her with eating utensils that she can manage easily will also help toward that goal—as will ignoring her sloppiness and contrariness.

Her skills and interest in self feeding will vary. At times she will absolutely insist on doing everything herself, and do rather an expert job of it; at other times she will drop things, or will want to be fed.

So how are you going to care nutritionally for this contrary, demanding, mercurial creature? In the following sections, I will attempt to define your job for you. I will try to give you some ideas about what you can be doing to promote good eating—and also to alert you to when you may go too far.

We will talk about nutritional adequacy, food selection, mealtime psychology, and other topics. But as we discuss these areas, there is one vital and central point that will come up again and again—in "managing" toddler eating, you must be aware of the division of responsibility:

You are responsible for <u>what</u> your child is offered to eat, <u>where</u> and <u>when</u> it is presented.

She is responsible for <u>how much</u> of it she eats.

If you cross these lines, you are going to get into trouble. You are setting limits for your toddler when you let her know that she can't bully you into offering different food than what you had planned. You are promoting her independence by allowing her to pick and choose from what is available.

Getting Enough of the Right Kind of Food

My major goal in this section is to reassure you that your child is actually doing OK. It is not to pressure you more to see to it that your child eats right. If you feel the pressure, let it be with respect to your family meal-planning. You can only expect yourself to get the right foods on the table. You can't expect yourself to get your child to eat them.

Often parents can relax once they know how little food children really need to eat. At the end of our solid feeding chapter, we talked about the basic four-food plan for the older infant. These same guidelines are appropriate for the toddler.

It is <u>most</u> important to be aware of child-sized portions. Too often we judge what a child "should" be eating by the quantities we, ourselves eat. It's easy to put too much on the plate and make the child feel overwhelmed by the amounts, sometimes to the point where he won't even try to eat.

Figure 8–2. Basic Four-Food Plan

1. *Milk—2–3 cups per day.* Two cups is adequate; more than three is inadvisable because it is then replacing other foods in the diet.
2. *Fruits and vegetables—4 servings per day.* An average adult serving is generally ½ cup or 1 piece (as commonly served). For a child we can say that a nutritionally-adequate portion size is one tablespoon per year of age or one fourth of the adult serving. Thus a child two years old will be taking two tablespoons of fruit or vegetables per serving, or a quarter of an apple or banana.

   An exception would be orange juice, which should be ⅓ cup daily, or the equivalent of another vitamin C source.
3. *Breads and cereals, enriched or whole grained—4 servings per day.* A child's serving is ¼ to ⅓ the adult portion size. The adult serving would be one slice of bread, five crackers, or ½ cup rice, cereal or pasta. Many children will eat disproportionately large amounts from this group, but that's no problem as long as minimum requirements from other groups are being met. Whole grains are appropriate and nutritionally desirable at this age; use them about half the time.
4. *Meats, fish, poultry, eggs, peanut butter, cooked dried beans—2 servings per day.* An adult's serving of meat is 2 to 3 ounces at a

meal. A child's serving is about ½ ounce, for a total of one ounce per day. If the child under age 3 is taking 2 cups of milk per day, 1 ounce of meat or equivalent is adequate to provide the protein requirement. A good source of protein should be offered at each meal.

Meat is often a problem for the infant and toddler, possibly due to difficulty of chewing and swallowing. Casseroles, hearty soups, eggs, fish, hamburger patties, barbecues, peanut butter and legumes* are often accepted better than plain meats.

Hot dogs and lunch meats are fine if limited to once or twice a week. High levels of salt, fat and nitrate make too-frequent consumption a concern.

*Cooked dried beans and peas such as navy beans, pinto beans, lima beans and split peas.

Let me emphasize some things about portion size. I said a good rule of thumb to use is one-fourth to one-third the adult portion size, or one tablespoon per year of age, whichever works better for the particular food. If you are judging bread or a piece of fruit, use the fraction. If you are portioning vegetables or say, rice, the tablespoon might be the easier guide. Give less than you think your child will eat and let him ask for more.

Most people are surprised at the small amount of milk and meat and other protein sources that are required to give enough protein. If there is any nutrient that is likely NOT to be deficient in the American diet it is protein. To repeat, 16 ounces of milk, plus one ounce of meat or meat substitute, provides an ample amount of protein for children up to three years of age. (After that the meat should go up to two ounces per day.)

Restated in more detail, the child one to three years of age needs about 23 grams of protein per day.* The amount of protein, in grams, in typical food sources is listed in the following table:

Figure 8-3. Levels of Protein in Commonly-used Foods

Milk	Grams Protein
Milk, 8 oz.	8
Cheese, cheddar, swiss, etc., 1 oz.	7
Cottage cheese, ¼ cup	7
Meat Group	
Meat, fish, poultry, 1 oz.	7
Egg, 1	7
Cooked dry beans & peas, ½ cup	7
Cooked soybeans, ½ cup	11
Peanut butter, 2 Tbsp.	7
Peanuts, 3 Tbsp.	7
Cashews, 5 Tbsp.	7
Almonds, 5 Tbsp.	7
Breads and Cereals	
Bread, 1 slice	2
Buns, biscuits, muffins, 1	2
Cooked cereals & grain, ½ cup	2
Breakfast cereal, 1 oz.	2
Vegetables and Fruits	
Vegetables, ½ cup	.5-1
Fruits & juices, ½ cup	.5

*All recommendations for levels of nutrients are taken from the Recommended Daily Allowances of the National Research Council, 1980. A table with the complete recommendations is in the Appendix.

Your child will probably eat more than this, and that is fine. Those portion sizes are intended to let you know the minimum he needs to eat to achieve a nutritionally-adequate diet. They are in no way intended for you to use in holding down the amounts he eats.

Evaluating the Diet. To evaluate your child's diet, give some casual attention to the distribution of choices among food groups to be sure that he is not consistently eating one group of foods so enthusiastically that he is completely excluding another group. This might happen on an isolated day or two, which is no problem, but if it happens too often, it could unbalance the diet.

Expect Variation. Many of us eat a nutritionally adequate diet on a weekly average, but few will meet all the minimum requirements every day. Even adults will eat significantly more calories one day than another. We might miss some vegetables or milk one day but consume extra the next. These same variations show up in children. When we discuss the daily food plan, interpret that as being an average of intake for several days, up to a week. Ideally, though, all the food groups should be offered every day; that way your family can regulate themselves in eating appropriate amounts.

Calorie Intakes. They will vary from day to day, and your child will eat as many calories as he needs. The child between one and three years of age will consume about 40 calories per inch of height. This will come out to be somewhere between 1,000 and 1300 calories per day. If you have ever dieted, you know how those seemingly small quantities of food add up. If your child is offered food at reasonably regular intervals, he will eat. No healthy child has ever voluntarily starved.

Milk Intake. Some children drink more milk than they should and will need to be limited so as not to spoil their appetite for other foods. Put a glass of water along with a glass of milk at your child's place, and then put the milk carton back in the refrigerator. That will encourage him to drink water for thirst, and begin to treat the milk as what it is: a food, not a beverage.

Some children do not drink enough milk. Most children, in fact, go through a time when they don't drink much milk. Generally, if you don't make a big issue of it, they go back to it eventually. If you worry or force or tell other people that Suzie won't drink milk, however, she will be reminded and taught that she doesn't like milk, and she might even feel she has to avoid milk on general principles.

Left alone, she will probably go back. While you are waiting for her to do so, you can utilize some information about calcium nutrition. Children from ages one through ten need about 800 mg. of calcium a day. They can get calcium from a variety of foods, although dairy products provide the best food sources, as you can see from the chart on the opposite page.

I will list (Figure 8-5) some tactics you can use for getting calcium into your child's diet, but don't go to great lengths to prepare special food. The chances that a child will refuse a food increase in direct proportion to your effort to provide it.

The footnote on p. 280 suggests using lactase to break down milk sugar for the lactose-intolerant child. Before and during the toddler period you will most likely only see lactose intolerance as a temporary problem following a major intestinal upset like viral enteritis. Even in groups of people who are extremely likely to become lactose intolerant as adults, lactase insufficiency doesn't appear before ages four or five.

Even relatively lactose intolerant children (who are not sick or recovering from acute diarrhea—see *Diarrhea* chapter) can drink some milk. They might get a little gas from it, especially at first, but the gas doesn't hurt them. (It's normal to have a variation in intestinal gas, even if there are no particular intestinal problems.)

If your child cannot tolerate something about the milk other than the lactose,* you should either try to substitute soy formula, or

---

*See the section on allergies at the end of the chapter.

Figure 8-4. Calcium in Foods.

Food	Amount	Calcium (mg.)
Dairy products		
Milk, fluid	1 cup	300
Milk, powdered	1 Tbsp.	60
Cheese, natural or processed	1 ounce	200
Cottage cheese	¼ cup	60
Yogurt	1 cup	300
Ice cream	½ cup	110
Cream cheese	1 Tbsp.	10
Meat and other protein sources		
Meat, poultry, fish	3 ounces	10–20
Canned fish with bones	3 ounces	250
Egg	1	30
Cooked dried beans	½ cup	70
Nuts and seeds	2 Tbsp.	20–40
Peanut butter	2 Tbsp.	20
Bread, cereal, pasta		
Bread	1 slice	25
Biscuits, rolls	1	25
Corn tortillas	1	60
Cooked and dry cereals	1 serving	15
Noodles, macaroni	½ cup	15
Vegetables and fruits		
Vegetables, average	½ cup	20–40
Green leafy vegetables, average	½ cup	100
Fruits, average	½ cup	20–40

Table 8-5. Suggestions for Increasing Calcium in the Diet

Use Dairy Products*

Make fortified milk: Combine 2 cups fluid milk, ⅓ cup powdered milk. Refrigerate before using. Substitute wherever you use milk. One cup fortified milk = 1½ cup regular milk.

Add flavorings to milk: strawberry, chocolate, soft-drink powders. Make eggnog, cocoa, milkshakes.

Make a "smoothie": Blend milk with fruit to make a milkshake-like beverage.

Use milk in some cooking instead of water: cooked cereal, soups, gravies.

Put powdered milk in baking: Add 2 Tbsp. powdered milk to each cup of flour. Store and use for all baking.

Put powdered milk in other cooking.
Ground beef: ½ cup per pound. Add water.
Casseroles: 2 Tbsp. per cup.
Vegetables: Make cream sauce.

Make desserts (use fortified milk): custard, pudding, rice pudding, pumpkin custard, cheese cake.

Use cheese in cooking: Macaroni and cheese, lasagna, tacos, grilled cheese sandwich, cheeseburgers, pizza.

Use High-Calcium Vegetables

Use legumes: bean or split pea soup, chili, three-bean salad, pea-pickle-cheese salad, kidney bean with cheese.

Use greens: In salads, soups, as a vegetable in casseroles.

*If your child gets intestinal gas or diarrhea from drinking milk, she may have a deficiency of lactase, the intestinal enzyme that digests milk sugar. You can buy lactase to pretreat milk. Use the brand name Lact-Aid®. Ask your pharmacist.

one of the hypoallergenic formulas. Both of these will give the calcium and vitamin D that you are counting on milk to provide. Don't use soy milk; it doesn't have the vitamin D of milk and is unpredictable about providing other nutrients.

Pasteurized goat's milk is a substitute for cow's milk that some people can tolerate. This may or may not be fortified with vitamin D; read the label. It is also low in folic acid, but this should not be a problem if a child is eating a variety of foods.

Calcium supplements don't work very well for the infant and toddler. Most supplements come in the form of tablets and the daily dose is four to six or more. It is an exceptional child who can, and will, swallow several pills a day. The only chewable I can find contains calcium phosphate, which interferes with iron absorption. Calcium in tablets is usually in the form of calcium lactate, and you will generally pay about the same amount for a day's calcium in tablet form as you do for milk. Calcium pills come with or without vitamin D. Which you should choose depends on whether your child is getting another good vitamin D source. Avoid bone meal and dolomite; they are contaminated with excessive amounts of lead and other trace elements.

Iron. Another nutrient that concerns us with the toddler is iron. Iron deficiency anemia continues to be a problem up until about age two years, particularly for children living in poverty.

There are two common nutritional errors that contribute to iron deficiency anemia in older infants and toddlers: 1) Overconsumption of milk (more than 16 to 24 ounces per day), with resultant low intake of iron-containing food; and 2) Poor snack selection; whereas meals commonly provide appropriate amounts of iron, snacks may provide calories with few nutrients of any sort.

The child who is one to three years old needs 15 mg. iron per day. With the exception of milk, the foods listed on the next page, eaten in child-size portions, provide significant iron.

Figure 8-6. Iron Content of Selected Foods

Food	Amount	Iron (mg.)
Meat and other protein		
Beef, pork, lamb	3 ounces	2–3
Poultry	3 ounces	1.5
Beef or chicken liver	3 ounces	8.5
Calves liver	3 ounces	14
Pork liver	3 ounces	25
Clams	3 ounces	5
Oysters	3 ounces	13
Other fish, shellfish	3 ounces	1–1.5
Egg	1	1
Nuts, average	2 Tbsp.	1
Seeds (sunflower, squash, pumpkin, average)	2 Tbsp.	2
Breads and Cereals		
Enriched or whole-grain bread	1 slice	0.7
Noodles, spaghetti, etc.	½ cup	0.7
Cooked or dry cereals	½–¾ cup	0.7
Multi-vitamin and iron supplement cereals	Iron content varies; read package.	
Fruits and Vegetables		
Green leafy vegetables	½ cup	2
Peas, mixed vegetables	½ cup	2
Other vegetables, average	½ cup	0.8
Prunes and dates	½ cup	2
Other fruits and juices	½ cup	0.6
Milk		
Whole, skim, 2% milk	1 cup	0.1 mg.

Miscellaneous
Blackstrap molasses	1 Tbsp.	3
Sorghum	1 Tbsp.	2.5
Molasses, medium	1 Tbsp.	1

Iron in meat, poultry and fish is absorbed several times as well as iron from vegetable sources.[9] It seems that these animal protein foods contain something we call a "meat factor," which also improves absorption of vegetable iron eaten at the same time as meat. Similarly, vitamin C sources consumed at the same time as other iron-containing foods will improve iron absorption.[9] "Meat factor" and Vitamin C also help each other out in iron absorption: if you take both at a meal, the iron absorption will be even further improved.[9] Examples of meals that would have both meat and vitamin C include hamburgers and coleslaw, spaghetti with tomato sauce, hot dogs and orange wedges.

Iron in egg yolk is poorly absorbed. In fact, unless you take vitamin C at the same time, egg yolk will actually impair iron absorption from other foods. Milk apparently neither enhances or blocks iron absorption from other foods.[9]

Limit liver consumption to twice a month. Eating too much liver will give too much vitamin A.

Vitamins A and C: As you run a rough check on your child's food intake, you will want to make sure that his food sources add up to a good amount of vitamin C almost every day (see p. 248 for a list of foods containing vitamin C), and a good amount of vitamin A every other day (see p. 246). Don't worry unnecessarily about temporary short-falls, however; as long as he is not suffering from any major illness, his food intake can drop 25 to 50% below the recommended allowances, and he will still be doing pretty well. Our nutrient requirements build in a "fudge factor," which means that we can eat somewhat less than prescribed quantities of nutrients and still be all right nutritionally.

If it seems like he just isn't eating any, say, high vitamin-A vegetables, you might want to see to it that he is offered some cantaloupe or apricot or peach nectar for a snack. But be subtle about it; you must not let him know that you are willing to substitute other foods for those he refuses.

Vitamin and Mineral Supplements. If your water is inadequately fluoridated, your child may need to take a fluoride supplement.* Beyond that, if you are preparing a nutritionally adequate diet, eating it yourself and presenting it in a neutral and matter-of-fact fashion, your child will not need to take vitamin-mineral supplements. Sooner or later he will eat well and will provide himself with an adequate diet.

Don't get too caught up in evaluating your child's diet. *Pay attention to whether he seems energetic and is growing well.* If observing his food intake and assessing it for nutritional adequacy is making you nervous, stop. He is probably doing OK. When I actually sit down to calculate nutrient intake in detail, I am always surprised at what odd diets add up to nutritional adequacy.

Pay at least as much attention to what you are offering (and the way you are offering it) as you do to what he is eating. Over-all, that will reflect his nutritional status much more clearly than any analysis of what he happens to accept on a few isolated days.

Food Selection

Before we get started on this section, let me issue a word of warning: Don't get so involved with planning and preparing nutritious food for your child that you forget that your ultimate job is *to parent*. Providing food will take some time and attention. Don't let it take too much.

---

*See the Supplemental Fluoride Schedule, table A-6 in the Appendix.

If you are running yourself ragged providing superior, homemade, delectable everything for your family, you may be sacrificing something else that is more important.

If you love to cook and it gives you more energy for other things, that is one thing. But if you see it as just another job, you will be perfectly justified in finding shortcuts, using good-quality mixes and convenience foods, and even taking in an occasional "fast-food" franchise.

Frozen vegetables are just as nutritious as fresh, and they take a lot less preparation time. It's great if you love to bake bread. You can, however, find good breads on the grocery-store shelf that are just as nutritious as the ones you bake yourself. It's fun to make yogurt and grow your own sprouts, but if you are getting up in the middle of the night to attend to them, the juice might not be worth the squeeze. And speaking of that, frozen orange juice is just as nutritious as juice you make yourself from fresh oranges.

Meal Planning. A meal should provide—

Protein: Meat, fish, poultry, egg, cooked dried beans, seeds or nuts.

A bread or cereal: Bread, bun, noodles, spaghetti, etc.

A fruit or vegetable or both.

Milk.

A nutritionally complete meal might contain only two food items, such as a tuna noodle casserole with peas and a glass of milk. Or everything could be separate, as with meat loaf, mashed potatoes, broccoli, bread and milk. Vegetables might be part of a combination dish, as in spaghetti and meat sauce. Fruit can be served as part of dessert, as in oatmeal raisin cookies, or given as a juice along with a meal.

You can evaluate some convenience foods, such as canned or frozen dinners or hearty soups—good menu choices for you and your toddler. You can just look at the product to see if it has vegetable and starch in it. To find out if it has enough protein, however, you will need to check the nutritional labeling. A toddler should be able to get about five grams of protein from a half-cup serving of main-dish food.

If everything doesn't fit into the meal, you can count on the snack to provide part of it. A fruit juice at a snack can help make up for a fruit or vegetable that wasn't eaten at the meal.

The hamburger, fried chicken, pizza and taco places offer nutritious choices for an occasional meal. If your child has milk or a milkshake (instead of pop) and some french fries or coleslaw, he can really come out quite well in getting a nutritionally-complete meal. These fast-food meals have two main drawbacks—their high sodium content and their lack of fruits and vegetables. (With the exception of batter-fried food, the fat content of fast foods is not too bad.) But such drawbacks do not become major problems if you don't go there too often.

Catering to Likes and Dislikes. In planning meals for your family, you will probably want to treat your child just like you do everyone else—by catering to a reasonable degree to her food preferences as you plan menus. But don't limit your menus to just the foods that you know your child will like. One good strategy is to include one food he likes with each meal; if the vegetable is a less-favorite one, have a bread or salad that your child usually likes.

I say *usually* likes, because another feature of this age group is that they will eat a food enthusiastically one time, and completely shun it the next, which is frustrating to say the least. You'll run out at one meal and have way too much at the next.

Short-order Cooking. You have the meal on the table, the toddler whines he doesn't like it, you insist he eat it, he refuses, and you say,

"All right, what will you eat?" That is short-order cooking. Don't do it. In fact, don't even get close to it. When your toddler complains he doesn't like something, ignore it. Don't give him the idea that you are concerned or upset about it or willing to substitute. Have his milk on the table when he arrives, put some bread on the table so he won't starve, give him some support in getting himself served, and leave him to his own devices.

Making Food Easy to Eat. Your toddler needs some help with certain foods. He can't chew tough and fibrous food too well, like meat, and too-dry food seems to get stuck in his mouth. Here are some suggestions to help the eating process along:
- Cut foods into bite-sized pieces, preferably before he gets there. He won't be able for some time to handle a knife, and is likely to have a tantrum about not being allowed to try—and another one about trying and failing.
- Make some foods soft and moist. If you have dry meat, have creamed peas. Make the mashed potatoes a little softer than you would for adults.
- Allow him to eat his foods at room temperature. Perhaps you can dish his up in a separate serving bowl so it can cool off or warm up a bit before he tries to eat it.
- Keep ground beef patties in the freezer to substitute when you have roasts or steaks that your child can't handle easily. Cook patties only long enough for the color to change to brown so it is still juicy. Meat is hard to eat, even for older children.
- Give salads without dressing and serve them as finger food.
- Make soups thin enough to drink from a cup or thick enough to spoon easily.
- Cook strong-flavored vegetables, such as brussels sprouts, in about an equal volume of cooking water and then throw away the water. You will be throwing away nutrients, but there's a better chance that they will be eaten.
- Prepare food well. Children accept foods better when they are

properly cooked with natural colors and textures preserved.
- Put a little extra color in foods. Children are interested in a little parsley in the hot dish or some carrot grated into the coleslaw.
- Put up with their idiosyncrasies about shapes. Children will often insist on having their sandwiches quartered, and if they are halfed, they will throw tantrums. Or they will think carrot sticks are inedible but will eat carrot dollars very happily. Orange wedges with the skins attached are often eaten better than sections.

You may delight in making little orange section boats and little gingerbread man sandwiches. I think that's fine for a party or special occasion, but not as a regular thing. I suspect parents who are willing regularly to go that far of having too much anxiety about their child's eating. I also know from experience that if I have gone to some trouble to make food cute and my child won't eat it, I feel disgusted and it is hard to ignore his refusal. Regularly providing cute food tends to confuse food with playthings. Food should look like FOOD, not like toys.

Mealtime Environment

To promote good attitudes about food and good nutrition, it is important for your meals to be <u>significant</u>, and <u>pleasant</u>.

By significant I mean that there needs to be a meal on the table. Someone in the household has to take responsibility for planning, purchasing and preparing the food. Significant also means expecting the family to show up to eat the meal, to pay attention to it, and to spend some time over it. Of course there are those unavoidable times when meals will have to be rushed, but if that is happening too often, you need to do some problem-solving.

Make mealtime pleasant. Don't argue, fight or scold at mealtimes, and don't let anyone else do it either. It is tempting to ventilate gripes at mealtime, because that may be the one reliable time when the family is together. Don't do it!

Consider Timing. Have your meals at whatever time works in your household. Don't be too concerned if your family eats at an unusual time—say has the evening meal quite late. The child this age is beginning to fit into the family's routine (instead of vice-versa). You can control the child's hunger with judicious use of snacks, so he will be able to wait and eat along with the rest of the family. This is important; one of the most powerful influences on your child's food acceptance is eating with you and seeing you enjoy a wide variety of nutritious food.

Seating Arrangements. Make any adjustments that may enhance everyone's comfort. Use whatever seating arrangement allows your child to sit at a convenient height in relation to the table. Her feet should be supported, as it is uncomfortable for anyone to have his feet dangling for any length of time.

Use a child-sized plate and utensils. A plate with low edges will give her a bang-board for pushing the food onto her fork or spoon. A smaller plate will help you regulate your portioning. Junior-sized silverware is a good size for this age, or a broad salad fork and a spoon work well. She should have a glass with a broad base that sits firmly on the table, and it should be small enough so that she can encircle it with her hands. If you are concerned about your floor, protect it some way, as there will be inevitable spills and dropping.

Occasionally children will ask to be allowed to sit at their own small eating table and chairs. That is fine and also comfortable for them, as long as they don't abuse the privilege by getting up and running around during the meal.

Eating Mechanics. Give her silverware, but don't insist that she use it. If she is allowed to look, feel, mash and smell while exploring new food, she is more likely to accept it. You'll be able to tell if she is truly exploring a new food, or just playing or messing around to get

289

you to react. Once she stops eating, it is time to let her get down from the table.

Don't worry too much about the mechanics of eating. Parents who make frequent demands on their children to eat, sit properly and use the napkin, interrupt their child's eating. Children either become rebellious or so preoccupied with the mechanics that they lose their interest in food. As your child matures, her dexterity will develop, and the spills, dropped food and utensils, and general mess will decrease. Developing wholesome attitudes about eating is more important, at this stage, than the niceties of table manners.

Enforcing Food Consumption. Don't do it! Your job is to get food on the table and to make it clear to everyone that they are expected to come to the table. Your job is <u>not</u> to enforce, cajole, trick or persuade them to eat. I often see fathers getting into the act as eating enforcer, particularly at dinner time. They take a hard line, insisting that the child <u>will</u> eat. In defense of fathers, I most often see them doing this when the mother is being overly-solicitous, worrying over food refusal, cajoling the child to eat, or even falling prey to short order cooking; because mother is so mushy, father has to be extra tough.

The role of disciplinarian is an important one; there are good and bad ways of filling it. You must not force, cajole, trick or otherwise interfere with your child's prerogative of deciding how much she will eat. What you CAN do is insist that she come to the table, be firm about limiting food availability to what is on the table, and refuse to allow her to complain about and criticize the food. And if mother shows signs of weakening and running for the peanut butter and jelly, you can remind her (diplomatically) that there will be another meal, and that your child is likely to survive very nicely until then.

Then you can go ahead and enjoy your own food, and refuse to allow your child to behave in a way that interferes with your own mealtime enjoyment. And don't forget to eat your vegetables.

Acknowledging Eating

You can acknowledge your child's willingness to try a new food, but don't praise him for eating a lot of it. That is interfering with his self-regulation. Giving him enthusiastic approval for his eating may teach him to eat just to please you. You want him to eat to please *himself*. Don't laugh at his mistakes, either. That is also paying too much attention to his eating, and will encourage him either to show off or to be embarrassed.

Reinforcing Desirable Behavior. Ignore undesirable behavior respecting food or eating, even if it means you have to remove your child from the table. Whenever you pay attention, or praise, coax or beg, or give in to his demands for food, you are paying attention to and rewarding bad behavior. Observe what you are doing that may inadvertently give attention to bad behavior. When you respond to his grocery-store crying and whining by buying him a candy bar, you are supporting his misbehavior. (You are also supporting your own weakness, because *you* get rewarded by *his* stopping crying.)

You can reinforce by paying attention, recognizing, and acknowledging appropriate behavior. Take time to eat and chat with your child at mealtime. Don't reserve your mealtime attention for the times when he is being naughty. If he misbehaves, put him down. When he behaves well, welcome him at the table and include him in the conversation.

Getting Ready to Eat. Children at times will get so tired or stimulated from play that they don't feel like eating. If you can manage it, a few minutes spent with him before offering the meal, perhaps reading a book to get settled down, can pay off in an improved appetite.

Other times they get so involved in their play that they don't want to come to the table. A five minute warning may help. Sometimes nothing helps, and your child will tell you he's not hungry anyway and will, on no account, eat. Tell him that that is his choice, but that you expect him to come to the table whether he eats or not and that you expect him to stay a while.

How long depends on your child. It needs to be long enough for him to get settled down and bored enough to realize that if he is going to have to sit there anyway, he might as well go ahead and eat, but not so long for it to seem vicious and punitive. (This situation is different from letting a fed child down from the table when he starts to misbehave. Here we have a hungry child who needs to be deprived of his other activity so he can know he's hungry.)

Food Acceptance

Depending on how much your child has to test you, you will probably have some showdowns over food. Don't, however, have them over what he will eat. Have them about what you will provide. You can't force him to eat his peas, but you can refuse to get up and make string beans as a substitute.

Your child may, or probably will, invite you to fight over his eating by refusing certain foods or whole meals. If you let him know you are concerned, he will get the upper hand, and manipulate you into doing all sorts of objectionable things to get him to eat. Don't overreact. Your only recourse is to ignore his food refusal and then decline to feed him when he comes around later panhandling for food. Don't order, beg, punish, force, reason or coax. You will always lose. And your child will lose, too, because he will be so busy struggling with you that he won't be able to eat well.

You won't avoid struggles by giving in to his demands. You will only postpone them. He needs to know he can rely on you to set limits on his behavior. If you give in, he will simply become more and more provocative until you are *forced* to have a confrontation with him. You might as well do it sooner rather than later.

Eat a Variety of Foods. If you are a finicky eater, you are likely to teach or allow your child to be the same way. Try new foods and attempt to teach yourself to eat a variety of foods. But go slowly; don't push it. Start out with a goal of taking one bite of a food you don't like. Once that becomes really quite tolerable, go to two bites. Don't expect yourself to eat a whole serving until you really like it. If you force too much on yourself too soon, you will feel revolted.

Change Undesirable Eating Behavior Slowly and Expect Setbacks. This goes for your own eating as well as that of your child. If you whittle away at undesirable behavior a little at a time, you will probably make major advances over time. If you try to do too much, too fast, you will relapse and may never make it.

Use Good Tactics for Introducing New Foods. Introduce new foods early. Acceptance of new foods is age-related. The older children get, the more likely they are to refuse new food. Observe the time of day when your child takes a new food most easily and give it to him then. This may be when he is most hungry. He may also accept new foods better if he is not too tired or excited. He will certainly accept them better if he doesn't feel pressure about it. The first time he is introduced to a new food, he may only look at it and not get around to eating it until the second or third time he sees it.

Do serve very small portions of a new or unpopular food. One pea or green bean has a better chance of being eaten than a whole big serving. Be judicious about demanding that he taste everything. This often works with minimum fuss, but be careful about establishing requirements. You'll lose. On the other hand, you might have a child who is suspicious of anything new, and then likes and eats it very well once he tastes it. Experiment and see what works for you.

Separate Rejection of You from Rejection of Your Food. Don't confuse the reason for your child's food rejection. That is easier said

293

than done, particularly if you like to pay a lot of attention to what your family likes, and struggle to find things that you think they will eat. You have to find a balance here, and one of the best ways I know of achieving it is to pay attention to your *own* preferences. Treat your own food likes and dislikes with as much respect as you do those of the rest of the family. Expect them to eat a less-favored food at times, simply because you *love* it. And if you make something you don't like, say so politely—to yourself.

Set realistic standards for yourself. You have to keep a lot of things in mind as you prepare your menus: cost, food availability, nutritional balance, the time you have available for preparation. With your busy life, you are simply going to have to resign yourself to the fact that some meals are not going to be all that hot.

Keep in mind that their not eating is not *your* failure. If you prepare acceptable food, it is not your fault if they won't eat. It's not their fault either. They just happen not to like it or not to feel like eating it. Children need to learn at home to cope with food they don't particularly enjoy. (From working in cafeterias, I know too many adults who throw tantrums when presented with food that doesn't happen to match their expectations.)

Don't Promote Food Jags. Don't ask your child what he wants for lunch. Make it and put it on the table. If he wants to eat a particular food every single day, let him ask for it ahead of time, and give it to him at snack time. Don't let him come to the table and refuse what you have prepared and demand the other food. Many times if you don't give children the idea that they have a choice about food selection, it won't occur to them. But at the same time, they need to learn to do some selecting. Snack time is a good time for that.

Snacking

People often think that snacking is bad for their children, and try to prevent eating between meals. That really isn't necessary or even helpful. *Children's energy needs are high, and they have a limited capacity for food, so they really need to eat every three to four hours.* The important thing is that you have control over the time of snacking and the type of food that is consumed.

Timing. Snacks should be offered midway between meals. They should be provided long enough after the previous meal so that your child knows he will have to go hungry for some time if he refuses the meal. This helps prevent the pattern of meal refusal followed by almost-immediate begging for food. You, too, will be much more inclined to refuse food handouts if you know that another feeding is coming up in only two or three hours.

Some parents, in their anxiety to feed their children will fall prey to this kind of tactic and end up feeding almost on demand all day. We particularly see this pattern in the child who is gaining weight slowly or growing less rapidly than average. The parent is understandably anxious about food intake and compounds the difficulty by giving in too easily to the child's food demands. In fact, these small feedings can actually decrease total calories and impair nutrient intake.

You may have to offer two snacks if you have a particularly long interval between meals. If children have an early lunch and a late dinner, it often works well to have a "heavy" snack (one with protein, fat and carbohydrate), two or three hours after lunch, and then a carbohydrate snack, such as fruit or crackers, later in the afternoon. A small amount of fruit or juice can help to tide your child over when you are dashing around getting dinner on. Some fruit or juice in the car on the way home from the day care center can prevent conflict later.

Regulation. The way to regulate snacks is to get there first. If you plan on a reasonably-consistent snack time, and get the food on the table, you will be able to manage timing, location and selection. If you feed your child before she is too hungry, she will eat a moderate amount. On the other hand, I will guarantee you a struggle if you wait until she is famished, and has already thought about what she wants to eat and where she wants to eat it. You may have to be firm about snacking either way, but at least you won't be asking for more trouble than necessary.

Selection. A snack that you want to last a while should contain some protein, some fat, and some carbohydrate, the same as a nutritious meal. It should be big and substantial enough to be filling for a hungry child. An apple or some carrots just don't do the trick when you are famished, even if they are filling for the moment; because they are only carbohydrate, they won't stay in the stomach long and your child will be hungry too soon before the next meal.

On the other hand, if it is only protein and fat, say cheese or peanut butter in celery sticks, it won't be as immediately satisfying, and may tend to be higher in calories. But if the snack contains all three major nutrients, it will be satisfying and should "stay with" the child, while still allowing her to be comfortably hungry in time for the next meal.

Figure 8-7 gives you some suggestions for nutritious snacks. However, any food that you consider appropriate for a meal is appropriate for a snack. Some parents are quite successful at sending a refused meal around again at snack time. This isn't as heartlessly sneaky as it sounds—maybe lunch has been eaten poorly because the child was tired before a nap.

Often snacktime is a good time to get the child to try new things. Maybe you can work in the servings of vegetables that are still missing in the day's food totals, particularly if you serve them raw or still-frozen. Many times children will accept as snacks foods that they ignore or refuse at meals. Experiment.

Avoid, in general, the kind of food that the advertising industry defines as snack foods. Chips, snack cakes (like Twinkies®), fruit drinks, and candies, all have very little nutritional value in relationship to the calories they contribute. In fact, nutritional surveys indicate that overall quality of the American diet is seriously diluted by snack selection. They show that meal averages look pretty good, but that when they are added in with snack patterns the quality goes down seriously. Poor-quality foods rob your child twice—once when they are eaten and a second time when the calories replace those of more nutritious food.

This is not to say that some of these questionable goodies should never be eaten. As available as they are today, it is probably wise to teach your children to manage them. Once in a while it is O.K. to make up a package of Kool-Aid® or to buy a small package of snack cakes to have along with a meal or a snack. But the trick is controlling the frequency and amount. Buy a limited quantity so it goes around once and then is gone. That way it doesn't force you to be the gatekeeper in rationing out what is left.

Even though it pains me to say this, even Kool-Aid and the snack cakes do make a nutritional contribution in the form of their calorie content. Most children are so active that they can satisfy all their nutritional requirements and still have need for more calories.

The purist in me, however, feels much more comfortable about giving sugary foods if they are hooked on to something nutritious. For a bunch of hungry and thirsty kids, I like to spike one part orange Kool-Aid with one-half to three parts orange juice. Ice cream, malts, oatmeal cookies and carrot-raisin cake are all basically nutritious foods, and they give the extra calories that most children need.

Sweets

It is valid for you to be concerned about sugar. It is not necessary to be terrified.

Americans consume a lot of sugar. Each American man, woman and child consumes on the average 130 pounds of sugar per

Figure 8-7. Nutritious Snacks

Vegetable Snacks:

Cut up fresh, raw vegetables. Serve with peanut butter, cheese, cottage cheese or milk* to get protein and fat. Add crackers or fruit juice to get carbohydrate.

Broccoli	Green beans
Carrots	Green peas
Cauliflower	Turnip sticks
Celery	Zucchini
Cucumber	

Fresh Fruit Snacks:

Slice or serve whole. Serve with peanut butter, cottage cheese, yogurt, ricotta cheese or milk to give protein and fat.

Apples	Berries	Peaches
Apricots	Grapefruit	Pears
Bananas	Grapes	Pineapple
	Melons	

Dried Fruit Snacks:

Serve with nuts, almonds, cashews, peanuts, or with seeds (pumpkin, squash, sunflower) to give protein and fat. *Be very cautious about giving seeds and nuts to young children.*

Apples	Figs	Prunes
Apricots	Peaches	Raisins
Dates	Pears	

*Use either 2% or whole milk to give fat.

Nuts and Seeds:

Peanuts, Pumpkin and squash kernels, Sunflower seeds.

Grain Products:

A. *Bread products.* Use whole wheat about half the time. Read the label to make sure the flour is enriched or whole grain. (The first listed ingredient should be *whole* wheat.) Try a variety of yeast breads and quick breads—whole wheat, rye, oatmeal, mixed grains, bran—plain or with dried fruit. Try rye crisps, whole grain flat bread, and whole grain crackers. Serve bread and crackers with cheese, peanut butter or a glass of milk to give protein and fat.

B. *Dry cereals:* Choose varieties with less than three grams of "sucrose or other sugar", *read the label,* per serving. Serve with milk to give protein and fat. Add dried fruits, nuts and seeds for variety and increased nutrients.

C. *Popcorn:* Try using grated cheese instead of salt and butter. Serve with milk or cocoa to give protein and fat.

D. *Cookies:* Bake your own, substituting ½ whole wheat flour for white flour. Try oatmeal, peanut butter or molasses cookies. Experiment with cutting down on sugar in recipes, often you can decrease sugar by ⅓ to ½. Serve cookies with milk to give protein (cookies already have fat).

Beverages:

A. Use fruit juices and vegetable juices rather than powdered or canned fruit drinks which are high in sugar and lower in vitamins.

B. Milk: Serve plain with bread, crackers, cereal, etc. Mix in blender with banana, other fruit or orange juice for a healthy milkshake. Try adding vanilla extract, honey, molasses, even a little sugar. Use chocolate and strawberry flavorings for an occasional treat.

year. That figures out to ¼ cup of sugar per person, per day. About 24% of the calories in the average diet come from sugar. Of that 24%, 14% comes from refined sugars like sucrose (table sugar), fructose, glucose, lactose and maltose. Four percent of the sugar comes from processed foods like corn syrup, corn syrup solids, maple syrup, honey and molasses. And only about six percent comes from natural sources like fruits, vegetables and milk products.

More than two-thirds of the sugar in the food supply is consumed in factory-made foods and only a quarter is in foods prepared with sugar in the home. Processors use sugar for sweetening, to help foods retain moisture, to prevent spoilage, and to improve texture and appearance.

It's very hard to avoid sugar and you needn't try. Used judiciously, sugar does improve the flavor and acceptability of some foods. Eaten along with a meal or a substantial snack, sugar won't send people off on sugar jags.

How Much Sugar. Your child does not *need* any added sugar at all in her diet. The natural foods we mentioned earlier, milk and fruit, have sugar in them. But even without these, the body can provide itself with sugar by manufacturing it from starch, protein and fat. But, whether the sweet tooth is born or made, most of us do have one. Sweet-tasting foods add considerable pleasure, as well as providing energy for our fast-growing, fast-moving children.

The U.S. dietary goals recommend that the amount of refined and processed sugar in the diet be brought down from the average level of 18% to about 10% of calories in the diet.[4] This is a pretty arbitrary figure—and a pretty drastic reduction. Short of being sure that sugar does not replace other nutritious foods in the diet, there is no real way of knowing how much sugar is "bad" for your child. But it might help you to relax about sugar intake if we are more specific, and with that in mind, I'll accept the figure of 10% as a sugar "allowance" and give you an idea of how much that is.

A child taking about 1300 calories per day, a rough guess of average calorie intake for the toddler, will have a sugar "allowance" of 130 calories per day. Each teaspoonful of table sugar gives 20 calories. You can figure a reasonable daily sugar allowance at six teaspoons or (30 grams) of sugar (or molasses, jelly, syrup or honey). A fast way of figuring a sugar "allowance," in teaspoons, for different calorie levels is to divide calories comsumed per day by 200: a person eating 1800 calories could have nine teaspoons of sugar.

Here are the amounts of sugar contained in some common foods:

Figure 8-8. Sugar Content of Common Sweet Foods

Food	Teaspoons of sugar
Candy bar, 1 ounce	7
Cookies, 1–3 inch	1–2
Brownies, 2-inch square	1–2
Frosted cake, two layer, 1/16	7
Fruit pie, 1/7 of 9 inch	6–9
Pumpkin pie, 1/7 of 9 inch	3–5
Ice cream, 1/2 cup	3
Chocolate milk, 1 cup	3
Milkshake, 10 ounces	9
Sweetened soda pop, 12 ounces	6–9
Kool-Aid,® 8 ounces	6

Source: U.S.D.A. Home and Garden Bulletin #72

You can figure sugar content of food by dividing the total amount of sugar in a recipe by the number of servings it makes. An apple pie recipe that serves seven and calls for ¾ cup sugar will have

36 teaspoons of sugar (3 teaspoons per tablespoon and 16 tablespoons per cup makes 48 teaspoons times ¾ = 36 teaspoons), or about five teaspoons (36 ÷ 7) per serving.

(These figures are lower than the ones you generally see in tables of "hidden sugar" in foods, although they are certainly high enough. I think other list-compilers must be figuring total carbohydrate, rather than subtracting out the starch from the sugar.)

Many nutritional labels tell the amount of sugar in an average serving of their product. Breakfast cereals do this, and declare it as grams of "sucrose and other sugars." Again, if you prefer to think in terms of teaspoons, convert by figuring five grams of sugar per teaspoon.

Having done all of this figuring, I want to put things back in perspective. I really don't want you to declare an absolute limit on your child's sweets intake, counting every cookie or glass of Kool-Aid.® I also don't want you to give free access to the candy and pop. Keep things in balance. See that your child is offered a variety of nutritious food, make most sweets nutritious, and offer the more-concentrated sweets only occasionally.

It is better to control or limit concentrated, low nutrient foods to an occasional use than it is to try to prohibit them completely. I know too many children who grew up in sugar-free households who load up on exactly this kind of food when they have a chance.

Using Sugar to Promote Nutritious Food. Good cooks use sugar to make food taste better. A teaspoon of sugar in a tomato dish takes the harsh edge off the tomato taste and makes the dish more acceptable, especially to younger tastebuds. A teaspoon of sugar in the frozen peas will give them a "just-picked" flavor.

Some desserts and sweets are very nutritious. Custards, puddings, oatmeal or peanut butter cookies, and pumpkin pie (you can skip the top crust) are all very nutritious desserts. If children like sugar on their (low-sugar) breakfast cereal, or enjoy flavoring in milk, or like jam on toast, those are valid uses of sugar. Just keep an eye on the proportion of sugar to other foods in the diet.

Desserts. Should a child be allowed to have dessert if he doesn't finish his meal? Yes! If you make dessert a reward for eating "well" (which usually means "a lot"), you will probably be encouraging your child to overeat twice: once at the meal and once when he eats dessert after he is already full. You are also teaching him that dessert is the only really-desirable part of the meal.

Make dessert something nutritious and put a serving of it at each plate at the same time as you serve the rest of the meal. So what if he eats it first. He will probably discover that he is still hungry and go on to eat the rest of his meal. If he is waiting and saving room for dessert, he will probably end up not satisfied and then harass you for more dessert.

Oral Health. Sugar promotes tooth decay by nourishing the acid-producing bacteria in the mouth. Mouth bacteria can learn to live on the sugar in milk (lactose) or the sugar in fruit (fructose) just as well as they can on table sugar.

The longer and more frequently sugar is in contact with the teeth, the more likely it is to cause tooth decay. If a child is sipping pop or fruit juice for a very long time, or fanning the refrigerator door satisfying his thirst with calorie-containing beverages, he will be bathing his teeth with sugar and promoting tooth decay.

Sugar in sticky foods will adhere to the teeth and remain in the mouth longer. Caramels and raisins, for example, stick to the teeth and also take a long time to eat, so both increase the risk of tooth decay.

Nutritional Concerns. The major nutritional problem with sugar is that it can displace other, more nutritious foods in your diet. Sugar in and of itself will not make you sick, cause insanity, or lead to any of the horrible maladies that are reported in the popular press. The only disease that we can really blame on sugar is tooth decay.*

I object to sugar-coated cereals, and their advertising, primarily because they teach kids that food has to be sweet to be good. Highly sweetened breakfast cereals dyed vivid colors disguise the delicious flavors of grains, and promote a substitute food that is more like candy than cereal. As I tell my children (and they hate it), "If you are going to eat candy, eat candy. If you are going to eat cereal, eat cereal. But don't eat that stuff and call it cereal."

We buy about two boxes of sugar-coated cereal a year for the kids to eat when we go on camping trips. They think it is a big treat and they wolf it down for snacks. They say they think I am being rigid and silly when I won't buy it all of the time. Too bad.

Too-frequent consumption of high-sugar food can send some kids and some older people on sugar jags, periodically recharging themselves with sugary foods. The body can overreact to a high sugar load and send blood sugar levels below fasting levels. This leads to more hunger and more sugar craving—and another sugar fix repeats the process.

Eating Problems

There is a mixed bag of typical eating concerns and questions that show up during the toddler period. I will lump them together in the discussion that follows.

Chewing and Swallowing Problems. An occasional child will get stuck at a developmental stage with his eating, and not move on in normal fashion to the next stage. He might insist on nursing instead of eating meals, or refuse to eat anything that is the least-bit lumpy

---

*Even diabetes is not "caused" by excess sugar intake.

long past the time when he should have been gumming more tex-
tured foods.

One of the causes may have been that he was not offered next-
stage food when he was developmentally ready. He may have been
sick or fussy when it was time to get him on table foods, or he may
have had an over-developed gag response that scared his parents into
backing off from teaching him to chew. For whatever reason, it is
important to get the toddler on grownup type food, with only
minimal modifications. That can create a problem, as the toddler can
be perfectly capable of carrying on a battle over just that issue.

To get him to progress developmentally, you will have to
change the texture and consistency of his food, and you will have to
be firm about it. You will have to slowly introduce an increasing
amount of texture and thickness into his food. If you are being slow
and patient and he still refuses, you will have to tough it out. Children are capable of refusing to eat for several days before they give
in and start to eat. But don't let him panhandle, and don't let him fill
up on milk and juice.

If he seems like he is having particular difficulty chewing and
swallowing food, or if he continues to do a lot of gagging, it is possible that he is having a real developmental problem. Talk with your
pediatrician about this, and ask him to refer you to a good occupational therapist. That professional is well equipped to evaluate patterns of oral musculature, and to work, if necessary, in promoting
appropriate developmental changes. An occupational therapist can
also help you to know if your child is really having a problem or he is
simply trying to manipulate you with food.

Overdependency on the Breast. The toddler should be eating meals
rather than breastfeeding at mealtime. Breastfeeding morning and
evening, or for snacks, is appropriate nutritionally, but breastmilk
consumption should not interfere with the developmental and nutritional advantages of meal-eating.

If your toddler has gotten stuck on breastfeeding, you will have to be firm about refusing the breast at mealtime. It may help if mother makes herself scarce and lets someone else feed him for a while until he gets interested in table food.

Overdependency on the Bottle. If you have waited until the toddler period to wean at mealtime, that bottle is likely interfering with food consumption and you should get rid of it. You may be able to avoid a confrontation by diluting the bottle milk and giving undiluted milk in a glass. Eventually your child may begin to prefer the milk in the glass and give up the bottle voluntarily.

If that doesn't work and you can't come up with any other indirect tactic, you are simply going to have to be firm about omitting the bottle at mealtime. You are highly likely to be tested strongly— but hold firm.

Don't make the mistake of giving a bottle right after a meal or letting him run around with a bottle. A bottle must be treated as a snack, and be controlled in time and location.

Allergies. Don't put yourself through all the hassle of catering to a food allergy unless it is really necessary. Many times when children who are assumed to be allergic are challenged with an offending food, it is discovered that they aren't even sensitive to it.

Most evidence for food allergies is pretty circumstantial, and misleading. As we said earlier, perfectly healthy babies will, at times, sound congested, spit up and get gassy. About one baby in ten, through no fault of his own or his parents, is downright impossible: fussy, wakeful, irritable, sensitive to almost everything. You could begin to link a particular food with these symptoms, if you happen to provide the food just before the symptoms appear, and remove it just as symptoms disappear.

But at the same time as I encourage you not to be over ready to label your child food-allergic, I want to caution you that true food allergy can be very serious for the few children who do react significantly to certain foods. Severe allergic reactions include extreme skin rashes, pronounced breathing difficulties, marked nausea and diarrhea, and shock. For some few children, ingestion of even a small amount of an offending food can be life-threatening. Those children must be under a doctor's care and parents must know emergency procedures.

In many cases it appears that children's food allergies are transient. As they get older, the food intolerance resolves itself and the offending food may be safely reintroduced into the diet.

Sometimes children's reactions to foods are not allergies at all, but just temporary problems brought on by disease. Intestinal reactions to foods may come and go with bowel disturbances, so are really in the category of sensitivities rather than allergies. For instance, viral enteritis (viral diarrhea) will often leave a child temporarily intolerant of the lactose in milk. Occasionally someone who has had an infection will become sensitive to the protein in milk. If all goes well and these substances are removed for a few weeks, the ability to tolerate them can be regained.

The most useful tool for diagnosing food allergy is removing, then challenging, with the offending food. (Skin tests are only partially successful in diagnosis.) In most cases, you can do the challenging at home by keeping the diet constant and varying the suspected food. However, food challenge can be dangerous if the initial reaction to the food has been serious or violent. The child who has had any marked reactions to food must be under a doctor's care and any food challenging must be done with a physician *present*.

Physical symptoms of allergic reactions to foods include: abdominal pain, vomiting and diarrhea; cough, runny nose and wheezing; skin itching and rash; headache and irritability; and shock. In addition to these physical syptoms, there are a number of pseudo-scientists who are selling books by saying that food allergies cause a number of behavioral problems, such as irritability, contrariness, sleeplessness, rebelliousness, and general nastiness. For the embattled parent, it is very tempting to believe that some external, definable, controllable force can be responsible for all these maddening traits.

It is extremely difficult to prove, or disprove, a food-allergy basis for a behavioral problem. (A good example is the research with hyperkinesis, which we will discuss in a subsequent section.) To prove that a particular behavior is caused by dietary intolerance, you have to keep the environment the same and change only the diet. Since behavior is so complex and changes so rapidly, it is very difficult to know whether the improvement is due to a change in diet or a change in other factors. A child may behave better after he is taken off Kool-Aid because he is sensitive to something in the Kool-Aid—or he may behave better because he is impressed by his mother's firmness in refusing to give in to his demands.

Eating and Behavior. People try to find nutritional solutions to problems such as hyperactivity, minimal brain dysfunction and learning disabilities. They aren't successful. To have a nutritional solution, you must have a nutritional problem. That is, a person can only be made better by nutritional supplementation if his symptoms are caused in the first place, by a nutritional deficiency. There is no evidence that any of these conditions is caused by nutritional deficiency. They are often *treated* with massive doses of nutrients, but the treatment doesn't work; in fact, at times it *causes* serious nutritional and physical problems.[10]

It is true that deficiency of almost any vitamin or mineral is likely to make someone behave differently, because he will be physically weak and susceptible to disease. People with iron deficiency anemia are lethargic and irritable. Some nutrients, such as niacin and thiamine, are particularly important for a steady and well-functioning nervous system. But if your child is eating a variety of foods and growing well, he is unlikely to be deficient in any nutrient.

Energy is the one nutritional factor that is likely to have an impact on your child's behavior. A child who is hungry is likely to be tired, irritable and contrary. Sometimes a hungry child is so contrary that he won't eat. The child who is very physically active and enthusiastic will often get so busy and involved that he won't notice he's getting hungry until it is too late. For a time, he will go on nerves and excitement alone, but will, eventually, collapse before your eyes into a screaming, unmanageable heap, or become even more frantically active in response to hunger.

The busy and active child is a likely candidate for a pattern of sugar jags, because he will want something he can get down in a hurry that will satisfy him in a hurry. Stand firm. Insist that he calm down and come to the table and spend some time eating. Once he gets there and finds out you mean business, he will likely eat just as enthusiastically as he plays. Be particularly careful to choose snacks for him that have a balance of protein, fat and carbohydrate.* He needs to have his food stay with him long enough so he can get some of his playing done. It's a real chore getting a person like this settled down and ready to eat. You'd better do what you can to provide food that will last him a while.

Hyperactivity. Beginning in 1973, the late Dr. Ben Feingold, a California pediatric allergist, argued that salicylates (naturally occurring compounds present in many fruits, some vegetables and a number of other foods), artificial colors and artificial flavors are causes of hyperkinesis. The Feingold diet eliminates essentially all manufactured baked goods, luncheon meats, ice cream, powdered pudding, candies, soft drinks and powdered and canned fruit drinks, as well as mouthwash, tooth paste and cough drops. The regimen also stresses includ-

---

*Look in the *Solid Foods* chapter, p. 239, for a table with protein, fat and carbohydrate content of foods, and in the *Regulation* chapter, p. 351 for a discussion on satisfaction.

ing the hyperactive child in food preparation, and encourages the entire family to participate in the diet program.

Because the Feingold regimen changes so many factors, it is hard to tell if it works and, if it does, what there is about it that helps. The child on this regimen is likely to get more attention as well as more firm limits. Because so many of the prohibited foods are high in sugar, the diet can improve nutritional status and help to prevent sugar jags.

Feingold claimed a marked improvement in over 50% of hyperactive children. Other, carefully-controlled studies have shown a much more modest response. A fraction of one percent of hyperkinetic children in controlled experiments show a mild decrease in hyperactive behavior. A very few preschool-aged hyperkinetic children appear to benefit significantly from the diet.[1,3]

Provided adequate vitamin C can be provided from "allowed" fruits and vegetables, the Feingold diet is not harmful to the child nutritionally. In fact, it may be helpful, because it strips away the high-sugar extras and forces reliance on home-prepared, basic foods. There is certainly nothing to be lost from eliminating artificial coloring and flavoring, nor is it all that difficult.

But the diet can limit a child's opportunities to eat out in many restaurants, and it will rule out the use of otherwise satisfactory convenience foods. The most serious drawback, however, may be that it could teach a child (and his parents) that his behavior is controlled by what he eats. It follows that if food controls his behavior, he (and his parents) can't, or won't have to. Thus he could be handicapped in the part of his social development that demands that he learn to curb and manage his emotional and behavioral responses.

If you are going to use this diet, I would encourage you to use it as an adjunct, not an alternative, to other behavioral and psychological counseling that you may enlist to help you evaluate and manage your family environment and your child's behavior. I would also encourage you to be subtle and matter-of-fact about your child's dietary restrictions. I don't think it's wise to emphasize any child's food intolerances or restrictions. You can be firm about food avoidance without making an issue of it.

Elevated Blood Lipids. Some few children may benefit from being started early on a special dietary regimen to control the amount of cholesterol and triglycerides in their blood.[2] These children have what we call "familial hyperlipidemia." They have inherited a marked susceptibility to heart disease, and are likely to be very sensitive to high levels of cholesterol or animal fats in their diet, and to react with elevated blood lipids. In some children this shows up as early as age two; other children don't show the family trait until they get into their twenties.

Children are at risk of having this trait if they have a close relative who has severe heart disease, particularly at a young age. Parents of this child should be tested to find out whether they have high blood cholesterol or triglyceride levels. If either or both of them do, the child should also be tested and followed to catch the trait if and when it appears.

Children who show signs of developing elevated blood lipids should be kept on a modified diet that limits saturated fats such as animal fat, coconut and palm oil, and hydrogenated shortening and margarine, and which substitutes, in moderation, polyunsaturated fats, such as safflower and corn oil. This diet also requires that use of cholesterol sources like egg yolks and liver be kept as low as possible. Get your doctor's advice about using this diet for your child, and consult with a dietitian for help in understanding and following it.

The course of action is less clear for people who do not have elevated blood lipids. Experts on heart disease have been arguing for years about whether everybody should follow a low cholesterol, modified fat diet in an attempt to lower the incidence of heart disease. Some consider the diet reasonable, moderate and desirable for everyone. Others think the changes are extreme rather than moderate, and say that such dietary intervention should be directed only to people who are clearly susceptible. I prefer to take an approach somewhere between the extremes. There are plenty of moderate and positive changes that can be made in the American way of eating that stop short of the therapeutic dieting we have talked about.

Avoidance of overeating and obesity is important.* Beyond that, Americans don't eat enough fruits and vegetables. They eat too little starch and too much meat, sugar, and fat. We could improve our diets and give our budgets a break if we would start using more meat-extender dishes like casseroles and soups, and even substituting beans for meat occasionally. We could eat a smaller portion of meat and a larger baked potato. We could choose lower fat cuts of meat and eat chicken or fish more often. We could cut down on frequency of frying. We could eat fewer sweets and drink less sugar-sweetened soft drinks.

All of these strategies would bring our diets back in better proportion to the basic-four food plan, which depends on the use, in moderation, of all types of foods to provide a healthful diet.

Vegetarianism. Children do fine on vegetarian diets as long as the diet is well-planned and includes milk, cheese and eggs. However, children on the more-restrictive vegetarian diets that omit animal protein sources may not fare as well. Some groups of vegetarian children are smaller than other children and have more problems with rickets, iron-deficiency anemia and malabsorption.[5]

For children, the major problem with the vegetarian diet is its bulk. Unless the cook makes a special effort to include fat with the meals, the vegetarian diet tends to be low in caloric density, and this makes it difficult for children to get their calorie requirement. Pro-

---

*This is <u>not</u>, however, the same thing as promotion of undereating and attempting to maintain excessive thinness. See the *Obesity* chapter.

tein can also be a problem. Legumes, seeds and nuts, in proper combination with grains, provide a high-quality source of the "meat and other protein" group. However, to get an adequate amount of protein from, for example, a beans and rice dish, a child would have to eat a volume of food that would be four to six times as great as if he were getting his protein from meat or cheese. Children who can't eat that much, and many don't, simply do not get enough protein.

One way in which insufficient protein limits overall nutritional status is by making the intestine less able to absorb fat. With poor fat absorption, a protein deficiency can exaggerate a calorie deficiency, and growth can fall off.

You must take some precautions if you want your child to be on a vegetarian diet.

- Continue to follow the basic-four food plan; substitute for the meat group, eggs, cheese, legumes (cooked dried beans such as kidney, lima and navy beans, or lentils) or seeds and nuts (especially peanuts). With the exception of legumes, vegetables are not good sources of protein but offer other important nutrients.
- Use vitamin D-fortified milk to provide calcium and vitamin D, as well as a concentrated source of high-quality protein and fat. If you are adamant about avoiding all animal products, substitute vitamin D and iron-fortified soy formula for the cow's milk. Do not make your own soy or nut milks or buy soy or nut milks from the health food store—these vary greatly in nutritional composition and generally do not give iron and vitamin D.
- Offer some concentrated source of animal protein at each meal, such as eggs, cheese or milk. Your child can get valuable amounts of protein from a vegetarian main dish, but he needs some help from a concentrated protein source in order to get enough total protein.
- Know what you are doing in combining vegetable protein substitutes for animal proteins. Study a reliable cookbook, such as *Laurel's Kitchen*.[11]

313

- Keep an eye on iron nutrition. About 3% to 8% of the iron in vegetables and grains (depending on what is in the rest of the meal) is absorbed, compared to about 20% of the iron in meat, poultry and fish. Without the well-absorbed iron and the "meat factor" from meat, poultry and fish, it will be more difficult for him to get and absorb enough iron from his diet. Be sure to keep him on iron-fortified baby cereal throughout the high-risk toddler period. Try to give a good source of vitamin C along with at least two of his meals every day to help him absorb his plant iron.
- Use whole grains only about half of the time, enriched refined grains the rest. Too much fiber in the diet can interfere with iron, copper and zinc absorption.[7] Enriched white flour, white rice and white macaroni products give some of the advantages of the grain without overloading your child with fiber.

There is nothing about the vegetarian diet that is inherently superior to the carnivorous diet. In fact, unless you have chosen to eat a vegetarian diet for philosophical or aesthetic reasons, you might consider drawing on the best features and enjoyable qualities of both. Use meat judiciously as a source of valuable trace elements, protein, iron and "meat factor." A small amount of meat in a largely legume and cereal dish can add flavor as well as nutritional value. Also learn to depend on legumes and grains as sources of protein, iron and trace elements. There are many wonderful dishes, including foods from other cultures, that are based on grain and legume combinations, such as Mexican tortillas and refried beans, Brazilian black beans and rice, and our own navy bean soup with crackers.

Fiber. For children as well as adults, it appears that a moderate amount of fiber in the diet helps good bowel function. The large intestine seems to work best when it has a certain amount of filling from a diet that has some indigestible residue of the sort that you get from whole grains, legumes, seeds and nuts and raw fruits and vegetables.

314

If a diet has a reasonable amount of fiber, it gives a stool that is formed, soft and somewhat bulky, and easy to pass without a lot of straining. Stools from a highly refined diet tend to be smaller, harder and more formed. If your child's stool is small and hard, it may hurt to go to the bathroom, and it could give her intestinal cramps.

To provide your child with enough fiber, offer an adequate amount of fruits and vegetables and use whole grain at least part of the time. Read the label on whole grain bread to make sure the first listed ingredient is WHOLE wheat. "Wheat flour" is not whole wheat, nor is "unbleached" wheat flour. It has to say WHOLE wheat. If your child won't eat whole wheat bread, try her out on graham crackers, brown rice or oatmeal cookies.

Don't overdo it on the whole grains, however. If she gets too much, it could backfire and give her diarrhea. Further, an extremely high-fiber diet, such as a vegetarian diet with a lot of legumes, seeds and nuts as well as whole grains, can cause nutritional problems.[7]

Looking Ahead.

Some day you will call your child to dinner and he will come willingly. Some day you will remind him to finish his dinner and it won't precipitate a major power struggle. When that day comes, your toddler will have changed to a preschooler and peace (relatively speaking) will come.

We're going to stop here in our discussion of feeding children. Although we are leaving off at the toddler stage, the nutritional and behavioral principles of feeding will remain the same as your child grows up.

Older children are easier to feed than infants and toddlers because they do not have such specialized nutritional and developmental needs. But they are also harder, because as they grow they increasingly develop their own ideas about what they want to eat and when they want to eat it.

With preadolescents, adolescents and teenagers, you will have to know when to be flexible and when to stand firm. You will likely have to loosen your controls on snack selection and eventually even meal selection. However, you will be wise to maintain consistent and reliable meals as the backbone of your family's food supply and to insist that your children, even your teenagers, show up for most meals. And it is appropriate for you to encourage snack selection that is nutritious and worthwhile. You will also be wise to insist on timing snacks so children are hungry for meals.

It is important to continue to be positive about your child's eating and food selection. You may have to overlook at lot to do that, but in the long run you will all be ahead. Children's nutritional status, at all ages, suffers from family criticism and interference.[8]

Selected References

1. American Council on Science and Health. Diet and Hyperactivity: Is There a Relationship? 1995 Broadway, New York 10023.
2. Breslow, Jan. Pediatric aspects of hyperlipidemia. Pediatrics. 62:510–520. 1978.
3. Consensus Development Conference. Defined diets and childhood hyperactivity.National Institutes of Health. IN Journal of the American Medical Association. 248(3). 290-292. 1982.
4. Dietary Goals for the United States, prepared by the Senate Select Committee on Nutrition and Human Needs, Superintendent of Documents, U.S. Government Printing Office. Washington, D.C. 1977.
5. Dwyer, J. T., E. M. Andrew, I. Valadian and R. B. Reed. Size, obesity and leanness in vegetarian preschool children. The Journal of the American Dietetics Association. 77:434–439. 1980.
6. Gerber Products Company. Current Practices in Infant Feeding. Freemont, Michigan. 1980.

7. James, W. P. T. Dietary fiber and mineral absorption. IN Spiller, G. A. and R. M. Kay. Medical Aspects of Dietary Fiber. Plenum. New York. 1980.

8. Kinter, Martha, P. G. Boss and N. Johnson. The relationship between dysfunctional family environments and the family member food intake. Journal of Marriage and the Family. August 1981. 633–641.

9. Monson, E. R., et al. Estimation of available dietary iron. The American Journal of Clinical Nutrition. 31:134–141. 1978.

10. Pipes, Peggy L. Special concerns of dietary intake during infancy and childhood. IN Nutrition in Infancy and Childhood. C. V. Mosby. St. Louis, 1981.

11. Robertson, Laurel, Carol Flinders and Bronwen Godfrey. Laurel's Kitchen. Nilgiri Press, Petaluma, CA. 1978.

9
Diarrhea

In most cases, the condition that is loosely termed "diarrhea" isn't diarrhea at all, but is simply an increase in the frequency or liquidity of the stools. True diarrhea of the kind that should concern you is better termed acute diarrhea. It is the sort that is caused by a virus or bacteria that makes the child truly sick—feverish or vomiting or both. With acute diarrhea you must be alert to the signs of dehydration, and vigilant about maintaining your child's fluid intake.

The child with other forms of diarrhea is generally not sick, but has chronic diarrhea. He has an increase in stool frequency that could be caused by any number of things—from teething to eating too much watermelon. The increased stool frequency of chronic diarrhea doesn't present the same threat of dehydration because such children remain thirsty and hungry, and their ability to absorb nutrients is not impaired.

You will need to make some dietary modifications to help your child recover from acute diarrhea. Other dietary modifications to *help decrease stool frequency associated with chronic diarrhea are optional—you would use them to help control the mess of diarrhea, not because they are necessary for the health of your child.*

Why are we talking about diarrhea in a book on nutrition?—Because diarrhea can have an impact on feeding.

For one thing, an illness causing diarrhea can spoil the appetite. For another, physicians and parents often react to diarrhea by putting children on various kinds of dietary restrictions; and sometimes the dietary restrictions are so drastic, or are applied so energetically that children actually end up not growing very well. In most cases the diarrhea itself doesn't cause the growth impairment. It is the diet.[5]

Although standard treatment regimens for diarrhea are improving, some health workers are extremely tenacious at clinging to traditional though questionably-effective therapies for diarrhea, because they know diarrhea can lead to dehydration. The diarrhea of the child who is truly ill, especially if it is accompanied by vomiting, fever, or both, can take a considerable amount of water out of a child's body. An infant cannot let his adults know he is thirsty, and can actually sleep himself into dehydration. If the dehydration goes too far, the child may have to be hospitalized and put on intravenous fluids. (While this is serious, it is unusual for this dehydration to get to the point of being life-threatening.)

Health workers, like parents, are also tired of diarrhea. Small children seem to have sensitive intestines that are easily upset by a variety of physical and emotional changes, from teething to going on vacation. So health workers spend a considerable amount of contact time with parents simply doing diarrhea counseling. The counseling often doesn't help and the diarrhea often doesn't go away. When my friend Mary Ellen announced her intention to resign her position as a pediatric nurse practitioner and go off around the world, she said the main thing she would <u>not</u> miss about her job was talking with parents about diarrhea.

Parents do worry. To them, an increase in stool frequency and wateriness is a sign that there is something wrong with their baby. And they know that diarrhea can be dangerous. But most diarrhea does not cause dehydration, and it is not harmful nutritionally. It is a terrible nuisance. Parents of infants with diarrhea do not hand their child to doting and dressed-up godmothers. Parents of toddlers with diarrhea do not visit friends with newly-carpeted living rooms.

Normal Bowel Habits

You need to know how to identify, evaluate and respond when normal bowel habits change into diarrhea. That is not easy, because nobody really knows what are and what are not normal bowel habits.[2]

Bowel habits vary greatly from one infant to another, and from one time to another for the same individual. The normal breastfed infant at 10 days of age is likely to pass 8 to 10 stools per day, and these stools can be loose, explosive, and vary in color from yellow to brown to dark green. On the other hand, a two-month-old breastfed infant not on solids may pass only one stool in two or three days. Some older children have one stool every three or four days. Others have two or three stools a day, again varying in consistency, color, and nature of passing.

Generally the most-desirable stool from the standpoint of comfort and convenience is a soft, somewhat-formed stool, that is easily passed without apparent straining. However, many healthy children pass watery stools with no apparent discomfort. Their stools are a problem only to their parents.

Overreacting to changes in bowel habits can be simply asking for trouble. When our Kjerstin was six months old, her stools changed from their usual—a formed, even semi-solid, once-a-day pattern—to a three-times-daily pattern that was consistently softer and almost runny. I was concerned and thought there was something wrong with her. We happened to be at the doctor's office for a regular appointment, and I told the pediatrician that I thought she had diarrhea. She told me quite abruptly that it was not diarrhea, that it was simply a change in bowel habits, that my daughter was really quite normal and there was no cause for concern.

I was miffed. I thought she had dismissed my concerns in quite a cavalier fashion, and that it was abundantly clear to me that she did have diarrhea. However, having been offered nothing else to do about it, I did nothing. I continued feeding Kjerstin as I always had—and I can't remember now if the stool frequency again changed back or if I just quit paying attention to it.

I am now grateful to that doctor for dismissing my concerns, however abruptly. I have seen too many other parents in very similar circumstances, who have been advised and supervised in treating the same kind of "diarrhea," to the detriment of all concerned. I have seen children put on liquids-only diets to "rest the bowel," or taken off milk for no apparent reason. At times I have suspected that dietary manipulations actually worsened the condition, and have seen parents positively dreading each bowel movement because they felt they must react to every change in bowel habits with dietary manipulations. I have seen children irritable and restless from hunger, and be allowed only crackers and juice because they were on some sort of a diarrhea-treating dietary regimen.

Types of Diarrhea

Diarrhea may be loosely defined as the passage of frequent, unformed or watery stools. It is a term, and a definition, that means little, because as I said, many babies and toddlers have a "normal" pattern of bowel movements that look very much like diarrhea.

A change in bowel habits becomes diarrhea when you have to change the socks as well as the pants—and it bugs you.

A change in bowel habits can also begin to look like and seem like diarrhea when your baby's bottom becomes red and sore after a few minutes contact with a dirty diaper, and he cries pitifully when you clean him off. While both of these conditions are highly undesirable, they are not critical or dangerous. A better term, and one that means something in terms of taking action, is acute diarrhea.

Acute Diarrhea. Acute diarrhea goes along with an infection, generally viral enteritis.* It can also come from contamination of food or drinking water with illness-causing bacteria. A child with acute diarrhea is likely to have fever, vomiting, or both, along with his diarrhea, so he is losing fluid from more than one place. To make matters worse, when a small child is ill or feels nauseated and has a sore throat, he is likely to refuse fluids as well as foods. As he begins to be dehydrated he will sleep more and refuse more, and may eventually end up seriously dehydrated.

The other major form of diarrhea, chronic nonspecific diarrhea, rarely becomes dangerous unless the child is not eating or drinking.

Chronic Nonspecific Diarrhea. Unlike the child with acute diarrhea, the child with chronic nonspecific diarrhea (which we will call "chronic diarrhea") is not sick. He eats well, appears healthy and energetic, has a normal pattern of growth and development, and doesn't seem to have any particular food sensitivities or intolerances.

---

*This may also be called viral diarrhea. It is characterized by sudden onset and is generally accompanied by vomiting and fever. Viral enteritis is often mislabeled as flu. Flu is influenza, which is primarily a respiratory disease. Its symptoms are cough, respiratory congestion, fever and muscle aching.

The child with chronic diarrhea simply has a bowel pattern which someone labels excessively frequent or watery (and probably with good cause, if that someone is cleaning up after it).

Chronic diarrhea comes in many forms. It can last a day or several months, it can appear intermittently or can be consistently present from day to day. There might be five semisolid stools a day or 10 liquid stools a day. Some people will even label as diarrhea the occasional runny bowel movement. Chronic diarrhea is one of the most frequent gastrointestinal complaints in childhood, familiar to every pediatrician and to too many parents.

Chronic diarrhea is not threatening like acute diarrhea because it is not accompanied by other dehydrating stressors. The child is well and alert, so he can let you know if he is thirsty, and if he drinks something he can keep it down. Because he is not feverish he will not be sweating excessively. And he will be hungry so he will be able to get his water and other electrolytes from food. Provided he is allowed to eat appropriately, he will be able to absorb the nutrients from his food and will remain adequately nourished.

It is hard to know what causes chronic diarrhea. Babies and young children react to changes or distortions in their diets with more-frequent and watery stools. They often get diarrhea when they are teething, have a cold, or have a change in water or schedule. Antibiotics will also cause diarrhea, probably because they disrupt the bacteria in the colon. At times, chronic diarrhea may develop following an acute bowel upset, although the child is no longer ill. Many times bowel habits return to their more-usual pattern once the stress has passed. Many times they do not.

Sad to say, many infants and toddlers have intermittent diarrhea lasting in some cases as long as three years. These children seem to have a normal pattern of growth and development and don't seem to have any particular food sensitivites or intolerances. This condition is hard to treat and treatment is frequently unsuccessful. (Although we will be looking at tactics in the next section.)

Chronic Organic Diarrhea. One of the persistent forms of diarrhea, chronic organic diarrhea, is distinguished from chronic nonspecific diarrhea by the fact that it is being caused by some disease process. The child with chronic organic diarrhea will show warning signs of the disease, including growth that drops off in weight and/or height, lung problems, abdominal pain, cramps, protuberant stomach, chronic fever, and blood in the stool.

If you see these signs you should let your doctor know so he can examine your child. Don't, however, alarm yourself unnecessarily. All children show lung congestion and have stomach aches from time to time, and it is normal for the young child to have a stomach that sticks out. It is only when these signs become marked that you should be concerned.

How Do You Manage Diarrhea?

Management of diarrhea first requires some sorting out of the type of diarrhea you are dealing with. You have to watch out for acute diarrhea; specifically, you must be prepared to take firm and prompt action to prevent the dehydration of acute diarrhea. Chronic, nonspecific diarrhea really presents more social and aesthetic problems than medical ones. Your goal in treatment of chronic diarrhea is somewhat diagnostic. By changing the diet you can find out what, if anything, is causing the loose and runny bowel movements, and, with any luck, get the stools to dry up a bit.

All the types of diarrhea are not the same. It's important to separate them out in talking about treatment, even if some of the principles of treatment are somewhat similar.

Managing Acute Diarrhea. The child with acute diarrhea is genuinely sick and in danger of becoming dehydrated. Your job is to see that that doesn't happen.

The Signs of Dehydration. Your job during the acute phase of your child's illness, is to: 1) maintain an adequate fluid intake to correct the fluid loss; 2) be alert to the signs of dehydration; 3) stay in touch with the doctor.

To assess if the baby is becoming dehydrated:

- Check his skin elasticity. Pinch a fold of skin on his abdomen. Does it spring back like it should?
- Check his mouth. Is it dry?
- Check the number of wet diapers. Is he still urinating?
- Check his fontanelle (the soft spot at the top of his head). Is it sunken?
- Check his eyes. Are they sunk back into his head?

If your baby is reasonably lively, taking oral fluids, and not vomiting excessively, you should be able to look after him at home, and not have to put him in the hospital.

If the first three symptoms begin to appear, increase your efforts to get him to drink more. The last two symptoms are later signs of dehydration. If your child's eyes or soft spot begin to sink in, you definitely should get in touch with your doctor.

Providing Oral Fluids. The amount of oral fluids you should try to get into your baby depends on his body weight. A baby up to 20 pounds will require about two ounces of fluid per pound per day to keep him hydrated. If he has diarrhea, is feverish and/or is vomiting, the fluid intake should increase to about three ounces per pound.[4]

The child over 20 pounds, because she has a smaller surface area relative to the rest of her body, and is better at concentrating her urine, doesn't need so much fluid. She can probably do all right on one to one-and-one-half ounces of fluid per pound.

In order to get this amount of fluid into your baby, you will have to keep at it frequently and insistently. Even when she is vomiting, she can take tiny sips of fluids; the older child can suck on crushed ice or popsickles. Good fluid choices include water, fruit juices, soda pop or ginger ale, jello and clear broth.

Beware of arbitrary rules about how long you should wait before you start to feed your baby again after she has had acute diarrhea, or about what you feed her.

When to Feed. Feed your child when she is hungry and interested in food. There is nothing to be gained by withholding food after she starts to get better, as long as the food is properly chosen.[6]

What to Feed. Food selection for a child recovering from viral diarrhea depends on the age of the child. Generally, keep the baby under age three months off cow's milk for up to a week.* Substitute a soy formula or hypoallergenic formula during that time. You should avoid cow's milk early on because the virus can change the young infant's intestine so it lets in whole protein molecules, which, in turn can cause an allergic response.

Continue to breastfeed. The lactose in breastmilk might make the stools more watery and gassy for a couple of days, but that problem will resolve itself. It is worth tolerating that to enable you to breastfeed. There is generally no other reason to avoid breastfeeding, since breast milk protein doesn't cause sensitivites like cow's milk protein does.

Keep infants and children over age three months off large amounts of cow's milk for about 48 hours after they start feeling better. The child still taking a lot of formula should be given soy or hypo-allergenic formula during this time. The child taking a substantial amount of solid foods can probably get along without milk for a couple of days. For the older child, the milk avoidance is primarily intended to eliminate lactose.[6] A viral infection often reduces the intestine's ability to digest lactose. (This is true for people of all ages.) If children continue to get lactose during that time, it will make their

---

*This is probably longer than is absolutely necessary, but it doesn't hurt to be a little extra careful in this case.

stools watery and gassy. Losing this extra fluid is, of course, more of a stress for the younger child, who has more difficulty maintaining fluid balance.

Figure 9-1 lists foods high in lactose. Limiting lactose intake to two or three grams at each meal or snack is probably a reasonable approach for the child recovering from acute diarrhea.

Figure 9-1. Lactose Content of Common Foods

Food	Quantity	Lactose, (grams)
Milk	1 cup	12
Yogurt	1 cup	10–15
"Hard" cheeses:		
Cheddar, Swiss, American	1 oz	1
Cottage cheese	¼ cup	2
Ice cream, ice milk	½ cup	5
Sherbet	¼ cup	2

With the exception of cow's milk and other foods containing lactose, resume a normal diet. Every family has a list of foods they turn to when people are sick or convalescing, and your family is probably no different. You may give starchy foods like toast and crackers, and such foods as eggs and cheese, and meats and vegetables when she has an appetite for them. Soups are good, like chicken noodle or vegetable beef. Don't go too heavy on fruits and fruit juices at first: it appears that young children react to excessive amounts by producing loose stools. But stay away from large amounts of custards, milk toast and yogurt.

It may also be wise to stay away from large amounts of sucrose, or table sugar, during that first couple of days after your child has viral diarrhea. In about one out of three cases children's ability to digest that sugar is impaired, as well.[3]

Routine Management of Chronic Diarrhea. Don't overreact to chronic diarrhea. Remember that looseness of stools is diarrhea only by definition. In many cultures, what we define as diarrhea is a normal bowel pattern. But there are some general procedures you should use in dealing with diarrhea:
• Continue to offer a balanced diet at the usual feeding intervals.
• Wait for the stress to pass before you assume you have a stubborn or chronic form of diarrhea.
• Keep your child as comfortable as possible.

   Diet. Continue to give a balanced diet, including all the foods that your child has been accustomed to having. Give the same formula, breastmilk or whole milk as always. It is only when children have had acute diarrhea that we recommend taking them off cow's milk, lactose, and sucrose for a while. Continue to give breads, cereals and crackers. Meats, fish, poultry, fat and vegetables should be given in the usual amounts. Go easy on fruits and fruit juices.

   There are a few things about diet that you should check or control more carefully for the child with non-acute diarrhea:
1. Make sure the diet has enough fat in it. There is some reasonably good evidence that diarrhea of the chronic, non-specific type may be caused or prolonged by a low-fat diet.[7] Some children who were put on low-fat diets by their families in an attempt to prevent heart disease or obesity developed diarrhea, and returned to more formed stools when given high-fat diets. Other children, who were put on low-fat diets as control measures for diarrhea, continued to have diarrhea, in some cases, for two or three years. Most of them improved when they were put on high-fat diets. The speculation is that the fat helps by slowing down the activity of the stomach and intestine.

   The diet of an infant and young child should have somewhere between 30 and 55% of the calories in the form of fat. To get this adequate level of fat, make sure you give formula, breastmilk or whole milk to a child under age two. Put a little butter, or, better still, margarine* on his bread and vegetables, and use meats, poultry and fish that have moderate amounts of fat in them. Make sure that a child taking 2% milk has at least one <u>extra</u> teaspoon of margarine or oil* for each glass of whole milk he <u>is</u> drinking.

2. Limit fruit and juice intake to two or three child-sized portions per day. Kids get loose stools from too much fruit, so there's no sense aggravating things. Of course, you know that prunes and figs contain a natural laxative, so keep those away from your child. Don't forget that fig newtons contain figs.

3. Hold down on sugar. Cut out the very-sweet candies, pops and desserts. If you have dessert, make it something that is not very sweet, such as ice cream or custard, and keep the portions moderate. A little sugar on cereal is OK, and a moderate amount of syrup on pancakes is fine, but be extra-conservative about sugar in general. If you give a child too much sugar, some may slip through into the large intestine and promote the fermentation and gas we talked about earlier.

4. Avoid artificial sweeteners. Not only is there some question whether sorbitol, mannitol and saccharin are safe for children, but there is also the problem that too much of these substances can give diarrhea.

Wait for the Stress to Pass. If teething appears to be the stress, you have little choice but to wait. You can try out some of the elimination tactics we will talk about later, but you may just have to tough it out. The same thing goes for colds, sore throats and the like.

As I recall, our Curtis had diarrhea every time we went on vacation. The first few times we took our home water along, but that really didn't seem to help. If we were gone long enough, eventually his stools went back to normal, but generally we would have to get back home before things would start to dry up again.

---

*The fat in margarine and oil appears to be better-absorbed by the young child than the fat in butter.

Keep the Child as Comfortable as Possible. That means, change a dirty diaper as quickly as possible. Sometimes, however, it seems that the stools are so irritating that you just can't be fast enough—their little backsides get sore and inflamed almost immediately.

The best thing is to make sure that the whole diaper area is greased generously with zinc oxide, petroleum jelly, or some other ointment that will stick on and leave a heavy protective coat.

Dietary Treatment of Chronic Nonspecific Diarrhea. After chronic diarrhea hangs on for a while, say over two or three weeks, and it begins to look like it's not going to go away by itself, you might want to (or be driven to) see if there is anything you can do about it. There are some dietary tactics you can try out to encourage your child's stools to be less watery and less frequent. They are tactics that won't hurt him, as long as you pay attention to maintaining a basically well-balanced diet while you experiment.

It's hard to tell what might help, or even if anything will help. One approach works for one child, another for another, and nothing for a third. The important thing is to list possible causes (or remedies), then go through the list, trying out one thing at a time. Wait at least a week after initiating one change before trying another, so you can tell what, if anything, helps.

1. Try a high-fat diet. Get a dietitian's help for this one. Keep eating records on your child for three or four days, and have the dietitian analyze the amount of fat that he generally takes. (While you are at it, have her evaluate his diet for any other distortions or inadequacies.) Then make a plan for increasing the fat in his diet, up to about 50% of his daily calorie intake.

    One university pediatrician reported about an 80% success rate using this approach for treating chronic, nonspecific diarrhea.

2. Eliminate sugar. This is a cumulative approach. To start with:
    a. Eliminate table sugar as completely as practically possible.

Avoid all obviously sweet foods.
- b. Eliminate citrus fruit and juice. Some children have specific intolerances to grapefruit and oranges and their juices. If that doesn't help, . . .
- c. Eliminate all fruit and juice. The goal here is to complete the process of getting rid of sugar in the diet, as well as to pick up on the occasional child who gets the trots from eating fruit.
3. Vary the milk.
   - a. If your child is on pasteurized milk, start out by using evaporated milk, diluted one-to-one with water. The theory here is that boiled milk is more easily digestible than pasteurized milk, and is likely to let less undigested nutrients escape into the large intestine.
   - b. Use lactase-treated milk or milk that uses some other carbohydrate source instead of lactose.
   - c. Avoid cow's milk altogether. The theory here is that it is not the sugar in milk but some other component that is causing a diarrhea-producing sensitivity.
4. Gradually introduce more whole grain. Start out by substituting whole grain about a quarter of the time for enriched white breads and cereals. Gradually increase to about 50%. It appears that in some cases shifting to a diet that gives more indigestible residue helps the colon to work better. It is important, however, to experiment gradually with this approach, as it can backfire. If a person gets too much fiber for his particular digestive tract, it can aggravate a case of diarrhea.
5. Include yogurt—about eight ounces per day. Use the unsweetened yogurt, and make it a little more appealing by putting in a teaspoon of sugar and a little fruit; it will still be lower in sugar than the store-bought presweetened type. Eating yogurt introduces lactobacillus bacteria into the colon. This can be helpful, providing the diarrhea is caused by overgrowth of less-helpful and diarrhea-causing colon bacteria. It is the same principle that

is used in the physician's prescription of acidolpholus culture. Some people swear by yogurt, or acidolpholus culture, as a way of controlling diarrhea caused by antibiotic therapy. Presumably, to be most helpful the yogurt "therapy" has to be instituted at the same time as the antibiotic therapy.

Keep in mind that if you are substituting yogurt for milk for an extended time, yogurt is lower than whole milk in two important nutrients: fat (if it is low-fat yogurt) and vitamin D. Both must be supplemented if low-fat yogurt is to substitute adequately for milk; and vitamin D must be supplemented with any type of yogurt substitution.*

6. If your child is developmentally ready, toilet train him. You *can* train a child who has diarrhea. They don't like being messy and will hold their stools. Then, as the stool gets to stay in the colon longer, more of the fluid may be absorbed and the stools may eventually be more formed.

I hope by the time you have gone all the way through this list that something has helped the diarrhea. Eventually your child will be toilet trained and he will be able to keep from messing. Colons, like children, grow up. Some day you will no longer know your child's bowel habits in intimate detail.

---

*Of course if you are making your own yogurt with vitamin-D fortified whole milk, it will be adequate in both nutrients.

Selected References

1. Cohen, Stanley, A., Kristy M. Hendricks, Richard K. Mathis, Susan Laramee and W. Allan Walker. Chronic nonspecific diarrhea: dietary relationships. Pediatrics 64:402–407. 1979.

2. Graham, G. G. Chronic "diarrhea" and diet. American Journal of Diseases of Childhood. 134:526. 1980.
3. Hirschhorn, Norbert. The treatment of acute diarrhea in children. An historical and physiological perspective. The American Journal of Clinical Nutrition. 33:637–663. 1980.
4. Holland, P. Diarrhea. Nursing (Oxford). 17:744–748. 1980.
5. Lloyd-Still, John D. Chronic diarrhea of childhood and the misuse of elimination diets. The Journal of Pediatrics. 95:10–13. 1979.
6. Sack, R. B., N. F. Pierce and N. Hirschhorn. The current status of oral therapy in the treatment of acute diarrheal illness. The American Journal of Clinical Nutrition 31:2251–2257. 1978.
7. ———. Role of dietary fat in chronic non-specific diarrhea in childhood. Nutrition reviews. 38:240–241. 1980.

10
Regulation of
Food Intake
and Body Weight

You can't control or dictate the
quantity of food your child eats, and you shouldn't try. You also
can't control or dictate the kind of body your child develops, and you
shouldn't try. What you can do, and it is a great deal, is set things
up for your child so she, herself, can regulate her food intake as well
as possible, and so she can develop a healthy body that is constitutionally right for her.

You can do this by providing her with regular and balanced
meals, and with the expectation that she come to the table and pay
attention to what she is eating. You can encourage her to get an
adequate amount of exercise. And you can seek the middle ground in
your feeding relationship by teaching her firm expectations of appropriate eating behavior, without dominating her with your own perceptions about quantity and choice.

Years ago, when I first began consulting in pediatrics, I made up a little feeding guide for infants, a guide to be distributed to parents by the nursing staff. The guide made recommendations, by age, for solid-food additions to the child's diet and told some of the reasons for the additions. I thought it was very nice, and that it would answer most of parents' questions.

However, about two days after they began using the guide, I got a call from one of the nurses: "the mothers want to know *how much* they should feed their babies." How much? I didn't know how much. I had raised three babies and I hadn't paid much attention to how much. That question really intimidated me: how was I going to tell them how much when I didn't know myself? What kind of nutritionist and mother was I?

I thought a lot and read everything I could and I realized that I still didn't know. There was nothing consistent on which to base a recommendation. I had looked at calorie requirements for infants (which varied), food-intake studies of infants (which varied), recommendations by pediatricians, nutritionists and nurses (which varied), and I had talked with parents about how much their babies ate (which also varied).

About the only thing I could come up with that made any sense was a guide to what was the *least* amount of solid food a baby could eat and still get his nutrient requirement, and that wasn't very much—either information or food. But, as far as saying how much a child should be eating, I was really stuck. I couldn't possibly answer.

I further began to realize that for me, or even the parent, to say *how much* was inappropriate and was taking away a right that belonged to the child. It was not for me to say how much, sitting in my office miles away from where the really-important decisions were being made. It was not even the parents' right to say how much a child should be eating, because the parent cannot experience the infant's hunger and desire for food: the parent can only respond to it.

Only the child could say how much, and that information was not going to fit on my neat little feeding guide.

How much is the topic of this chapter. *How much* should a child be eating? Like all questions without easy answers, the response to this one will take a while.

Food Regulation

The way you decide how much a child should eat is different from the way you decide what a child should eat. Nutritionists can tell you types and amounts of food that will provide a nutritionally-adequate diet. But again, nutritionists can't tell you how much to feed—only your child can tell you that, through communication of his own internal cues of hunger and satiety.

Proper child-feeding depends on a division of responsibility: You are responsible for what your child is presented to eat. He is responsible for what and how much he eats.

To go into more detail, you are responsible for:
• Controlling what food comes into the house.
• Making and presenting meals.
• Insisting that children show up for meals.
• Making children behave at the table.
• Keeping kids "on task" with their eating.
• Regulating timing and food at snacks (no food right before dinner).
• And all the things your grandmother said: no fanning the refrigerator door, no candy before dinner, etc.

However, parents are NOT responsible for:
• How much a child eats.
• Whether he eats.
• How his body turns out.

You will simply have to risk it.

Predicting Calorie Requirements. The parents who asked for guides on *how much*, wanted information that I simply couldn't give and that no one else could, or should, give.

Whether people are *willing* to give it anyway is another matter. Let me give you a couple of quotes from an article on "managing feeding," written by a pediatrician who is also a university professor of medicine:[3] "Parents are not likely to look up calorie charts, so it is necessary to give them guidance as to volume needed as growth continues." He goes on to describe how he figures out how much to tell parents to feed their children, and finishes by saying that this "provides approximately the caloric intake recommended by infant nutritionists."

That pediatrician has us nutritionists all wrong. We don't say what quantity an infant *should be* eating; we ask how much a child *is* eating. Particularly when growth is taking place, I do not presume to be able to dictate to *anyone* how much they should be eating. There are too many things I don't know about and that nobody knows about: activity level, calories required for growth, and ability of the body to squander and conserve calories in response to changes in food intake, and behavioral and psychological consequences of manipulation of food intake.

Every five years a committee of the National Research Council publishes the Recommended Dietary Allowances.[10] The Committee is made up of respected nutritionists who summarize current nutritional knowledge and make estimates about levels of nutrients required for health. Over the years they have had a very hard time making recommendations for calories. In 1980 they found their way out of their dilemma by stating that "allowances must be individually adjusted," based on "observations of appetite, activity, growth and weight gain in relation to the extent of deposits of subcutaneous fat."

The table reproduced below is from the current RDA book. The committee got the energy levels from observations of the food intake of large groups of people. Notice that at every age level there are wide variations in calorie levels.

Figure 10-1. Mean Heights and Weights and Recommended Energy Intake

Category	Age (years)	Weight (kg)	Weight (lb)	Height (cm)	Height (in.)	Energy Needs (with range) (kcal)		(MJ)
Infants	0.0–0.5	6	13	60	24	kg × 115	(95–145)	kg × 0.48
	0.5–1.0	9	20	71	28	kg × 105	(80–135)	kg × 0.44
Children	1–3	13	29	90	35	1300	(900–1800)	5.5
	4–6	20	44	112	44	1700	(1300–2300)	7.1
	7–10	28	62	132	52	2400	(1650–3300)	10.1
Males	11–14	45	99	157	62	2700	(2000–3700)	11.3
	15–18	66	145	176	69	2800	(2100–3900)	11.3
	19–22	70	154	177	70	2900	(2500–3300)	12.2
	23–50	70	154	178	70	2700	(2300–3100)	11.3
	51–75	70	154	178	70	2400	(2000–2800)	10.1
	76+	70	154	178	70	2050	(1650–2450)	8.6
Females	11–14	46	101	157	62	2200	(1500–3000)	9.2
	15–18	55	120	163	64	2100	(1200–3000)	8.8
	19–22	55	120	163	64	2100	(1700–2500)	8.8
	23–50	55	120	163	64	2000	(1600–2400)	8.4
	51–75	55	120	163	64	1800	(1400–2200)	7.6
	76+	55	120	163	64	1600	(1200–2000)	6.7
Pregnancy						+300		
Lactation						+500		

In most cases knowing the amount of calories that an infant or child is consuming is really unimportant, and just a matter of curiosity. Figuring that out for a normal child capable of making his needs known is a lot of unnecessary work, and may even be a detriment because it imposes an unnecessary element of external control. The child comes equipped with all the tools that are necessary to "individually adjust . . . energy intake on the basis of appetite, activity,

338

growth and weight gain." Our role in that process is not to figure out and provide a carefully calibrated number of calories. Our role is to feed him and see how he grows.

Predicting Calorie Intake

About the only time that parents and health professionals should get into the business of trying to figure out and manipulate calories is when there is something that is complicating the growth process. If the child is ill or has some physical disability that makes food intake more difficult, or that distorts energy output, then it may be necessary to manipulate calories. For instance, a child with a neuromuscular disease has a hard time eating and tends to burn more calories because of spastic muscle movements. A child with heart defects uses more energy breathing and circulating blood, and also has a more difficult time taking in food. In both cases we would want to know about how much that child is eating, because it might be important to try to increase calorie intake. In a similar way, if an apparently normal child seems to be growing poorly, knowing how much he is eating will help us judge whether we have a dietary or a medical problem.

Defending Constitutional Weight

But sometimes that child's growth potential and ability to regulate overcomes even our best efforts to manipulate it. Years ago a pediatrician asked me what I would recommend to increase the growth rate in little Alice Black. Alice was six months old, a beautiful, alert little child. However, she had gained only 3 lb. and 5 inches since birth. Alice's parents had taken her for a chromosomal examination and for endocrine tests to find out if anything was wrong with her. But no one could really say. Actually, other than her size, nothing really WAS wrong with Alice. She was just tiny.

The parents, of course, were concerned. They wanted to be sure that they were doing everything they could to encourage Alice to grow. But they said that she was very emphatic about how much she wanted to eat, and cried and fussed when they tried to encourage her to take more food. We decided we would try concentrating her formula.

We knew we would have to be careful in doing this. For one thing, we knew that giving her more nutrients and less water per unit volume of formula could dehydrate her. The doctor was alert to this, and saw her frequently to watch for any signs of dehydration. We also knew that we might just make Alice fat with our extra calories, so the nurse weighed and measured and plotted her carefully to make sure that if she got an acceleration in growth rate that it would occur in both height and weight. Alice was perfectly proportioned, and we didn't want to spoil that.

Then we set about modifying the formula. Since she was taking a formula that had more protein than she really needed, the first thing we did was add a little syrup, increasing her calories by about 7%. Alice responded by decreasing her volume of intake by 7%. Since that hadn't worked, we put her back on the regular formula while we reevaluated, and she immediately increased her volume back to its previous level. We then speculated that Alice may not have liked the increased sweetness of the syrup carbohydrate, so this time we tried fat, figuring that would change the flavor less. We again increased the calories by 7% and, once again, Alice was ahead of us. She cut her intake by 7%. Back on the normal feed went Alice, and back to the previous volume went the intake.

Our last try was simply concentrating the regular formula. We carefully took out some of the water to concentrate it by 7%; and Alice again decreased her intake. At that point, we gave up. Our only other option would have been to put a tube down and force-feed her, and none of us wanted to do that.

The parents decided that they simply had to support the growth pattern that was normal for Alice. They moved away and the last time I saw them Alice was nine months old, and weighed nine pounds. She was feeding herself tiny amounts of food from the table. She was pulling herself up and walking around things and startling everyone because she looked like a newborn.

I think those parents behaved in a very moderate and responsible way: they did what they could and then they left it up to Alice. Alice's father was a nutritionist, and he was as fascinated as I was by her ability to regulate her food intake and her growth. If Alice stays that small it will be hard for her, but at least her parents won't make it harder by struggling with her over her food in attempts to change her body.

The Body's Regulation

The body will regulate if you let it—or, at least some of the time, in spite of what you do to it. Your body has powerful regulatory systems built into it which allow it to maintain a more-or-less stable pattern of weight. There are systems of regulating food intake as well as systems for conserving or squandering calories metabolically, in response to deficits or excesses in calorie intake.[5]

If you look at yourself a moment, you will realize that in the last year, in spite of all the different ways that you have lived, eaten, drunk and exercised, that your weight has probably stayed pretty stable. Regrettably, even if you have tried to lose or gain weight you probably will have found that once you relaxed your efforts to modify your food intake, your weight returned to very near its original level. Even if you are ten pounds heavier or lighter than you were a year ago you will have missed an exact balance of calorie output and input by an average of only about 100 calories per day. You can hardly call that gluttony—or starvation.

341

The way growing children regulate is even more remarkable. Not only do they need calories for general bodily maintenance, as do adults, they also need the right amount of calories for growth. They get taller and heavier, and usually weight increases proportionally to height. Generally once children are established on a smooth pattern of growth for height and weight they adhere to that pattern very well.

And their level of food intake will reflect their needs. As their growth velocity varies, their food intake also varies to match it. The same thing happens with a variation in exercise levels. It is all automatic; the child can do it all himself with his own feelings of hunger and satiety. All you have to do is provide the food.

This physiological reality is in marked contrast to the societal view of body weight. According to the latter view, you choose a particular body weight or physique and you work to achieve it by managing your eating and exercise.

Even this wouldn't be so bad if the societal standard for body weight were broader or more realistic. Unfortunately, the standard is *thin*, and many people have a mind set about body weight that is consistently 10 or 20 pounds less than what their body appears to want. Even the standards for children are thin, to the extent that a parent of a blocky or chubby child often feels he is doing something wrong. The aesthetic standards may have little to do with good health. Most children go through a chubby stage. For adults, body weight as much as 20% above "normal weight"* does not appear to impair health (see the discussion in the *Obesity* chapter).

Many people spend their time engaged in a struggle to force their weight below its physically preferred level, or "set point." What they don't seem to realize is that to a considerable extent body weight is constitutionally determined, that physical, behavioral and

---

*"Normal" body weight is generally accepted as that defined by the Metropolitan Life Insurance Company, Actuarial Tables, 1959.

metabolic processes tend to defend that body weight, and that achieving a different body weight will be accomplished only at considerable cost.

The chart on the next page (Figure 10-2) gives a view of the complexity of the process which maintains body weight.

Most of us are aware that eating and exercise have an impact on body weight and on each other. Most people do not know, however, that there are other, and perhaps more powerful, physical, behavioral and psychological mechanisms that defend body weight.[4]

When people undereat, they get hungry and become preoccupied with food. Conversely, when they overeat they feel full and, if pressed too much to overeat, feel a very strong aversion to food. These are behavioral reactions which exert pressure to restore "normal" food intake.[4]

Physiological mechanisms work in the same way. When people undereat they feel tired and decrease their exercise, whether they realize it or not. Their involuntary muscle activity (heart and lung action, etc.) also decreases slightly. Metabolic rate, the rate at which the body uses energy, goes down as another way of conserving calories,[4] and there is accumulating evidence that people who undereat radiate less heat from their skin and thus conserve calories.[5] When you diet you get cold more easily.

When people overeat, the converse is true. Metabolic rate increases, heat radiation increases, and energy levels increase. For some people, this increase appears to be enough to defend body weight. Others just get fat.

Some experimental volunteers who are overfed require considerably more calories than predicted to gain over their normal "set point." Once the surfeit is ended, they lose back to their previous levels, after cutting calorie intake less than would be expected. Conversely, some underfed volunteers have to establish a larger than predicted deficit in food intake to achieve weight loss, and then gain back very readily.[4]

343

Figure 10-2. Regulation of Body Weight.

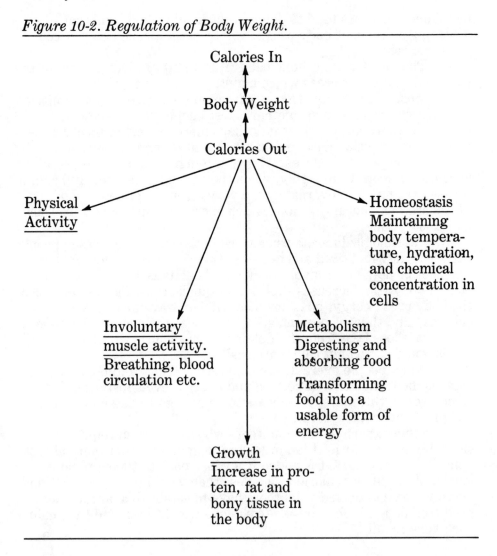

The point is that to overwhelm the tendency to regulate body weight appears to require considerable stamina. In fact, it could be that our attempts to manipulate body weight can backfire, and promote the very thing we are trying to prevent or cure. If underfed children become hungry and preoccupied with food, they will be likely to overeat when they get access to food. If overfed children become nauseous and revolted by food, they will be likely to undereat when they get a chance.

Parental Behavior and Children's Eating

Generally, children eat best when their parents are neither overmanaging or overpermissive. Mothers of small bottle-fed babies use more pressure tactics to get their babies to eat, such as pushing the nipple into the mouth, juggling it, and imposing a frequent set feeding routine. And the more active and controlling the mother, the less the baby eats.[9]

Appropriate parental attention may be a factor in obesity as well. Mothers of fatter children, ages four to eight years, talked less to their children during mealtimes, were less responsive, gave less approval, and made fewer efforts to control inappropriate behavior during mealtime.[1]

Teenaged girls, as well, showed poorer diets and higher frequency of low-quality foods when they came from families who were highly critical of their food intake.[7]

But undesirable as they are, poor eating habits may not be your worst problem if you interfere with food regulation. If the parent-child relationship about food is distorted, it is likely to distort the whole relationship. If you are attempting to manipulate or control your child's eating, it can spoil your relationship and it can have a far-reaching impact on your child.

Your attitude about your child is reflected in the way you feed your child. If you have an attitude of curiosity, relaxation and trust,

345

you will watch for his cues and respond to them. You will depend on information coming from him and be willing to let him develop the body that's right for him. On the other hand, if your attitude is one of responsibility and control, you will not be able to be trusting. You will have to supervise eating closely, and monitor growth, being ready at all times to step in and curb or influence the growth pattern.

Your child learns about himself and about the world from the way he is fed. Can he be trusting? Is the world trustworthy? If he has to fight and struggle for every mouthful of food, then it is likely the world is not very trustworthy at all. If his needs are met, on the other hand, in a supportive and consistent fashion, then it is likely that the world is trustworthy and he can, in turn, allow himself to depend on others.

In these feeding interactions he will also learn whether or not he has the capability to influence others. If he has to fuss and fight and struggle mightily to get his needs met, or if what he gets has little or nothing to do with what he wants, then he is likely to think of himself as not having much clout in the world. On the other hand, if other people respond to him in a prompt and appropriate fashion, he learns that what he wants and needs does matter and that other people will respond to him.

The way health professionals teach you to feed your child will have an impact on your attitude about your child. If we get out our growth charts and our feeding tables that specify quantities, then we are teaching you to be controlling. If we supervise your child carefully at all times to make sure he isn't getting fat, and take preventative action at every step of the way, we are teaching you to be controlling. And, worst of all, if we encourage you to put your child on a diet, we are encouraging you to be controlling in a way that is absolutely guaranteed to disrupt the entire family. That is very serious business.

A child can outgrow a diet that is less-than optimally chosen, as long as it is offered supportively and lovingly. However, outgrowing deeply ingrained attitudes about self and the world is devilishly difficult.

It appears, then, that a child has a growth potential that he tends to maintain and defend, and that to change that or modify it requires the most persistent of efforts. Further, it appears that any sort of major effort to manage or modify food intake can backfire and promote the very things we are trying to avoid, whether it is over-growth or undergrowth. And finally, parents who are either too over-involved or too under-involved with their children's eating appear to have children who eat less well.

The task that presents itself then, is to find the middle ground. What are the appropriate types of parental involvement and management, that are helpful and productive for children? And, further, how can parents set things up for their child so he can regulate well?

The Regulation Process

People regulate their food intake by getting hungry, by eating, by becoming full and satisfied, and by stopping eating. Your child's body will regulate if you let it. Your job is to support that process; to help set things up for your child so regulation works as well as possible.

More specifically, you need to train your child in deliberate, attentive consumption of satisfying and enjoyable food. Your key to accomplishing this goal will be your willingness and ability to tune in on and trust your child's signals of food regulation.

Make Eating Times Significant. From the very first, it is important for you to give your time and attention to feeding your child and paying attention to him, always observing and problem-solving to make sure the feeding process goes well. For the infant, that means using a system of trial and error to find out why he pulls off the nipple, or fusses, or spits up, or seemingly terminates feeding too soon. For the older child, it means paying attention to what promotes good eating, and managing him and the situation in such a way that he can eat well. We talked about this at length in the *Toddler* chapter.

Your willingness to give children the time and attention they need to allow them to eat well can have a big impact on how much they eat. As an extreme example, babies who are cared for coldly and impersonally do not thrive. Old studies from orphanages showed that babies left alone in their cribs had a higher death rate than those that were regularly fed, stimulated and cared for. The theory was that the understimulated babies died from lack of love. However, we suspect now that while the babies might indeed have died from lack of love, the major factor in their deaths was lack of food. The babies who were left alone were also fed rapidly and inattentively. The caretakers interpreted any interruption in the feeding as a sign of satiety and stopped feeding rather than soothing the baby and giving her time to go back to nursing. As the babies were fed less and less, they became less demanding, got less stimulation, and finally they became so lethargic and seriously undernourished that they became ill and died.[12]

Manage the Eating Environment. Keep food and reminders of food out of the picture until it is time to eat. You want your child to pay attention to his food and enjoy it thoroughly at eating time. Then you want him, as much as possible, to forget about it the rest of the time. If he is not thinking about food, he won't be panhandling and badgering all the time, or munching along in stomach-souring, appetite-spoiling little dibs and dabs.

I have yet to meet a child who has not been struck by a terrific hunger pang when the ice-cream truck drives up. Or one who is not immediately reminded of a cookie when he arrives at the home of the favorite aunt who always seems to have her cookie jar well-stocked. I would not for the world tell you that trips to the ice-cream truck are taboo or that the favorite aunt and the child have to be deprived of the delights of the cookie ritual. What I am saying is that there are external circumstances that remind people to eat, and that there are certain of these external circumstances that you can manipulate in regulating when and what a child eats.

If you have a cookie jar sitting on the counter and it is generally kept well-filled, it is likely that your child will have a fairly high frequency of cookie wanting. As a further example, if your child regularly eats in front of the TV set, he may set up an association between turning on the TV and wanting a snack, and may at times be reminded of eating when he really isn't hungry.

To manage the eating environment:
1. Set up the eating situation so that when he eats, he eats only. No TV, no comic book, no trucks.
2. Limit eating to one or two appropriate places in the house.
3. Keep food, as much as possible, out of sight.

Environmental control is a major tactic that is used by behaviorists to encourage and help people who want to lose weight. There, the goal is to cut down on eating. Our goal here is not to cut down on eating, but TO MAKE EATING IMPORTANT AND WORTH-WHILE.

Food Distribution. You want your child to come to the table hungry, so he is interested in eating and so his appetite heightens his interest and awareness of food. We do not want him to come to the table starved, so he is either too cranky to eat or so famished that he simply wolfs down his food and gets a stomach ache. Which it is to be depends on how often he eats.

Except for the increased incidence of cavities with all-day nibbling, we really can't say much about an optimum eating pattern. The pattern of food intake that promotes the most positive comfort and energy is a pretty individual matter and one that you may more-

349

or-less have to explore with your child. In general, depend on three
meals a day and vary the snacks according to his needs.

Select Foods that Help Regulation. A well-selected meal, with a
good distribution of protein, fat and carbohydrate, can help your
child regulate his food intake. Each of these nutrients has a role to
play in inducing some of the many satiety factors that let your child
know that he has had enough to eat.

The pattern of satisfaction you get from each when consuming
each separately appears to be different from the pattern of satisfaction from all of them consumed together. To be more specific about
this, using a series of graphs, we will speculate about what happens
to your sensation, level, and duration of satisfaction from consuming
carbohydrate, protein or fat. Generally these graphs present a
simplified version of the physiological parts of satiety.* The repre-
sentation ignores the psychological parts, like quality and taste, and
the personal parts, like preference and emotional state. They tell you
how and when the fuel from the meal becomes available, how long it
is likely to last, and how the physical properties of foods are likely to
affect your sense of satisfaction from eating. But before we can get to
the fun part, you have to have a lesson in food composition.

Food Composition. There are three major sources of calories
in the diet: protein, fat and carbohydrate (sugar and starch). The
only other nutrient that gives calories is alcohol. There is a table of
the protein, fat and carbohydrate content of foods in the *Solid Foods*
chapter, Figure 7-4. You get protein from the meat group as well as
from milk and milk products. You also get protein from cooked dried
beans and peas, and in small amounts from breads and cereal products.

---

*The whole issue of satiety is extremely complex. I have purposely oversimplified, to
give a general picture of how the nutritional components interact to *generally* affect
satiety.

Fat is often a separate food such as butter or oil, but it is often also contained IN foods, where it may not be noticeable. Most meats have fat in them, as do many dairy products. Fat is often used in food preparation, as in frying or in buttering or creaming vegetables. Fat is also used as a spread or as a dressing on other foods.

Carbohydrate comes in two forms: the *simple*, or sugar form, and the *complex*, or starch form. (The basic chemical structure of both forms is sugar, and starches are essentially made up of dozens of molecules of sugar, linked together.) The important difference, metabolically, is that starch has to be broken down chemically before it can be made available to the body, whereas sugar is virtually ready to be absorbed, as is, from the intestine. Sugar can be transported into the blood stream very promptly with very little digestive action.

Starch is found in cereal products, like noodles, rice and breakfast cereals and anything made with flour. Starchy vegetables such as potatoes, corn and lima beans are also good sources of carbohydrate. Sugar is found in nature in fruits and honey, and in sugar cane and sugar beets. Of course, the last two are refined and used mainly as brown or white sugars. Fruits and fruit juices, as well as cookies, cakes, candies, pop and sweetened fruit-flavored beverages are all major sources of sugar in the diet.

Take a look now at the "Satisfaction" charts. Each of the charts measures "satisfaction" on the left-hand side, or vertical axis; it has no number on it because it is really a general sort of feeling that is actually made up of several factors. It is hard to calibrate because it is so subjective. On the horizontal axis is time, which is also an approximation. How quickly you feel satisfied after you eat has something to do with bodily state (including mental state), as well as with the food itself—so these lines will have to be imprecise.

Sugar. Figure 10-3 (next page) demonstrates the kind of satisfaction response a child would get if he were at a fasting or hungry level and consumed only sugar. That sugar might be fruit or fruit juice. It might also be some kind of "sweet," like jelly beans or hard candy, or pop or a sweetened fruit drink. (Many sweets, like cookies, cake or candies, have fat in them as well as sugar, so you don't get the same kind of response.)

Figure 10-3. Satisfaction from Consuming Sugar.

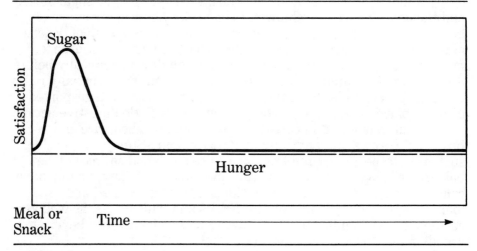

Notice that the satisfaction response to sugar is quite fast. In this case, the feeling of satisfaction probably comes from an increase in blood glucose, which is apparently one of many signals to the body that it has been fed. But the curve drops off just as fast; the sugar doesn't have much staying power. Once it is used up, the child who has had a sugar-only meal or snack will again be hungry and may even be cranky and unmanageable because of it. The sugar didn't MAKE him cranky; it just let him down before he got too far.

Starch. let's consider a sugar and starch meal, say one consisting of orange juice and dry toast. As you can see by the graph in Figure 10-4, the addition of the starch helps some in terms of extending the satisfaction period. The starch has to be disgested before it can be absorbed, and it can't be digested all at one time, so the nutrients get into the blood stream more slowly and over a more extended time.

Figure 10-4. Satisfaction from Consuming Sugar and Starch.

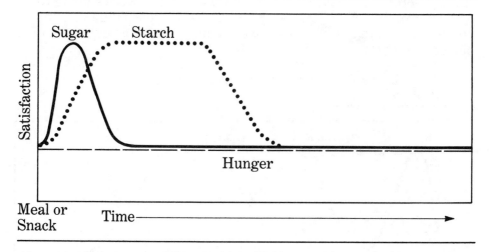

The nutrient that enters the blood is still glucose, because when starch is digested it is absorbed and carried in the blood stream as glucose. The sugar from starch is burned up by the body cells just as fast as that from refined sugar, but because it gets to the blood more slowly, it is likely to last longer.

With bread and starchy foods like cereals we are also adding other components of satisfaction: bulk and chewing. Bread is solid and it is bulky, so it gives your stomach a feeling of having something in it. Depending on the kind of bread you are eating, you are also going to do a greater or lesser amount of chewing. Some people depend heavily on chewing to let them feel that they have had enough to eat, so a tougher bread, like toast or bagels, is likely to give them a greater feeling of satisfaction than they get from squishy "sandwich bread."

   Protein. But let's say we know better than to have just juice and dry toast. We have been watching TV and have seen the ad for the high-protein breakfast cereal, and that is what we are going to have: a protein-fortified cereal, juice, and also some skim milk. In adding protein to our breakfast, we are likely to get a response to our breakfast that looks like the one below.

Figure 10-5. Satisfaction from Consuming Sugar, Starch and Protein.

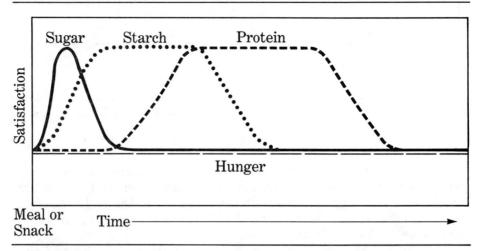

   The protein helps make our breakfast last longer. It takes a while for the protein to get to you, because it has to be broken down in the intestine into amino acids before it can be absorbed into the blood stream.

Eating a source of protein adds still another component of satisfaction to the diet: that of circulating amino acids* in the blood stream. Like increases in blood sugar, it appears that the body is able to sense increases in blood amino acids, and uses that as one of the bits of information supporting a sense of satisfaction. Skim milk is one of the few sources of protein in the diet that doesn't also have some fat associated with it. Egg white is a source of fat-free protein, and some very lean fish is almost fat free, but most sources of protein come associated with varying amounts of fat.

Fat. Once you add fat to an otherwise fat-free meal, you are likely to have quite a different picture of satisfaction. Let's have our same cereal-and-milk-juice breakfast, only now let's have a source of fat with it, like 2% or whole milk on the cereal instead of skim milk.

Figure 10-6. Satisfaction from Consuming Sugar, Starch, Protein and Fat.

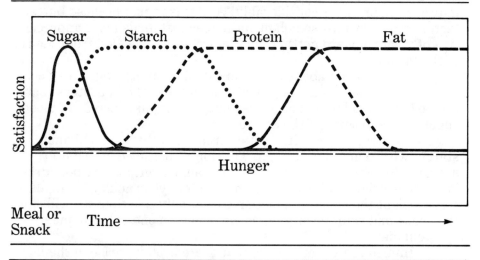

---

*Amino acids can also be broken down to glucose in the blood stream.

Fat is digested and absorbed slowly, so fatty acids from fat digestion get into the blood stream after sugar and amino acids, and fat is released to the blood stream over a more extended period of time than the other nutrients. But more importantly, presence of fat in the meal slows down the rate at which the whole meal is used. Fat retards the emptying time of the stomach. It keeps food in the stomach where it can be released more slowly to the intestine. Once there, it is digested and absorbed at a moderate rate, so that all accompanying carbohydrate and protein are also available to the body more slowly and over a more-extended time. So fat mixed with a meal makes the meal stay with you longer.

Also, when you include fat in the meal, you add on a couple of other components of satisfaction. One of them is just simple pleasure. Fat carries the flavor in food; addition of fat allows you to taste the food better and more acutely. You can taste the cereal when you have 2% milk rather than skim milk. A little butter on the vegetables improves their flavor considerably. And it isn't just because butter tastes so wonderful—somehow fat makes tastebuds more appreciative of what they are getting, and improves satisfaction from the rest of the meal.

Fat has a metabolic effect on satisfaction, as well. Fatty acid level in the blood stream is probably another of the indicators that the body uses to know that it has enough, and, like increased blood sugar, helps to turn off the desire to eat.

Omitting Starch. If we start from the other end and omit starch, we see another pattern. This might be called "the dieters' special." But for dieters or for anyone, a meal without carbohydrates is not so special at all because it may distort your ability to regulate. Let's look at the same satisfaction curve, only this time we will skip the sugar and skip the starch, as we would on one of the popular "protein diets."

Immediately you can see that there is an increase in the lag time before the arrival of satisfaction from this meal. Because the

protein breaks down so slowly, and because the meal has fat in it, it
can take quite a while before you feel satisfaction from the meal.
Your body will still manufacture its essential blood glucose from protein. However, the process takes a while, and that slows down the
blood glucose response. Furthermore, without the bulk of starch we
will be missing the full, substantial feeling of stomach filling and comfort.

Figure 10-7. Satisfaction from Consuming Protein and Fat.

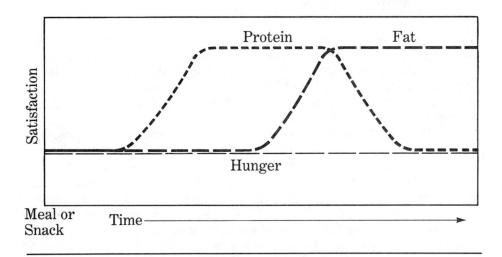

A major factor in food regulation, then, is to plan a meal to
include carbohydrate, protein, and fat, because they work best nutritionally when they are consumed in combination. It is easier to regulate the amount eaten at a meal that includes all three because all the
physical cues of satisfaction are present to signal you when to stop
eating.

You can vary your snack selection depending on the response
you want. If you want the snack to last two or three hours, choosing
all three major nutrients is a good strategy. If, however, it is five
o'clock and dinner is at six and your child is desperate from hunger, a
glass of juice or an apple might be a better choice. The fruit sugar is
quickly satisfying and has a good chance of allowing him to be hungry
a short time later.

Do you get the idea? Remember, A MEAL (OR SNACK)
THAT YOU WANT TO BE IMMEDIATELY SATISFYING, AND
ALSO TO LAST A WHILE, MUST HAVE PROTEIN, FAT AND
CARBOHYDRATE IN IT.

Treat High Calorie Foods with Respect. Before we leave the topic
of food composition and food regulation we need to discuss the regulation of very high caloric density foods: the foods that are high in
sugar, or high in fat, or both. These foods are harder to regulate.
They are very delicious and they are very concentrated calorically; it
is easy to eat too much of them.

With a particularly delicious meal of any nutrient composition,
it is the same: it is very easy to enjoy too much and end up eating
more than you would ordinarily. But, overeating at times is not all
that bad. Even people who are what I consider "normal" eaters
overdo it at times and eat until they feel quite full. It appears that
the body's process of food regulation is flexible enough to compensate
for this; it regulates food intake on a daily basis as well as on the
basis of longer periods of time. Overeating for one day or for a period
of several days is usually followed by a day or a period of undereating, as the body in some way accounts for those calorie excesses and
balances the ledger.

Teach Him to Savor the Flavor. But at the same time I say
this, I would also like to make the point that eating a great deal is
not the only way to get full value out of a particularly delicious food

or meal. There is another way that you can use, and it is a way that you can demonstrate and teach your child. That way is to be very attentive to your food—to taste and savor and expose all of your taste buds. Essentially, you can eat like a gourmet, getting all the sensations and pleasure out of the food that you possibly can. You can look at it, smell it, anticipate it, feel your teeth sinking into it, feel it in your mouth and taste it as you pay great attention to chewing it thoroughly, and generally doing as careful a job of eating as you can.

Approaching eating in this way can allow you to get a great deal more satisfaction out of the same or maybe even less food. And that is important when you are eating a food that is relatively high in calories. In fact, I would say that the higher-calorie the food you are eating, the more careful you should be to savor it. That way you won't have to overeat to enjoy it.

I am reminded of the old story of the man, finishing his lunch and asking for a second piece of pie: "This one is to taste. The other piece was so good I forgot to taste it." Too bad. The second piece never tastes as good, because part of the hunger is gone.

Make Wise Social and Emotional Use of Food. The problem is not that people eat when they are celebrating or depressed or lonely. The problem is that they do it poorly. Eating well can be wonderfully satisfying and relaxing. Many people comfort or soothe themselves with food, even though they try not to. And because they think it's wrong, they eat rapidly, or inattentively, or in some way that doesn't allow them to get the emotional solace they seek.

To allow food to be helpful for you emotionally, you have to be clear about what you are trying to do with food—and do it well. If you are depressed, it is a very good idea to take extra good care of yourself—find yourself something you really like to eat, put yourself in an environment that you find very pleasant, and be aware of letting the pleasure of the food raise your spirits. If you are uptight, food can relax you, if you will slow yourself down and concentrate, and allow the rhythm of the eating process to smooth you out.

This is not to imply that you should give your child a cookie when he scrapes his knee or is bored. It is certainly more appropriate to offer comfort or your reassurance that he can get interested in doing something. However, sooner or later he is likely to use food, to some extent, for emotional reasons. When that happens, you need to help him learn how to: first, respond appropriately to his emotional needs; and second, use food as productively as possible.

Maintain an Active Lifestyle. Getting an adequate level of exercise is essential to helping your body regulate appropriately. Exercise helps:
1. Tune the food regulation mechanism.
2. Burn off extra calories and body fat.
3. Maintain a good level of muscle tissue.

Tuning the Food Regulation Mechanism. We know very little about activity and food regulation in children, beyond knowing that children will vary their food intake to provide appropriately for their level of physical activity. We don't know whether this holds true for children, but adults must achieve a certain level of physical activity in order to regulate well.

As illustrated by Figure 10-8, when adults are at the extremes of physical activity (that is, markedly sedentary or very active), their food intake becomes disproportionate to their actual needs. A person in the sedentary range, rather than eating very small amounts of food to provide for the low requirements of the inactive lifestyle, actually tends to increase food intake above what he needs. At the other, and much less common, extreme of intense exercise, food intake tends to fall off, instead of increasing to very high levels to match the requirements of the exercise. The weight response is predictable. The sedentary, overeating person gains weight, where the exhausted, undereating person loses.[8]

Figure 10-8. The Relationship of Food Intake to Physical Activity.

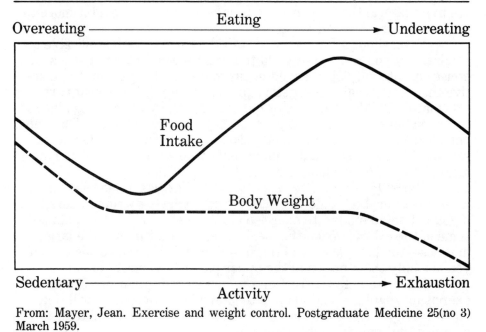

From: Mayer, Jean. Exercise and weight control. Postgraduate Medicine 25(no 3) March 1959.

Theoretically at least, you can make up for inactivity by conscious attention to regulating your food consumption at a level that will allow you to maintain your body weight. But that is going at it the hard way. It is much more functional, direct, and more likely to be successful to give your body the exercise it needs to regulate in a positive and automatic way.

The level of exercise that will allow you to accomplish automatic regulation appears to be an individual matter. The tall, thin person is likely to maintain his weight pretty well if he does little else all day but turn on the TV set. On the other hand, those of us who are more lateral than linear have to move around quite a bit more to achieve that sort of self-regulation.

Even though I have used *adult* data, they seem applicable to children—if you want your child to regulate well, let him get his exercise. A naturally placid child needs more encouragement to be active than a physically energetic child, especially if his parents are also placid. Children of all ages benefit physically from being allowed to roam about in as large an area as they can safely handle. They also benefit from a family recreation pattern that includes moderate, pleasurable exercise—and from parents who are capable of turning off that anti-exercise machine, the TV set.

Burn Off Extra Calories and Body Fat. Exercise uses up calories—everybody knows that. But not everybody remembers that if you get some moderate exercise after a meal it helps to squander some of the calories from the meal. Exercise that moves the large muscles—the hips, legs, and thighs—demands more calories than if you use only the muscles in the upper part of the body.

Exercise helps correct errors in weight regulation. If you are exercising regularly and happen to gain a little weight, it will take more energy for you to carry yourself around and you will tend to exercise that weight right off again.

Maintain Muscle Tissue. Regular exercise builds muscle tissue at the expense of fat. Since muscle tissue is more active metabolically than fat, the leaner body needs more calories to support it. Since lean tissue burns more calories than fat tissue, there is more of a margin of protection against eating too much and overshooting energy requirements.

In the whole area of food regulation we are dealing with a delicately balanced interaction of nutritional, behavioral, physical,

and psychological factors, an interaction that we know little about—
and even less how to manage or manipulate. Because the process is
so complex, we must be extremely careful about intruding upon it.
Changing or overruling the body's ability to regulate food intake and
growth potential can only be done against odds, and with the possibility of unacceptable cost. We can only speculate on the consequences of intruding on weight regulation.

We have talked about social cost to the feeding relationship,
and psychological cost to the infant. We can only wonder about physical and metabolic costs of producing a more-efficient body that maintains itself on less calories.

Our whole discussion of regulation supports what we have
been talking about all along: Trust the child's natural growth process.
Feed the child and see how he grows.

Selected References

1. Birch, L. L., D. W. Marlin, L. Kramer and C. Peyers. Mother-
   child interaction patterns and the degree of fatness in children.
   Journal of Nutrition Education 13:17–21. 1981.
2. Brazelton, T. Infants and Mothers. Delacorte, 1969.
3. Eisenberg, Bernard. Managing feeding problems in a busy
   pediatric practice. IN Problems Relating to Feeding in the First
   Two Years. Ross Laboratories, Columbus, 1977.
4. Jordan, H. A. and Levitz, L. A behavioral approach to the problem of obesity. Obesity and Bariatric Medicine 4:58–59. 1975.
5. Keesey, R. E. A set-point analysis of the regulation of body
   weight. IN Stunkard, A. J. OBESITY. W. B. Saunders,
   Philadelphia, 1980.
6. Keys, A. et al. The Biology of Human Starvation. University of
   Minnesota Press. Minneapolis, MN. 1950.

7. Kinter, M., P. G. Boss and N. E. Johnson. The relationship between dysfunctional family environments and family member food intake. Journal of Marriage and the Family. April, 1981.
8. Mayer, J. Exercise and weight control. Postgraduate Medicine. 25(3). March 1959.
9. Politt, E. and S. Wirtz. Mother-infant feeding interaction and weight gain in the first month of life. Journal of the American Dietetics Association. 78:596–601. 1978.
10. Recommended Dietary Allowances. The National Research Council, National Academy of Sciences, Washington, D.C. 1980.
11. Rose, H. E. and J. Mayer. Activity, calorie intake, fat storage and the energy balance of infants. Pediatrics 41:18. 1968.
12. Whitten, C. F., M. G. Pettit, and J. Fischoff. Evidence that growth failure from maternal deprivation is secondary to undereating. Journal of the American Medical Association 209:1675–1682.

11
Obesity

It is worth attempting to prevent obesity in children. While the obese infant has little increased risk of remaining obese until adulthood, the risk is greater for the fat preschooler, and greater still for the fat adolescent. Unfortunately we really don't know how to go about prevention. Dieting doesn't work, and we don't know what does.

However, despite the dismal reality of dieting failure, parents are regularly persuaded, by their own concern and by advice from others, to attempt to withhold food from their supposedly too-fat children. This often causes a struggle over food intake, with suffering and distortions on both sides.

Parents are deprived of a harmonious relationship with a contented child. The child is deprived of the security of knowing he will get enough to eat. Because he may be forced to go hungry, the child becomes preoccupied with food, prone to overeat when he gets the chance, and limited in the attention and energy he devotes to other pursuits. Dieting is generally sporadic. The pain of dieting is tolerable only for so long, and diets are abandoned, to be started another *day when motivation is higher or obesity appears to be a greater threat.*

It is vital that our attempts at prevention do no harm. Our tactics must be moderate, positive and permanent and our goals realistic. The essential task is to set things up for the child so his natural ability to regulate his food intake is distorted as little as possible by outside influences.

While accurate statistics on obesity are hard to find, it appears that less than 10% of infants who are obese become obese adults. The risk of developing adult obesity is increased to about 25% for the obese preschooler, and 70% for the obese adolescent.[13] The person who is obese as an adult has a considerable chance of remaining obese throughout his life.

Clearly, prevention of obesity is extremely important. The catch is being able to do it.

The Dilemma of Obesity

Here is our dilemma: We don't know how to define obesity, what causes it, how to cure it, or even how to prevent it. We have very little way of knowing what to predict or expect from a child. Some people seem to be genetically predisposed to obesity, and we have little way of knowing who they are or how to overcome that genetic tendency. We don't know if dieting helps or harms the situation or, indeed, if it has any effect at all.

We know that people who diet tend to reduce their metabolic rate, so they lose weight more slowly than predicted and regain the weight more easily. Most of the time when people lose weight they regain, and often they regain to a higher weight than before. If they manage to maintain their lowered weight, it is usually because they are able to tolerate a consistently lowered calorie intake, by accepting to some degree the symptoms of starvation, and usually, at the same time are able to maintain a consistent meticulous exercise program.

Most children lose their baby fat as they get older. We don't know if weight loss programs help or hinder this. If a program sets up struggles and anxiety around eating, it is possible that it hinders weight control.

Pressures to be Thin

Despite this sobering reality, most parents are concerned about obesity, and feel bound to intervene if their child shows signs of getting too fat. And their concern has been encouraged by health professionals. Physicians have charged themselves with the responsibility of preventing obesity in future adults by pressuring parents to keep their babies and little children slim. We nutritionists and dietitians have done our share in speaking out about the dangers of obesity and by promoting weight reduction efforts.

Like Dr. Frankenstein, I fear we have created a monster. But unlike Dr. Frankenstein, we have not done it alone. Gradually, over the last 30 years or so the national preoccupation with slenderness has increased to the point where it is now a major aesthetic concern, and even an obsession. Health issues have gotten lost as standards of appearance have become more and more narrow and unrealistic, and as people have done increasingly harmful things to themselves to lose weight.

Diet companies have become big business, many of them promoting severe, nutritionally-inadequate and expensive weight reduction regimens. To achieve weight loss, even people with a moderate or nonexistent excess in body weight are apparently willing to put up with "cures" that are physically more harmful than the condition itself. Many weight reduction regimens are so severe that they can only be justified when the obesity presents a serious health risk.

Physical Consequences

The health consequence of obesity is a very individual thing. However, it appears that at least moderate degrees of fatness are less of a health hazard than we had thought. People who are moderately overweight—up to 20% above currently-accepted standards—have been found in recent studies to reflect a health picture that is as good or better than that of thin or even normal-weight people.[7]

Above that level, obesity does appear to increase health risk. However, it is extremely difficult to sort out how much of a health risk it really presents. The obese person often has a history of erratic and poor nutrition, and fluctuation in body weight brought on by attempts to lose weight. Weight reduction diets may be severe and nutritionally inadequate. In particular, popular high-protein weight-loss diets are high in fat and often produce elevated blood lipids. Many times, rebounds from weight reduction diets are also nutritionally inadequate, and cause elevated blood lipids as people compensate with high fat foods that were previously forbidden. And even if a diet is low in fat, any weight gain causes blood lipids to increase, and may contribute to the process of heart disease.

Consequences of Chronic Dieting

In this struggle to achieve thinness there are not only physical casualties, but also emotional and social casualties. Disorders related to eating are on the increase: 1) Compulsive eating; 2) Bulimia,* which may include ritual vomiting (to compensate for eating and to

---

*Bulimia (or bulimarexia) is stuff-purge cycling. People with this disorder gorge themselves with food, and then get rid of the calories or weight by vomiting, exercising compulsively, or abusing laxatives or diuretics.

control weight); and even 3) Anorexia nervosa—self-imposed starvation. People with such eating disorders are preoccupied with food and with dieting, have distorted perceptions of their bodies, and are excessively concerned about body weight. Their struggle with eating and with body weight takes on the proportion of a major life issue, one that postpones or overshadows all other considerations. Taken to the extreme, it becomes a major disability.

Confusion about Normal Eating. Parents who are very concerned about their own weight reflect their concern in the way they feed their children. They are so preoccupied with preventing obesity that they forget about promoting normal growth. Parents who are chronic dieters have often forgotten what it is like to eat normally, as they veer between the extremes of the weight reduction diet and the compensatory eating that follows it. Because they are themselves confused about normal food regulation, they are confused about their child's food regulation. They feel constrained to manage and regulate that child's food intake.

And we health practitioners do our share—or maybe more than our share—to encourage that interference, with our willingness to weigh and measure and plot and devise strategies. At times, I am sorry to say, we get carried away by our enthusiasm, as did one of my associates when he advised a breastfeeding mother to restrict her chubby daughter to five, rather than seven feedings a day. He neglected to find out that the mother was already being careful not to overfeed her little girl. The mother tried to follow the advice, but fortunately gave up after two very trying days with her fussy infant. She was a wise mother. She acknowledged the doctor's warnings about increased risk of obesity but decided that she wasn't willing to follow the restricted regimen at the risk of losing her breastmilk or spoiling her relationship with her daughter. She was able to see that trying harder to restrict her daughter's food intake was making the situation intolerable for both of them.

That mother was right. Overenergetic attempts to regulate body weight may do more harm than good. In the first place, too little food, no matter whether it is wonderfully balanced, nutritious food, can cause nutritional deficiencies. If a person, particularly a growing person, is not allowed to eat enough, there is no way he or she can be optimally nourished. In the second place, overmanagement of the feeding process can cause distortions in self image and in the feeding relationship. Parents and children become locked in a struggle about eating, a struggle that distorts and damages not only the feeding process, but the over-all relationship. Third, overreaction to moderate degrees of overweight may, in the long run, promote more severe forms of obesity.

We discussed the hazard of too little food in the chapter on calories and normal growth, and we will deal with the third hazard later, as we discuss causes and control of obesity. Right now it is important for you to get a clear fix on the second: the impact of over-managing on the feeding process. This is best illustrated by a horror story.

Distorted Eating—the Story of Mary. Mary was suffering from bulimia; she was obsessed with food and with dieting, disliked and distrusted her body, and ate in a bizarre and extreme fashion. She would diet severely, so severely that she virtually starved herself. Then, when she couldn't stand the pain any longer she would stuff herself, and then she would vomit.

She wouldn't just eat enough to satisfy her hunger, because as far as she was concerned an amount of food sufficient to satisfy her was extreme overeating. Once she had by her standards overeaten, she would go on an eating binge, stuffing herself in a frantic fashion, eating whole cakes and butter by the spoonful, and virtually depleting the family food supply. Then, when her stomach became so bloated and painful that she could hardly stand it, she would vomit. She used her finger, pushing it far down her throat so she could retch again and again until she had no more left to throw up. Sometimes that would be the end of it. Other times she would repeat the pattern, stuffing and purging herself repeatedly in the course of a day.

Mary perceived herself as being fat, although she was not fat. She was about 5-foot, seven inches tall. She was heavier than "model" thinness, weighing 147 lb. And she was gorgeous. She was very nicely proportioned. In fact, she was perfectly voluptuous. She had the kind of body you only see in a teenaged girl—a very womanly body with a special kind of firmness and strength and physical vitality. But Mary didn't like her body. She said she was too fat and said she was so ashamed of her size and shape that she stayed home a lot, avoiding her friends and their activities.

Part of her distress about her body came from high school standards of body shape and size, and standards of thinness. Part of her distress came from the modeling school to which her parents were sending her in hopes that it would "make her feel better about herself." (In reality it just made her feel worse to be around all those skinny women with all that emphasis on appearance.) But the most powerful pressure came from home.

Mary's mother was thin, the kind of disciplined-looking thinness you only get when you work on your weight, and work hard. She had the model look about her—starved. That is a different kind of look than the one people get who are constitutionally thin, because those people look for the most part like their flesh covers their bones and like they are strong and healthy. Mary's mother looked fragile, and there was a quality of being forced about her, as if she constantly had to drive herself, physically and emotionally.

Mary's father was thin, too, but not excessively so. But he was the one who voiced their concern about Mary's "overeating." He said that Mary had always eaten a lot, and wondered how much it was normal for someone of her age to eat. In fact, he said, Mary had eaten a lot ever since she was born. When she had still been in the hospital, the nurse had brought her into the room and said "Your little girl certainly eats a lot—she had two whole bottles." Of course they thought eating a lot meant Mary would get fat, so they set out to prevent that. (Actually, I wondered if Mary was hungry when she was born—had her mother gained enough weight during pregnancy?)

From that day forth, Mary and her parents engaged in a struggle over her eating. From observing other parents with their supposedly overweight babies, I can guess what that struggle was like. I would guess that Mary's parents tried to feed her less than she really wanted to have. She has a lot of spirit, and I would bet that she was not willing to go hungry without a struggle. I'll also bet that she fussed and cried until she got more to eat. How long she had to fuss probably depended on how able her parents were on any given day to tolerate her fussiness. Her crying was no doubt upsetting, and the only way they could stop it was to do the one thing they didn't want to do—feed her.

I wonder if they got support from the pediatrician for their tactics. If the concern about obesity and the approach to its prevention was as energetic as it is today, I would say that they did get support. In fact, they may have been subjected to pressure and suspicion by the doctor, because Mary managed to get the food that she needed, and to grow and stay on the chubby side despite all their efforts to keep her thin. It's possible that the doctor assumed that they were not energetic enough in their efforts to restrict Mary's food intake, and put even more pressure on them.

Mary grew into what they perceived as being a chubby toddler, and by the time she was three she was sneaking extra food from wherever she could get it. Her first memory of mealtime is of her mother dishing up her plate for her with a limited amount of carefully-selected food. And she cried at the memory of never getting enough unless she sneaked to do it. For Mary, not getting enough food felt very much like not getting enough love. Her parents said they were doing it for her own good, but I wondered how much of their own egos were involved—how important it was for them to have a thin and what they perceived as being more-beautiful daughter.

Distorted Eating Attitudes and Behavior. Mary's eating response was extreme, but it is not unusual. Many people are so upset and obsessed about their eating and body weight that they really think of little else.

Hers is a very common attitude in people who are fat and who have spent their lives trying to be thin. In most cases they speak with resentment of the struggle that they had with their parents over food and their weight, and they carry their hurt that, no matter what else they accomplished in their lives, until they lost weight it wasn't good enough. Those people have kept their fat, and have become well schooled in their negative attitudes about their bodies. And they are completely deprived in their eating—they simply don't feel entitled to eat well. Even with all their dieting, they view their eating as being shameful and out of control. They fear that if they ever stop dieting and eat what they want, they will gain terrific amounts of weight.

The people who <u>don't</u> come into my office are the ones who would be able to tell the success stories. These are people who were chubby children who were allowed or helped to grow up to be normal-weight adults. I know that these people exist because the great majority of obese infants do grow up to be normal-weight adults.

I do, however, see a few success stories of another type. These are fat children who grew up to be fat adults, and still maintained a good attitude about eating and about themselves.

Learning Eating Behavior

Hilde Bruch, a psychiatrist who works in the field of eating disorders, says that she sees two different types of attitudes among obese people. One fat person will see the obesity as being a part of him, a body feature, and not the most important feature at that. He will have a sense of his capabilities and opportunities, and generally get on with his life. In contrast, another fat person will see the obesity as being the absolutely most important thing about him. He will see his fatness as a complete barrier, one that absolutely has to be removed before he will be able to get any sense of achievement or satisfaction out of life. Bruch says the thing that makes the difference is parental attitude. In the growing-up years the family of the first type will have supported him and recognized his potential in many areas. They may have regretted his overweight, and have even tried to help him get rid of it, but ultimately they maintained their perspective about his real sense of worth.[1]

The parents of the immobilized type of obese person, on the other hand, are quite different. As long as their child is obese they see something as being fundamentally wrong with him, they identify it as their failure, and they devote themselves to correcting the obesity. They take the child around from one weight specialist to another, demanding that somehow the child be made thin. And the more intrusive the helpers, the poorer the outcome—the more likely that the child will see himself as a fat person who will never be successful unless he gets thin.

We must be careful that our efforts at preventing or managing obesity do not go too far. It is clear from the discussion we just had that there is very real need for caution. We are entirely too glib and too casual about interfering with the process of food regulation, both in ourselves and in our children. Intruding on balance of food and weight regulation can be tremendously disruptive. Anything that we do to intervene must be done with a real sense of our own limitations.

You must also face up to a hard truth: Despite your best efforts, in some cases a child is simply going to be fat and there won't be anything you can do to change it. Then the task will be that of raising a child who, despite a handicapping condition, can be as physically and emotionally healthy as any other child.

Trying to Understand Obesity

In the area of obesity, our limitations are very real. As I said earlier, we don't even know how to define obesity. We don't know when a child crosses the line between a normal and desirable amount of body fat, to an amount that is excessive and undesirable. We don't know what causes obesity; people who are obese seemingly do little out of the ordinary to cause them to be fat and, once fat, only the most extraordinary behavior will allow them to be thin. And, since we don't know what causes the problem, we also don't know how to treat it.

The traditional treatment of overweight has been reduction in food intake. The fact that this course, if followed, results in weight loss does not necessarily mean that obesity results from excess calorie intake. Despite our national pastime of dieting, we still are a nation of overweight people. Would the problem be worse if we didn't diet, as so many people who struggle with their eating and their weight fear, or is all of our dieting really a factor in promoting the problem? Nobody knows.

But we have to do the best we can. Right now, let's spend some time talking about what we know and what we speculate about obesity: definition, cause and cure.

Before we get into our discussion of causes of obesity, we need to have a word about vocabulary. I will refer to the physical condition of having an excessive amount of fat on the body in a number of ways. I will call it "excessively fat," "obese," (which means the same thing) and simply, "fat." My use of the word "fat" is not intended to be derogatory. If anything, it is intended to desensitize a perfectly good and descriptive word that has too-often been used in a derogatory fashion. There is a "big beautiful woman" movement starting in California that insists on the use of the word *fat* to describe themselves. They say dignifying that term is as important for them as it was for blacks to adopt a reference for themselves that was dignified. I agree. When I use the word fat, I am thinking along those lines.

"Overweight" and "heavy" are terms I have avoided. Many "heavy" people are not fat at all—their weight comes from muscle and bone, or from a broader-than-average torso.

Defining Obesity. Parents dread being told their child is fat. Not only is there social stigma attached to fatness, but most people are experienced enough about dieting and struggles to manage weight to know that it is a long-term, disruptive and discouraging process. Defining a child as obese puts pressure on parents to begin this process.

Sadly, the diagnosis of obesity is often made on the basis of the most casual of observations. A child may look fat, and, even though fatness is normal for the infant and toddler, parents will be told the fat is excessive. Some standards say a weight above the 90th percentile of weight indicates obesity, even if his height is also in the upper percentile.

Other people are more methodical and reasonable at defining obesity in children, saying that a child can be suspected of being excessively fat if he or she is in the 95th percentile, *weight for height*.[3] If you remember our discussion in Chapter 4, this refers to the plotting which tells you whether a child is proportionally thin (less than 50th percentile) or "thick" (over 50th percentile). Whether that thick child is also fat is another story. Again, a heavy child may have a barrel chest or have heavy bones or have very muscular arms and legs.

The growth charts can be particularly helpful in watching for disproportionate increases in weight. From the growth chart in the example in Figure 11-1, it is apparent that the little girl grew

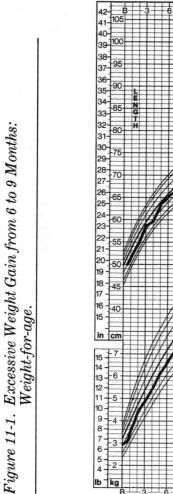

Figure 11-1. Excessive Weight Gain from 6 to 9 Months: Weight-for-age.

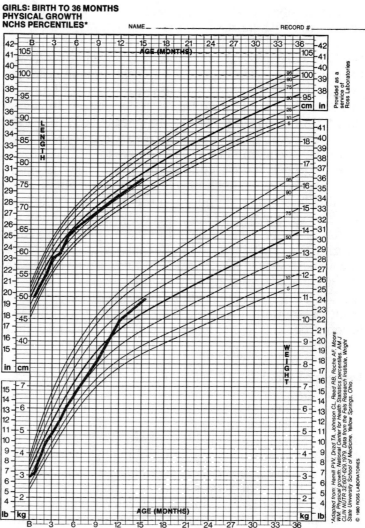

GIRLS: BIRTH TO 36 MONTHS
PHYSICAL GROWTH
NCHS PERCENTILES*

NAME _____ RECORD # _____

AGE (MONTHS)

LENGTH

WEIGHT

AGE (MONTHS)

*Adapted from: Hamill PVV, Drizd TA, Johnson CL, Reed RB, Roche AF, Moore WM. Physical growth: National Center for Health Statistics percentiles. AM J CLIN NUTR 32:607-629,1979. Data from the Fels Research Institute, Wright State University School of Medicine, Yellow Springs, Ohio.

© 1980 ROSS LABORATORIES

Provided as a service of Ross Laboratories

appropriately and was nicely balanced in weight and height, right
around the 25th percentile, until age six or possibly nine months.
Then her weight began to increase and, at age 15 months has reached
the 75th percentile; it is hard to predict whether it will level there or
keep on going. Clearly, some exploration is in order for this child,
particularly when we plot weight for length (Figure 11-2) and find an
increase from the 50th to the 95th percentile. In reviewing her history with her parents, we will be particularly interested in changes.
Has there been a big change in her eating style or her level of activity or her social and emotional environment? What is she eating, and
is she eating in a developmentally appropriate fashion?

Before we launch into our discussion about the causes of obesity, it is important to underline the point we made in the last chapter. The tendency is to appropriately regulate body weight. The
tendency is not, as is believed by many people, to continually gain
weight. We don't have to be eternally vigilant about "keeping it
down" with diet and exercise. And we don't have to be eternally
vigilant about preventing overgain in a child. The tendency is for a
child to grow in a smooth and fairly-predictable fashion and for the
adult to maintain a reasonably stable adult weight. Because the regulation process is so flexible, it takes a persistent and powerful force
to disrupt it.

Causes of Obesity. Obesity may be caused by any combination of
five factors:
1. Overeating
2. Underexercise
3. Social or psychological influences
4. Slow or inflexible body metabolism
5. Genetic predisposition to any of the above

Eating. Fat people of all ages do not eat more than people of
normal weight. In fact, in many cases fat people actually eat less.
For every obese child who eats a certain amount, there is a child who

Obesity

Figure 11-2. Weight-for-length Plotting of Figure 11-1.

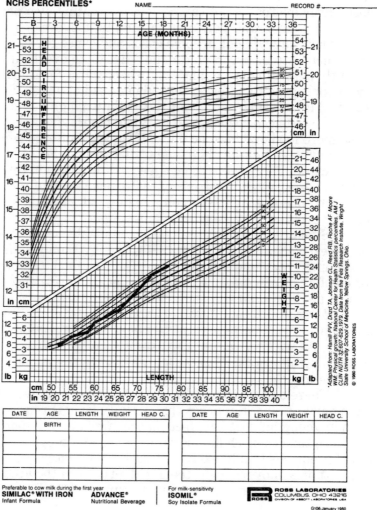

remains lean on the same amount. But saying that obese people don't necessarily overeat is not saying that overeating won't cause obesity.

As I have said, persistent attempts to override a child's satiety signals may win out in some cases and cause the child to overeat. There may also be errors in the diet that force overfeeding, like consistently mistaking the infant's signals of thirst for signals of hunger and inappropriately offering formula instead of water. Some children may find it particularly difficult to regulate a highly-palatable diet and will overeat in response to it. Some laboratory animals will consume more food and become obese if they are offered a delicious (to them, anyway) high-fat, high-sugar diet instead of the standard laboratory chow. There seem to be species differences in this predisposition to overeating on the basis of taste; one group of rats is able to maintain normal weight even on a highly-palatable diet, whereas another group will overeat and gain weight.

Similarly, if food is too readily available, some children may eat excessively and gain weight. If there is a family eating style of consuming great amounts of wonderful, rich food, or of offering food for comfort or reward, one child may get fat in response to it, even though another child will stay slim.

Exercise. Maintenance of an adequate exercise level is probably the single most important factor in the prevention and control of obesity. As we said earlier, consistent activity stabilizes body weight by burning off calories and fat stores, tuning the appetite and developing muscle.

There appear to be marked differences in activity levels from birth onward, and it appears that activity level is related to leanness, even in young infants. The fact that lean infants are more active, and eat more than their chubbier counterparts,[10, 12] suggests a constitutional predisposition to exercise that is also related to food regulation. Studies of overweight teenaged girls show they too eat less but move less than their normal-weight counterparts. By that age it is hard to tell whether constitutional or other factors (like embarrassment or difficulty moving) promote the inactivity.

But even if exercise is constitutionally influenced, environmental influences can also have an impact. A child's level of physical activity will vary for instance, depending on whether his parents are active and responsive, or more sedentary and placid. Parents vary in their willingness to let their children take risks and explore. A very cautious or controlling parent may be less likely to allow rough playing, and thus significantly curb the child's physical activity.

Social and Emotional Factors. There are certainly social and emotional factors in overweight. People in a variety of circumstances misuse food as a way of coping with stress or resolving conflict. Carried to excess, this can cause obesity.

A child's disruption in food regulation is at times the product of a disturbed family environment. Disturbed families are rigid, have poor communication patterns, and a high level of unresolved conflict. Because of their own problems, such parents show inappropriate levels of control and concern with children. They may be so over-managing that a child's failure to eat dessert provokes a family crisis, or so underinvolved that they do not even know where their children are at night.

Children in disturbed families develop patterns of coping that help them get by. They may become depressed and lethargic, or active and delinquent. They may choose overeating as a way of conforming, or gain excess weight as a way of rebelling. It appears that for a child to use food as a way of coping, rather than naughtiness or fingernail biting, eating has to be an issue in the family.[9]

Dieting appears to help set up the pattern of using food to cope. Compared with "normal" eaters, people of all weights who are chronic dieters tend to overeat rather than undereat in response to stress.[4] If a child has been raised dieting, he is likely to continue this pattern, and may also show periods of pronounced weight gain throughout his life.

Parents with hangups about their own eating send their children very mixed messages about eating. Most obese mothers are chronic dieters. (Because they are obese—not because they are mothers.) They often prefer thin babies, and can be very concerned about preventing obesity in their children. However, they tend to over-interpret hunger in their babies (they feed rather than looking for other causes of fussiness), BUT spend less time feeding. They also are more likely to use external cues for regulating feeding, such as time and quantity. To make matters worse, obese parents are prone to pressure from health professionals about preventing obesity in their children.[2, 14]

But obese mothers are not the only ones who have hangups about eating. Remember that Mary's mother was thin—but very preoccupied with eating. Slender parents who assign a lot of importance to physical fitness can have real conflict about feeding their children.

As a consequence, a child's eating experience may be inconsistent, erratic and emotionally charged. If the adult is anxious and inconsistent about feeding, the child can grow up with unreliable access to food, and having to struggle to get enough to eat. She may learn to distrust her own perception of her need for food, since it appears so often to be in conflict with her parents' ideas. On the other hand, if the parent is too ready to feed, the infant may grow up over-interpreting the need for food. She may learn the habit of using food for taking care of all kinds of discomfort, and end up eating more often than if she were depending on hunger as a cue for eating.

While we can say that many people appear to overeat, under-exercise and gain weight for social and emotional reasons, there are no consistent personality patterns in obese people. Obese people are no more depressed, dependent, anxious or uncontrolled than anybody else. They may simply have chosen a way of coping that disrupts their ability to regulate body weight.

However, even for people whose eating and weight are clearly related to psychological and emotional factors, resolving the emotional issues will not necessarily allow the person to lose weight. Psychotherapy has a very poor track record for promoting weight loss. Its benefit is in helping people feel better about themselves and improve their lives—at *any* weight level.

And finally, eating, or failing to eat, can have a major impact on people's emotions. People who are starving, whether or not the starvation is self imposed, become irritable and depressed and lose interest in other activities. They become tired and weak and think of little else but food. To function well emotionally you have to have enough to eat.

Metabolism. Body metabolic rate can have an automatic adjustment mechanism which serves to defend body weight at a preferred level. In starvation, metabolic processes slow down, muscle mass dwindles, voluntary activity decreases, and heat generation decreases.[6] These variations in metabolic efficiency can stack the deck against the person who tries to lose weight.

Dieters hit plateaus at low-calorie levels of eating, and have to restrict themselves even more severely to lose more. To maintain reduced body weight, they have to maintain continued food restriction.

A while back Erma Bombeck was lamenting confirmation of something she already knew. As she put it, thinking about food can make you fat. She had run across some research that was done at Yale showing that people who diet and are hungry and preoccupied with food may actually increase body efficiency with their preoccupation. Chronic dieters, when presented with a good-looking aromatic, sizzling steak, made more insulin in response than people who were not dieters.[11] Insulin increases body efficiency and promotes fat storage. In such cases, paradoxically, dieting may make us fat, if food deprivation makes people respond physiologically to food and less active metabolically.

The idea that there are metabolic differences that predispose to obesity has been almost totally rejected by physicians. Most doctors persist in their conviction that fatness is caused by overeating alone, and insist that the only way to control obesity is to stop overeating. Nutritionists and physiologists, who know more about metabolism, are less convinced that they know the answers. Indeed, they know it may be many years before they can be at all sure what is going on metabolically.

Until then, we know enough about metabolic responses to starvation to make us cautious. Drastic decreases in food intake, especially when they are not accompanied by increases in exercise, can shift metabolism into low gear and promote the regaining of any lost weight. Tactics for preventing or controlling obesity must therefore be selected with an eye to avoiding decreases in metabolic rate.

Genetics. Overeating and underexercise may turn some children into fat adults and have no effect on others, because of their different inherited factors.

Body build is inherited; a tendency to obesity appears to be inherited as well. Studies of identical twins who were separated early on and raised by different adoptive families found that the twins' weight resembled each other more than they did those of the adoptive families. From these studies come the often-quoted figures that if both parents are obese, the child has about an 80% chance of obesity; if one parent is obese, the odds drop to about 40%, and if neither is obese the chances drop to about 10%.

A person may be genetically programmed with respect to body composition, activity, sociability, aggressiveness, docility and even sharpness of sense of taste, all of which can in turn have an impact on energy balance. Other factors are even more clearly tied to genetics. Body build is a genetically-determined factor which has a

384

major impact on body weight and body composition. And as much as I hate to say it, *set point* of body weight may also be largely constitutionally determined.

According to the set point theory,[6] the body works actively to defend body weight at a certain preferred level. Weight, rather than varying in response to other factors, actually is kept very stable. Appetite and calorie expenditure appear to adjust in an attempt to defend body weight.

The set point idea is worrisome because it appears so hard to influence it. What if some people simply have an inherited tendency to be fat? What is to happen to them? Do they have any chance of maintaining normal weight with that kind of genetic handicap?

Those are absolutely impossible questions. There may, however, be some room for maneuvering. Genetically-obese strains of mice don't get as fat if they are offered ample opportunity for exercise; and to turn it around, the fattening of farm animals genetically-selected for tendency toward fatness can be accelerated by penning them. That gives hope that exercise can really make a difference.

To avoid getting fat, one who is genetically predisposed to obesity will probably have to be consistently careful about both diet and exercise. In fact, it appears that a genetic predisposition to fatness is better overcome with exercise than with diet, because the metabolic slowdowns that are produced by dietary restrictions can be at least partially reversed by increasing exercise.

Perhaps the issue should be considered in terms of controlling the *degree* of fatness. It may be that the genetically obese person will be somewhat fat in any event, and that is something that he will simply have to live with. Over-reaction to moderate degrees of fatness might only make the situation worse.

Diets and Other Cures

I am not going to spend a lot of time talking about cures or controls for obesity, because as I have said, very little has worked—once people become fat, it is extremely difficult for them to become and remain thin.

Almost twenty years ago, when I first went to the University of Wisconsin hospitals, we thought that the high-protein, low carbohydrate frequent-feeding diet was the answer. It turned out not to be. About that same time there were some people who were saying that the complete starvation diet was the answer. It wasn't. Then there was the protein-modifying fast. No, again. Five years ago, we thought that the behaviorists had the answer. What they did helped, but it wasn't the answer.

All of these approaches were based on the idea that overweight people are overeaters. Or, even if they weren't really overeaters, if they were willing to cut down on calories from their present level, and were patient in waiting for change, that eventually they would lose weight. That may be the answer, but there aren't that many people who are patient enough, long enough to find out.

Even people who are able to adhere to weight reduction regimens, and lose significant amounts of weight, simply do not maintain it. Difficult as it is to lose weight, the truly difficult part seems to be maintenance of weight loss. It seems that once the active phase of the program is discontinued, people usually regain to their previous weights, and often gain more.

Those are the hard facts. I think it is unrealistic to give some sort of paternalistic peptalk about how you can and must keep your child thin. It is possible that nothing you can do will keep your child thin, and that eventually you, and your child, and I, and all the rest of your helpers may have to face up to that fact.* At that point we may all need to tell ourselves that we have been moderate and consistent in our efforts and at least we have done no harm. We might

---

*If reconciling yourself to your child's weight is very difficult for you, you might consider getting professional counseling. Your strong feelings about your child's weight are probably related to the way you feel about yourself.

even have done some good. Your child might be more slender and more healthy physically than he otherwise would have been had we not tried.

To summarize: It appears that the obese person has a predisposition to energy storage, and that once the fat is stored it is very difficult to get it out of storage. Attempting to get rid of fat by use of weight reduction diets, particularly severe ones, may only make the problem worse. Calorie deficits reduce exercise and body metabolism, and increase hunger and preoccupation with food. Rebound eating from weight reduction diets, in combination with slowed metabolism and exercise, sets the dieter up to regain the weight, and often to store even more fat, which is, again, difficult to lose.

Preventing Excessive Weight Gain

Since we are concerned about *prevention*, and since we are working with growing children, it seems to me that our task is reasonably clear. We must try to prevent the weight-gaining phase of the obesity. We must try to prevent energy intake that is in excess of the amount that the child needs for growth, maintenance and activity. We must be vigilant, and we must do it in a way that is consistent. That means that we cannot use extreme methods that we can't tolerate for long, because rebound from the extremes is likely to exaggerate fat accumulation. We cannot, as one of my neighbors said to her chubby son, give up ice cream forever.

We are not talking about supervising every bite your child eats. Children, and adults as well, vary in their hunger and appetite from day to day. Children must be allowed to eat as much as they are hungry for. It is our task to set things up for the child so that his natural ability to regulate his food intake is being distorted as little as possible by outside influences. And we have to set things up for you so you know when you have done what you can. You need to be able at some point to leave the problem, and yourself, alone. You mustn't end up feeling responsible for every bite that your child eats.

Our task is made immeasurably easier if the child is active. Activity improves his ability to regulate his eating, increases lean body mass, and helps him to use up excessive calories.

Take particular note that I do not define outcome in terms of *weight loss.* I said the goal is to *lose fat.* There is a difference. A child eating moderately and exercising well can be successful in losing fat and gaining lean, and yet not show any difference on the scale. Since fat tissue contains about five times the calories of lean tissue, he could actually be losing calories from his body and still have a stable body weight. Eating in moderation can reduce fatness while sparing the loss of lean body mass, whereas severe dieting causes the loss of much more lean (relative to fat) tissue.

Defining Goals. In order to keep yourself feeling successful, it is important to be clear about what you can expect and realistically shoot for. If you are working on obesity prevention, you should keep in mind that you are basically trying to maintain a smooth and balanced weight-to-height ratio as your child grows.

The boy in Figure 11-3, although his weight was at a higher percentile than his height, maintained his pattern until he was about six years old. Then his weight began increasing rapidly until, at age 11 years, it had reached the 90th percentile. (By that time, he was well over the 95th percentile, weight for height—Figure 11-4.) The goal for him was to get his rate of weight gain to slow down so his height could catch up to it. Figure 11-3 shows that he accomplished that by the time he was 14.

Weight loss is not desirable for a rapidly growing child. For one thing, it could impair growth. For another, it could hook you into a cycle of depriving and then compensating with food. If a child loses some weight as a fringe benefit, say, from the change of seasons or from making some changes in family food selection, that is fine. I would hope, however, that that would not be more than a pound or two a month, and the younger the child, the less the amount. Keep in

Figure 11-3. Weight Variation in Boy from 9 to 14 Years of Age.

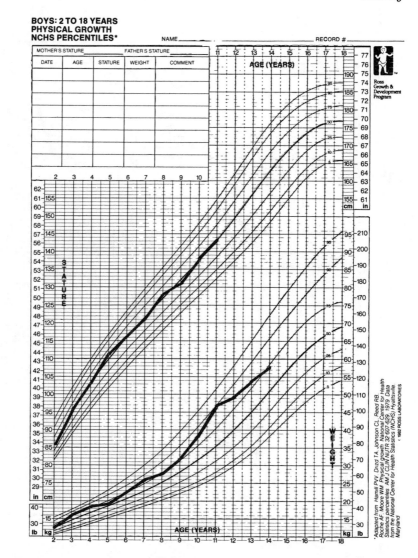

389

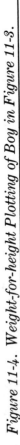

Figure 11-4. Weight-for-height Plotting of Boy in Figure 11-3.

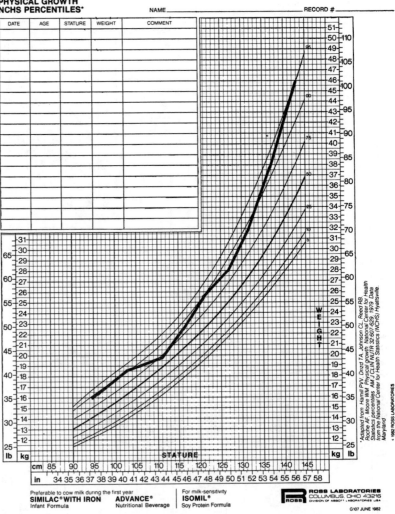

BOYS: PREPUBESCENT PHYSICAL GROWTH NCHS PERCENTILES*

NAME_____   RECORD #_____

DATE	AGE	STATURE	WEIGHT	COMMENT

Adapted from Hamil PVV, Drizd TA, Johnson CL, Reed RB, Roche AF, Moore WM. Physical growth: National Center for Health Statistics percentiles. AM J CLIN NUTR 32:607-629, 1979. Data from the National Center for Health Statistics (NCHS) Hyattsville, Maryland

© 1982 ROSS LABORATORIES

Preferable to cow milk during the first year
SIMILAC® WITH IRON   ADVANCE®
Infant Formula   Nutritional Beverage

For milk-sensitivity
ISOMIL®
Soy Protein Formula

ROSS LABORATORIES
COLUMBUS, OHIO 43216
DIVISION OF ABBOTT LABORATORIES USA

G107 JUNE 1982

mind that a child's weight is supposed to be increasing, and if it is instead going down, that can indicate quite a calorie deficit.

Strategy for Weight Control

The tactics that I am going to suggest now have the best chance of producing the results that we have just described, with minimal negative side effects. There are five important principles in the control and treatment of obesity in children:

1. We must prevent overeating. We must be careful to maintain sufficient but not excessive calorie intake (on the chance that we are dealing with a child who is very efficient at using his calories).
2. We must maintain a sufficient level of exercise (to maintain lean body mass, enhance food regulation and compensate for any inherited abnormalities in energy regulation).
3. We must be careful to avoid anything that will be likely to reduce metabolic rate, such as severe calorie deficits or restriction of physical activity.
4. We must be careful not to do anything that even *feels* like deprivation (as that sets up behavioral and possibly metabolic patterns, like excessive insulin production in anticipation of eating, that promote food-seeking and possible calorie storage).
5. We must select tactics that are positive enough and non-intrusive enough that they have a good chance of becoming a permanent part of life. We simply must not choose extreme methods which will be abandoned whenever the going gets tough.

In dietary management, the key strategy is prevention of overeating. Prevention of overeating is absolutely, unquestionably and emphatically NOT the same thing as promotion of under-eating. The latter is dieting, no matter how you disguise it.

As you no doubt have gathered by now, I am a real extremist about moderation. And nowhere are my views more extreme than in the area of dieting. I am unconditionally opposed to putting a child on

391

a weight reduction diet. We just don't know how many calories are needed by any one growing child, and we don't know whether our restrictions will impair growth and development. But that is not the worst of it. I consider the outright food deprivation characteristic of some diets to be so harsh and disruptive that it extracts a great penalty from the parent, the child and the relationship. YOU MUST NOT MAKE A CHILD GO HUNGRY. Enforced hunger implants in a child the fear that she won't get enough to eat—or the feeling that she is not entitled to eat. I have pointed out that that can be very destructive, in terms of long-term attitudes toward self and about eating.

Although we are avoiding dieting, we still have some ways of modifying a child's food intake. There are many indirect, subtle and moderate approaches you can use without making a major point to the child that you are managing his eating and are concerned about preventing obesity.

Your child is entitled to learn to trust his body. If you are too intrusive, you can spoil that trust. For example, you can make a big issue out of cooking meals and avoiding desserts, and you can make your child feel singled-out and deprived. Or you can generally cook in a low-fat, low-sugar way and opt for desserts only occasionally, and your child will grow up thinking that is how people eat. The tactics I am proposing represent the kind of firm and reasonable discipline that I think is appropriate for any generally healthy child.

Eating Behavior. Teach and model for your child slow, attentive and focused eating behavior. Your aim is to get her to pay attention to her food so she can get as much satisfaction as possible whenever she eats. Part of doing this is for her to pay attention to herself while she is eating, so she can be aware of her enjoyment and can tell when she is feeling full and satisfied. Meals and snacks that are truly satisfying can help cut down on the amount of times she ends up grazing for food, perhaps searching for the satisfaction that she missed at mealtime. If she is eating slowly and in an attentive fashion, it is likely that she will feel satisfied on less food, and it is less likely that she will overeat.

The first thing to think of to encourage slow and attentive eating is to model that kind of eating yourself. If you gobble your food, chances are your child will, too. If you enjoy and savor your food, your child will get the idea.

Teach your child to eat like a gourmet, not like a gourmand. A gourmand is greedy, a glutton. A gourmet is a connoisseur of good food. She gets considerable enjoyment out of eating, and enhances that enjoyment by being very aware of the food. She looks at the food, smells it, anticipates it, and when she eats it, she does so attentively and carefully, paying attention to the textures and flavors and temperatures as she chews thoroughly before swallowing. Eating in this way, the gourmet comes to realize that it doesn't take a great deal of food, even if it is wonderful food, to be truly satisfied.

But even great gourmets have to start somewhere, and you can start with your child by helping him slow his eating rate. Encourage him to put his fork or his sandwich down between bites, and not pick it up again until his mouth is empty. Encourage him to chew thoroughly, being careful to crush all the pieces and bits of food in his mouth. Coach him in keeping the food off the back of his tongue, because if it goes back that far it gets swallowed automatically, whether he is ready or not. And remind him not to wash his food down when it is still half-chewed. Again, be a good model for all of these behaviors.

There is room for firmness in encouraging this behavior in your child. I do not consider it too harsh and intrusive for you to insist that your child chew his food well and pay attention to his eating. Some people make a game of learning this, with family members reminding each other. Sometimes a timer helps, with the condition that the first helping must last a certain amount of time. For the child who hurries through her meal so she can get back to playing, you might try requiring her to be at the table a certain amount of time, whether she is eating or not. That would be just an interim tactic, however, because if she is sitting there with all that food around she could be reminded to eat more.

Food Selection and Meal Planning. Your ability to control the source of supply is your major advantage in influencing your child's eating. You can't determine how much your child eats, but you can control, most of the time, what is presented to him to eat. There are some good strategies you can use to help your child regulate his eating.

Provide Meals and Make Your Meals Significant. Having set and reliable eating times gives a child a sense of order and predictability. This predictability seems to have an impact on perceptions about eating. It seems that people who are in the habit of eating at regular times are less likely to pick up food at odd times. Even the hungry animal will be less inclined to seek food if it is not its established time to eat.

Plan Meals that are Satisfying. You can help your child to regulate his eating appropriately by the way you plan your meals. As you recall, when we were talking about food regulation we said that the components of satisfaction are: a) the relative levels of various nutrients in the meal (glucose, amino acids, fatty acids); b) the amount of stomach filling; c) the amount of chewing involved; and d) the amount of enjoyment and appetite satisfaction from the meal. As much as possible, in planning meals, try to provide the components of satisfaction. Translated into meal planning, this means:

• Include protein, fat and carbohydrate.
• Include something of low caloric density.
• Include something chewy.
• Include one or more food items that your child is likely to enjoy.
• Be moderate in the use of high caloric-density foods.

Protein, Fat and Carbohydrate. Reread our discussion in the *Regulation* chapter (p. 350), and pay particular attention to the discussion on the "dieters special" (p. 356). Don't be tempted to omit starch; it won't work.

Low Caloric-density Food. Bulky, low-calorie foods let your child chew and fill up without adding too many calories. If you can dilute out the overall caloric density of the meal a little with some low-calorie vegetables, that makes the meal somewhat easier to regulate.

The low-calorie foods that your child is likely to enjoy the most are fresh vegetables like carrot or celery sticks. And he will be likely to continue to enjoy them as long as he doesn't get the idea that they are a form of penance, and something you have to eat when you are too fat.

The lowest caloric-density foods that I can think of are the vegetables that I have listed in Figure 11-5.

These low-calorie vegetables end up supplying a moderate number of calories overall, even with a reasonable addition of cheese sauce or some butter. But use your head. A friend gave me a recipe for a zucchini casserole that called for a stick of butter and a cup of sour cream. The recipe said it served four people, which would figure out to 300 extra calories in fat for each serving. She said the recipe was delicious, and I have no doubt that it was. If you have a passion for that particular dish, that's fine with me; enjoy yourself. But don't kid yourself that just because it has zucchini in it that it is low in calories. That is the same thing as kidding yourself that carrot cake or zucchini bread or french fried onion rings are low in calories.

Something Chewy. Chewing is important for satisfaction as well as for promoting a strong attachment of teeth to the jaws. The raw vegetables described in the previous section can do double duty as something chewy as well. Also think of bagels or other tough breads, or a piece of steak, or some nuts or crackers.

Figure 11-5. Low-calorie Vegetables.

Asparagus	Eggplant
Bean sprouts	Endive
Broccoli	Greens—beet, chard, turnip,
Cabbage	kale, etc.
Carrots	Lettuce
Cauliflower	Mushrooms
Celery	Green onions
Chicory	Okra
Chinese cabbage	Pea pods
Cucumbers	Pepper
Escarole	Radishes
Romaine lettuce	Summer squash
Sauerkraut	Tomatoes or tomato juice
Spinach	V8-Juice
String beans—green or wax	

Something Your Child Likes. If you are going to make the meal significant for your child you will need to include something that she likes. That might be something as simple as a good bread. It might be a favorite casserole or a vegetable. If you are going to allow high caloric-density foods at all, I would really encourage you to include them at mealtime—don't imprint in your child the idea that the only way to get "treat" foods is to snack.

Be Cautious about High Caloric-density Foods. Anything that is fried or prepared with a lot of additional fat is going to be high in calories. Anything that is high in sugar may be also high in fat, and the combination of both makes for particularly high-calorie food. Because these foods are so delicious, and because each mouthful carries such a caloric whallop, they merit special attention. It may be that some people, like some animals, have a particular taste for fatty or sugary foods, and will overeat and get fat if given too-free access to them. Children in general, and some children in particular seem to love sweets.

It is a good idea to limit the frequency of particularly high-calorie, low-nutrient foods, and you can develop strategies for doing so. For example, kids don't have to have candy bars all that often, and it isn't really necessary to send potato chips in the school lunch every day. Most of us probably don't have to have desserts after every meal. And even if we really do prefer fried chicken, there are other ways of preparing chicken that can be most enjoyable, that you can use every other time or so.

The more you reduce the frequency of the high-calorie foods, the more you are cutting down on calories from those foods. You don't have to cut them out altogether. Nor do you have to make your changes all at the same time. If your children are accustomed to potato chips every day, you might just plan to run out before the end of the week. You can make gradual shifts in your menu planning, and a lot of times no one will even notice.

Don't Be Afraid of Starchy Foods. It is a surprise to most people to learn that breads, potatoes and other starchy foods are really quite moderate in caloric density, especially when compared with the foods that they often accompany, such as meats and cheeses.

People worry about eating starch because they think it is fattening. I talk with a lot of mothers who won't feed their children *any* "starchy" foods. They say their children love bread, potatoes, noodles and cereal, but that they really don't dare to give them to them for fear they will get fat. They should stop reading the "diet" books and relax. The idea that starch shoots straight into fat storage in the body is largely a myth. Starchy foods are not all that concentrated in calories, and they are so filling that they are easier to regulate. And they are satisfying because they are tasty.

Watch the Beverages. Here is where you get to discover the real, true, hard-nosed rigid me, because I am extremely opinionated about beverages. I think kids should avoid almost all beverages except for water, milk and juice, and that the last two should be consumed in moderate amounts. I think that pop should be saved for special occasions only, and I think that fruit-flavored powdered or canned beverages are an abomination—although I think their occasional use is unavoidable. (Actually, powdered or liquid fruit drinks are no worse nutritionally than pop, but the way they are advertised as being so nutritious and wonderful for kids irritates the dickens out of me.) Children should not expect that everything that they drink be flavored in some way. As you can see by the table below, drinking lemonade or pop, or even juice or milk in response to thirst can provide an awful lot of excess calories, and it can kill the appetite for other nutritious food. Water is still the best thing for thirst, and children should be encouraged to drink it.

Figure 11-6. Calories in Common Beverages

	Calories in 8 ounces
Whole milk	170
2% milk	120
Chocolate milk	250
Pop	100
Kool-Aid	100
Lemonade	100
Fruit juice	80–120
Canned fruit drinks	120

If a child is drinking rather than eating his food, or if a child is overdoing on the milk and juice, you may have to impose a limit. Depending on age, children need two to four cups of milk a day and, I think should be allowed an absolute juice maximum of about 3 to 6 ounces per day.

You can make and enforce a rule in your house: no juice or milk except at meals or snacks. Imposing a limit on milk might be easier if you keep the milk carton off the table and provide a glass of water to take care of thirst.

Control the Eating Environment. Set things up for your child so that as much as possible she is encouraged to eat intentionally, in response to a deliberate decision to eat. Reminders for eating (which often lead to unintentional eating) include being in the presence of food, and being in a place where food is usually eaten. In some cases these reminders are so powerful that they overwhelm a child's attention to his own hunger and appetite as a basis for making the decision to eat. The point is that it is helpful to the child to control eating stimuli, so that as much as possible he is encouraged to eat on the basis of hunger and satiety. You can decrease eating cues and encourage a deliberate decision to eat by controlling food access, and in effect complicating eating.

Control Food Access. As much as possible keep food out of sight and make it difficult to get at. Keep cookies in an opaque container on the top shelf. Keep candy in the refrigerator, and use the candy dish for paper clips. Your child may know the foods are there but he won't think of them as often as if they were sitting right out in the open.

You can control food access at meals, too. Try not to have a laden serving platter sitting in front of the child. Anybody will eat more fried chicken if they are looking at a big mound of it directly in front of them. Anticipating the second helping also makes it more difficult to tune in on and enjoy the first. Some people have simply stopped having serving dishes on the table, and serve directly from the pans on the stove or sideboard.

The child can serve himself, but the parent can still play the role of encouraging moderation. You can reassure the child that if he wants more, he can have more, but in the meantime he can pay attention to what he has on his plate and decide later if he is still hungry.

If a child eats too fast and then wants more, you can say, "Well, you ate that pretty fast. Why don't you just sit here a couple of minutes and see if you still want it." Then, if he does, be sure you deliver, or else he won't trust you the next time.

Complicate Eating. You can set things up to make eating consume time and effort, and thus force a deliberate decision to eat. You can forbid eating in the family room and in front of the TV. You can tell a child that he can eat if he wants to, but he must be sitting at the table to do it. Of course, "sitting at the table," for children five to seven years old, has a broad definition. Kids that age wiggle, stand up with their foot on the chair seat, and rock the chair back and forth and from side to side, and turn around and swing their feet. When asked to sit still they are puzzled—as if that was what they were doing all along. But, it passes, and until then, "sitting" means being within one foot of the chair.

Encourage Exercise. Appropriate eating regulation and weight control are absolutely dependent on exercise.

For weight management, the goals in exercising are threefold: expending calories, promoting and maintaining lean body mass, and fine tuning the food regulation mechanism.

Exercise that accomplishes all three goals most effectively is that which requires movement of the whole body, but particularly of the larger muscles, like the thighs and hips. For example, comparable exertion while walking or running requires more calories than does paddling a canoe, and swimming requires more calories than either. Exercise also requires adequate time spent in motion. Sports like soccer and swimming require more sustained movement than baseball or bowling, where the activity is sporadic.

When you set out to modify exercise, just like modifying eating, it is important to be both *moderate* and *consistent*. And as with eating, setting realistic goals, and adopting positive and pleasurable ways of going about it are also essential, in order to have an exercise program that will be maintained over the years. And years it will take. It won't work to go all out and get your child involved in a high-intensity exercise program that, like the diet, will be abandoned when the going gets rough. You may well get a rebound from that just like the rebound from dieting.

There are a number of ways you can encourage an increased level of activity.

Encourage Your Child to Play Sports. If there is a choice, encourage the sports that require more energy. And be sure that you let her play the sport for fun and recreation. Watch your own competitiveness and your own ego involvement. She doesn't have to be great to get what she needs from a sport.

Encourage Children to be Mobile. Let them get around in as much space as they can handle. For the toddler that may mean the living room or the back yard. For the older child that may mean walking 12 blocks to school or riding the bike to the library a couple of miles away. It's no great kindness to lug kids around to their activities when they can make it themselves. They will kick and complain and resist, but once they have gotten themselves used to things, they feel so independent and pleased—and sure it was all their own idea.

Build in Energy-burning Habits. Take the stairs rather than the elevator and take your child along. When you are looking for a parking place, talk to yourself about how it takes no more time to park further out and walk in than to drive around looking for a closer parking place. Encourage your child to put his things away as they accumulate, rather than doing it all at one time. And if he complains about having to go ALL THE WAY UPSTAIRS, turn a deaf ear.

Develop an Active Family Recreation Style. It helps if you like biking and hiking and playing badminton. If you don't, I don't know what to recommend for you, other than to say that surely there is some kind of active recreation SOMEWHERE that you can enjoy with your child. Some families are taking up square dancing or raquetball.

Regulate Television Watching. Television entraps children in one position and keeps them passive. Television ads also remind them to eat. Some behaviorists recommend having a child earn TV time with physical activity, matching every hour of TV with an hour of physical activity. I think the idea is good, but the proportion may be way off. Physical activity is much more important for children than TV, and time spent should reflect that.

The tactics that I have suggested to you, both for diet and exercise, are all indirect, moderate and positive. They cannot, however, be utilized without effort and consistency and discipline. The problems they address won't get "solved" permanently. You will still be setting limits on your child's eating. You will still have showdowns with him about eating in front of the TV or snacking right before dinner. It may take your energy and time and commitment to be sure that your child is presented with opportunities to exercise. And you will clash when you insist on his biking or walking rather than having you drive him. As the woman advised us when we bought our shetland pony, be firm, fair, and follow through.

I wish that I could say that if you do all of this that your child will not be fat. I can't promise that. All I can say to you is that you will have done what is reasonable and moderate, and stands the best chance of helping your child to achieve normal weight. At some point you may have to decide, as did the parents of little Alice in the last chapter, that although you regret the direction that growth is taking, you simply have to support your child in the pattern that is normal for her. If your child is too fat, you will have to let yourself off the hook of feeling that you are responsible, or that you have done something wrong. Eventually your child may get thinner. The chances of that are increased if you keep your efforts moderate, consistent and positive.

If your child seems to be heading for excessive fatness, there is a great deal you can still do to help. You can define the problem in a way that permits a solution. Instead of trying to fix things by getting your child thin, you need to help your child at her elevated weight to be as physically, socially and emotionally healthy as possible. You can be clear and consistent about your love and caring. You can be understanding and supportive about the difficulties of being a fat child, but you mustn't be overprotective. That will only teach her to use her fat as an excuse for not taking risks or taking responsibility for herself.

You can dress her attractively and not settle for ugly clothing. Heavy people can look absolutely stunning if they know how to dress well, and your child can, too. You can teach her ways of being assertive and not allowing other children to hurt her or bully her. You can allow her to respect her body by encouraging her to participate in activities at which she can be successful, and by letting her feel that her eating is appropriate. Even if other people think that overweight people are overeaters, she doesn't have to think that of herself.

All of this is very difficult. The societal values and attitude are quite the opposite, and you may have feelings that get in the way of your being able to be positive and supportive. Again, if you find you are unable to accept and support your child, at *any* weight, you should consider professional counseling.

In most instances you can best help your child by supporting her as she conducts her own affairs. But in some cases you can be helpful by intervening with other adults—the teacher or gymnastics instructor or scout leader or grandparent who puts pressure on the child to lose weight. At some point it may be necessary to say to them: "Your job is not to make my child thin. Your job is to help him learn to like and accept himself as he is."

A good teacher will help a child to achieve a sense of accomplishment and status in the classroom that has nothing to do with fatness or thinness. A good gymnastics instructor will be positive and flexible in what she expects from the child, adjusting demands to fit the capability of the youngster. A good scout leader will help children to get past discrimination, and reinforce a sense of worth in individual differences. And a good grandparent will treat that child like the greatest person in the world, just like all good grandparents do.

Selected References

1. Bruch, Hilde. Eating disorders; Obesity, Anorexia Nervosa and the Person Within. New York: Basic Books, Inc. 1973.
2. Dubois, S., D. E. Hill, and G. H. Beaton. An examination of factors believed to be associated with infantile obesity. The American Journal of Clinical Nutrition. 32:1997–2004. 1979.
3. Fomon, S. J. Nutritional Disorders of Children. Prevention, Screening and Followup. DHEW Publication No. (HSA) 76-5612. 1976.
4. Herman, C. P. and J. Polivy. Restrained eating. In Stunkard, A. J. Obesity. W. B. Saunders. Philadelphia. 1980.
5. Huenemann, R. L. Environmental factors associated with pre-school obesity. Part I and II. Journal of the American Dietetics Association 64:480 and 488. 1974.
6. Keesey, R. E. A set-point analysis of the regulation of body weight. In Stunkard, A. J. Obesity. W. B. Saunders, Philadelphia. 1980.
7. Keys, Ancel. W. P. Atwater memorial lecture: Overweight, obesity, coronary heart disease and mortality. Nutrition Reviews. 38:297–307. 1980.

8. Mayer, Jean. Some aspects of the problem of regulation of food intake and obesity. New England Journal of Medicine 274:610–616, 662–673, 722–731. 1960.

9. Minuchin, S., B. L. Rosman and L. Baker. Psychosomatic Families. Anorexia Nervosa in Context. Cambridge: Harvard University Press. 1978.

10. Purvis, G. A. Infant Nutrition Survey. Gerber Products Company. 1979.

11. Rodin, J. Has the distinction between internal versus external control of feeding outlived its usefulness? In G. A. Bray (ed.), Recent Advances in Obesity Research: II. London: Newman Publishing, Ltd. 1978.

12. Rose, H. E. and J. Mayer. Activity, calorie intake, fat storage and the energy balance of infants. Pediatrics 41:18. 1968.

13. Weil, W. B. Current controversies in childhood obesity. The Journal of Pediatrics 91:175–187. 1977.

14. Wooley, S. C. and Wooley, O. W. Obesity and women—I. A closer look at the facts. Women's Studies International Quarterly. 2:69–79. 1979.

12
The
Feeding
Relationship

T*he feeding relationship is all the interactions that go into working it out with your child about feeding. To be successful in feeding your child, you have to be able to share responsibility with him: You, the parent, are responsible for what he is offered to eat. But he is responsible for how much of it he eats. To share that responsibility, you have to be accepting of your child's abilities and limitations in feeding and responsive to his messages that let you know what, when, and how much he wants to eat.*

If you establish a positive feeding relationship with your child, you increase his chances of being well nourished, and of having healthy attitudes about eating and about himself and the world. Disruptions in the feeding relationship can produce an overly finicky child or one who eats too much or too little.

You might be having trouble with feeding because you have had poor advice about food and eating, because your child has been sick and you feel like he is vulnerable, or because you are having some emotional difficulties. If feeding is a struggle that just doesn't seem to get resolved, you should get some professional help in finding a solution.

We have talked about the feeding relationship in other chapters. It is important enough to talk about it in more detail here. The relationship you establish with your child in feeding can affect his food acceptance, nutritional status, growth and the way he feels about himself and about the world.

The feeding relationship is all the interactions that go into working it out with your child about feeding.[5] Parents come equipped with their ideas and attitudes and feelings about themselves and about their child. Children bring their temperament and genetic makeup[6]. And they work it out between them. Or fail to.

Let me illustrate.

Parental Behavior and Children's Eating

Kathy and her little boy were having a difficult time with feeding. He wasn't growing very well, and she had been told by the doctor that she "had to get him to eat more." And she tried. She figured out what he generally ate and presented it to him in the ways he liked it. And sometimes he ate and sometimes he wouldn't. He was getting rather naughty at mealtimes, and she was getting angry with him and more and more desperate about his eating.

We talked some along the lines I used in the "Toddler" chapter, about how she needed to be in charge of food selection, but that she should keep the pressure off him with eating. I suggested she simply present the food to him and let him pick and choose.

That got her started thinking. As she put it, she said to herself, "I wonder what's going on here." So she observed, and thought about it and tried to figure it out. And she noticed that she *was* offering him a variety of foods from the family meal, but she was offering them *one at a time*. And he was playing the toddler's favorite game: he was saying "No" and watching her try something different. With a lovely game like that, what child would want to stop it by eating the first thing he was offered?

So *she* stopped playing. And it helped. But it also didn't help. Their meals are now more tranquil and he is developing more of an interest in his food. But he is still growing slowly and she is still worried about it, although she tries not to let him know it.

Kathy and her husband have probably done all they can at this point. They have given their son a more complete physical examination to find out if anything is the matter with him. Nothing appears to be, so they are going to have to do the most difficult thing of all— wait and see how it all turns out.

Kathy was able to change her feeding situation because she was flexible and had some energy to devote to it. Claire's parents were a different matter. Their physician encouraged them to see a dietitian because their eighteen-month-old daughter was falling off her growth curve. They were having such pitched battles with her about eating that they were "afraid the neighbors would think we were beating her." The father would hold her head and force a spoonful of food between her lips, and she would scream. They could not explain why, although she ate virtually nothing at home, she reportedly ate "very well" at the day care center.

The dietitian advised the parents to stop pressuring her about her eating, to simply present the food to her, give her some help getting started, then leave her alone to do her own eating.

The dietitian told me about it, and I called them back a few weeks later. The mother said that the advice had been helpful. She had stopped forcing her daughter, and although "Claire's eating is still the pits, I don't worry about it any more."

On the other hand, while the mother had stopped pressuring her daughter, the father was still at it. He kept a bowl of food in the living room while they watched TV, and when Claire was distracted he slipped a spoonful of food in her mouth.

I asked the mother why she didn't tell the father to stop, and she said she hadn't thought of it. I wondered afterward if she was really interested in helping her daughter, or was more concerned about allowing herself to stop feeling responsible.

There is a lot to think about in working it out with your child about feeding. Helping you to work it out with your child is the focus of this chapter.

A Division of Responsibility in Feeding

Proper feeding demands a division of responsibility. It is your basic guideline in feeding children.

The parent is responsible for what is presented to eat.
The child is responsible for how much and even whether he eats.

Children will eat—it is normal to eat and grow properly. They have their own built in hunger and appetite and their own regulators that let them know when they need to eat and when they have had enough to eat. (I talked about this in the "Calories and Normal Growth" chapter, and talked about it more in the chapter, "Regulation of Food Intake.") Parents do not have to *make* children eat. But sometimes it gets to *look* like that, because the parent gets started pushing and the child gets started resisting, like with Claire. And eating gets lost in the struggle.

Children eat best when parents recognize their needs and go along with them. Children have their own unique sense of timing and pacing in the feeding situation; they have their own food preferences and vary in their eating capabilities. You really have to assume that all those characteristics are fine, and simply take it from there. If you behave otherwise and impose your own expectations, you get in the way of eating.

Research gives guidelines for feeding relationships. People have a lot of opinions about what it takes to make a child eat well. Some opinions work, others don't. Fortunately, we have more to go on than opinion. There has been quite a bit of good research on effective feeding, and we can use it to guide us.

Mothers vary in their approach to feeding. As part of her interest in infant attachment, Mary Ainsworth observed 26 mothers and their babies in the feeding situation.[1] She noted an enormous range of behaviors.

Seven mothers were very sensitive to their babies' signals and skillful about their feeding. They presented the food so the baby could take it easily, and they enjoyed each other in the feeding situation.

Three mothers were eager to get their babies on a schedule. To achieve that, they ignored their hunger and staved them off so long that they became over-hungry and upset. As a consequence, the feedings were tense and unhappy.

Four were impatient. They said they were feeding on demand, but they seemed so eager to be finished caring for their babies that they put them down whenever they paused or smiled or fussed during the feeding. Perhaps because the mothers wanted to get the feedings over in a hurry, the nipple holes were too big so the babies choked and gagged and paused in the feeding. When they paused, the mothers assumed they were full and terminated the feedings.

Five of the the mothers overfed their babies, some to gratify them and some to fill them up so they would sleep a long time. In the latter case, the babies spit out the nipple, struggled and tried to avert their heads. But the mothers were determined to get the food in, and they did. Needless to say, the feedings were also tense and anxious.

In five of the cases, the feeding was absolutely arbitrary in timing, pacing or both. In each case, the mother was having personal problems such as depression or anxiety that made her detached and insensitive to the baby's signals. These mothers put their babies away for long periods and either tuned out the crying or failed to perceive it as a sign of hunger.

Feeding times were erratic, as were feeding styles. Sometimes the mothers forced their babies to eat long past the point where they indicated they were full, and sometimes they interpreted any pause as satiety and stopped feeding. Feeding was at their own whim, and showed little reflection of the baby's wishes. Ainsworth commented in one case that a mother's determined stuffing of her baby "had to be seen to be believed."

Although she did not measure how much the babies ate, Ainsworth did note that the overfed babies were heavier, and the babies who were fed erratically and terminated too soon were underweight.

Feeding tactics can make a child fail to thrive. A nutritionist in Texas, Ernesto Pollitt, wondered specifically if mothers' behaviors could produce underfed children. He was working with Puerto Rican children who were not growing very well. In fact they were growing so poorly that they were classified as "failure to thrive," a diagnostic term that refers to serious growth failure. Pollitt compared their mothers' feeding techniques with techniques of mothers of babies who were growing well, and observed that the mothers of the poorly-growing babies were very active during feeding. They did a lot of nipple-moving and wiping and arranging of their babies and generally disrupted the pace of the feedings.

Children's characteristics affect feeding. A researcher in England, Peter Wright[7], wondered if there were characteristics of the baby that encourage their mothers to be overactive in feeding them. Wright compared the mothers of low birth weight babies with those of normal weight babies and further subdivided the groups into bottle-fed and breast-fed babies. He found that the bottle feeding mothers were more active with low birth weight babies. And the more active they were, the less the babies ate. Mothers would ignore their babies' responses and screw the nipple into the baby's mouth whether or not he was turning toward the nipple or rooting for it.

The moderately-active bottle feeding mothers in both low and normal weight groups had babies who grew better. On the other hand, all breast-fed babies grew about the same, whether they were low or normal weight. Even the babies' smallness didn't (or couldn't) encourage overactive breastfeeding. One of the advantages of breast-feeding is that you *can't* be over managing. You have to share the responsibility for feeding whether you want to or not.

In short, Wright found that parents' concern about their child's nutrition and growth often showed up as pressure tactics in feeding. Tiffany Field[3], a specialist in developmental disabilities, observed the same thing, both with parents of premature babies and with those who were post mature (born considerably after their due date). She observed that after babies were designated as being "at nutritional risk" pressure tactics in feeding began to emerge. Parents (and health workers) did more jiggling of the bottle and pulling the nipple in and out and jostling the babies.

We can understand why they did that—when someone seems to need help it is natural to try to help. But, ironically, the "helping" tactics backfired—the children ate less, rather than more, when feeders got pushy.

How it feels to the child. It is clear from the previous discussion that good nutrition and appropriate food regulation depend on the establishment of a positive feeding relationship between parent and child. The impact of this relationship becomes more clear if we imagine what it must be like for a child who is, after all, essentially a captive audience in the feeding situation. He is absolutely in his adults' power to satisfy his needs.

Hunger is a very powerful and potentially painful drive. Whether a child learns to fear or accomodate hunger depends on his early experience with feeding. If he cries to be fed and someone shows up promptly and feeds with some sensitivity to his abilities and preferences, he associates hunger with pleasure and it makes him look forward to what happens next. But if his caretakers are slow or inconsistent about responding to his hunger cries, or forceful and insensitive about feeding, it can make him feel anxious and desperate when he gets hungry.

There are lots of feeding experiences that can frighten a child. He might have to wait a long time to eat when he is hungry—so long, in fact, that he might wonder (on whatever primitive level babies and young children wonder at) if he will *ever* get fed. He might get started eating and then have to put up with a lot of interruptions. That could be frightening again, especially if his feeder is in the habit of stopping the feeding before he really gets satisfied. He might have food forced on him when he really doesn't want it. If you have ever had to eat when you really weren't hungry, or experienced the nauseated, too-full feeling that comes from having overdone it, you know that is not a pleasant experience. Someone commented that it "feels like the food grows in your mouth."

Children need help in recognizing and sorting out what they are feeling. A sensitive caretaker can help a child differentiate hunger from loneliness from wet pants. But if a parent is insensitive and repeatedly overlooks messages coming from the child or, worse, simply ignores or overrules those cues, the child doesn't become aware of what he is feeling. He never learns to express his wishes or feels the dignity of having his needs accepted and acted on by another person.

Eventually, the child loses track of what he is feeling and simply goes along with what his grownup expects of him. He still has the feelings, but he has trouble interpreting them, or, eventually, learns to ignore them. When he gets older, he likely will be embarrassed about a hunger or desire for food that is in conflict with what his mother or father seems to think is appropriate.

A few examples of feeding relationships. Most people successfully work out the feeding relationship with their children. The relationships or solutions might not be the ones I describe in this book, but they work. A few negative experiences won't ruin feeding forever. Things can go badly for a while, and people can still work it out.

Problems with communication. A colleague told about learning with his infant son, Jerrod, to use the bottle for feedings after the boy had been breastfed for the first five months. Their problem was that in the feeding process Jerrod would suck all the air out of the bottle and the nipple would collapse. Then the father would pull the nipple out of Jerrod's mouth to let more air into the bottle, intending to resume the feeding.

But Jerrod didn't know that. To him, having the nipple removed from his mouth meant the feeding was over. And *he* was still *hungry*. So he fussed angrily whenever they paused.

Eventually Jerrod learned that the feeding would continue after the interruption. He began voluntarily letting go of the nipple, waiting a few moments (while the air bubbled back into the bottle), and then going back to feeding. They worked it out, but it took some real patience and sensitivity on the father's part.

Sometimes you have to look farther afield to find the source of a feeding difficulty. This same colleague told another feeding story about his older son, Eric. Eric, too, was breast and bottle fed. He took to the bottle quite well, but started fussing at the breast. In fact, he seemed quite angry when his mother tried to feed him, and fussed and fumed for about 20 minutes before he settled down to nurse well.

414

The mother was concerned enough about it to call the nurse practitioner, who did a very careful and creative job of problem solving. It turned out that when the father was feeding his son, instead of cuddling him in the crook of his arm he was stretching him out in front of him on his lap. Eric preferred that, and he was putting up a fuss to let his mother know that he wanted her to change, too. Obviously, she couldn't, so my colleague had to change. He had to feed Eric cuddled close to him. And Eric didn't like it one bit. He cried and fussed and objected for an hour that first bottle feeding before he finally settled down to eating. After that, he protested less and less and, finally, the problem was solved.

Overmanaging feeding. The research we talked about earlier demonstrated that some children do not grow very well because their caretakers don't pay enough attention to them. Sometimes that inattentiveness comes in the form of the *wrong kind* of attention. Brian's mother said she had to force in every mouthful her son ate or he wouldn't eat at all. At age three, he took an hour and lots of pressure from his mother to eat a simple meal. And he was falling off his growth curve.

Brian had been born at the 50th percentile, where he stayed for the first fourteen weeks while he was breast fed. Once solids feeding was initiated he didn't grow as fast, and his growth fell to the 10th percentile by age 18 months. Then he started to grow faster again, and returned to the 50th percentile by 26 months. But, once again, over the next ten months his growth fell, and when I saw him at 34 months it was below the fifth percentile.

The circumstantial evidence was pretty strong that the problem was Brian's mother's overbearing behavior. During the time when he was growing better, she had been ill and unable to keep her usual tight control on him. But when she got better, she went back to putting a lot of pressure on his eating. And he fell off the growth curve again.

A parent's insensitivity to a child's cues can clearly take the form of being overbearing. But not all children fight back the way Brian did. Some are docile and allow their parents to overstuff them deliberately. I was astounded to watch one example in an airport.

I heard a timer going off near me, and located the source as a woman holding a baby who looked to be about five months old. She stopped her timer, and took from her bag a jar of baby food and one of those horrid little syringe-action feeders. She loaded the syringe, and from that, loaded the baby. No other word describes it. She simply saw to it that he consumed what she wanted him to consume. When the food was gone, she returned the apparatus to her bag (I hope she at least washed it the next time she got near water) and reset her timer.

The baby was just like a little slug. He was absolutely placid and totally uninterested in what went on around him. My imagination may have been too fertile, but it seemed to me he felt very hopeless.

Withholding food from a "fat" child. If you feed (or try to feed) a child less or more than he really wants, it can produce the opposite of what you want. Children who are overfed become revolted by food and prone to undereat when they get a chance. They also become skillful at manipulating their parents to do what they want them to do by refusing to eat.

On the other hand, children who are underfed become preoccupied by food and prone to overeat when they get the chance. Recently I worked with a two year old boy, Todd, whose parents were very concerned with his "overeating." As they told it, Todd wanted second helpings even when he had eaten quite a lot. He was "always" asking for food. When they put out a plate of cheese and crackers for their company, Todd was right there, eating steadily as long as the supplies held out.

His weight fluctuated modestly, and MAY have been increasing disproportionately to his percentile curve. But to his parents, his weight pattern was beside the point. They saw his EATING as being abnormal, and that is where their major concern lay.

416

Mother was bulimic. She was thin, but very concerned about her weight and always putting pressure on herself to lose. She starved herself and then binged and then vomited, sometimes two or three times daily. She had absolutely no faith in her ability to automatically regulate her food intake, and was always curbing and restricting herself. Or attempting to. And she treated Todd the same way.

As I explained to the parents, the more they tried to restrict Todd's eating the more pressure he put on eating. He felt like he had to put up a struggle to get food.

To help Todd, his parents had to get the pressure off him. To do that, I treated the mother's eating to help her relax and trust her own food regulation processes. I also worked with both parents in understanding Todd's ability to regulate his own food intake and setting reasonable limits for him. It helped—Todd stopped being so demanding about food, and the last I saw them they had had company and Todd ate a couple of crackers and went off to play.

Emotional deprivation and food regulation. Sometimes children overeat because their parents are so preoccupied with their own problems that they can't provide for their childrens' emotional needs. The children try to provide for themselves instead with food and they get fat. That seemed to be what was happening with Ben. He had gained 23 pounds between his third and fourth birthday, during a time when he should have gained about seven pounds.

Ben's parents were doing what they shouldn't and failing to do what they should. Ben was very picky about what he ate and Mother short-order cooked for him. He had unlimited access to the refrigerator and made use of it a lot. But even those factors shouldn't have made him gain like that. He had been running the show with eating since he was about 18 months old, and he hadn't gained too much weight before.

In the last year Ben's family had been under a lot of pressure. They had adopted another child and they were planning a move they weren't happy about. It appeared that Ben was feeling anxious, and his anxiety was coming out in the form of extra eating. And his parents weren't good at putting limits on him. His mother said she didn't want to tell him no because she was afraid he wouldn't like her. And his father simply expected that Ben would know how to behave, and if he acted out the father would get very cold and not talk to him.

Ben was looking for limits, and no one was giving them. His eating behavior became more and more unacceptable until finally his parents took some action. Why he acted out in the area of eating I do not know. Another child might have become really naughty or wet his bed. Ben may have known that his mother couldn't take much defiance, and this was a quiet kind of defiance that she could handle.

I worked with them in setting some moderate and reasonable limits similar to those I described in the "Toddler" chapter. It seemed to be helping some, but the mother was so insecure and the father was so withdrawn that I really wonder how much they were able to do on their own. When they moved away, I suggested counseling for them, and hope they got it.

Recommendations for parents. By now, you have undoubtedly developed a bad case of medical student's hypochondria. No doubt you recognize every mistake you have ever made and have decided that you are doing a rotten job with feeding. You've undoubtedly made some mistakes; that doesn't mean you have failed as a parent. But if you are having the same struggle over and over again and can't seem to resolve it, you had better get some help. Neither you or your child is enjoying the relationship if you are struggling all the time.

Find an early childhood expert—a family counselor—and find out what makes it hard for you to be positive and sensitive with your baby. You might be worn out or overstressed or feel overly insecure. You might be getting pressure from others. You might have a difficult baby and could use some tips on being successful with him. Or all of the above. But don't assume that just because you have some struggles at times that you are doing everything all wrong.

We have all made our errors in feeding. At times we have filled a baby "too full," or have been distracted or in a hurry and not really let our baby eat until he had enough. But babies, and parents, can make up for their errors in feeding. A child who gets too full at a feeding will simply not eat as much the next time, or will wait longer before he gets hungry the next time. A baby who is underfed will get hungry sooner.

The reason the children we talked about earlier showed the effects of errors is that they were repeated, time after time. The caretakers were so inattentive to their children's needs that they just kept doing the same things over and over again. And when that happens, child and parent get caught in a downward slide and matters just get worse and worse.

Overfed children become placid and hopeless and eventually give up on having any say about their feeding. Underfed babies become less energetic and demanding. So they get less to eat the next time. In some really severe cases babies demand so little and eat so little they can't survive.

Practical Approaches to Children's Eating

In previous chapters, we have talked about practical approaches to feeding infants and toddlers. It is worth summarizing here so you can see how approaches complement and contradict as your child grows up. Some of his needs remain the same; others become different. You have to be able to adapt as he progresses.

Feeding in infancy. The infant's emotional task is to become aware of and trust both self and the world around. To do that, he needs a caretaker who is accepting of him, curious about him, and generally goes along with what he seems to want and need. The parent's task is to look for and accept information coming from him. Generally, you try to figure out the small infant, find out what he wants, what works with him, and how to make him comfortable.

Your most important tools are patience, perserverance, and a willingness to develop ways that work. To help you in your quest for effective methods, here are some nipple feeding skills that we can summarize from our earlier discussion.

Nipple feeding. During early infancy, your baby's only feeding skills are his instinctive ability to root for the nipple, to suckle and to swallow. He can't sit up and can only be held supported. It makes the greatest kind of sense with a child this age to cuddle him and feed him by nipple.

In both "The Milk Feeding" and "Breastfeeding How-to" we went into nipple feeding in some detail. Figure 12-1, Nipple Feeding Skills, summarizes effective approaches.

Figure 12-1. Nipple Feeding Skills

- Hold the baby securely but not restrictively. He needs a little room for wiggling and moving around, but not so much that he feels like he might fall.
- Hold the bottle still at an appropriate angle. Don't jiggle it. This is a place where breastfeeding has the advantage. Did you ever try to jiggle a breast? Well, you know what I mean.
- Stimulate his rooting reflex by touching his cheek. He'll turn, mouth open, toward the touch. If he's not hungry, he won't show a rooting reflex.
- Allow time and patience for learning. It takes some children, such as the premature child, a long time to really get good at sucking from a nipple. Take time to enjoy the accomplishment once you do it: don't rush right in to spoon feeding.
- Feed according to his times, or GENTLY work toward a routine. Regularity of behavior (or lack of it) is a temperamental thing[6]. If your baby is born irregular, only time will change him.

- Let him determine how much he wants to eat. It will vary from time to time and day to day. Don't withhold food or force more than he wants.
- Let him decide how fast he will eat. Get the nipple to flow at the right speed so he can handle it. You might have to hand express some breast milk if it is flowing too fast or change the nipple size in a rubber nipple.
- Talk to him in a quiet and encouraging manner while he eats, but don't overwhelm him with attention.
- Let him pause in the feeding. Give him enough time to go back to eating if he wants to.
- If he stops to fuss, soothe him and again offer the nipple. Don't force more food—you are just checking to see if he has had enough.
- Keep the feeding smooth and continuous. Avoid disrupting it with wiping, unnecessary burping, checking the amounts and arranging clothing and blankets.

Spoon feeding. Spoon feeding demands of parents much the same skills and sensitivity as nipple feeding did. Keep in mind that there is a LOT to learn in eating from the spoon. A baby has to figure out how to get the food off the spoon and into his mouth. He has to move his tongue in a different way than he does with nipple drinking, or the mush will just come right out on his chin. He has to get the food to move back in his mouth and, finally, down his throat. And to begin with, he isn't used to the feeling of the hard spoon in his mouth, and he doesn't even know that that soft stuff IS food. Very puzzling.

To help your baby learn, you need to be patient and reassuring. You need to give him the feeling that he is in control, that you are not simply going to impose something on him without his having any say in the matter.

To allow him to retain control, wait until he is developmentally ready. He should be able to sit up, open his mouth (or close it) when he sees something coming and direct his hands where he wants them to go. Sitting puts him in position to look at the food and reach out and touch it. He will be able to turn his head toward and away from the spoon, to participate in the feeding and to let you know what he wants.

Again, your instincts are the important guide to what works and what doesn't. Figure 12-2, Spoon Feeding Skills, offers some suggestions about your approach.

Figure 12-2. Spoon Feeding Skills

- Hold your baby on your lap to introduce solids. He'll be braver.
- Support him well in an upright position so he can explore his food.
- Have him sit up straight and face forward. He'll be able to swallow better and be less likely to choke.
- Wait for him to pay attention to each spoonful before you try to feed it to him.
- Let him touch his food—in the dish, on the spoon. You wouldn't eat something if you didn't know anything about it, would you?
- Feed at his tempo. Don't try to get him to go faster or slower than he wants to.
- Talk to him in a quiet and encouraging manner while he eats. Don't entertain him or overwhelm him with attention, but do keep him company.
- Allow him to feed himself with his fingers as soon as he shows an interest.
- Stop feeding when he indicates he has had enough.

You have to accept it when your child indicates he has had enough. If you try to force beyond that point you probably won't get anywhere and you may turn him off on eating. He'll show you he is full by turning his head away from the spoon, by refusing to open up for the spoon or by spitting the food back out again. Show him you trust him by stopping feeding at that point.

Feeding the toddler. Feeding the toddler and dealing with the toddler is lots different from working with an infant. The toddler has had a chance to establish trust and self awareness. Now his job is to discover and confirm that he is a person separate from his mother (or person who takes care of him the most). The only way he can do that is to explore and exert himself. He will become oppositional, because by saying "no" to other people he proves he is separate from them.

The healthy toddler is engaging, curious, energetic and re-calcitrant. If you treat him like you did when he was an infant, and simply accept and support his desires, you will be failing him utterly. He needs reasonable and firm limits in order to feel secure. You don't have to make up the limits. The toddler is generally an aggressive little explorer who needs a lot of room to find out about the world. But he will go too far and he will get on your nerves and he will violate your civil rights and endanger himself and property. You will recognize it when you see it.

To help you distinguish reasonable limits from harsh intrusions, it helps to elaborate on the division of responsibility we talked about earlier. Figure 12-3, Control of Feeding in the Toddler, separates responsibilities in feeding.

Keep in mind that you are responsible for what your child is offered to eat, he is responsible for how much. In the toddler period, you add on the responsibilities of timing and location. You no longer feed the toddler on demand—you ask him to come to the table with the rest of the family. And you time his snacks so he can last until mealtime. You also have to decide if you want eating done at the table or will allow eating elsewhere.

It is important to be concerned enough about a child's eating that you plan, cook and present meals and snacks in a positive way. It

Figure 12-3. Control of Feeding in the Toddler

The parent is responsible for
- Selecting and buying food
- Making and presenting meals
- Regulating timing of meals and snacks
- Presenting food in a form a child can handle
- Allowing eating methods a child can master
- Making family mealtimes pleasant
- Helping the child to participate in family meals
- Helping the child to attend to his eating
- Maintaining standards of behavior at the table

The parent is NOT responsible for
- How much a child eats
- Whether he eats
- How his body turns out

---

is equally important not to get *so* concerned that you take responsibility for getting food IN to your child. Getting meals on the table regularly is difficult enough without devoting yourself to getting people to eat them.

Unacceptable mealtime behaviors include crying and whining, making a big fuss about eating generally or about particular foods, making a *provocative* mess (there will be a mess, but this kind is where the child seems to be trying to get your goat), and running back and forth from the table when parents are still eating. If your child's behavior is interfering with YOUR mealtime enjoyment, it is probably unacceptable and he should be allowed to get down. Most times, parents put up with misbehavior because they hope their child will eat a few more bites. Let him down when he loses interest in eating. There will be another snack or another meal, and he can eat then.

Hungry children are very businesslike about their eating. It's when they start to get full that they become distractible and the other behaviors start to show up.

Beyond the toddler period. Individuating was the toddler's task. Integrating is the preschooler's task. By the preschool period, a child knows who he is, he is just getting better. After the toddler period, the preschool period is EASY.

The preschooler's eating skills continue to develop and improve. He gets better at chewing and swallowing. He gets neater and more consistent at using utensils to eat and at drinking from a cup without spilling. He takes pride in his eating abilities and likes eating with the rest of the family.

Remember that. Almost everyone knows that children like to gain skills and feel pride in mastering their world. But when it comes to eating, grownups forget that important fact. For some reason we regard eating as different, and that unless we make it happen, the child will never really grow up with his eating. It's not true. At least, not to start with. You can make it true by putting a lot of pressure on eating, but without pressure it really isn't so.

Children can recognize pressure on feeding even in its most cleverly disguised forms. A child development researcher in Illinois rewarded one group of preschoolers for trying new food[2]. Another group of preschoolers was simply introduced to the foods with no kind of expectation about their eating. A few days later, they again presented the new food to the two groups of children. The rewarded preschoolers were *less* likely to go back to the new food than the ones who had been allowed to approach the food in their own way. It appears that children recognize even the most positive enticement as pressure and react negatively to it.

As children grow, their eating grows. For a couple of years now, my children have all pretty consistently been using utensils when they eat. The youngest is 13. My teenaged children accept a wider variety of foods now than they did when they were smaller, and they continue to experiment. Just the other night, Lucas, aged 15, looked at a salad I had been making for the last eight years and announced that he was going to try it. I had never noticed that he wasn't eating it. After he tried it, he allowed as how it wasn't so bad. High praise, indeed!

I would recommend that you not get too eager about having your children grow up with eating. You will have a long wait.

The feeding relationship changes as children grow up. They are always able to take the initiative with feeding, and the wise and sensitive parent supports them. But as a child progresses from infancy through preschool, school age, adolescence and the teen years and finally, (sob, hooray) leaves home, he develops more and more autonomy with his eating.

At some point you have to trust your child to make all his own eating decisions, but you will still exert an influence, for good or ill. Your child will carry with him your habits, attitudes and expectations about eating.

Selected References

1. Ainsworth, M. D. S. and S. M. Bell. Some contemporary patterns of mother-infant interaction in the feeding situation. IN Ambrose, Anthony: Stimulation in Early Infancy. New York: Academic Press, 1969.
2. Birch, L. L., D. W. Marlin and J. Rotter. Eating as the "means" activity in a contingency: effects on young children's food preference. Child Development 55(2):431–439. 1984.

3. Field, T.: Maternal stimulation during infant feeding. Developmental Psychology 13:539–540, 1977.
4. Pollitt, E. and S. Wirtz. Mother-infant feeding interaction and weight gain in the first month of life. Journal of the American Dietetic Association 78:596–601, 1981.
5. Satter, E. M.: The feeding relationship. Journal of the American Dietetic Association 86: 35–6, 1986.
6. Thomas, A. and S. Chess. Genesis and evolution of behavioral disorders: from infancy to early adult life. The American Journal of Psychiatry, 141:1–9, 1984.
7. Wright, P., J. Fawcett, and R. Crow. The development of differences in the feeding behavior of bottle and breast fed human infants from birth to two months. Behavioural Processes 5:1–20, 1980.

13
Eating
Disorders

To have an eating disorder, you need two main ingredients: *A disruption in eating and a significant emotional problem. Generally when we think about eating disorders, we think about anorexia nervosa and bulimia and the adolescent or adult. While these difficulties don't appear in small children, other eating problems severe enough to be called eating disorders can exist. In early childhood, an eating disorder might take the form of poor growth or excessive weight gain, severe finickiness or major battles with parents about eating.*

Particularly with the young child, an eating disorder is not the child's alone—it is a disorder in the way the whole family operates. In the eating-disordered family, parents are having emotional problems that they can't explain or have great difficulty resolving. They might unconsciously distract themselves from these problems by becoming too preoccupied with their child. Or they might be so preoccupied with their own problems

*that they can't provide emotionally for their child, and she shows
her distress with changes in her eating.*

*The best way to avoid eating disorders is to have a well-
functioning family. If there are signs of prolonged and serious
problems with eating, get an evaluation by a therapist who works
with children and families. Distortions in eating can be an early
warning sign of distortions in family functioning. Early correc-
tion can make a big difference in the way your family operates.*

A few years ago a 16-year-old girl, we'll call her Cindy, came to
my office wanting help with a weight reduction diet. She thought she
was too fat and wanted to do something about it. Cindy was 5 foot, 6
inches tall and weighed 150 pounds. She had a broad, strong body,
and had trouble finding clothes that fit and looked nice on her. She
was an excellent basketball player, trained a lot, and was so lean that
she wasn't even having her periods. She wasn't too fat, but she was
very unhappy about her blocky body and had been dieting to change
it.

Cindy had gone to one of the commercial weight loss organizations, paid her $500.00, and they had put her on a 800-calorie diet.
She went in to be weighed every day and stuck to her eating plan
religiously, but she didn't lose any weight. So the counselors in the
program advised her to cut her calories down to 500 per day.

Cindy tried to do it, but at that point her will power started to
slip. She no longer could stick to the diet and she began cheating—a
little candy here, an extra piece of bread there. Then she began
cheating a *lot.*

She went on eating binges, then suffered agonies of remorse,
subsequently redoubling her efforts and then giving in again to the
temptation to overeat. Almost all her thinking time was devoted to
her eating and weight problem. She became preoccupied with her
eating and weight and felt upset and bad about it almost all the time.

She underate at meals and nibbled at food before and afterwards. She became depressed and didn't have much energy for her friends or sports. She was crabby around home, and that didn't help her feelings about herself.

Not only was Cindy having trouble losing weight, but she also began to worry that she had an eating disorder. Just before coming to see me she had read an article in the student newspaper written by one of her classmates who was anorexic. The article described her exact symptoms—preoccupation with food and weight, lack of energy, irritability, erratic eating habits, anxiety about her physical appearance, negative feelings about herself.

Cindy *was* having some major difficulty with her eating, but she didn't have an eating disorder. She certainly wasn't anorexic: Her weight wasn't low enough. To be anorexic she would have to have lost a significant proportion of her body weight[1]. Despite all her dieting struggles, she hadn't lost anything. She didn't even qualify to be a bulimic. (That's the disorder where people starve, then binge, then purge in some way, by vomiting, starving, overexercising or abusing laxatives.)

She *was* doing that, but definitions of both anorexia nervosa and bulimia *go on to say* that the person has to have some significant emotional difficulty that is perpetuating the problem. Aside from her eating, Cindy didn't seem too upset about anything. It seemed to me that her behavior and her preoccupation with the process came more from her severe dieting than from anything else. Dieting is a form of starvation, and people who starve show exactly the symptoms that Cindy complained of.

Reactions to food deprivation. During World War II, Ancel Keys, a nutritionist from Minnesota, did a starvation experiment with 36 young men who volunteered for the study as an alternative to military service[3]. His intent was to duplicate concentration camp conditions so people who had been incarcerated during the war could be understood and cared for. During the first three months, the men ate normally while their behaviors, personalities and eating patterns were studied in detail. Then for the next six months, they were restricted to approximately half their former food. This was followed by three months of rehabilitation, during which the men were gradually refed.

During the starvation phase they lost 25% of their body weight, and eventually got to the point where their weights stabilized on the low calorie level. And they developed all the symptoms Cindy was complaining about. They thought about food a great deal, and when they did get a chance to eat, their table manners were eccentric. They hoarded food and lost interest in other activities. Because they were getting along on less calories they had a difficult time staying warm.

For the most part, the subjects became tired, depressed and hard to get along with. But their emotional responses to starvation varied widely. Some appeared to tolerate it fairly well, while others displayed severe disturbance following weight loss. They became confused and irrational, and one even had to have a psychiatric hospitalization.

At times some would lose control of their food intake and overeat, often enormously. When they did that, they were critical and disgusted with themselves.

When they went off the study and had access to food, for a time they ate a great deal. At a given feeding they would eat long past the apparent point of satiety, seemingly stuffing themselves in their attempts to get filled up. And they gained weight back to, or near to, their previous levels. But they were fatter than before: They had lost proportionately more lean tissue during their starvation and then had regained more fat.

While many of Cindy's symptoms made her look like she had an eating disorder, those symptoms may have also been coming from her severe food restriction. Keys' subjects were not eating disor-

431

dered: They very easily gave up their starvation and went back to eating. People with eating disorders cling to their distorted relationship with food as if they need it.

So that became the central question in distinguishing whether Cindy had an eating disorder: How willing and able was she to give up that distortion and go back to normal eating?

I wasn't *sure* whether Cindy had an eating disorder until after we treated her eating. She was able very readily to get herself weaned off the dieting and back to eating normally again. And once her eating changed, her symptoms went away.

The deprive-overeat cycle. Cindy's cyclical eating demonstrated what Keys and his young men demonstrated: The body will defend itself against starvation. If you over-deprive yourself, you will, sooner or later, react by overeating. Because Cindy had access to food and was being deterred from eating only by her will power, her eating took on a cyclical pattern that is very typical both of the dieter and of the person suffering from an eating disorder. Table 13-1, Binge-Purge Pattern, illustrates that circular pattern.

Like Cindy, most people who come in for help see their problem as overeating, and want help controlling their chaotic eating behavior. They are surprised when I tell them the real problem is their dieting and depriving, *not* their overindulging.

They deprive themselves of food, and the symptoms accumulate. Actually, those symptoms are no more or less than the body's defenses against starvation that we talked about earlier. The symptoms increase the pressure to seek food and to eat and help insure survival. For a while dieters can stand the pain, but finally they give in to food. Since they don't give themselves any deliberate permission to eat, they figure they have blown it, so they might as well go ahead and eat a lot. And they do. They eat until they are really full.

It's interesting that often the "seasoned" dieter doesn't even actually have to GO on a diet to set off this reactive overeating. Just

432

Figure 13-1. Binge-Purge Pattern

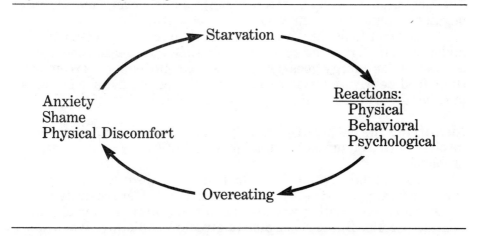

thinking about it will do it. They remind themselves that they "shouldn't" be eating something, or look at the new fashions and remind themselves to lose some weight, and off they go on an eating binge. They have gotten so sensitive to the negative feelings associated with dieting that they run away before they ever get there.

So they binge, and at first, often only momentarily, it feels like a great relief to give in to food. But as the eating progresses to *over*eating, the remorse sets in. They feel overstuffed, uncomfortable and disgusted with themselves. They are ashamed of their lack of control and anxious about not being able to manage their eating. So they purge in some way. And then they starve and start the cycle all over again.

Tolerating the reactions to starvation and holding out against hunger takes a lot of energy. That's what the weight loss "experts" are selling: A cheering section to help their clients keep going. The businesses that charge more provide a cheering section every day, along with the extra motivation that paying a lot of money provides. The motivation is really only some energy to help overcome all those negative symptoms of starvation.

So what happens when the dieter is tired or depressed or under stress? Right, she goes off her diet. But the reason she goes off is because her energy goes down and she can no longer overcome all those food-deprivation symptoms. It's not so much that she *over*eats in response to stress, but rather that she *stops under*eating.

Identifying the eating disorder. By definition, an eating disorder involves both a significant distortion in eating AND an emotional problem[2].

I said I didn't think Cindy had an eating disorder, and my subsequent experience with her supported that. Her frustration and concern about her eating was causing her considerable pain and was limiting her life. But she was able to give up her dieting. When she did that she became more trusting of her body's ability to regulate, and most of those negative feelings went away.

Cindy had the usual adolescent concerns about friends and boyfriends and school and parents. But she didn't seem to be in a lot of distress about her situation. Things seemed to be going reasonably well with school and friends and, particularly, she and her parents had a pretty good relationship. Things were good at home. I was surprised that her parents were willing to invest so much money in enabling their daughter to lose weight. But when we talked about it they confessed they actually were uncomfortable with the attempt, and they appreciated my helping them call a halt to it.

Cindy's parents seemed to feel that their daughter was just fine the way she was. They recognized that she didn't have a very *stylish* body, but they thought she was really very attractive and they were proud of her athletic ability. Her mother offered to go shopping with her, and she helped Cindy persist in trying on clothes until she found some that looked good on her. (As the dapper young clerk at the clothing store said, "Dressing well is the art of deception.") Cindy and her parents worked out a good solution. Even though they had momentarily gotten caught in our society's mania for thinness, they didn't have much trouble getting out of it.

Contrast Cindy with Mary, the girl with bulimia we talked about in the "Obesity" chapter. Mary's parents had "dieted" her virtually from birth because they thought she had a big appetite and they were afraid she would get too fat. Mary had struggled with her parents and with food all her growing-up years, and by age 19 had become bulimic.

When Mary and I worked on her eating, she couldn't let go of her obsession with her weight and eating. Part of the problem was that she felt so bad about herself, and she thought that if she could be thinner she would feel better. And, miserable as her bingeing and vomiting was, it had some side benefits for her.

As long as she was involved with that she didn't have the time or energy to worry about her other problems. But the real, underlying problems were her feelings about herself and her relationship with her parents. Mary had a low self esteem that reflected her parents' doubts about her. They felt uncomfortable with her weight and wanted her to get thinner. At least part of their concern was that her appearance reflected on them. They couldn't see how much pain it was causing her and how bad she felt about herself.

Mary's parents had their own problems. It was apparent to an outside observer that they weren't getting along very well with each other. But they denied it. Instead of working out their problems with each other so they could be helpful to Mary, they *distracted* themselves with concern about Mary. And she obliged with her eating disorder.

Mary's eating couldn't get any better until she felt better about herself. And she wasn't getting any help from her family. It was truly an eating disorder: Not only was her eating significantly distorted, but she was having considerable emotional difficulty.

My recommendations for her treatment included dietary management to resolve the problematic eating and psychotherapy to deal with social and emotional issues. I recommended family therapy so her parents could figure out what kind of pressure they were putting on Mary and stop it. Mary was willing, but her parents weren't. At her young age, and without their support, she wasn't able to improve very much.

The continuum of eating behavior. Eating behavior exists on a continuum, with normal balanced weight regulation on the one end and anorexia nervosa on the other. Table 13-2, Eating Behavior Continuum, illustrates that.

Normal balanced food regulation depends on internalized signals of hunger, appetite, satiety and awareness of body levels of energy and fatigue. We talked about all this in detail in the chapter, "Regulation of Food Intake."

At the other extreme, anorexia nervosa involves almost exclusively external regulation of food intake based on what the person *thinks* she should be eating, not what she *feels* like eating. In between the extremes are varying degrees of awareness and control of hunger, appetite and satiety.

Methods of regulating body weight also vary along this continuum. At the "normal" end, weight is determined largely by genetics, which influence not only body contours but also calorie need and energy level. At the other extreme, body weight is almost totally regulated externally. That is, the person chooses a particular body weight and struggles to achieve it by dietary manipulation, whether or not that weight is constitutionally appropriate. In some cases, the person imposes external control and ignores feedback from her body to the point of starvation, as in cases of anorexia nervosa.

In between the extremes there is a spectrum of eating behaviors ranging from dieting for cosmetic reasons to obsessive food managment dominated by the fear of obesity. In the category of

Table 13-2.   Eating Behavior Continuum

Normal Balanced Weight Regulation	*Normal Voluntary Weight Reduction*	*Midrange Eating Disorders*	*Anorexia Nervosa*
Internal food regulation	Some external eating, weight control	Increasing external eating, weight control	External food regulation
Weight constitutionally determined	External weight regulation		

―――――――――Decreasing Attention to Body Cues―――――――――⟶

"midrange eating disorders" are the bulimics, the sports anorexics I'll talk about later, and a group of people I have come to call the "failed chronic reducers." They are the people who diet and fail at dieting repeatedly, and end up feeling intensely negative about themselves and about the process.

The farther you go along the continuum the harder it is for people to get better. Some people in the midrange category can resolve their difficulties pretty easily. Others feel so much emotional pressure that it is about as difficult for them to get better as it is for the anorexic. Cindy was probably just across the solid line from normal eating. Mary was probably off to the right very close to anorexia nervosa.

Notice that the vertical line between "normal balanced weight regulation" and "normal voluntary weight reduction" is a solid line, whereas the other vertical lines are dashed. The most major change is made in crossing that first line. Once the person crosses that solid line and initiates dieting, she begins to show the symptoms of starvation. As dieting becomes more restrictive, the symptoms become more pronounced. Further changes are subtle and simply involve more and more external control and less and less responsiveness to body cues.

When a person starts dieting, she first begins ignoring and attempting to overcome automatic food regulation processes. She has to substitute a considerably more laborious and willful process. There is a price to pay for that. She can no longer trust her body's ability to regulate. She has to ignore to some extent hunger and appetite. She has to deprive herself, either in quantity or type of food. And when she deprives she becomes preoccupied with food and with herself. Dieting makes people narcissistic.

Sports anorexia. Another eating pattern that can generally be included in the "midrange eating disorder" category is sports anorexia[6].

An increasing number of kids who are out for sports like skating, gymnastics, running and wrestling are being encouraged to lose weight as part of their training. The wrestlers diet to "make weight." (It is seen as an advantage to wrestle in lower weight categories.) In running, gymnastics and skating, correlations are being made between performance and body fatness.

Jo was a skater, doing well but perhaps not really top caliber. She worked very hard at it, and had a lot of support from her parents for her efforts: They were eager for her to excel. Her sister had been very successful at gymnastics, and they thought it had helped her be popular. Jo was having a difficult time making a particular turn, and her coach told her she thought she could do it better if she lost a little weight—maybe five pounds. So she lost her five pounds and things *might* have gone better—it was hard to tell.

So she lost another five pounds. And so on. Before long her weight had dipped into the anorexic range, she had become very preoccupied with eating and weight, she had started to cut off contacts with her friends ("all they want to do is eat"), and her skating had begun to slip.

After about six months of this, Jo's parents became concerned enough to get her into treatment. She recovered quite rapidly. Part of her treatment was working with her coach and her parents to set more realistic goals for her skating. And part of her treatment was to help her feel better about herself in general so her skating wasn't so vital to her self confidence.

She is still skating and is taking pride in her good performances, even when they are not the tops. She is enjoying it more, and enjoying her friends more. Her parents have adjusted some of their attitudes, too. They take pleasure in her accomplishments, but they aren't so determined that she take top honors. And they can see that she doesn't have to earn her way with friends.

Sports anorexia generally can be turned around much more readily than the other types. In many cases, the kids are functioning better in the first place, and the families are more positive and flexible to begin with. Plus, the disorder gets identified more quickly. In any type of eating disorder, the more quickly you can intervene the better off you are.

Eating Disturbances in Early Childhood

Disturbances in family feeding styles and attitudes about eating generally show up long before a full-blown eating disorder develops. One mother of a fourteen-year-old anorexic commented that she ". . . just knew something would go wrong with this girl's eating. From the very first, her eating was strange. I would put as much formula as she should have in the bottle, and she would just *wolf* it

439

down and cry for more. She never seemed to be satisfied with what I gave her." It had never occurred to that mother that she wasn't giving her daughter enough food.

Some eating disturbances in early childhood are great enough to be called eating disorders in their own right, not just forerunners of a later condition[5]. The childhood eating disorder might take the form of failure to thrive, obesity, excessive finickiness, or vehement and prolonged struggles between parents and children about eating.

In the early childhood eating disorder you see a distinctively inappropriate level of parental control, a stubborn resistance to change on the part of all parties, and very intense feelings on all sides. Emotional struggles between the parents are typically so great that parents are unable to provide for childrens' emotional needs.

Let's make some distinctions between eating disordered and non-eating disordered situations using some examples from the "Feeding Relationship" chapter. You may remember Claire, the poorly-growing toddler we talked about on page 408, whose parents force-fed her until she screamed. Claire likely had an eating disorder. (For ease in writing, I'll say the *child* had an eating disorder. But, particularly with a young child, it is very apparent that the eating disorder is not the child's alone—it is a disorder in the way the whole family operates.) I didn't have a chance to test that, because I didn't get to know the parents, nor did I try to get them to change.

Five of the mothers I talked about from Ainsworth's feeding observations (p. 410) probably had eating disorders—the arbitrary mothers. They were so caught up in themselves and unaware of their babies' needs that they actually cared for them based on their own needs or convenience. Sometimes mothers would feed when babies weren't hungry; other times they failed to feed even when they screamed from hunger.

On page 415 we talked about three-year-old Brian, whose mother tried for an hour at each meal to force him to eat (as he fell from the 50th to the 10th weight percentile). On page 416 there was two-year-old Todd, who was being restrained from eating by his bulimic mother. Both of these boys had eating disorders. Parents and children were emotionally over-intense and rigid in their interactions; they were unable to resolve their difficulties on their own.

Ben gained 16 extra pounds in a year during which his parents were having a difficult time. In a short treatment centered around his eating, his parents were able to make some improvements in their dealings with Ben. But I predict relapse unless his mother can get started feeling better about herself and his father can become more warm and available to his family.

In the "Feeding Relationship" chapter I also described some relationships that were not disordered. Kathy and her little boy were not. He gained very poorly, and she just had to let him eat the way he wanted to. (She was providing appropriate food in a supportive manner and she had had him checked out medically.) And neither did my colleague who got into problems attempting to bottle feed his breast-fed sons. All of those situations could have led to horrendous misunderstandings and struggles between parent and child. But they didn't. Both parents were sensitive and flexible enough to work it out with their children.

Avoiding the Eating Disorder

We will hope that the issue of treating an eating disorder does not come up for you. If it does, acknowledge it and get in for help as quickly as you can. All families have problems. Some families, some times, get stuck and can't seem to resolve a problem. The good families are the ones who are honest with themselves about it and get help.

I hope I have made it clear that an eating disorder is not just the problem of the affected child. It is an indication that things are not going well in the family as a whole. A good counselor will understand that, help you figure out what there is about your family that isn't working and help you fix it. You may have to shop around some to find someone who is helpful, but the effort is worth it. It's very difficult to change the way you interact with other people, but if things go well in therapy, you can look forward to functioning better than you ever have before.

Enhancing emotional functioning. From the standpoint of prevention, your best chance of avoiding eating disorders is in having a well-functioning family. Parents must be helpful to each other in seeing that the family works. Fathers in the highly distorted feeding situations that Ainsworth studied should have been able to see what was going on and get help for their wives. Brian's father should have talked with his wife about the way she was handling feeding, rather than just letting her do her thing.

To function well as a couple and as parents, you need to function well as individuals. You need to feel good enough about yourself to be able to pay attention to another person and get a feeling for what it is like to be in that person's place. The mother of the anorexic I talked about earlier was so self preoccupied she couldn't make the most basic observation about her infant daughter.

When you function well as individuals and as a couple, you will have the intuition to interact positively with your child. You will be able to establish the good feeding relationship we have been talking about throughout this book. *You will be able to respect your child and depend on him, appropriately, to take the lead with feeding.*

Avoid intruding on food regulation. Resist in yourself and your child the tendency to diet, especially vehemently. We went into this at length in the *Obesity* chapter, so I will just summarize here. Trust the body's ability to regulate. Any interventions made with regulation should be made moderately and indirectly, such as changing the type or availability of food in the house or the family meal schedule. You should never impose food restriction or food excess on a child, or in any way try to manipulate his growth. Any interventions should be made with the motive of *preventing* overeating or undereating, not *promoting* it.

Eventually your child may get to the point where she wants to diet and lose weight, but you don't have to cave in to the pressure. You can let her know that you are willing to have low-calorie foods available, and that you will plan meals that generally aren't so high in sugar and fat. Don't cook "diet" meals, or you will become enraged at her when she goes out for french fries with her friends.

You can be supportive without giving in to pressure to buy a membership in an expensive weight loss business like Cindy's parents did. And you can be firm about expecting your child to attend most family meals, and steadfast in your faith that good nutritional habits are important for your child. The adolescent makes a lot of his own food choices, but parents should still function in finding out (tactfully) what those choices are, making suggestions, and encouraging her to take good care of her body. Don't preach, just express your concern.

You can get after your dieter when you see her nibbling too much between meals and remind her that she would be better off eating a little more at meal time. And, yes, you can tell her to get out of the refrigerator right before meals. Making meals important and satisfying is one helpful way of preventing being caught up in that deprive-overeat cycle we talked about earlier.

The dieting athlete. Here are some facts to help you withstand the dieting pressure on the athlete in your house.

Optimum body fat percentage for competition is higher for an adolescent than it is for an adult[4]. If your child's coach is setting body fat percentage goals, make sure the goals are appropriate for adolescents. Adolescents may do better at body fat levels 30% to 50% higher than levels established for adults.

There is nothing to be gained by severe dieting. Excessive weight loss, especially the type that is achieved by a crash program right before the competition, impairs rather than enhances performance. Wrestlers who had crash dieted just before a competition suffered in endurance and skill, even when they had gained most of their weight back after the weigh-in[8].

The best tactic is to decrease food intake moderately—say cut 500 to 1000 calories per day off normal intake. Even if she isn't eating much to begin with, no child should eat less than 1200 calories per day. Children need at least 1200 calories to cover their nutritional requirements. They should continue to follow their coaches' instructions about training. (Since gymnastics and figure skating do not expend many calories, it may be necessary for an athlete attempting to keep her weight down to to add on walking, running, biking, or another energy-expending exercise.) And whatever weight level they achieve using these modest methods should be the weight at which they compete.

If a young athlete has to use heroic methods to lose, i.e., severe dieting or exhaustive exercising, it will probably detract from fitness and performance. We are talking about the law of diminishing returns here: If children have to punish their bodies to get their weight or fat percentage down, it is likely they will impair performance. And studies have supported this conclusion[4].

As I pointed out in the "Obesity" chapter, our national attitude about weight is distorted. You will have to keep a level head not to be swept away by it. In eating for sports as well as in establishing good feeding relationships in all areas, you have to feel your way through your situation. If you and your family are functioning well, you will be doing what you can to prevent an eating disorder. A how-to book like this one is (I hope) helpful, but knowing what to do is no substitute for good instincts.

Selected References

1. American Psychiatric Association: Diagnostic and Statistical Manual of Mental Disorders, Third Edition. American Psychiatric

Association, Washington, D.C., 1980.

2. Bruch, H.: Eating Disorders: Obesity, Anorexia Nervosa and the Person Within. New York: Basic Books, 1973.

3. Keys, A. J., Brozek, A., Henschel, O., Michelsen, O., and Taylor, H. S.: The Biology of Human Starvation. Vols. 1, 2. Minneapolis: University of Minnesota Press, 1950.

4. Pipes, Peggy L. Nutrition in Infancy and Childhood. Times Mirror/Mosby. St. Louis, 1985.

5. Satter, E. M.: Childhood eating disorders. Journal of the American Dietetic Association 86: 357–61, 1986.

6. Smith, N. J. Excessive weight loss and food aversion in athletes simulating anorexia nervosa. Pediatrics 66:139–142, 1980.

7. Thomas, A. and Chess, S. Genesis and evolution of behavioral disorders: from infancy to early adult life. The American Journal of Psychiatry, 141:1–9, 1984.

8. Tipton, C. M. Consequences of rapid weight loss. IN Haskell, W., et. al. Nutrition and Athletic Performance. Proceedings of the Conference on Nutritional Determinants in Athletic Performance, San Francisco, CA, September 24–25, 1981. Bull Publishing, Palo Alto, 1982.

Appendix

Table A-1

Food and Nutrition Board, National Academy of Sciences—National Research Council Recommended Daily Dietary Allowances[a] Revised 1989
Designed for the maintenance of good nutrition of practically all healthy people in the U.S.A.

Category	Age (years) or Condition	Weight[b] (kg)	Weight[b] (lb)	Height[b] (cm)	Height[b] (in)	Protein (g)	Fat-Soluble Vitamins Vita-min A (μg RE)[c]	Vita-min D (μg)[d]	Vita-min E (mg α–TE)[e]	Vita-min K (μg)
Infants	0.0–0.5	6	13	60	24	13	375	7.5	3	5
	0.5–1.0	9	20	71	28	14	375	10	4	10
Children	1–3	13	29	90	35	16	400	10	6	15
	4–6	20	44	112	44	24	500	10	7	20
	7–10	28	62	132	52	28	700	10	7	30
Males	11–14	45	99	157	62	45	1,000	10	10	45
	15–18	66	145	176	69	59	1,000	10	10	65
	19–24	72	160	177	70	58	1,000	10	10	70
	25–50	79	174	176	70	63	1,000	5	10	80
	51+	77	170	173	68	63	1,000	5	10	80
Females	11–14	46	101	157	62	46	800	10	8	45
	15–18	55	120	163	64	44	800	10	8	55
	19–24	58	128	164	65	46	800	10	8	60
	25–50	63	138	163	64	50	800	5	8	65
	51+	65	143	160	63	50	800	5	8	65
Pregnant						60	800	10	10	65
Lactating	1st 6 months					65	1,300	10	12	65
	2nd 6 months					62	1,200	10	11	65

[a] The allowances, expressed as average daily intakes over time, are intended to provide for individual variations among most normal persons as they live in the United States under usual environmental stresses. Diets should be based on a variety of common foods in order to provide other nutrients for which human requirements have been less well defined.

446

Food and Nutrition Board, National Academy of Sciences—National Research Council Recommended Daily Dietary Allowances[a] (Continued)

Category	Age (years) or Condition	Weight[b] (kg)	(lb)	Height[b] (cm)	(in)	Protein (g)	Vita-min C (mg)	Thia-min (mg)	Ribo-flavin (mg)	Niacin (mg NE[f])	Vita-min B$_6$ (mg)	Fo-late (μg)	Vita-min B$_{12}$ (μg)
								Water-Soluble Vitamins					
Infants	0.0–0.5	6	13	60	24	13	30	0.3	0.4	5	0.3	25	0.3
	0.5–1.0	9	20	71	28	14	35	0.4	0.5	6	0.6	35	0.5
Children	1–3	13	29	90	35	16	40	0.7	0.8	9	1.0	50	0.7
	4–6	20	44	112	44	24	45	0.9	1.1	12	1.1	75	1.0
	7–10	28	62	132	52	28	45	1.0	1.2	13	1.4	100	1.4
Males	11–14	45	99	157	62	45	50	1.3	1.5	17	1.7	150	2.0
	15–18	66	145	176	69	59	60	1.5	1.8	20	2.0	200	2.0
	19–24	72	160	177	70	68	60	1.5	1.7	19	2.0	200	2.0
	25–50	79	174	176	70	63	60	1.5	1.7	19	2.0	200	2.0
	51+	77	170	173	68	63	60	1.2	1.4	15	2.0	200	2.0
Females	11–14	46	101	157	62	46	50	1.1	1.3	15	1.4	150	2.0
	15–18	55	120	163	64	44	60	1.1	1.3	15	1.5	180	2.0
	19–24	58	128	164	65	46	60	1.1	1.3	15	1.6	180	2.0
	25–50	63	138	163	64	50	60	1.1	1.3	15	1.6	180	2.0
	51+	65	143	160	63	50	60	1.0	1.2	13	1.6	180	2.0
Pregnant						60	70	1.5	1.6	17	2.2	400	2.2
Lactating	1st 6 months					65	95	1.6	1.8	20	2.1	280	2.6
	2nd 6 months					62	90	1.6	1.7	20	2.1	260	2.6

[b]Weights and heights of Reference Adults are actual medians for the U.S. population of the designated age, as reported by NHANES II. The median weights and heights of those under 19 years of age were taken from Hammill et al. (1979). The use of these figures does not imply that the height-to-weight ratios are ideal.

[c]Retinol equivalents. 1 retinol equivalent = 1 μg retinol or 6 μg β-carotene. See text for calculation of vitamin A activity of diets as retinol equivalents.

[d]As cholecalciferol. 10 μg cholecalciferol = 400 IU of vitamin D.

[e]α-Tocopherol equivalents. 1 mg d-α tocopherol = 1 α-TE. See text for variation in allowances and calculation of vitamin E activity of the diet as α-tocopherol equivalents.

[f]1 NE (niacin equivalent) is equal to 1 mg of niacin or 60 mg of dietary tryptophan.

Food and Nutrition Board, National Academy of Sciences—National Research Council Recommended Daily Dietary Allowances[a] (Continued)

Category	Age (years) or Condition	Weight[b] (kg)	(lb)	Height[b] (cm)	(in)	Protein (g)	Minerals Cal-cium (mg)	Phos-phorus (mg)	Mag-nesium (mg)	Iron (mg)	Zinc (mg)	Iodine (μg)	Sele-nium (μg)
Infants	0.0–0.5	6	13	60	24	13	400	300	40	6	5	40	10
	0.5–1.0	9	20	71	28	14	600	500	60	10	5	50	15
Children	1–3	13	29	90	35	16	800	800	80	10	10	70	20
	4–6	20	44	112	44	24	800	800	120	10	10	90	20
	7–10	28	62	132	52	28	800	800	170	10	10	120	30
Males	11–14	45	99	157	62	45	1,200	1,200	270	12	15	150	40
	15–18	66	145	176	69	59	1,200	1,200	400	12	15	150	50
	19–24	72	160	177	70	58	1,200	1,200	350	10	15	150	70
	25–50	79	174	176	70	63	800	800	350	10	15	150	70
	51+	77	170	173	68	63	800	800	350	10	15	150	70
Females	11–14	46	101	157	62	46	1,200	1,200	280	15	12	150	45
	15–18	55	120	163	64	44	1,200	1,200	300	15	12	150	50
	19–24	58	128	164	65	46	1,200	1,200	280	15	12	150	55
	25–50	63	138	163	64	50	800	800	280	15	12	150	55
	51+	65	143	160	63	50	800	800	280	10	12	150	55
Pregnant						60	1,200	1,200	320	30	15	175	65
Lactating	1st 6 months					65	1,200	1,200	355	15	19	200	75
	2nd 6 months					62	1,200	1,200	340	15	16	200	75

Table A-2

Table of standard weight for height for women suggested for use by the American College of Obstetricians and Gynecologists (30)*

(Height without shoes, plus 1 inch)

	lbs.
4'-10"	= 104
4'-11"	= 107
5'-0"	= 110
5'-1"	= 113
5'-2"	= 116
5'-3"	= 118
5'-4"	= 123
5'-5"	= 128
5'-6"	= 132
5'-7"	= 136
5'-8"	= 140
5'-9"	= 144
5'-10"	= 148
5'-11"	= 152
6'-0"	= 156

*Weights were taken from Metropolitan Life Insurance Company, Actuarial Tables, 1959, for heights in inches without shoes plus one inch. For patients under age 25, one pound should be deducted for each year.

Table A-3

Nutrient content of human milk and cow's milk

Constituent (per liter)	Human milk	Cow's milk
Energy (kcal)	690	660
Protein (gm)	9	35
Fat (gm)	45	37
Lactose (gm)	68	49
Vitamins		
Vitamin A (IU)	1898	1025
Vitamin D (IU)	22	14
Vitamin E (IU)	2	0.4
Vitamin K (μg)	15	60
Thiamine (μg)	160	440
Riboflavin (μg)	360	1750
Niacin (mg)	1.5	0.9
Pyridoxine (μg)	100	640
Folic acid (μg)	52	55
Cobalamine (μg)	0.3	4
Ascorbic acid (mg)	43	11
Minerals		
Calcium (mg)	297	1170
Phosphorus (mg)	150	920
Sodium (mg)	150	506
Potassium (mg)	550	1368

Nutrient content of human milk and cow's milk (Continued)

Constituent (per liter)	Human milk	Cow's milk
Chlorine (mg)	385	1028
Magnesium (mg)	23	120
Sulfur (mg)	140	300
Iron (mg)	0.56–0.3	0.5
Iodine (mg)	30	47
Manganese (μg)	5.9–4.0	20–40
Copper (μg)	0.6–0.25	0.3
Zinc (mg)	4–.5	3–5
Selenium (μg)	20	5–50
Flouride (mg)	0.05	0.03–0.1

From Pipes, Peggy L.: Nutrition in infancy and childhood, ed. 2, St. Louis, 1981, The C. V. Mosby Co.; adapted from Hambreaus, L.: Proprietary milk versus human breast milk in infant feeding, a critical approach from the nutritional point of view. Pediatr. Clin. North Am. *24*:17, 1977; Siimes, M. A., Vuori, E., and Kuitunen, P.: Breast milk iron—a declining concentration during the course of lactation, Acta Paediatr. Scand. *68*:29, 1979; Vuori, E.: A longitudinal study of manganese in human milk, Acta Paediatr. Scand. *68*:571, 1979, Vuori, E., and Kuitunen, P.: Concentrations of copper and zinc in human milk, Acta Paediatr. Scand. *68*:33, 1978; and nayman, R., and others: Observations on the composition of milk-substitute products for the treatment of inborn errors of amino acid metabolism: comparisons with human milk, Am. J. Clin. Nutr. *32*:1279, 1979.

Table A-4

Nutrient content of commercially available milk-base formulas

Nutrient (per 100 ml)	Amount
Energy (kcal)	67
Protein (gm)	1.5–1.6
Fat (gm)	3.6–3.7
Carbohydrate (gm)	7.0–7.3
Vitamin A (IU)	165–260
Vitamin D (IU)	40–42
Vitamin E (IU)	0.9–1.5
Vitamin C (mg)	5.4–5.7
Thiamine (μg)	52–69
Riboflavin (μg)	57–100
Niacin (mg)	0.6–1.0
Pyridoxine (μg)	40–42
Vitamin B_{12} (μg)	0.1–0.2
Folic acid (μg)	5–10
Calcium (mg)	44–54
Phosphorus (mg)	33–46
Magnesium (mg)	4.1–5.2
Iron (mg)*	Trace–1.3
Zinc (mg)	0.36–0.5
Copper (mg)	.041–.062
Iodine (μg)	6.7–10

*Iron-fortified formulas contain 12 mg of iron/32 oz; others contain only a trace.

From Pipes, Peggy L.: Nutrition in infancy and childhood, ed. 2, St. Louis, 1981, The C. V. Mosby Co.

Table A-5

Nutrient content of soy formulas (soy isolates, vegetable or soy oil, corn syrup solids and/or sucrose)

Nutrient (per 100 ml)	Amount
Energy (kcal)	67
Protein (gm)	1.8–2.5
Fat (gm)	3.4–3.6
Carbohydrate (gm)	6.4–6.8
Vitamin A (IU)	167–250
Vitamin D (IU)	40–42
Vitamin E (IU)	1.0–1.5
Vitamin C (mg)	5.4–7.3
Thiamine (μg)	40–52
Riboflavin (μg)	62–104
Niacin (mg)	0.7–0.9
Pyridoxine (μg)	40–41
Vitamin B_{12} (μg)	0.21–0.30
Folic acid (μg)	5.3–10.4
Calcium (mg)	70–83
Phosphorus (mg)	50–63
Magnesium (mg)	5–7.81
Iron (mg)*	1.0–1.2
Zinc (mg)	0.3–0.5
Copper (mg)	0.04–0.06
Iodine (μg)	1.5–4.7

From Pipes, Peggy L.: Nutrition in infancy and childhood, ed. 2, St. Louis, 1981, The C. V. Mosby Co.

Table A-6

Supplemental fluoride dosage schedule (in mg F/day*) according to fluoride concentration of drinking water.

Age (Years)	Concentration of Fluoride in Water (ppm)		
	Less Than 0.3	0.3 to 0.7	Greater Than 0.7
Birth to 2	0.25	0	0
2 to 3	0.50	0.25	0
3 to 13	1.00	0.50	0

*2.2 mg. sodium fluoride contain 1 mg fluoride.

From Council on Dental Therapeutics. In Accepted Dental Therapeutics, ed. 38 American Dental Association. Chicago, 1979.

A-7   Table of Figures

Index